THE COURSE OF AMERICAN
ECONOMIC GROWTH AND DEVELOPMENT

THE WILEY SERIES IN

AMERICAN ECONOMIC HISTORY

RALPH L. ANDREANO
Editor

Ralph L. Andreano
THE NEW ECONOMIC HISTORY:
RECENT PAPERS ON METHODOLOGY

Louis M. Hacker
THE COURSE OF AMERICAN ECONOMIC
GROWTH AND DEVELOPMENT

THE COURSE
OF AMERICAN
ECONOMIC
GROWTH AND
DEVELOPMENT

LOUIS M. HACKER

JOHN WILEY & SONS, INC.

NEW YORK • LONDON • SYDNEY • TORONTO

Library of Congress Catalogue Card Number: 75-105384

Cloth: SBN 471 33840 0   Paper: SBN 471 33841 9

Printed in the United States of America

10 9 8 7 6 5 4 3 2 1

To BLANCHE SPECKMAN and BLENDA LARSON

INTRODUCTION TO THE SERIES

Research in economic history has literally exploded in the past decade. The purpose of this series is to make this research available to students in a set of interchangeable books on American economic history from earliest times to the present. Not only is there a lengthy time lag required to bring this research into the classroom in conventional textbook form, but the text itself would be massive in order to capture fully what economists and historians have been writing about America's economic past. The Wiley series aims to give a breadth and depth to American economic development not now possible in a single, unsupplemented, conventional text. The series includes books both by historians and economists that represent new and fresh thinking, that challenge old concepts and ideas, and that contribute to a new understanding of the main contours of American growth and the human welfare consequences of that growth. The past ten years have witnessed not just a "new economic history" but a "new history." The books in the Wiley series will bring to the student and the classroom a needed dialogue between historians and economists that will reshape our thinking about America's economic growth and development.

Ralph Andreano

INTRODUCTION TO
THIS VOLUME

I

No historian has contributed as much to the interpretation of American economic development as has Louis Hacker. His pathbreaking study, *The Triumph of American Capitalism,* first published in 1940, presented a provocative and challenging view of America's past. The ideas in that book have continued to provide stimulation to new research and thinking in economic history. It is appropriate, therefore, that the first volume in a series devoted to new thinking on this subject should be written by Louis Hacker. It is his work that has given to the new economic historians unconventional hypotheses that begged for explicit theorizing and empirical measurement.

One reviewer of the manuscript of this book termed Hacker "the doyen of American economic historians," and it is a justified tribute. His *The Triumph of American Capitalism,* his biography of Alexander Hamilton, and many other books and articles on American history have made, more recently his *The World of Andrew Carnegie, 1865–1901,* his long career one of impressive and concrete scholarly achievement. Professor Hacker is now 70 years old, but his scholarship is still young, refreshing, and meaningful.

In the present volume Professor Hacker has taken a reflective look at the course of American development. And the result is a pugnacious, provocative, and free-swinging survey of American economic history. The book is vigorously written, full of insights and comments on the recent literature, and challenges many of his own earlier views. The book may not please all historians or economists but they will not find it dull. As one reviewer stated: "If 'new' economic historians do not get too upset about

Hacker's criticism of economists' work . . . [the book] would be an excellent teaching tool for new economic historians." But the traditional economic historian also is well served by Hacker because, for the most part, he is extremely suspicious of modern economic theory and modern statistical analysis as substitutes for the careful, less impressive, but just as meaningful approach of the conventional institutional historian. There is, therefore, much to argue about in Hacker's book, and it is in every respect a welcome contribution to the methodological debate that has raged between historians and economists in recent years.

II

At the substantive level Professor Hacker's book includes a number of still challenging ideas. In *The Triumph of American Capitalism,* Professor Hacker used the Revolutionary and Civil Wars as the catalytic agents in bringing about change. In the present book, these two epochal events still occupy a central role in Hacker's interpretation of how economic and political forces worked to shape the American future. But it is how men and ideas were shaped by these events and not impersonal market forces that concern Hacker, and he has carried this approach far beyond that limited to the implications of the Revolutionary and Civil Wars. The present book is, therefore, much broader in scope than Hacker's previous work. Moreover, the ideas first expounded in *The Triumph of American Capitalism* are greatly expanded in coverage and time. The chapters on the 1930s and the post-World War II period are particularly useful extensions of Hacker's underlying concern with the factors and forces that move men to move nations. Hacker has also given much more attention in this book than in his previous work to social and institutional factors in 19th-century growth patterns. The discussion of the plantation system is particularly illuminating, as is Hacker's analysis of the impact of education, the role of labor organizations, radical increments and the impact of the values of the business community on the post-Civil War dynamics of industrialization. He has taken advantage of new research whenever applicable and the result is a dialogue in narrative form between Hacker, his old views, those he has changed, and the rest of the historical profession.

III

One of Hacker's substantive concerns in this volume and in his earlier work is the premise that a linear relationship exists between equality of opportunity and progress and welfare. Although this perspective is analytically useful when one is interested, as Hacker is, in the broad forces shaping national economic development, it does bias one's interest in the equity and distributional consequences of the growth process. Do empirical tests of income distribution, of poverty levels, or of welfare levels justify equality of opportunity as a working premise? Much of the work of the "new economic history," forcefully discussed here by Hacker, has, ironically, nearly the same broad analytical objective as does Hacker: to explain the major determinants of American economic growth. The perspective, however, is not of men and ideas but from the premise of market forces and their transformation by largely internal but also external economic stimuli. Productivity growth and efficiency in the allocation of resources for growth over time thus tend to dominate historical questions to the neglect of those of equity and welfare distribution. There are challenges here for both "new" and "old" economic historians. American economic problems in the 1960's, as Professor Hacker discusses so well, are largely distributional ones. The role of human capital in the growth process, just beginning to be examined by economic historians "new" or "old," casts an entirely new perspective on the historical forces shaping the growth of the American economy. Professor Hacker has made a contribution to this view, and it is appropriate to suggest that economic theory and modern statistical analysis can also yield just as valuable results as traditional historical scholarship. Whatever methodological differences exist, all historians share the same objective of historical truth, accuracy, and deeper understanding of national accomplishments and failures. I welcome Professor Hacker's contribution to this goal.

Ralph Andreano

PREFACE

The title of this book seeks to indicate its intention. It is an introduction
to the factors and forces responsible for the economic *growth* (quantitatively measured) and the resulting social and institutional *development*
(qualitatively analyzed) of the United States. All this is done in a historical
setting. The methodology—the tools used in the examination—are those
of both economics and history; and therefore this book can be used with
profit by students of either discipline as a brief *vade mecum* rather than as
a full-dress economic history. I say *vade mecum* advisedly. First, there is a
consistent theoretical viewpoint being pursued here, with which the reader
may or may not agree. Second, the book can be employed best as a com-
panion both to the many collections of readings and documents in American economic history recently appearing (the work of either economists or
historians) and to specialized studies in particular fields—which is the plan
of this series on American economic history. All of this permits flexibility
of discussion and greater student participation in the classroom.

My theoretical viewpoint, the fabric I have woven together, is made
up of the following strands. I do not think that quantifiable economic
variables (such as size and character of the labor force, capital creation and
investment, money supply, and expansion of the market) are all that are
needed to make models to test growth and to predict and manipulate its
future direction. In its generally accepted sense, economics deals with the
study of the allocation of available productive resources, which are limited,
for the satisfaction of alternative needs, which may be infinite. But—in a
larger social and political sense—its sweep covers the whole of human welfare. The latter is what the early giants—David Hume, Adam Smith,
Thomas Malthus, David Ricardo, Karl Marx, John Stuart Mill, Alfred
Marshall (and to this company should be added John Maynard Keynes)—
had in mind when they used (or it was used to describe) the rubric "politi-

cal economy" as the subject of their writings. These men had no trouble in communicating their ideas and intentions to a wider reading public—and to the shapers of public policy—than was to be found among professional economists alone.* For these reasons, I find it difficult to accept the theoretical positions of the "new economics" (of the neo-Keynesians) and the "new economic" (econometric) history.

To get at both the course of American economic growth (as measured by real per capita GNP and the capital/output ratio) and development (improving social and political attitudes and commitments and a more equitable allocation of the national product), one must throw a wider net. The climate of opinion (which rejected or accepted entrepreneurship and its leadership); social and political moods and postures; stability or conflict in class relations; the presence or absence of mobility in society; law and the law courts; the impact of labor radicalism; and political decision making (again with rejection or acceptance)—these singly or severally have played a large, perhaps the larger, role in retarding or encouraging growth and in holding back or advancing development. The analysis pursued by the historian must be in terms of both economics and human (and therefore often not predictable) institutions.

My mentors and guides in such an exercise are J. A. Schumpeter and Karl Marx rather than the American Keynesians and the neo-Keynesians. Schumpeter and Marx before him (Schumpeter, refusing to take Marxian economics seriously, always acknowledged his debt to Marx as a social philosopher and historian) were institutionalists, for they sought to weigh the dynamic rather than the static influences or impulses at work in historical time for progressive change. More particularly, both addressed themselves to these questions: What were the elements of vitality in capitalist entrepreneurship? And did these spend themselves—for Marx, because of inevitable dialectical conflict, and for Schumpeter, because of capitalism's "creative destruction"? If this were true, must public decision making (communism, socialism, the "welfare state") replace the private decision making of the capitalist entrepreneur and the (more rather than less) free market place?

Here I part company with both Marx and Schumpeter † as well as with the American Keynesians and the neo-Keynesians—with Marx and Schumpeter, because I do not think that industrial capitalism in the

---

* The distinguished English economist Sir Roy Harrod discusses and deplores the current failure in communication of present-day economists in the delightful essay "How Can Economists Communicate?" in the *Time Literary Supplement* (London), July 24, 1969.

† At any rate, with the Schumpeter of *Capitalism, Socialism, and Democracy* which (the internal evidence seems to indicate) was written before his *Business Cycles*.

United States has built the engines of its own undoing; with the American Keynesians, because I do not believe that only social (public) investment can maintain effective demand and insure high employment; and with the neo-Keynesians, because I am dubious about their position that massive public intervention (through fiscal manipulation, guideposts for industry and trade unions, and an "incomes" policy—wage and price controls) is necessary for sustained growth.

To me, therefore, growth and development in the United States is a historical process, and there was a number of way stations or peaks in the stated combined progress upward toward economic stability, higher per capita real income, improved productivity, maintained high employment, and social—perhaps even distributive—justice. The narrative is broken up into a discussion of these turning points in American history. Political economy—in addition to having to do with ways and means by which, broadly, human welfare is achieved or frustrated—perforce gives attention to the structural aspects of an economic society: the organization and production of agriculture, manufactures, transportation; the labor force and its composition; banking and the money supply; foreign trade and the balance of payments; international capital movements; urbanization; and education. Such discussions, in brief, and really only in their effects on growth and development, I have also included.

This book says many things I have written elsewhere; for I have been studying and publishing books and articles about these "forces and factors" for much of my mature life. For reading this manuscript, and for the comments they have made, I am indebted to the editor of this Series, Ralph L. Andreano, and to two young scholars, one the economist Lloyd J. Mercer of the University of California, Santa Barbara, and the other the historian Morton Rothstein of the University of Wisconsin. The friendliness with which these young men have received my efforts to fit my views of economics and history together proves there is really no "generation gap" when scholarship (if not ideology) is involved. And I am grateful to the librarians of the Columbia University library and the University of Rhode Island library for their many courtesies.

Louis M. Hacker

New York, New York, 1969

ACKNOWLEDGMENTS

The author acknowledges with thanks to the authors and their publishers their kind permission to print quotations from the following works:

Joe S. Bain, *Industrial Organization,* copyright © 1959. New York: John Wiley & Sons, Inc.

Carl Bridenbaugh, *Cities in Revolt,* copyright © 1955. New York: Alfred A. Knopf, Inc.

Richard C. Caves, *American Industry: Structure, Conduct, Performance,* 2nd ed., copyright © 1967. Englewood Cliffs, N. J.: Prentice-Hall, Inc.

Donald Dewey, *Monopoly in Economics and Law,* copyright © 1959. Chicago: Rand McNally & Co.

Douglas F. Dowd, in "Slavery as an Obstacle to Economic Growth: A Panel Discussion," in *Journal of Economic History,* Vol. xxvii (December 1967), copyright © 1967 by The Economic History Association. New York: New York University Press.

Albert Fishlow, *American Railroads and the Transformation of the Ante-Bellum Economy,* copyright © 1965 by the President and Fellows of Harvard College. Cambridge: Harvard University Press.

Milton Friedman and Anna J. Schwartz, *A Monetary History of the United States, 1867–1960,* copyright © 1963 by National Bureau of Economic Research. Princeton: Princeton University Press.

J. K. Gailbraith, *The Great Crash, 1929,* copyright © 1955. Boston: Houghton Mifflin Company.

Eugene D. Genovese, *Political Economy of Slavery,* copyright © 1965. New York: Random House, Inc.

Julius Grodinsky, *Transcontinental Railway Strategy, 1869–1893,* copyright © 1962. Philadelphia: University of Pennsylvania Press.

Bray Hammond, *Banks and Politics in America from the Revolution to the Civil War,* copyright © 1957. Princeton: Princeton University Press.

Seymour E. Harris, ed., *American Economic History,* copyright © 1961. New York: McGraw Hill Book Company.

Walter W. Heller, *New Dimensions of Political Economy,* copyright © 1967 by the President and Fellows of Harvard College. Cambridge: Harvard University Press.

Richard Hofstader, ed., *Progressive Movement, 1900–1915,* copyright © 1963. Englewood Cliffs, N. J.: Prentice-Hall, Inc.

John W. Kendrick, *Productivity Trends in the United States,* copyright © 1961. New York: National Bureau of Economic Research.

Gabriel Kolko, *Triumph of Conservatism,* copyright © 1963. New York: The Free Press of Glencoe of The Macmillan Company.

Simon Kuznets, *National Income and Its Composition,* copyright © 1941. New York: National Bureau of Economic Research.

Cleona Lewis, *America's Stake in International Investment,* copyright © 1938. Washington: The Brookings Institution.

W. Arthur Lewis, *Economic Survey, 1919–1939,* copyright © 1949. London: George Allen & Unwin, Ltd.

Frederick C. Mills, "Productivity and Economic Progress" (Occasional Paper 38), copyright © 1952. New York: National Bureau of Economic Research.

National Bureau of Economic Research. Conference on Research in Income and Wealth, *Trends in the American Economy in the Nineteenth Century,* copyright © 1960. New York: National Bureau of Economic Research.

———, *Output, Employment and Productivity,* copyright © 1966. New York: Columbia University Press.

Ralph L. Nelson, *Merger Movements in American Industry, 1895–1965,* copyright © 1959 for the National Bureau of Economic Research. Princeton: Princeton University Press.

Douglass C. North, *Economic Growth of the United States, 1790–1860,* copyright © 1961. Englewood Cliffs, N. J.: Prentice-Hall, Inc.

J. A. Schumpeter, *Business Cycles,* copyright © 1939. New York: McGraw Hill Book Company.

Peter Temin, *Iron and Steel in Nineteenth Century America,* copyright © 1964 by the Massachusetts Institute of Technology. Cambridge: The M.I.T. Press.

J. A. Willburn, *Biddle's Bank, The Crucial Years,* copyright © 1967. New York: Columbia University Press.

CONTENTS

XI. THE PROCESSES OF INDUSTRIALIZATION AFTER THE CIVIL WAR

XII. CHALLENGES TO A MARKET ECONOMY

XIII. THE PROGRESS OF THE ECONOMY AND ITS INSTABILITIES

LIST OF TABLES

THE COURSE OF AMERICAN
ECONOMIC GROWTH AND DEVELOPMENT

I

PRELIMINARY OBSERVATIONS

ENTER THE ''NEW ECONOMICS'' AND THE ''NEW ECONOMIC HISTORY''

There is no reason why economists, like other mortals, whether working in the arts and humanities or the natural sciences or indeed in the broad area of popular culture, should not yield to the whims and vagaries of fashion. Of course, as a rule, there is a pacemaker: some bold or, less frequently, truly creative man or woman, some person, like a new star suddenly appearing in the heavens, who fires the emotions and quickens the imagination; or someone neglected by his contemporaries and only dimly remembered, who is rediscovered. A style is set—the vast majority of us are followers rather than leaders—and all the stops are pulled, all the changes rung.

There is suddenly fresh life. Hundreds, hitherto mute or inert, are stirring; they write or paint or compose, make new designs or furniture or stage scenery; or they proclaim a new morality. There is a rush to read, see, and hear the new creations and to follow the new prophets. The fury of activity is accompanied by one of talk; the current mode is hailed, the old pityingly condemned and discarded—for the time being.

Out of all this stir and bustle, one or two Promethean challengers and creators emerge—in our own time a Yeats and Pound, a Joyce and Proust, a Picasso and Bonnard, a Stravinsky and Bartok, a Wright, Le-Corbusier, Einstein—to lift the spirit and help the mind and the senses to roam, whatever the age and the vicissitudes of men. They are the real romantics; the rest become classical or baroque. The classical repeat skillfully but endlessly the new ideas or forms, giving back in a thousand ways what the ruling taste expects of them; the baroque only embellish amusingly or outrageously what has become accepted canon.

In economics the towering ones, the romantics, have been Smith, Ricardo, and Marx, the founders of whole systems; the modern-day one is Keynes, although seriously flawed. Among Keynes's classical heirs, I suppose, one includes Paul A. Samuelson and the neo-Keynesians who seek to supply the dynamic qualities for growth and development that Keynes left out. Among the baroque there is undoubtedly J. K. Galbraith, who has never forgotten the theory of stagnation Alvin Hansen, his Harvard colleague and mentor, taught him, with overtones of the leading role of Thorstein Veblen's engineers—later, technocrats—in the market economy. Among the baroque, too, one might include the econometric historians who, following a strange kind of historical materialism, hold that only economic causation, as measured by statistics (or their mathematical reconstruction) can unerringly trace the causes and path of a country's growth and development. Thus history becomes "scientific" as economics and socialism became "scientific" in Marx's hands. Once again predictability is possible.

The combination of classical and baroque elements in economic history is a fashion today in the American universities. Along with acceptance—of a dynamic and not a static Keynes, of mathematics as the only tool of analysis—has gone rejection. The "traditional" historians have been unceremoniously dumped into the lumber room. Admittedly, they had never been blind to the forces and factors that have brought change, hopefully for development and possibly for growth, but their tools allegedly have been inadequate. The documentary study of what people have said and done—originally to create and then to remold institutions, attitudes, values, the decisions of private persons and public policy makers—have not been enough. For them must be substituted the new touchstones.

These consist of the following: theory, based on economic (rather than political, social, or psychological) hypothesizing; the testing of such conjectures or hunches by a use of statistical data or, if they are inadequate (and the farther back we go in time the less reliable they become), mathematics to fill in the lacunae; and the employment as the primary benchmark of the processes of growth and development, from which all theorizing, testing, and general laws are to start and proliferate.

History, then, is central. For if the real concern of economics is growth, the use of Marxian economics is not meant: the dialectic linked with polarization and the class struggle is old hat. The economics is neo-Keynesian, based on the quantitative measurement of changes and advances in the real national income. Then only the study of history, powerfully reinforced by theory (to segregate the limited number of significant independent variables or causal factors) and econometrics (to test the validity and viability of these), will supply those invariant laws that explain the past and serve as guides to decisions and policy making.

In this fashion the growth of a developed country will be "scientifically" determined; and the creations of the small models or machines (small because the variables by definition—though "significant"—must be limited) will serve to manipulate the larger, real ones (which, it is true, are also being pulled and hauled by social, political, psychological, and personal forces, but no matter) of the countries and peoples that should be developed.

The economists are thus to be the king pins. In an earlier time (Carlyle's or Emerson's) they were presumed to be the Hero-Philosophers, Hero-Prophets, Hero-Priests, or Hero-Kings. More recently (Veblen's or Dewey's) they were the technicians or technocrats (Galbraith has resurrected them); but if we use neo-Keynesianism and econometrics the economists will be our guides and therefore our lads. Keynes needed supplementation, because his analysis was in terms of equilibrium—after all, he had been brought up by Alfred Marshall—at less than full employment. To seek to furnish the growth factor (on the demand side) has been the effort of two economists working independently, the Englishman, Roy Harrod and the American, Evsey D. Domar. More sophisticated models (on the supply side) have been those of the American, Robert Solow, and the Englishman, J. E. Meade. Put simply, having in mind the goal of full employment, the Harrod-Domar model functions through a capital-output ratio in time; that is, the amount of capital required to achieve a net output or national income, and therefore growth; better still—to correct for increases in population—real per capita national income.*

What are the variables the econometricians are to isolate and measure? Usually, population (but, more particularly, the labor force); savings and investment; market expansion (the domestic market, of course, but possibly more important the foreign one); urbanization; technology and productivity; and investment in human capital—the improved education and health of the working population.

Out of this mix—in varying proportions at different times—the American economy grew. (Discontinuously and suddenly? Continuously

* Dates are interesting. The Harrod theory appeared in 1948, Domar's, in 1957, Solow's, in 1956, and Meade's, in 1961. Keynes died in 1946.

in time but gradually? There is room for quarreling and the quarreling
has broken out.) True enough, the public policy of government appeared
at one point or another, but not so much to initiate as to help forces
that were already functioning. Wars, revolutions, independent political
decisions (based on prestige, glory, national rivalries), and the appearance
of private innovators were out: they were the results rather than the
causes of the interplay of the few independent variables that really
counted.

All this is bravely asserted and new analyses have been presented by
(as they call themselves) econometric historians; history textbooks are being rewritten. These efforts have been applauded by other economists.
Thus Douglass C. North's *The Economic Growth of the United States.
1790–1860* (1961), which presents the purposes and illustrates the methodology of the "revolution" in their most elegant form, was hailed in
these words by two reviewers in *The Journal of Economic History,*
June 1962:

> Prior [to this] . . . most American economic historians enmeshed them-
> selves in description and institutional change; their writings never ade-
> quately reflected an understanding of the interaction between economic
> theory and history and the parallel gains derived therefrom, nor did they
> always direct their primary attention to the *growth process.* (Italics original.)

Four years later an anonymous English writer in *The Times Literary
Supplement,* April 7, 1966, had already seen the successful completion of
the "revolution":

> In America the new econometric history, less than ten years old, is
> already sweeping all before it. Resting upon an alliance between the mathe-
> matically sophisticated tools of measurement and the construction of elabo-
> rate theoretical models, it promises a *definitive* solution to such problems as
> the economic efficiency of slavery and the contribution of the railways to
> American economic growth. (Italics supplied.) *

Peter Temin, an American economist, who, incidentally, has done
very good work in the history of the American steel industry, is not so
sure, but he does not want to throw the baby out with the bath water:
after all, he uses the tools of econometrics himself. Temin puts his finger
on a fundamental difficulty. If we are to measure growth by real national
income, we come head on against the really insoluable problem of the
use and efficacy of index numbers in time. Writing in the same English
journal, July 28, 1966, Temin makes this shrewd observation:

* Despite the enthusiasm of the English writer, English economic historians have
been slow in following the American lead. No signs of a "revolution" here.

The methodological problem has implications for the economic ones. Can we find a definitive evaluation of the contribution of railroads to economic growth if we cannot measure economic growth *definitively?* Obviously not. We may find answers for questions such as this that will satisfy us now. But as our views of the world change and as the relative values of different commodities and different activities change, our answers to questions such as this may be expected to change also. The use of quantitative tools brings precision, but it cannot bring *objectivity* to the study of history. (Italics supplied.)

Temin then goes on to do some salvaging, again using the case of the importance of the American railroads to the country's growth. What is to be said in favor of the new econometric historians is that the questions being raised and the hypotheses being used to answer them are explicit. The "traditional" history has depended on implicit assumptions. (Really? Macaulay's Whig interpretation of English history? Albert Mathiez's and Georges Lefebvre's Marxian interpretations of the French revolution? Christopher Hill's Marxian interpretation of the English revolution in contradistinction to Macaulay's?) But to continue with Temin:

By making these assumptions explicit, the new economic historians are attempting to increase *the area within which reasonable men can agree.* The use of explicit theoretical models provides the reader with the opportunity to understand thoroughly what the investigator is doing and therefore to make a *reasoned decision* as to whether he agrees with the way the questions have been posed. (Italics supplied.)

The examples Temin uses give us small comfort. Both Robert Fogel and Albert Fishlow, two American econometric historians, have applied their tools and skills to measuring the contribution of the railroads to growth. Using one set of assumptions, Fogel concludes that the social savings for railroads were less than 5 per cent of the national income in 1890. The railroads, in short, were not important to growth because there were alternative and more efficient means of transportation, as measured by investment. Fishlow, using another set of assumptions, concludes that the rate of return on railroad investment before the Civil War was in the neighborhood of 15 per cent, about twice as high as the rate of return for the economy as a whole, measured by the rate of return on low-risk bonds. The railroads, because they represented an efficient use of resources and investment, therefore made important contributions to growth.

Temin, in other words, is not asking us to agree but to choose: just as we can choose between Macaulay and Hill (depending on whether we are Whigs, modern-day Liberals, or Marxians). Temin, in effect, is saying this, for he concludes his article with these observations:

All history is a reconstruction, and all history reflects the views and interests of the historian. Econometric history differs from previous investigations only in its attempted precision, precision that represents a contribution—not opposition—to history.

Still another econometric historian has thrown this whole "counterfactual" kind of study into a state of complete confusion. McClelland * is harsh with both Fogel and Fishlow in their efforts to measure the social savings of the American railroads; both, in their work, are confronted by "a serious data shortage." In particular, he regards Fogel's "impressive cerebral and statistical manipulations" as leaving "with most readers a credibility gap of the first magnitude." Fishlow comes off no better: his "estimation techniques . . . are also suspect." McClelland damns both with faint praise by ending as follows:

> In both works can be found a wealth of information concerning railroads and the multitude of strands that run between this single innovation and the fabric of American development. Their central question, however—the net benefit to the economy from the existence of the railroad in 1859 or 1890—remains essentially as they found it: an unsolved mystery.

Douglass North, who had been accepted everywhere as the bellwether of the econometric historians—he had led off the "revolution" with his *The Economic Growth of the United States, 1790–1860* (1961) in a brief 215 pages of text; summarized the whole of American economic history with his *Growth and Welfare of the American Past* (1966) in an even briefer 192 pages; he had given direction to the discussions in the annual meetings of the American Economic Association, and made *The Journal of Economic History* the organ of the movement—in less than a decade was being challenged.

David,† another econometric historian, casts serious doubts on all that North and the others following him have been saying. Using the same methodology of mathematical reconstruction, but with another set of assumptions, he categorically denies that the long-term rate of growth of aggregate product per capita had undergone a significant acceleration "somewhere during the period between 1815 and 1860" (North's phrase). David comes up with these conclusions:

First, there was no long-term trend, no secular acceleration, in the per capita real product in the pre-Civil War period.

---

* Peter D. McClelland, "Railroads, American Growth, and the New Economic History: A Critique," *The Journal of Economic History*, March 1968.

† Paul A. David, "The Growth of Real Product in the United States Before 1840: New Evidence, Controlled Conjectures", *The Journal of Economic History*, June 1967.

Second, his own mathematical reconstructions put the rate of growth per capita real product near 1.3 per cent per annum for both periods 1800–1835 and 1835–1855, as well as for the entire span of the young Republic's life, 1790–1860.

Third, after the Civil War, the long-term rates of growth were around 1.8 per cent per annum.

David does not want to say in so many words that the American Industrial Revolution was not already on its way in the ante-bellum years. He is content to raise a question, albeit somewhat wryly:

> Or will we [the econometric historians] attempt to refurbish with cast-off Rostovian* garb, the now very unfashionable idea of the Industrial Revolution "taking hold" in the United States only after the northern victory in the Civil War?

At any rate, David ends in this fashion:

> At present, it seems, a far more sensible solution would be to abandon the whole idea that significant, portentous stirrings of urban-industrial development within the predominantly agrarian ante-bellum economy must have been immediately reflected in a discontinuous and permanent alteration of the per capita real product growth rate, or in a parallel shift of the aggregate capital–formation ratio.

AN INSTITUTIONAL MODEL OF AMERICAN GROWTH AND DEVELOPMENT

This excursion through an intricate, combined maze does lead us out into the open again. North admits that the theoretical hypotheses to "shape the direction of quantitative research" have been slow in appearing. In fact, "A decade or more of concentrated research on economic growth has yielded meager results for the quantitative economic historian." There is, then, no general theory, no magical talisman, or, better still, no "open sesame" to unseal the cave in which knowledge and certainty are hidden. (Plato had other notions about the cave, but of course

---

* The reference is to W. W. Rostow's declaration in *The Stages of Economic Growth*, 1960, based on the Harrod-Domar calculus of the capital–output ratio, that the "take-off" of the American economy, that is, the start of the Industrial Revolution, took place during 1843–1860. David says: "cast-off" because of the rough treatment Rostow received at the hands of Fogel, then Fishlow, and then North. Cf. Fogel's *Railroads and American Economic Growth: Essays in Econometric History*, 1964; Fishlow's *American Railroads and the Transformation of the Ante-Bellum Economy*, 1965; and North's *Growth and Welfare in the American Past*, 1966.

he was discussing something else.) This is not to say that model building cannot fruitfully be employed, in highly limited degree, for the analysis of quantifiable short-run determinants of income. Nor, on the other hand, does this mean that the historian's painstaking assemblage of facts will lead, sooner or later, to their falling into patterns. Theory—that of the economists, but also that of the political scientists, social anthropologists, and sociologists—must play an important part for the historian in trying to ascertain how a nation developed and why change, at certain points in its evolution, occurred.

There is a theory, then, that guides the analysis being pursued in this book. Two sets of hypotheses in particular: that of J. A. Schumpeter's seminal idea of entrepreneurship, when new men can emerge in a fluid society to reactivate, or start in new directions, the economic processes; and that of William Graham Sumner's equally seminal idea of the folkways and the mores. The mores—based on the accepted ways by which a people think and act, but which have dynamic characteristics—are real and right. The mores guide the courts and legislatures; the mores support private rights and lead to social welfare. As early as 1900 Sumner had outlined this theory of social organization and change; in his *Folkways* (1907) he presented it with a dazzling virtuosity. Two passages are quoted here. The first is from paragraph 31 and the second is paragraph 34.

> The notion of right is in the folkways. It is not outside of them, of independent origin, and brought to them to test them. In the folkways, whatever is, is right.

> When the elements of truth and right are developed into doctrines of welfare, the folkways are raised to another plane. Then they become capable of producing inferences, developing into new forms, and extending their constructive influence over men and society. Then we call them the mores. The mores are the folkways, including the philosophical and ethical generalizations as to societal welfare which are suggested by them, and inherent in them, as they grow.

This book, which deals with the broad forces and factors, as well as the reasons for change—the sudden leaps forward—responsible for the growth and development of the American economy, is based on the following characteristics of the American mores.

Americans were Europeans; but part of their heritage is rejection and part is acceptance of European attitudes, commitments, and institutions. Both rejection and acceptance have been woven into the mores. We shall look at the elements of rejection first.

The *American climate and its way of life have always been capitalist.* This means that neither feudalism (a hierarchical society of status, in which economic production was largely on a nonexchange and nonprofit basis) nor mercantalism (a system of state power guided by political considerations and making the economic processes subservient to and directed by them) was brought over by the Europeans who departed for the America that was to become the United States in the seventeenth and eighteenth centuries.*

The greater number of emigrants by far were the unwanted simple (rather than gentle) folk of the countryside and the small towns. Many left voluntarily; some were forced; a few were assisted. They came when they could pay their passage as freemen; the larger number, certainly in the one hundred years, 1650–1750, came as bond servants. The Negroes started as indentured servants; but, beginning in the third quarter of the seventeenth century, they were brought over as slaves and remained slaves. The whites, after a brief period of indenture, also became freemen. They were for the most part young men and women with skills, or skills soon acquired as bond servants (important, because here was the human capital so badly needed in a new country). These people had been the victims of war and famine (the Irish in the seventeenth century and the Palatinate Germans in the eighteenth), religious persecution (the English Puritans and Quakers in the seventeenth century), ecclesiastical and economic oppression (the Scotch-Irish in the eighteenth century). They came because the doors of economic opportunity at home, that is to say, easy access to property (and this is what capitalism boils down to), were tightly shut).

When they settled down to plow, till, and harvest cash crops, they did so as freeholders, for either by purchase (the freedom dues that bond servants frequently received) or as squatters (with subsequent purchase) access to real property was easy. They left behind, in consequence, the medieval land system and its hangovers of tenure and organization. In Europe, the cultivators of the soil were copyholders (tenants for three lives) or cottagers (laborers with habitations but without land). The common lands and their harmful effects on animal husbandry continued to exist, and villages continued to dominate planting programs.

The possession of a freehold, in fee simple, made it possible to disregard Europe's ancient and manorial rights. Because this was so, the American did not have to live in a village, observe the village planting program, pay dues—whether in work or cash—to the landlord, and use

---

* I first began to speculate about the rejection/acceptance symbiosis as early as 1940 in *The Triumph of American Capitalism* and continued in the Introduction of *The Shaping of the American Tradition*, 1947, and the Inaugural Lecture as the Harmsworth Professor at Oxford, 1948. A full presentation of my theoretical position is to be found in the Introduction to *The World of Andrew Carnegie, 1865–1901*, 1968.

his public utilities. He could live where he pleased—and he chose to live in the center of his farm away from his neighbors; he could plant what he liked—and more and more (because he was part of a money and market economy) he chose to grow staples; he had water and subsoil rights and the rights to devise, encumber, and bequeath his property as he elected.

The newcomers left behind them Europe's corporate organization —in industry, trades, the churches, and the state. The medieval world had been founded on corporate authority, whether of manor, guild, or church. Even as it dissolved, hangovers persisted into early modern Europe. The corporate guilds survived—although in England many became privileged trading companies and new corporations made their appearance—as regulated companies and joint-stock companies, and monopolies flourished, frequently with crown support (one of the devices of the statism, or *dirigisme,* of mercantilism).

The guild system, with its control over wages, apprentices, production, and new capital investments, was not transplanted to the New World. Whether as entrepreneur or worker, the American again was a free man: to found new towns, open his own establishment, move where he pleased, and trade where and when and under whatever conditions he chose.

The European system of monopolies had interesting effects on Americans, for they continued to be fearful of them. Up to the outbreak of the American Revolution there were not more than a half dozen business corporations in the American colonies. (By contrast, between 1789 and 1800, American state governments chartered more than 300 such corporations.) Jefferson opposed the creation of the First Bank of the United States (1791) by Congress because to him it was likely to become a monopoly. Jackson successfully fought the rechartering of the Second Bank (1832) because he said it had become one. Corporate charters—except in banking and transportation—were granted only with the utmost caution in early America, and the hostility to corporate power prompted Congress in 1890 to pass the Sherman Antitrust Act to curb monopoly and maintain fair competition.

Easy access to property led to that other aspect of capitalism: acceptance of the uneven distribution of wealth and income and the private decisions made by entrepreneurs. The inevitable corollary was receptivity to industrial and commercial innovation and change. If the man who became wealthy did so because he was an innovator, good for him; did he not reduce costs, market new products, and increase productivity? If old skills were displaced and machinery and plant became quickly obsolescent, the whole of society benefited along with him.

If doors of opportunity were open and people could rise, fluidity in the class structure was inevitable. The class hostilities and class exploitation, which Marx put his finger on as the hallmark of (European) industrial capitalism, did not appear; and the efforts of American radicals, in the third quarter of the nineteenth century and in the first quarter of the twentieth century, to preach class war and struggle, were unavailing. All Americans who worked (except the Negroes) belonged to the middle class: the European Marxist characterization of American workers as proletarians and American farmers as peasants was simply grotesque.

In every country of Europe from which the seventeenth- and eighteenth-century colonists came established churches existed and many survived into the nineteenth century. Established churches meant not only the curbing of dissent but they possessed great legal and financial powers and dominated education. Americans were concerned with the corporate authority of established churches and moved against them, but not all at once. Although churches were established in colonial America, it should be noted that for the first time in our modern era church and state were separated in the four colonies of Rhode Island, Delaware, New Jersey, and Pennsylvania. With the creation of the Republic, Americans proceeded to disestablish churches in the states and, through the first Amendment to the Constitution, prevented the federal government from setting up an established ecclesiastical authority. By the end of the first quarter of the nineteenth century the surviving state-established churches of New England were gone.

Freedom of religious worship (and the absence of political disabilities as regards dissenters, nonconformists, and non-Christians) became the law of the land. Nonestablishment and disestablishment had another important consequence: it compelled lay, and increasingly public support of education, and the common (or public) school (running through the elementary grades initially) soon became a responsibility of local authority. The founders of the Republic saw the significance of education of the American people from the start, and provision for congressional support of local schools in the new West (through the device of land grants) in the Land Ordinance of 1787 was one of the great commitments—unique at that time and continuing unique, as far as Europe was concerned, far into the nineteenth century.

Education further made possible the improvement of human capital; it was no accident that the productivity of the American worker so quickly surpassed that of the European, as all foreign observers readily admitted and wondered over as early as the 1830s. From this it followed that the real wages of the American labor force were always the highest in the world. As the pioneers moved westward, there sprang up everywhere in their midst the little white churches and the little red schoolhouses—both local and symbolic of their independence of corporate authority.

The *Americans have always regarded themselves as middle class.* Because there was no transmission of feudal institutions, because, as the young John Adams said in the midst of the Stamp Act controversy, America was not burdened with a "canon and feudal law," the political, social, and psychological consequences were immense. "Middle class," here, did not mean a second estate, permanently fixed, between a privileged nobility at the top and the dispossessed land and industrial workers at the bottom. As Hartz,* has remarked, the middle class American, because there was no feudal society to challenge, "lacked the passionate middle-class consciousness which saturated the liberal thought of Europe." The young Tocqueville caught this at once in his journeyings up and down the new United States when he said (and Hartz made the observation the motto of his book):

> The great advantage of the Americans is, that they have arrived at a state of democracy without having to endure a democratic [i.e., social] revolution; and that they are born equal, instead of becoming so.

One caveat: a social revolution was the purpose of the Radical Republicans after the Civil War. In seeking to redistribute the land ("forty acres and a mule") and ensure the Negroes of the South equal civil and political rights and access to education, the Radical Republicans hoped to give to the newly established freemen the same secure place in the American world and the same opportunities to rise that were available to the whites. Because the Radicals failed, Americans have inherited the tragic consequences of this "unfinished" revolution.

"Middle class" in the United States meant social mobility—movement up but also movement down—and before too long its broad arrow was "one man one vote." "Middle class" also meant a pragmatic and non-doctrinaire attitude toward political thinking and political participation. It was Locke, as we shall see, who became the guide to Americans, not Condorcet, Rousseau, or, for that matter, the conservative de Maistre or the radical Marx. In consequence, if European feudalism left not even vestigial traces, European socialism made few converts. As Hartz properly observes, "Daniel Shays, frightening as he was to Governor Bowdoin and the Continental Congress, could not become anything like Babeuf or even Winstanley." Shays (by dubious devices, it is true) was trying to make his property rights secure; redistribution never entered his mind.

* Louis Hartz, *The Liberal Tradition in America,* 1955.

The dream of the New England Puritans to set up, in Bruchey's [*] words "a divinely planned society of fixed classes," "a Bible Commonwealth in which the Saints of Church and State would govern a community of the elect," could not survive for long; the realities of easy access to property in land and a scarce labor supply were too compelling to be blown away by the thunderings of magistrates and preachers and the threats of hell fire.

The same was true of Virginia and the Carolinas. A gentry that occupied large estates sought to ape the English aristocracy socially and politically but could not bloom and flourish in the European sense. To maintain its economic position it was constantly engaged in selling off part of its own land or in land promotion schemes, creating in the process the freeholders whose possession of property gave them the right to vote —and to challenge any attempts at the establishment of prescription.

In his "Advice to a Young Tradesman" (1743), Benjamin Franklin, in the secular terms of the eighteenth century, described the compromise with their religion (because they were living in a market economy) at which late-seventeenth-century New England Calvinists and Pennsylvania Quakers had already arrived:

> In short, the way to wealth, if you desire it, is as plain as the way to market. It depends chiefly on two words, *industry* and *frugality;* that is, waste neither *time* nor *money,* but make the best use of both. Without industry and frugality nothing will do, and with them every thing. He that gets all he can honestly, and saves all he gets (necessary expenses excepted), will certainly become *rich,* if that Being who governs the world, to whom all should look for a blessing on their honest, endeavours, doth not, in his wise providence, otherwise determine. (Italics original.)

Work, to the Americans, has always been invested with dignity. Work, to the American, was a proper and self-respecting pursuit not only because of the Protestant Ethic but because of the conditions of the world in which he lived and by which he could rise. However, the theory of mercantilism—which the colonists rejected and against which they fought in the American Revolution—was founded on the debasement of human labor. Mercantilism held that the wealth of the world was fixed, that only a strong state power could get a nation a larger share of it, and that the wealth of a people was derived from its foreign trade. A nation's foreign trade could expand, at the expense of its rivals, only because it was able to keep its domestic costs of production down. The wealth of a nation, therefore, was in its labor supply engaged in the pro-

[*] Stuart Bruchey, *The Roots of American Economic Growth, 1607–1861,* 1965.

duction of goods and services for export; and the size, docility, and poverty of its workers made possible the riches of the state.

Who were the workers? Collectively, England called them "The Poor." Right into the last quarter of the nineteenth century the term, "The Poor," was still used to designate the English working class.

The moral and social consequences of this conception were these: "The Poor" were needed, and they were assured the right to work by apprenticeship laws, labor contracts, and guild restrictions; but they also had the duty to labor. Public authority used persuasion and discipline; in the last resort—through the institution of the workhouse, established in England at the end of the seventeenth century—it employed coercion and punishment. The rights of "The Poor" were set forth in the great Elizabethan Statute of Artificers. The medieval apprenticeship period of seven years was extended to most of the highly skilled industries, labor contracts were to run for at least a year, and the local magistrates were given the power to fix minimum but also maximum, wages.

Work was demanded; but the worker was held in contempt. He was badly fed, ill clad, and wretchedly housed, while lay and ecclesiastical moralists constantly called attention to his improvidence and indolence. In 1724, when tens of thousands of young men and women were streaming out of England and Ulster to come to America, most of them as bond servants, Daniel Defoe could write:

> To begin with the labouring poor, they are indeed the Grievance of the Nation, and there seems an absolute necessity to bring them, by severe regulations, to some State of immediate Subordination.

In 1771 Arthur Young, who twenty years later was to describe with great pity the sad lot of the French peasant, could say this of his own countrymen: "Everyone but an idiot knows that the lower classes must be kept poor or they will never be industrious." William Temple, in 1770, guided by the same certainty and seeking to enhance the trade and commerce of England, set out a detailed program of workhouses, reduced real wages, and positive encouragement to population growth.

The differences between the colonists and the mother country in the concept of work constituted an unbridgeable chasm. Of what little avail, therefore to try to prove (one of the exercises of present-day econometric historians) that the English Acts of Trade and Navigation, by which England in its colonial relations sought to make secure its mercantilist ideas, created a viable economic system!

The *American, in his attitudes toward himself and the institutions he created, has always been a pragmatist.* The American conception of the nature of man is largely English in its origins, rather than French or German, for he has tended to follow Locke, Bentham, and Mill rather than Condorcet, Rousseau, or Hegel. The belief that man could shape his own destiny and achieve welfare by his own striving; the assumption that freedom could be maintained, whether because of natural right or beneficent law, not in a social order so much as through it; the hope that equality of opportunity was realizable only by the creation of demo-cratic institutions—this optimistic faith Americans acquired from Eng-land, and this is what I mean when I say that along with rejection came acceptance.

The early settler brought to the American continent the Protes-tantism that clothed with dignity the individual and his rationality and made his personal conduct the basis of a Christian life. Locke's ideas— in religion, psychology, education, politics, economics—buttressed at every point this hopeful view that man could order his existence suc-cessfully. As a consequence Locke powerfully influenced not only the founders of the American republic but the first two generations of Amer-ican thinkers as well. Locke was replaced, in very considerable measure, by John Stuart Mill, who, starting with utility instead of natural right, nevertheless came out at the same place.

We are what our experiences make us, taught Locke. What better justification had Americans for their confident belief that a broad educa-tional system was the means of guaranteeing the continuance of the demo-cratic way of life and the assurance of equality of opportunity? Men have certain inalienable rights. Was not this the basis for the necessity to up-hold the individual's right to dissent against an oppressive church and an authoritarian state? Political power must be widely dispersed. What better support could one find for the whole theory of the separation of powers and popular sovereignty? The universe is orderly; it is ruled by law. Was not the Rule of Law the shield men had against prescription and tyranny? The Rule of Law—again, whether based on natural right, as Locke had it, or a constitution, as Bentham insisted—protected the citizen against the coercive conduct of his fellows and the state.

Man was egoistic; man was selfish; and man sought his personal happi-ness; but at the same time man was rational, and because this was so he was capable of self-improvement. Reason curbed egoism, prudence tem-pered selfishness, and self-improvement and social well-being became inextricably linked. This belief in rational behavior, this determination to defend man's individuality, and this devotion to welfare are English notions—and, by adoption, American.

Thus in 1863 John Stuart Mill, in his justly celebrated essay *Utili-tarianism,* observed:

Yet no one whose opinion deserves a moment's consideration can doubt that most of the great positive evils of the world are in themselves removable, and will, if human affairs continue to improve, be in the end reduced within narrow limits.

Americans are committed to the Rule of Law. One of the greatest heritages that Americans acquired from England has been the Rule of Law, which, as Dicey put it (in 1885), "excludes the existence of arbitrariness, of prerogative, or even of wide discretionary authority on the part of government." Out of long English experience in shaping the supremacy of law have flowed the following:

Constitutional government, which can be changed only through orderly processes.

Representative government and the supremacy of the legislature over the executive. To make this certain the legislature is invested with control of the purse strings and the defense establishment.

The protection of the rights of the individual by exact procedural guarantees. What the English wrote into Magna Carta, the Petition of Rights, the Habeas Corpus Act, the Bill of Rights, the Act of Succession Americans have written into the first ten amendments of the federal constitution and into their state constitutions. Free men have the rights of conscience, speech, the press, and association; they have the rights of jury trial, protection against unreasonable searches and seizures, and a hearing, according to "the law of the land," which is fully safeguarded by "due process." They have the right to continue to dissent, even to the advocacy of violence, until such point at which incitement or conduct may jeopardize the lives and property of others and the security of society itself.

MERCANTILISM: WHAT IT WAS AND ITS IMPACT ON COLONIAL AMERICA

I have said that the American colonists were brought up in a mercantilist society; from the beginning of the eighteenth century they were restive under its rules and restraints; they were constantly at odds with the English royal governors whose purpose it was to see that they complied (hence the growing importance of the provincial legislatures to confine the executive power); and from 1763 on, when, in the interests of empire, England began to tighten the screws, they moved toward rebellion.

Mercantilism, as a system of state power, with public authority controlling and directing the nation's economic life, generally obtained in western Europe from the sixteenth through the eighteenth centuries. (England, it should be noted, was not completely free of it until the repeal of the Corn Laws in 1846 and of the Acts of Trade and Navigation in 1849.) Broadly speaking, this statism, or *dirigisme,* had these purposes: to create a self-sufficient empire and defend it; to stimulate foreign trade and by these processes to achieve a favorable balance of payments; to store treasure (bullion) thus acquired to be used to strengthen the royal prerogative and the military and naval establishments for the purposes of maintaining peace at home and of beating off foreign rivals and expanding at their expense. Colonies were to be established and new ones wrested in war for the glory and profit of the empire and the security of the realm. Even Adam Smith, critical as he was of the whole program of restraint and regulation, much as he hoped that the "natural system of perfect liberty" would be restored, declared, on the eve of the American Revolution as he viewed the empire, that "defence is . . . of much more importance than opulence."

So much for purposes; the methods for their accomplishments were these:

National Unification

The dynastic royal houses brought the unruly nobility to heel, broke down the localism of the towns, worked to bring the guilds under national control, and sought to eliminate internal barriers to trade (successfully in England; less so in France).

Protectionism

Protectionism was made up of import and export duties for revenue but, more particularly, to stimulate home industries and keep the foreigners out. Along with it went regulation, intervention, and participation. The state imported artisans, granted bounties, staked out monopolies, itself invested in enterprise and trading companies, compelled private citizens to do similarly, and sometimes put up state workshops. To top this off it imposed an elaborate code for the supervision of the home industries (presumably to protect quality in the export trade; often to keep out competitors) and regulated wages (again to further foreign trade).

Bullionism

The state labored to increase the money stock of the nation. It sought precious metals in mines (Spain was lucky; England was not); its ships preyed on the plate ships of those who had them, by war, privateering, and piracy (the Dutch, French, and English against the Spanish). Best of all, money stocks, gold and silver bullion, were to be acquired through the export industries and a favorable balance of payments.

This is not so naïve as it seems, given the nature of the western world in the sixteenth and seventeenth centuries. If, as mercantilists argued, "plenty" was "a dead stock" and production for export the key to survival and strength, it was proper to encourage population increase and the labor of children, to use the colonies exclusively for the purposes of the metropolis, and to pile up the precious metals so that England could defeat—and dispoil—the Dutch, Spanish, and French. The eighteenth century was something else again. The trouble was that England continued to follow Thomas Mun and not Jean Bodin, John Locke, and Adam Smith.

Colonialism

Empire building was an integral part of mercantilist doctrine and policy. To make possible the establishment of colonies the mercantilist states chartered trading companies, gave them the right to erect colonies and "pacify" the native populations, and extended exclusive trading privileges. Once the colonies were settled elaborate legal codes were drawn up whose purposes in general was to compel the colonials to produce raw materials (for reprocessing, for home manufacture, to avoid dependence on foreign sources) and to absorb the finished goods of home industry. Balances were to be paid in bullion. Where were the colonials —if their balance of payments was adverse—to get specie? Mercantilist writers and policy makers never said. Realistically, the colonists got specie from the spoliation of the natives and their enslavement for work in the mines (Spanish and Portuguese), from the Negro slave traffic (Spanish, Portuguese, Dutch, English, and American), and from piracy and illegal trade (American). They sought to devalue foreign coins and to expand their own money supply by paper issues—the first, a form of debasement of the coinage, the second, for the easing of credit to facilitate internal promotions.

As controls from the metropolis multiplied to include almost all aspects of economic activity, the American colonists in the eighteenth century fell back on two devices to survive and, hopefully, to grow: the expansion of their own money supply and illegal trade with the Dutch in Europe, the foreign Sugar Islands in the Caribbean, and the enemy in time of war.

Broadly speaking, the English program of colonial relations (which meant regulation and restraint; *dirigisme* again) included these ideas and methods:

1. The passage of the Navigation Laws and their supplementation as conditions warranted. Their purpose was to give the metropolis control of the carrying and export trades and to confine the colonies to the production of primary goods, most, but not all, of which England needed and which were to be exported to England alone. From the point of view of the empire the concern over English shipping meant wresting sea supremacy from the Dutch (the first act was passed in 1651) and keeping it by building up the naval and mercantile fleets and training seamen for them.

2. The prohibition of colonial manufactures from intercolonial and foreign trade.

3. The management of the colonial money supply, which meant outlawing a colonial coinage, putting a ceiling on the devaluation of foreign coins, and seeking to limit the issuance of paper money.

4. Setting up a carefully devised and successfully functioning administrative and judicial machinery for the enforcement of these restraints.

It is idle to argue that the English were not fully aware of the purposes on which they were embarked or that, while filling their statute books with laws and their administrative codes with orders and prohibitions, certainly up to 1763 they regarded with benevolence colonial law breaking. This is not so; there was no "salutary neglect." Thus in 1726 a member of the Board of Trade (the chief regulatory agency) declared:

> Every act of a dependent provincial government ought therefore to terminate in the advantage of the mother state unto whom it owes its being and protection in all its valuable privileges. Hence it follows that all advantageous projects or commercial gains in any colony which are truly prejudicial to and inconsistent with the interests of the mother state must be understood to be illegal and the practice of them unwarrantable, because they contradict the end for which the colony had a being and are incompatible with the terms on which the people claim both privileges and protection. . . . For such is the end of the colonies, and if this use cannot be made of them it will be much better for the state to be without them.

Even the wise Adam Smith, writing as late as 1776, was of two minds when he contemplated the Acts of Trade and Navigation. Thus in his Fourth Book "Of Colonies" he could write:

> Agriculture is the proper business of all new colonies; a business which the cheapness of land renders more advantageous than any other. . . . In new colonies, agriculture either draws hands from all other employments or

keeps them from going to any other employment. There are few hands to spare for the necessary and none for the ornamental manufactures.

But then he could also write:

> The liberality of England, however, towards the trade of her colonies has been confined chiefly to what concerns the market for their produce, either in its rude state, or in what may be called the very first stage of manufacture. The more advanced or more refined manufactures even of the colonial produce, the merchants and manufacturers of Great Britain choose to reserve to themselves and have prevailed upon the legislature to prevent their establishment in the colonies, sometimes by high duties, and sometimes by absolute prohibitions.

Nineteenth-century American historians knew what the Navigation System was all about, whereas present-day historians, political and econometric, back and fill. Thus J. L. Bishop, in his excellent *History of American Manufactures,* Vol. 1 (1861), states:

> The several measures thus adopted for engrossing the colonial markets, by a monopoly of the export and import trade, by prohibition of manufactures, by bounties on raw materials and upon the exportation of English manufactures, gave a vast impulse to the productive industry of the mother country. The result demonstrated the value of the plantation trade, and of the policy pursued, and led to renewed recommendations of the same system, and increased manifestations of jealousy and vigilance in regard to Colonial attempts at manufacture.

Later in the same volume Bishop says flatly: "[It was that] legislation, which was the cause of the separation."

With regard to prohibitions of and restraints on the colonial money supply John Jay Knox, in his equally notable *A History of Banking in the United States* (1900) says:

> This interference by Parliament with the right of the colonies to avail themselves of the supposed blessings of paper money either directly by their Treasuries or by means of banks, excited the most intense indignation, and was one of the causes that led to the final break.

It was under such a regimen that the American colonies were planted and grew over the long period from 1607 to 1776. We must next determine why they began to challenge it.

II

THE AMERICAN REVOLUTION

THE EXPANDING COLONIAL WORLD

The American Revolution came out of the climate in which the colonists grew up, and this was a compound of many things: three thousand miles of sea which separated the mother country from the settlements in the New World; the ease with which the wild lands could be penetrated, subjugated (including the native Indians), and a living wrested from them; the involvement of England, fully half the time from 1689 to 1763, in foreign wars, so that the metropolis's restraints and prohibitions could be violated with a fair chance of escaping detection and punishment; the increasing controls over the purse being achieved by provincial legislatures—and, in consequence, the subordination of royal governors to the assemblies. All had led to manifold and subtle psychological changes. Whether the colonists stoutly asserted their loyalties to the crown, enrolled in the provincial militias to march against the French and Spanish, or sent our privateers to prey on their ships, they were Americans and not Englishmen; they were a "nation" by whatever broad or narrow terms that somewhat elusive concept is defined. They had been "born equal"; and circumstances (the ease of access to property), law (the English common and constitutional law), the absence of prescription, and the creation of settled political institutions had helped to keep them so.

Over the evolving years, from the mid-seventeenth century on, their various ways of activity, their economic patterns, had been formed and life had become easier. Many had prospered. Nine-tenths of them were engaged in agriculture but this did not mean self-sufficing farms. True enough, on the family farms there was a good deal of home production: the making of wooden fence posts and utensils, potash and pearl ash (for soap), spinning, weaving, tanning, and the fabrication of clothing (wool and leather) and animal harnesses. But Americans lived in a market economy based on cash and credit. Surpluses had to be and were produced to pay taxes and mortgages and to buy the necessities that even jacks-of-all-trades, no matter how resourceful, could not produce: guns and powder, salt, rum, iron, and hardware. To improve farming capital only surpluses or supplementary work (hunting, trapping, logging, and shipping with the fishing fleets) could accomplish the draining of wet meadows, the building of barns and silos, and the buying of herds and flocks.

The colonial agricultural community divided itself into three groups. In the New England provinces, where the terrain was rocky and hilly and the winters long and severe, mixed, or general, farming was the rule: the production of hay and corn, meat animals, and some wheat, dairying, and fruits. Even so, staples had appeared by the eighteenth century—beef cattle and hogs, horses and oxen, and surpluses of butter, cheese, honey, wool, and flaxseed (to be shipped to Ireland for the linen weavers)—and the products of the farmer's off-hours: deerskins, furs, barrel staves and heads, and the cod and whale fisheries. All of these moved into channels of trade, either at local stores or mills in exchange for goods and services or into the hands of the Connecticut Valley merchants who sent them to the towns or directly to the West Indies.

In the middle colonies, on large farms with excellent soil and terrain and a long growing season, wheat was planted and harvested to be shipped or milled into flour as the great articles of commerce. Wheat and flour

TABLE 1

COLONIAL POPULATION (IN THOUSANDS)

	1630	1660	1690	1720	1750	1770
New England	2	33	87	171	360	540
Middle	—	5	35	103	296	556
Southern	2	36	88	192	514	994
Totals	4	74	210	466	1,170	2,090

Source. *Historical Statistics of the United States*, 1960, p. 756.

and more beef cattle, hogs, and work animals were destined for the West Indies and the intercolonial trade.

In the southern colonies, after the last quarter of the seventeenth century, plantation wares, produced by Negro slaves as the labor supply, flourished. All were commercial crops. Virginia and Maryland planters grew tobacco to be sold (under the Navigation Laws) in England and Scotland. The tidewater planters of the Carolinas and Georgia raised rice, indigo, and some cotton. Not all were plantation lords or gentlemen farmers. There were family farms, on less advantageous soil, in the back-country or up rivers, in both the middle and southern colonies, where the round of living and working was much as it prevailed in New England.

All of this—agricultural production and expansion and the movement of surpluses into trade; hunting, trapping, woodworking, and the fisheries; the quick absorption into the work force of white bond servants and Negro slaves; the availability of and easy entrance into land along the Connecticut, Hudson, Delaware, Potomac, and James rivers—led to a great and almost steady growth in the American population. Table 1 lists the estimates for the original thirteen colonies by regions for 1630–1770. The figures are in thousands and include whites and blacks. By the outbreak of the Revolution Negroes made up one-fifth of the total; in the southern colonies, 40 per cent.

The colonial businessman was a merchant, usually an undifferentiated merchant, who maintained a retail store and, if he lived on a navigable river or in a seaport, a warehouse and dock for the wholesale trade. In the country he ran a grist mill, fulling mill, paper mill, or (in New Jersey and Pennsylvania) an iron works. In the seaboard towns he was interested in shipyards, rope-walks, canvas and sail-making shops,

TABLE 2

COLONIAL CITIES

	1630	1660	1690	1720	1760	1775
New York	300	2400	3900	7,000	18,000	25,000
Philadelphia	—	—	4000	10,000	23,750	40,000
Boston	—	3000	7000	12,000	15,631[a]	16,000
Charleston	—	—	1100	3,500	8,000	12,000
Newport	—	700	2600	3,800	7,500	11,000

[a] Actual census.

Source. Carl Bridenbaugh, Cities in the Wilderness, 1938, pp. 6, 143, 303; Cities in Revolt, 1955, pp. 5, 216.

ships, the fisheries, and (in Rhode Island and Massachusetts) rum distilleries. He extended book credit to his customers and suppliers and lent
them money. He was a land promoter and a land speculator. In the
southern colonies many of the earlier merchants were the factors, or
agents, of English houses, who worked with their capital to buy cash
crops of tobacco, indigo, and rice on consignment and sold on credit to
the planters.

The country merchants lived in the inland towns. On the seaboard
they occupied the five colonial cities, only one of which, Charleston, was
in the south. Table 2 lists the estimates of their population as they grew
and flourished in the period between 1630–1775.

THE MACHINERY OF MERCANTILIST CONTROL

As I have said, during the course of this century and a half the colonists
had learned to take for granted that theirs was an expanding world, with
the further opportunities, not chimerical but real, that were always available to the bold and enterprising. When, suddenly, doors were banged
shut, the restraints and prohibitions ever present in the mercantilist system were reasserted, supplemented, and, this time, enforced with all the
administrative machinery and authority available to the crown. Their
world was not only shaken but its survival was threatened. The young
Alexander Hamilton, writing in the first number of *The Continentalist*
in July 1781, had put his finger on it when he said: It had been a "narrow colonial sphere [in which Americans] had been accustomed to move,
not of that enlarged kind suited to the government of an independent
nation."

The reassertion of royal authority came in the 1760s and 1770s. The
mercantilist program was once more proclaimed, and there was no alternative to grasping the nettle—that is, to opt (by war) for a political freedom whose psychological, social, and intellectual roots had grown so
sturdily. It is important to look at this "narrow colonial sphere" and see
how Americans, frequently by violation of law, were forced to live in it
and how the tightening of restraints from the early 1760s on compelled
them to challenge the crown.

The Acts of Trade and Navigation were the centerpiece of the mercantilist system. The first one, really a statement of policy, was enacted
by Parliament in 1651 and was followed by the laws of 1660, 1663, 1673,
1696, and 1733. Their broad purposes have already been described, but
some of the details require filling in.

The Act of 1663 showed clearly enough what the English mercantilist lawmakers were about. Called the Staples Act, its intention was to make certain that London and Bristol were the entrepôts for all the finished goods the colonials might need. As Andrews * put it, the act meant "the making of England the staple for all European goods imported into the colonies, that is, the imposing of the requirement that all commodities from other countries which were wanted in the plantations should pass through England as the sole exporting center before shipment overseas to America." The implications were plain enough. England made and bought cheap and sold dear. Carriage to England had to be in "lawful shipping, lawfully manned." (Only countries of origin could ship to England; otherwise, goods had to be carried in English vessels. The fact is that most of the cargoes brought to America from the mother country were in English ships. This meant freight earnings, an important item in the English balance of payments.) Transshipment, too, meant export duties, warehousing, other handling charges, and commissions and interest (particularly for the southern planters who bought on credit). All this was put on the price.

The colonists could not trade directly with the East (the monopoly of the East India Company), but they could with European countries south of Cape Finisterre, a promontory on the northwest Spanish coast. Adam Smith dryly explained why:

> The parts of Europe which were south of Cape Finisterre are not manufacturing countries and we were less jealous of the colony ships carrying home from them any manufactures which could interfere with our own.

Only "nonenumerated articles" could go to southern Europe, which also included the famous Wine Islands, Madeira (Portuguese) and the Canaries (Spanish). Nevertheless, the enterprising colonial merchants quickly took advantage of the small opening left them, for they earned freights, sold more than they bought, and disposed of their ships into the bargain. One of the amusing consequences was that affluent colonials learned to drink Portuguese Madeira and port, Spanish sherry, and Italian marsala, instead of French claret.

The "enumerated lists" were a characteristic mercantilist device. Regularly added to, they meant that certain specified commodities produced in the plantations overseas (as a rule the outstanding colonial raw materials, always excepting northern foodstuffs) were to be exported only to England either for processing or for transshipment to Europe north and south. Thus freights were earned, duties collected, and primary products for English manufactures made certain. The Acts of 1660 and

* C. M. Andrews, *The Colonial Period of American History,* 1934.

1663 "enumerated" the following: sugar, cotton, tobacco, ginger, indigo, and various dyewoods. Those of 1704 and 1705, molasses, rice, naval stores, hemp, and masts, yards, and bowsprits. That of 1721, copper ore and beaver and other furs. That of 1764, whale fins, hides, iron, lumber, potash and pearl ash, and raw silk.

American historians who like to say that mercantilism was not wholly restrictive, for England gave as well as took away, point to the facts that the Americans were granted the monopoly of the growth of tobacco, whereas its culture was banned in England, and that the colonial production of naval stores (tar, pitch, resin, and turpentine) was offered bounties in 1705 and of indigo in 1748.

It will be observed that in the first place all of these were enumerated. In the second, England could not grow tobacco profitably. The fact is that England consumed relatively little tobacco (not quite 3.7 per cent of the 100.5 million pounds imported in 1773); most of it went to the European continent, with the English merchants making the profits from the processing and the freights. Worse still, because tobacco was so tightly controlled, the leaf was sold in a monopoly and manipulated market, so that the colonial planters got the short end of the stick. After the Revolution England imported 45.5 per cent of the American crop in 1799 and 22.7 per cent in 1840. In the third place, England had stripped itself of its timber to make charcoal for its iron industry, and if it was to build ships it sorely needed naval stores (to caulk ship bottoms), masts, yards, and bowsprits. The enumerated potash and pearl ash also are to be noted: they result from the burning of wood.

The act of 1673 put an export tax on enumerated goods at the port of clearance. The Act of 1696—whose targets were the sizable colonial smuggling into Holland and growing Scottish competition (ended in 1707 when Scotland became part of Britain, perhaps a mixed blessing because Scottish merchants were then able to establish their factors and stores in the southern colonies)—resulted in a tight administrative machinery. Admiralty courts, sitting without juries, were set up to plug the holes: to try smugglers who sought to avoid taxes by shipping illegally, English-built ships were to be registered; and the highly competent Board of Trade was established to watch the colonies and report malfeasance or nonfeasance to the Privy Council and Parliament.

The act of 1733 was the famous, or notorious, Molasses Act. Despite admiralty courts and because the mercantilist program made it impossible for the northern colonies to maintain a favorable balance of payments, northern merchants and ship captains had to go adventuring and venturing. They found rich pickings in the Spanish, French, Dutch, and Danish islands of the Caribbean, the so-called Sugar Islands. To protect its own plantations in Jamaica, Barbados, and the Leeward Islands—Parliament laid prohibitory duties on foreign sugar (5:5 d. per 100 pounds), molasses (6 d. per gallon), and rum (9 d. per gallon) imported into the American colonies. These levies were replaced in 1764 by the Sugar Act, an outstanding reason for the hue and cry that preceded the act of revolution itself.

To go back to the machinery of control. The Privy Council, the Board of Trade, the Secretary of State for Colonial Affairs, the Treasury, the Admiralty and its courts, the Commissioners of Customs, and the royal governors sent overseas spent a good deal of their time on colonial matters. The Board of Trade was there as watchdog; but much more. It prepared the colonial civil list, the judiciary being a particular concern. It had the right to deny charters, or patents, to English companies that sought to invest in the colonies, where home industries or financial interests would be hurt. It had the power to review colonial legislation— for colonial legislatures, also, tried bounties, tax remissions, and public investments to support native industries—and, when laws were unfriendly, to recommend their disallowance (veto) to the Privy Council. It cracked the whip over the royal governors (they were placemen who depended largely on the crown for their maintenance—rather than on the niggardly provincial legislatures) and prepared and sent out specific instructions which ordered them to veto colonial legislation when assemblies became too ambitious or defiant.

The Board of Trade ranged far and wide. The Privy Council, on the commissioners' request, disallowed colonial legislation on such matters as export duties on colonial raw materials required in English manufacture, the granting of exemptions that favored colonial shipowners in the carrying trade, and import duties on foreign wines and liquors and on English merchandise. When this last became a general practice, the commissioners of the Board issued blanket instructions to the royal governors to veto laws that imposed duties on European goods imported in English vessels (1724) and on the produce or manufactures of Great Britain (1732) and those laws under which the natives of a province were given preferential treatment over British subjects (1732).

The Privy Council was called on again and again to disallow legislation that placed prohibitive duties on the importation of Negro slaves and interferred with the free transport of felons overseas. Both the Board and the Privy Council were aware of the great English slave-carrying trade which was bound to be affected by such legislation, and their solicitude was plain. (The Royal African Company was chartered by the crown in 1662 with a monopoly to set up "factories"—settlements, stores, and forts—on the Guinea Coast. The size of this enterprise may be judged by its capitalization of £111,000.) Finally, in 1731, when the colonies persisted in their efforts to pass such bills, the royal governors received circular instructions to veto legislation that interfered with the free entry of Negroes and felons. (How much the forcing of Negro slavery on the colonies rankled is to be noted from these two items. In 1774 George Washington, with other Virginians, subscribed to this resolve, "We take this opportunity of declaring our most earnest wishes to see an entire stop forever put to such a wicked, cruel, and unnatural trade." In 1776 Thomas Jefferson's original draft of the Declaration of Independence—later struck out—named the Negro traffic as one of the "injuries and usurpations" visited on the colonies by the crown.)

In 1706, 1707, and 1708 the commissioners called on the royal governors to veto acts passed by Virginia and Maryland assemblies that provided for the establishment of new towns. The following reasons were given: new communities must inevitably lead to a desire to found manufacturing industries; they would draw off labor and capital from the countryside and tobacco growing would suffer. The retardation of urbanization was a consequence, for, as Russell * pointed out, "Largely as a result of the government's determined attitude in the matter, comparatively few laws for this purpose were enacted in the plantations."

Nothing was too minute to escape the commissioners' attention and quick action. I cite only two; the dates will be noted. In 1705 a Pennsylvania statute to foster the shoemaking industry was disallowed on the grounds that, as the Board said, "It cannot be expected that encouragement should be given by law to the making of any manufactures made in England . . . it being against the advantage of England." In 1756, when a Massachusetts statute to build up a linen industry was disallowed (by this time the export of flaxseed to Ireland had become important), the Board as roundly declared, as it had a half-century earlier, "The passing of laws in the plantations for encouraging manufactures, which any ways interfere with the manufacture of this kingdom, has always been thought improper, and has even been discouraged."

It can be seen, therefore, that the few occasions on which Parliament intervened were not flashes in the pan; Privy Council, Board of Trade, Parliament, all labored ceaselessly in the interests of the same grand design. In 1699 Parliament passed the Woolen Act, which barred colonial wool, woolen yarn, and woolen manufactures from intercolonial and foreign commerce. In 1732 the Hat Act prevented the exportation of hats (they were made of beaver, one of the "enumerated" commodities) out of the separate colonies, restricted colonial hat makers to two apprentices

---

* E. B. Russell, *The Review of American Colonial Legislation by the King in Council*, 1915.

who were to serve seven-year terms, and forbade Negroes to work in the industry. The Iron Act of 1750 struck at an important industrial development which attracted and trained a large labor force (whites and Negroes) and involved sizable capital investments in colonial America.

Iron deposits had been found in western Virginia and Maryland and in New Jersey and Pennsylvania. Iron plantations sprang up, so called because they were located in the country amid great stands of timber that could be cut and burned down to charcoal, the basic fuel of the blast furnaces. Here flourished many small works, which combined furnaces, forges, and charcoal-making ovens, and large quantities of crude iron—pigs and bars—were turned out for sale to blacksmiths to be beaten into chains, ploughshares, and axheads. The next step followed: the establishment of rolling and slitting mills and plating forges to make nails and sheets out of wrought iron.

It was at this point that Parliament intervened. The colonial production of crude iron was all very well: England's ironmongers needed iron for their finished hardware, an important article of commerce, with a large market in America itself. Colonial finished iron was something else again. The Act of 1750 therefore put crude iron on a free list and denied to colonists the right to extend the manufacture of wrought iron by banning the erection of new slitting and rolling mills, plating forges, and steel furnaces. In 1764 iron was "enumerated."

All this makes the idea of "salutary neglect" just plain silly. Earlier American historians, less concerned with English susceptibilities than later ones and less inclined to weigh pros and cons "judicially," knew how pervasive the whole program of mercantilist restraint and prohibition was, as English commentators and writers were also fully aware. Thus Swank * stated:

> The first Lord Sheffield declared [1783] that "the only use and advantage of American Colonies or West Indies island is the monopoly of their consumption and the carriages of their produce." McCullough, in his *Commercial Dictionary* [1832], admits that it was "a leading principle in the system of colonial policy, adopted as well by England as by other European nations, to discourage all attempts to manufacture such articles in the colonies as could be provided for them by the mother country." Dr. William Elder, in his *Questions of the Day* [1871], says: "The colonies were held under restraint so absolute that, beyond the common domestic industries and the most ordinary mechanical employments, no kind of manufactures was permitted."

C. P. Nettels, an outstanding modern-day historian of the American colonies, is one of the few to agree with Swank, Bishop, and, inciden-

* J. M. Swank, *The History of the Manufacture of Iron in All Ages*, 1892.

tally, this writer.* In a comprehensive review of the character and effect of English mercantilism Nettels † says: "Thus there was no more important ingredient in Eiglish policy than the determined effort to retard or prevent the growth in America of industries."

In this commentary on the mercantilist system much has been made of the prohibitions put on the appearance and the restriction of colonial manufactures. It is unrealistic to argue, as too many historians have done, that Americans would not have engaged in manufacturing in any case. Manufacturing, up to the end of the eighteenth century, was based on hand and not machine production, and Americans not only had in abundance the needed product markets (wool, iron, fuel, flax, wood, furs and hides) but, even more important, the factor markets of a working force (the Negroes could be taught skills, as they were in the iron industry), capital, great entrepreneurial ingenuity, as well as outlets at home in the rising middle class and abroad in the Sugar Islands, where they had comparative advantages. America would have been a serious rival of England and probably would have worsened it, for American workers were better and its entrepreneurs more venturesome.

Then why, with independence, did not manufactures in the United States spring up and flourish, as Alexander Hamilton, in his famous *Report on Manufactures,* so persuasively claimed they would? Three observations may be offered. First, the outbreak of the European wars in the early 1790s turned American capital and skills to the highly profitable ship-building and carrying trades (in 1790 Americans laid down more than 29,000 tons of ships, at least equaling the amount built on the eve of revolution, and in 1815, almost 155,000 tons).

Second, the cession of western lands by Britain in the United States and the Louisiana Purchase encouraged the investment of capital in land promotions and the surplus labor of the eastern farms to move west, across the Alleghenies and into the rich agricultural region of the Northwest Territory. The United States—federal government and states—did everything necessary to stimulate these activities. They passed easy land laws in which squatting was legalized, extended credit for land companies from the state banks, and, best of all, facilitated western movement and settlement. Road building across the wide prairies (the best agri-

* As early as 1935 I made the same analysis in "The First American Revolution," *Columbia University Quarterly,* September 1935, and more fully, in *The Triumph of American Capitalism,* 1940.

† C. P. Nettels, "British Mercantilism and the Economic Development of the Thirteen Colonies," *Journal of Economic History,* Spring 1952. For a contrary view see L. A. Harper, "The Effects of the Navigation Acts on the Thirteen Colonies," in R. B. Morris, Ed., *The Era of the American Revolution,* 1939 and his "Mercantilism and the American Revolution," *Canadian Historical Review,* March 1942.

cultural country in the world) was made possible by the financial assist-ance of the federal government; and the states—the federal government bowing out, although Secretary of the Treasury Albert Gallatin had laid out an imaginative and extensive federal plan in 1808—began to finance canal construction. Railroading followed soon thereafter, as early as 1830.

Third, the Industrial Revolution—machine manufacture, factory and cheap wage labor, a machine-tools industry, larger towns and cities with the external economies these created—was fully launched in Eng-land before the first quarter of the nineteenth century was over. American entrepreneurs could not compete; and, because American tariffs con-tinued low right up to the eve of the Civil War, even the American market was easily invaded by and saturated with English manufactured goods. It was no wonder that the American businessman continued largely as a merchant; and it is typical of the prevailing mores that Free-man Hunt, when he sat down in 1856 to sing the praises and accom-plishments of the American entrepreneurs, called his collection of essays *Lives of American Merchants.*

MERCANTILIST RESTRAINTS ON THE MONEY SUPPLY

Control over the colonial money supply was an integral part of the whole policy of mercantilist restraint. Virtually from the beginning the Amer-ican colonies sought to expand their money: they were in a market economy; money was the basis of credit; their unfavorable balances of payments drained off foreign and English coins; and, England, on its part, moved in the opposite direction. Americans pressed into service commodities (tobacco, rice, corn, hides), whose values were fixed by the provincial assemblies, but the Crown warned the colonists that they could not impair contracts by setting prices for commodities contrary to those stipulated in agreements. They tried (notably in Massachusetts in 1652) to remint foreign coins and create their own currency; in 1684 such practices were outlawed. They attempted to stop the export of coin; in 1697 the Privy Council disallowed such efforts. By statute (in Mary-land, Virginia, and also in Barbados and Jamaica), the Spanish pieces of eight were revalued from 4s/6d up to 6s/8d in an effort to keep the coins at home (and to pay off English creditors with a depreciated cur-rency); these laws were disallowed. The result was that the tobacco and sugar colonies were stripped of their coin, but the general distress com-pelled Parliament in 1704 to fix the value of the pieces of eight at 6s and four years later to prescribe prison sentences for those violating the regulations.

Paper money had to be resorted to. This was of two sorts: "bills of credit" (really tax-anticipation warrants), which were issued by most of the provincial governments, and bills that were printed and circulated by land banks (some were public, some private) against land mortgages.

The first such bills of credit made their appearance in 1690 in Massachusetts: England had declared war on France, American colonials were marching off to the north, and funds were needed to supply them; at the same time, the increasingly pressing demands of businessmen had to be satisfied. Because these were short-term bills, their maturities were fixed (with taxes earmarked to meet them) and they were not to be considered legal tenders. Within the first third of the eighteenth century all of New England, New York, New Jersey, Pennsylvania, both Carolinas, and Maryland had emitted such bills. They constituted a floating supply of money for these reasons: before too long all the bills were invested with legal-tender quality so that private debts as well as public obligations could be discharged with them; in fact, some colonies added compulsion, providing for fines for refusal to accept the bills; maturities lengthened, and they lost their character of tax-anticipation warrants, for assemblies stopped earmarking taxes, renewed bills when they came due, or substituted what were called "New Tenures" for "Old Tenures." Frequently the two kinds of bills existed side by side.

Beginning in 1712 (in South Carolina), land banks set up by the provincial governments made their appearance, thus adding to the public notes. Their bills were usually issued against rural land mortgages, but in New England, against town lots and houses as well. There were large numbers of these banks and many failed (particularly in South Carolina and New England, where issues were against poor securities), but those of Pennsylvania, New Jersey, New York, and Maryland continued solvent because of the greater restraint exercised in the making of loans. In Pennsylvania, where a provincial land bank was in continuous operation from 1723 on, the interest it earned over twenty-five years paid all the costs of operating the public services and direct taxes could be dispensed with.

Rhode Island—its businessmen plagued by unfavorable balances of payments, as their ventures continued to expand—went off the deep end in regard to land-bank bills. From 1715 to 1750 there were something like eight separate issues, the total emission coming to £400,000. The value of the bills (in relation to sterling) naturally fell, in some colonies only moderately (New York and Pennsylvania), in some sizably (Massachusetts, Connecticut, North Carolina), in two very sharply. In Rhode Island in the 1750s the ratio of paper to silver was 26 to 1 and in New Hampshire, 24 to 1.

With these considerable additions to the money supply, what was the effect on prices? Unfortunately, an index of wholesale prices for Rhode Island is not available. The one we have is based on the prices of Philadelphia, New York, and Charleston.* With 1850–1859 as 100, the index rose from 58.6 in 1720 to 84.3 in 1774, about 44 per cent over 54 years, or less than 1 per cent annually. Hardly inflationary, considering the expanding economy.

For Boston † we have an index of the price of an ounce of silver in paper shillings. With the year 1700 as the base, the price rose quite steadily from 7 shillings in 1700 to 38.5 shillings in 1746 (450 per cent) and then leaped to 60.0 shillings in 1749 (or 900 per cent in 50 years.) This clearly reflects the severe balance-of-payments problem in New England. As we shall see, New England (as well as New York and Philadelphia) merchants were compelled to obtain bills of exchange in triangular trades to satisfy their obligations in England.

Was the emission of paper money designed to permit debtors (usually farmers) to fob off their creditors? Some thought and said so, in the 1740s; later Americans, writing in the 1890s when the controversy over free silver became so heated, said so too and roundly condemned the colonists for being repudiationists. This assumes that the colonists knew nothing about money and that their intentions were always suspect.

We are more knowledgeable about money today than the highly reputable economists of the 1890s were, and, by the same token, we can see that the colonists understood what they were about. In 1749 a committee of the Rhode Island Assembly, seeking to explain what was happening in that colony, had this to say:

> Where balance of trade is against any country, that such part of their medium of exchange as hath a universal currency [coin] will leave them, and such part of their medium [paper] as is confined to the country will sink in its value in proportion as the balance against them is to their trade.

The fact is that a careful reading of the very large and highly controversial colonial literature about money appearing in the first half of the eighteenth century shows that not debtor farmers but alert, enterprising, and deeply perplexed (because of balance of payments) businessmen—merchants, promoters of new ventures, and advocates of public improvements—were the ones who clamored for more money. They were

---

* *Historical Statistics of the United States,* 1960, p. 772.
† *Ibid.,* p. 723.

sorely tried by inadequate liquidity in a developing economy. Adam Smith, toward the end of *The Wealth of Nations,* recognized this need, for in talking of Scotland and the American colonies, both bereft of the hard metals, he observes that they were forced to resort to paper issues because "it is not the poverty, but the enterprising and projecting spirit of the people, their desire of employing all the stock which they can get as active and productive stock, which has occasioned their redundancy of money."

As early as 1682, all sorts of people in the colonies began to write about money—and the debate continued hot and heavy up to the outbreak of the Revolution—clerics, public officials, a printer (Benjamin Franklin), a doctor (the redoubtable William Douglass), as well as merchants and land-bank promoters.* They talked of the money supply (some wanted less, some wanted more) with all the skill and not a few of the subtleties of modern-day analysts; for in writing of money they also discussed its effects on trade, the balance of payments, immigration, business recession, and growth.

The contractionists complained about the high living of their contemporaries; check imports, they said, and there would be no balance-of-payments difficulties and no necessity for increasing paper issues. Douglass, a contractionist, thundered again and again, in pamphlets issued in 1738, 1740, 1741, and 1743, that legal tenders were the work of debtors, hard pressed and squirming to escape, who put upon their creditors. It was Douglass who threw off Adam Smith (in an early part of *The Wealth of Nations,* Smith, following him, referred to the legal tenders as "a scheme of fraudulent debtors"); and it was Douglass whom the economists of the 1890s trailed after sheep-fashion.

Benjamin Franklin entered the lists as an expansionist in 1729, and his pamphlet is an amazingly modern and sophisticated analysis of the role of money. The colonies needed more to encourage the ship-building industry and other arts and crafts, to stimulate immigration and build up the labor supply, and to give a lift to investment and employment. An earlier expansionist, in 1716, argued for a land bank in Massachusetts so that it could promote public works (a bridge across the Charles River, a canal through Cape Cod) and help in the development of a large number of private enterprises (slitting mills, glass works, the manufacture of linen, and the growth of hemp and flax).

It is Douglass who scored, however, for he was seen and heard in London, and there can be no doubt that he played a large part in raising

---

* See the interesting collection of these outpourings in A. McF. Davis's *Colonial Currency Reprints, 1682–1751,* 1910–1911.

the wind about the very ambitious Massachusetts Land Bank and Manu-factory scheme of 1740. The bank was capitalized at £150,000 and in a single year issued notes totaling £40,000. The English Board of Trade—alarmed over the fact that the project might prove to be more than a land bank (its bills at the end of 20 years were to be payable in produce or finished goods, hence "manufactory," and part of the bank's capital subscription could be paid in its own bills or in the same produce or manufactured articles)—cracked down at once. The Massachusetts assem-bly had chartered the bank; this time the Board of Trade turned to Parliament and in 1741 the bank was outlawed by statute, with the en-suing ruin of many of its backers, the father of Samuel Adams among them. Thence forward the descent into Avernus was swift.

The Board of Trade had regarded with suspicion this growth of legal tenders and had tried to control them with its customary devices of disallowance and instructions to royal governors, laying down these general principles: that the amount of public bills to be issued was to be limited to the actual requirements of the colonial governments; that there be fixed maturities and no reissues; and that they not become legal tenders. All this was unavailing, however, and again Parliament was resorted to.

In 1751 a statute forbade the New England colonies from making any further issues of legal tenders for private transactions; the only exceptions were emissions that covered current public expenses and the financing of war costs. In 1764 this so-called Currency Act extended the prohibition of legal tenders to all the colonies and required that they be sunk at the expiry dates. The Act of 1773 opened the door a crack by specifically permitting, within the restrictions of the 1751 and 1764 laws, the continued issue of public bills and their use as legal tenders for the discharge of obligations due governments.

The restraining act of 1764 raised a general outcry. Benjamin Franklin told the House of Commons that restrictions on paper money were alienating the colonies from the mother country. In 1774, as the breach widened, the First Continental Congress roundly condemned the restraining act as a violation of colonial rights.*

---

* In recent years, there has been renewed interest in colonial monetary history. See R. A. Lester, *Monetary Experiments: Early American and Recent Scandinavian,* 1939 and E. James Ferguson, "Currency Finance: an Interpretation of Colonial Mone-tary Practices," *William and Mary Quarterly,* April 1953. In the 1960s, as a result of American balance of payment problems, monetary theorists have been attracted to the colonial experiences once more. See the articles by M. L. Burstein and J. A. Ernest in *Explorations in Entrepreneurial History,* Spring-Summer 1966 and Winter 1968.

THE UNFAVORABLE BALANCE OF PAYMENTS AND EFFORTS TO ESCAPE

Direct trade of the colonies with England and their balance of payments, to which passing reference already has been made, must now be examined in detail. Put simply, in regard to direct trade, from the beginning of the eighteenth century (the figures are fairly good starting with 1697) the northern colonies had an unfavorable trade balance which continued to increase until it became very large in the decade, 1761–1770; the trade balance of the southern colonies was favorable up to the end, but the gap kept on narrowing—so much so that during 1761–1770 the imports of Maryland and Virginia from England exceeded their exports. The southern colonies' exports, all largely sought after and encouraged by the English, were tobacco, indigo, rice, furs and hides, and naval stores.

Table 3 tells the story succinctly of the direct colonial trade with England.

TABLE 3

COMMERCE OF AMERICAN CONTINENTAL COLONIES WITH ENGLAND,
SELECTED YEARS (ANNUAL AVERAGES IN THOUSANDS OF POUNDS STERLING)

	Exports to England			Imports from England		
	1701–1710	1730–1741	1761–1770	1701–1710	1730–1741	1761–1770
New England	37	64	113	86	197	358
New York	10	16	62	28	92	349
Pennsylvania	12	14	35	9	52	295
Maryland-Va.	205	394	468	128	207	491
Carolina	14	177	330	22	94	262
Georgia	—	—	36	—	3	40
Total	268	665	1,044	273	645	1,795

Source. Historical Statistics of the United States, 1960, p. 757.

Table 4 shows the relative role of the American colonial trade in the whole English picture. The total of American continental imports and exports may be compared with those of the British West Indies and India. The increasingly greater importance of the Sugar Islands to England helps to account for the pressures on the American colonies that began to grow during the 1760s.

TABLE 4

ENGLISH COMBINED IMPORTS AND EXPORTS, SELECTED YEARS AND AREAS
(ANNUAL AVERAGES IN THOUSANDS OF POUNDS STERLING)

	1701–1710	1731–1740	1761–1770
American Continental Colonies	556	1,313	2,843
British West Indies	942	1,781	3,406
India	582	1,179	2,516
Ireland	579	1,045	2,850
Total Empire	2,802	5,751	12,651
Total Europe	7,673	10,555	11,740
Grand Total	11,069	18,919	25,930

Source. David Macpherson, *Annals of Commerce, Manufactures, Fisheries and Navigation,* Vol. 3, 1805.

No figures are available for the balance of payments; that is, the services (freight, insurance, commissions, interest), gold and silver, and capital investments that move in international commerce along with the imports and exports of goods. Considering their direct trade with England, the northern colonies did have earnings from the carriage of freights and the sale of ships. These additions were not enough to pay for the heavy imbalance in imports; on the invisible services of freights and insurance in all likelihood the northern colonies had an unfavorable balance. In consequence, northern merchants had to develop all sorts of additional trades—with Newfoundland, southern Europe, the Wine Islands, the Sugar Islands, and Africa—to discharge their obligations to the mother country. On the other hand, the southern colonies acquired almost all of their services (their freights, insurance, commissions and interest) from England. The upshot was that because these costs were so heavy, their favorable balance of trade turned into an unfavorable balance of payments, against which there were no offsets by earnings from trading voyages elsewhere. That this was so is demonstrated by the fact that the floating obligations of southern planters to English merchants were converted into long-term debts or capital investments—mortgages on land and on Negro slaves. These sums have been estimated to have been about 4 million pounds by the outbreak of the Revolution. England afforded no such relief to the northern colonies; the capital investments in the region were so slight as to be unimportant. In contrast, it is interesting to note that the size of the capital stake the English had in their own Sugar Islands was about 60 million pounds, another important reason why, when it came to the crunch, they were favored over the continental colonies.

Why did the northern colonies fall so far behind in their direct trade with England? They were producing surpluses of wheat and corn, provisions, cattle, work animals but they could not be sent to England. Up to 1767, the mother country was an exporter of "corn," (the small grains, and also beans and peas); and after 1767, an importer, but by this time the quarrel between England and the colonies had already boiled up. They were producing surpluses of fish which were virtually barred from England because they would compete with the English fishery industry of the North Sea and the Newfoundland banks. They could export masts, yards, bowsprits, naval stores, iron, furs, deer skins, whale oil, whale fins and flax seed. Little enough pay for the English manufactured goods—textiles and dry goods, notions, hardware, house furnishings—the northern colonies were buying in such growing quantities.

Hence the development of these additional trades, which included the movement of services as well as goods. The upshot was, in all of them, that the northern merchants ran up favorable balances of payments which were converted into foreign bills of exchange and foreign specie to pay off English creditors and to add to their own money supply.

Newfoundland-Nova Scotia

To these famous fishing grounds (fished not only by the English but the French, Portuguese, and Dutch as well) went fishing tackle, flour and bread, salt, provisions, and rum; in return came fish, usually cod (dried at home for re-export), and bills of exchange and specie.

Wine Islands and Southern Europe

To the Azores, Madeira, and the Canaries went the dried fish, barrel staves and heads, cattle and work animals, rice, and the ships themselves; back came light and fortified wines and bills of exchange and specie. To Spain, Portugal, and Italy were exported dried fish, rice and ships; in return came fruits and wines and again bills of exchange and specie.

Sugar Islands and Africa

This route developed into a great triangular trade—it became the basis of the strength and vitality of the northern commercial economy (and also its Achilles heel!)—the movement of goods and services that employed all the ingenuity of an impressive trading people. Out of Salem, Boston, Bristol, Newport, New Haven, New York and Philadelphia (and also the river towns of Middletown, Hartford, and Albany) went the small, swift ships of the northern merchants, loaded with the necessities that the sugar planters of the West Indies demanded and could not produce for themselves—cattle and work animals; lumber, staves, heads, and hoops; wheat, flour, and salted provisions; salted cod for the slaves; and ships. Back came indigo, cotton, ginger, allspice, and dyewoods (much of this for re-export to England); foreign bills of exchange and specie; and, above all, sugar and molasses for manufacture into rum in the scores of small distilleries in Massachusetts and Rhode Island. The colonies learned to drink the rum themselves (too often they mixed it with strong beer, vinegar, or cream in vile concoctions!); they bartered rum (and trade goods) with the Indians for their furs and hides, they sold it to the Newfoundland fishermen, and they used it to trade with the African chiefs of the Guinea Coast who sold their tribesmen and the Negroes they kidnapped or captured in war into the unholy slave traffic.

Frequently ships would set out eastward to the African coast as the first leg of the journey. Here went rum, iron bars, dried fish and trade goods. Small quantities of ivory, gum and, beeswax and, most important, large numbers of Negro slaves were picked up in exchange. The second leg of the journey led westward across the famous Middle Passage to the Sugar Islands, where the slaves would be sold and cargoes of sugar and molasses loaded. The profits took the form of bills of exchange (on London, Paris, Madrid, Amsterdam, or Copenhagen), silver pieces of eight, and gold guilders and louis. The northern merchants thrived on this and waxed rich, for two reasons: their West Indian trade was diverted more and more to the foreign Sugar Islands where prices of sugar and molasses were cheaper and there were no export duties; and until 1763 it was easy to return home and land cargoes without paying import duties—either by smuggling them in or by suborning local customs officials.

In the Caribbean, along with the British plantations of Jamaica, Barbados, and the Leeward Islands, similar settlements had been established by the French (Martinique, Guadaloupe), the Spanish (Cuba, Hispaniola), the Dutch (Curaçao, St. Eustatius), and the Danes (the present-day Virgin Islands). These colonies, too had begun to grow sugar—this was notably true of the French—and by the third decade of the eighteenth century they had become serious rivals of the English. Not only was the English sugar-planting economy inefficiently operated— it was run by stewards or managers, while the owners lived in great luxury in England—but a heavy export tax (4½ per cent) was levied at the island ports; and because sugar was an "enumerated" article it had to go to England first before being re-exported (with the additional costs of handling, profits, and freights).

The English and the Americans knew this. Adam Smith referred to the "superiority" of the French planters, and John Dickinson, a colonial, alluded to the English in this contemptuous fashion: "By a very singular disposition of affairs, the colonies of an absolute monarchy [France] are settled on a republican principle; while those of a kingdom in many respects resembling a commonwealth [Britain] are cantoned out among a few lords vested with despotic powers over myriads of vassals and supported in the pomp of Baggas by their slavery."

The foreign growers usually settled on their plantations, and owner-operations achieved real economies; there was diversification (instead of the single cropping of the English), with coffee often rotating with sugar; their sugar was not burdened with duties and was not "enumerated" so that marketing costs were lower. Besides, a number of foreign islands had free ports—the Dutch St. Eustatius, the Danish St. Croix— which American merchants regularly used for market and price intelligence, warehousing, and transshipment as they moved through the numerous islands of the area, buying sugar and molasses and selling their flour and wheat, and dried fish. As a result, foreign sugar and molasses could be had 25 to 40 per cent cheaper, and with the "safe conducts" for ships and cargoes to the French islands that were easily obtained in the free ports and the smuggling of the sugar and molasses into the colonies (the Molasses Act of 1733 was circumvented without any real trouble) it was understandable why the English sugar islands began to languish and colonial merchants became bolder and richer. By the late 1750s, when the traffic was at its height, at least 11,500 hogsheads of molasses reached Rhode Island annually from the foreign islands, as against 2500 from the English; in Massachusetts the ratio was 14,500 to 500.

Small wonder that the pressures on Parliament from the English sugar interest intensified—the illegal trade in the West Indies had to be stopped—and, beginning in 1760, the whole elaborate administrative machinery of English mercantilism moved into action.*

---

* It was inevitable that the econometric historians should seek to evaluate British imperial policy quantitatively. See R. P. Thomas in *The Journal of Economic History*, December 1965, in which he came to the conclusion that the Navigation Acts were not oppressive. He was challenged by R. L. Ransom in the same journal, September 1968 and Thomas replied, *op. cit.* A New entry to the debate was G. M. Walton in the same journal, September 1968. He expressed dubiety about the triangular trade with Africa as the apex, but said nothing about the balance of payments.

THE TIGHTENING OF CONTROL

Even before the Seven Years War (French and Indian War) was over in 1763 the English crown set about closing doors and tightening screws. In 1761, to catch the colonial smugglers, local courts were directed to issue and recognize the doubtfully legal writs of assistance (general search warrants). In 1763 the peacetime navy (the war had ended) was converted into a patrol fleet with powers of search (also illegal) on the high seas. In the same year absentee officials in the customs service (up to then, placemen) were ordered to their colonial posts. A vice-admiralty court for all America was established in 1764, and the number of local admiralty courts (sitting without juries) was increased. In 1768 a new board of customs officials, resident in America, was created. Informers were to be rewarded out of captured illegal cargoes. Customs officials were to be protected from damage suits for seizures of ships and goods, and stricter registration and inspection of vessels was ordered. Suits involving informers and cases having to do with customs duties were to be tried in the admiralty courts; and to protect the judges from local retaliation their salaries were to be paid out of the customs revenues.

The Sugar Act of 1764 reduced the duty on molasses from 6 to 3d, but it raised the duty on refined sugar and banned entirely the importation of foreign-island rum. The same act required American customs officers to post bonds and keep full records; the smuggled cargoes caught by naval ships were to be sold, and officers and ratings were to share in the proceeds; all colonial ships, even those in the coastwide trade, were required to observe all the formalities of port clearance.

So much for illegal trade with foreign islands. Having embarked on this course of making mercantilist restraint work, crown officials pressed into other areas in which laxities had developed. The "enumerated" lists were expanded to include lumber, hides and skins, pig and bar iron, and potash and pearl ash. In 1764 the Currency Act was passed, and in the same year certain kinds of French and oriental dry goods were taxed for the first time. High duties were put on wines from the Wine Islands and on wines, fruits, and oil imported directly from Spain and Portugal. In 1765, the importation of foreign silk stockings, gloves, and mitts was forbidden, and in 1766 Parliament ordered that cargoes of all remaining "nonenumerated" articles (largely flour, provisions, and fish) bound for European ports north of Cape Finisterre be discharged first at English ports. None of this had to do with direct taxes; "taxation without representation" was not involved. The crown was determined to protect the English Sugar Colonies, compel the Americans to send their raw materials to England and to buy British, and get as much as it could out of carry-ing trades.

I am not arguing that the direct taxes imposed by the Stamp Act of 1765, the Townshend duties of 1767, and the Tea Act of 1773 did not inflame opinion; the point is that these revenue laws only exacerbated the hostilities the tightening of mercantilist regulations had produced. Hard times had set in because of these laws, the stringency of credit, the Currency Act, and the stoppage of the easy money that had flowed into the colonies, due to British military expenditures. Hard times and admin-istrative oppression will make a well-to-do middle class of merchants restive and rebellious. When to this was added the *coup de main* directed against the southern planters in the Proclamation Line of 1763 and the Quebec Act of 1774, then men of property, loyal subjects of the crown, North and South, became united in their resistance.

The great planters of the southern colonies had always been interested in the wild lands beyond the Appalachians; they had acquired, by crown grant or purchase, large tracts on which they set up land promotions or permitted squatters to settle. As settlers moved in, the land promoters also financed trade with the Indians, thus assuring the steady flow of fur skins and hides for export to England. In short, land promoters (and speculators) preceded the Daniel Boones into Kentucky and Tennessee. When in 1748 the young George Washington set out to survey the lands around the waters of the upper Potomac, he went as the representative of a great colonial landlord (Fairfax) and, in his own right, as the scion of a rich land-owning family; and when he bought up soldier bounty claims, after the French and Indian War was over, he was taking the risk—as other large Virginia planters were—that the western lands would be kept open for entry and settlement.

At home the English crown officials had other ideas. They insisted that the western territories wrested from the French had to be pacified and that orderly governments had to be established first; hence the so-called Proclamation Line of 1763, which shut off the whole area beyond the western crest of the Appalachian Mountains to colonial land dealers and fur traders and ordered the abandonment,of the newly established settlements. Imperial agents, and not the colonial governors, were to administer the region. All this was declared to be temporary; colonials were prepared to assume that a final policy would restore their rights of entry, exploitation, and trade and would recognize the ancient colonial charters with their western claims. These were vain hopes; in 1774, when the Quebec Act was passed, the English intention became clear.

The vast trans-Allegheny West was to be kept as wild land, where the fur and hide trades could flourish and timber and wood products would continue as important articles of commerce, rather than for the founding of settlements, farther and farther distant from crown controls. The recipients of the royal bounty, in the shape of great tracts of land, were to be British (English and Scottish) merchants, army officers, and rich landlords, and not the colonials; all their land schemes went aglimmering. This pattern had already emerged between 1763 and 1774 when such grants were made to British subjects in Canada, Nova Scotia, Florida, and Prince Edward Island—all areas directly accessible to British merchants. As for the western fur trade, it was to be regulated from the newly established province of Quebec. Western furs, which had been moving to Philadelphia and New York, were to go to Montreal—with English merchants and companies financing the traffic and deriving the profits.

This combination of circumstances—plus the other so-called Coercive and Restraining Acts of 1774—led to the summoning of the First Continental Congress of 1774, to which delegates from all the colonies came. It established the Continental Association, an embargo agreement, which was so successful that in 1775 English imports virtually disappeared. In resolutions passed April 6, 1776, the Second Continental Congress declared the Acts of Trade and Navigation null and void and ordered an end put to the colonial slave trade. By this time the war for independence had already broken out.

III

THE CONSEQUENCES OF THE
FIRST AMERICAN REVOLUTION

THE INADEQUACIES OF THE
ARTICLES OF CONFEDERATION

The course of the Revolution was an uneven and uncertain one, as most revolutions are, at times civil war and reconstruction at home—to crush the loyalists, to effect drastic political changes, and even to redistribute property—being regarded as more important and being pushed more energetically than organization for military victories in the field. The defeat of the British at Saratoga was a turning point: it brought France (she entered into an offensive and defensive alliance with the "United States in Congress") and then Spain and Holland back into war with Britain. Loans and gifts from these European allies helped to shore up the faltering finances of the Continental Congress. By 1781, after the victory at Yorktown (in which a French army and navy had participated), Britain had had enough: it was more important to preserve domestic tranquility (in England there was outspoken opposition to the war) and to protect the far-flung empire from her European enemies than to crush the Americans. In 1783 a formal peace was signed.

The Treaty of Paris recognized the independence of the United States and ceded to her the vast, unsettled lands beyond the Alleghenies, as far as the Mississippi on the west and the Floridas on the south; it also gave

44

Americans the right to fish the Newfoundland banks and agreed to evacuate American territory without carrying off any property (i.e., Negro slaves). The United States, on its part, promised British creditors the recovery of their prewar debts (British garrisons continued to occupy the western posts to spur this on) and the restoration of the rights and property of the loyalists. To this extent the American peace commissioners returned empty-handed: Britain refused to open its own ports and those of its Sugar Islands freely to American commerce.

It was one thing to obtain peace abroad; it was another to assure the success of the Revolution at home. It was not until 1787 that the *political* means for survival, stability, and future growth were forged; from 1781 until 1789 it was really (despite outward semblances of economic recovery) touch and go. It was the Constitution, and through it the establishment of a strong central government, that saved the nascent American Republic.

The war had been fought by an alliance of the thirteen states acting through the Continental Congress. It was not until March 1781 that the Articles of Confederation (a league of friendship of sovereign states) had been ratified. No executive or judiciary had been established, and the powers vested in the Confederation Congress (each state delegation voted as a unit and nine votes were required for the passage of important legislation) had been narrowly circumscribed. By the Articles Congress could make war and peace, support an army and navy, enter into treaties of alliance, borrow money, regulate the coinage and weights and measures, establish a post office, and manage Indian affairs. It was given control over the new national domain as a result of the cession of their western claims by the states, and it enacted two important pieces of legislation in consequence: the Land Ordinance of 1785, which provided for the organization of the new territory and its eventual formation into states, the guarantee of the political, civil, and property rights of settlers, and the prohibition of slavery; and the Land Ordinance of 1787, which became the basis of American land law. This legislation established these important principles: that surveys were to be made and parcels of land of fixed and uniform size (a section was defined as one mile square, or 640 acres) laid out before sale; that sales take place at auctions (minimum price one dollar an acre) and be paid for in specie or in loan-office certificates reduced to specie; that military warrants be honored from this public domain; and that at least one lot in each township be set aside on which to build public schools.

Yet the Confederation Congress could not tax to support and develop a central authority. It had no control over the money supply, it could not regulate domestic or interstate commerce, and it could not protect property. To meet its own requirements and to service the foreign debt (how otherwise could it obtain foreign credits?) it was permitted to levy requisitions on the states. This was a slender reed to lean on, for between 1783 and 1789 the states honored only 25 per cent of the requests thus made, and by 1786 the total income of the central government was less than one-third of the annual charges on the national debt. Because of the accumulation of unpaid interest, by the end of the decade of the 1780s the debt had reached an estimated total of $52,788,000.

In 1781, and again in 1783, Congress had urged the states to grant it power to levy on imports an ad valorem duty of 5 per cent, the proceeds of which were to be used for debt management; because this required unanimous consent and because Rhode Island and then New York refused to accede, any hope of restoring the public credit went aglimmering. This, and the fact that the states played politics with the requisition system to their own advantage only (they paid Congress's debts in their own way or used moneys requested to perform federal functions within their own territories), compelled Robert Morris, whom the Congress had made Superintendent of Finance in May 1781, to resign in November 1784. With his strong hand gone, drift set in.*

Outwardly there were signs that freedom was giving spur to enterprise. The removal of British restraints and prohibitions led to increased activity as new companies (some joint-stocks, some limited partnerships, engaged in scores of different and hitherto interdicted ventures) made their appearance: commercial banks, land promotions for the development and settlement of the western lands and for urban growth, the building of public improvements (turnpikes, canals, bridges, river and harbor channels), and small manufactories in iron, woolens, paper, glass, wood products, and the exploration of new avenues of foreign trade. State legislatures, only too eager to encourage the creation of joint-stock companies, authorized by special charter 11 of them between 1781 and 1785, 22 between 1786 and 1790, but, with the emergence of the Republic, as the pace quickened, 114 between 1791 and 1795.

Commercial banks (to write up deposits, to discount commercial paper, and to make accommodation or term loans for more ambitious projects) emerged for the first time in America, and met with immediate success. The Bank of North America (chartered by the Congress) was

* E. James Ferguson, who is suspicious of Morris and who revives the generally discredited charge of a conspiracy of the monied interests to force the creation of a powerful "nationalist" government, admits it in this fashion: "In any case, they [the states] preferred their own devices and when they raised money in compliance with requisitions, they often disbursed it themselves for federal purposes." See his *The Power of the Purse. A History of American Public Finance, 1776–1790*, 1961.

established in Philadelphia in 1781; the Bank of New York (chartered by the legislature) began to function in 1784; so did the Massachusetts Bank in Boston in the same year; before the decade was over four more had made their appearance (in the 1790s the new banks thus chartered came to a total of 27). Thus financial assistance was readily available to private enterprise—and to get-rich-quick schemes, particularly wild-land promotions and speculations—but the want of credit for farmers was a fatal weakness in the country's financial structure and led to the difficulties and alarums and excursions of 1785–1787.

Foreign trade got off to a good start; direct trade with France, the Netherlands, the Baltic region, and the Orient was open, but it dropped sharply with England and the adverse trade balance mounted: in the two years 1784 and 1785 imports from England came to £6,000,000 and exports to England totaled only £2,000,000. A British Order of Council of 1783 created serious impediments in the direct trade with the British Sugar Islands and, although there was a certain amount of smuggling, the regulations hurt New England shipping and products. Only to a certain extent did the expansion of the trade with the Dutch take in the slack—by the end of the 1780s American exports to the Netherlands came to about one-half those sent to Britain—and although Dutch merchant-bankers were prepared to underwrite American commerce the precariousness of the country's public finances led to an understandable caution.

Despite all the new ventures in trade and industry and the great promise of America—in its vast, unsettled continent, its rich natural resources, and the skills and energy of its population—the boom began to peter out. The balance of payments was unfavorable; too much of the newly created capital had become illiquid, being tied up in speculation schemes (land promotion; the purchase of returned soldiers' land warrants); after 1784, the Confederation Congress could no longer obtain credit from the Dutch bankers, and agricultural prices were dropping. In 1785 and 1786 specie began to flow out of the country, the premiums on foreign bills of exchange rose, credit was tight, and interest rates went up. The recession of 1785–1786 was followed by a spotty revival; toward the end of 1787 wholesale prices began to slip once more, and their decline continued until the middle of 1789. It was not until the Republic was established that a steady upward advance began to take place. The restoration of the public credit was the key to economic revival and political stability, for by 1786 the central government to all intents and purposes was bankrupt.

At the beginning of 1784—apart from outstanding bills of credit (i.e., Continental paper money, which Robert Morris had reconverted with a heavy write-down)—the Congress's indebtedness in specie was

$39 million, broken down as follows: foreign debt, including arrears of interest, $7.9 million; loan office certificates (in effect, war bonds) $11.6 million; unliquidated certificates of indebtedness (to suppliers and to those whose property and products had been requisitioned by army officers), $16.7 million; unpaid interest on domestic debt (so-called "indents"), $3.1 million. To this must be added the indebtedness of the states—largely incurred for war purposes—and this came to $21 million.

The annual interest charges on the Congress's foreign debt were $375,000 and on the domestic debt, $1,500,000. Because of their inability to pay these sums, the arrears kept on piling up. Those of foreign interest grew from $67,037 to $1,640,071 between 1787 and 1789, and those of domestic interest grew from $3 million to $11.5 million in the same period.

During the same years, 1784–1789 the receipts of the central government totaled $4.6 million. Requisitions on the states brought in only $1.9 million; miscellaneous sums produced $338,000; loans from Dutch bankers came to $2.3 million. More than half of the Dutch funds were raised in the single year 1784, and were used to pay interest on older loans and finance imports from Holland. In the two years, 1785 and 1786—the years of recession when foreign aid would have been so helpful—Dutch loans amounted to a meager $100,000. Helpless because of the holding back by the states of the levies requested of them, the Congress' financial office was compelled to turn to the further issuance of certificates of indebtedness in order to finance its modest civil and military requirements. These certificates sank so low that they were publicly valued at fifteen cents on the dollar.

The states continued to go their separate ways, as the breakdown of the requisition system indicated. In addition, they were using their control over foreign trade to seek advantages for their own merchants. It is true that the erection of barriers to impede domestic commerce did not exist, for reciprocity among the states generally took place. Furthermore, American-made goods and American ships were exempt from import and tonnage duties, and foreign goods imported in American ships enjoyed lower rates. But quarrels and irritations broke out: New Jersey and Connecticut tried to win away some of the foreign trade entering New York, and New York retaliated by taxing foreign goods reaching her by way of her neighbor states.

The complex of state regulations, imposts, and tariffs not only made the flow of foreign commerce difficult but—more important—it prevented the use of a weapon (commercial pressure) against those countries, Britain and Spain in particular, that were discriminating against American ships and products. All the states laid duties for revenue purposes; starting in 1785 they began—frequently on top of earlier schedules—to establish tariffs for protection. Rhode Island led off the procession and was quickly followed by Pennsylvania, Massachusetts, Connecticut, Georgia and Virginia. The tariff rates were uneven from state to state; some had no tariffs at all, and the advantages that protection might have produced turned into liabilities.

States were quarreling among themselves about the use and regulation of the rivers and bays that served two or more of them and about boundaries and land claims. The first led to the meeting of the Annapolis Convention of 1786, but it ended abortively, for only New Jersey, Pennsylvania, Delaware and New York joined Virginia in sending delegates. The second brought on hard feeling—and blows that cost lives. Connecticut, on the basis of its ancient charter, claimed a portion of northern Pennsylvania. New York, New Hampshire, and Massachusetts could not, or would not, settle among themselves the boundaries of the region that was to become the state of Vermont and there were border forays in consequence.

State paper money (new bills of credit) was introduced, as states, during the recession of 1785–1786, attempted to add to the money supply at the same time that some of them (Massachusetts was an outstanding case in point) raised taxes to fund and extinguish their public debts. By the end of the war most states had put a stop to the use of their bills of credit as legal tender for private obligations, but the outflow of specie, tight money, and mounting rural indebtedness prompted seven states to reissue bills and to invest them with legal-tender rights. These states were Pennsylvania, South Carolina, North Carolina, New York, New Jersey, Georgia, and Rhode Island. All kinds of motives were advanced: states said that they wanted to pay their share of the Confederation foreign debt (but they did not), pay the bounties that soldiers had been promised, help in the redemption of loan-office certificates, lend on farm mortgages, and buy up surplus farm crops.

Whatever the intentions—some were laudable, some were not, by modern standards of fiscal and monetary management—a number of states overshot the mark. The Pennsylvania and New York issues depreciated slightly, but the North Carolina paper dropped by 50 per cent in value in three years. In New Jersey the depreciation was so sharp that its paper was not being accepted for private transaction, whereas in Georgia and Rhode Island paper ended by being worthless. Rhode Island embarked on the same reckless course it had followed in the colonial period: it sought to compel the acceptance of its legal tenders by a "forcing" provision—a fine of £100 for the first failure to comply and another fine of £100 and loss of citizenship for continued recalcitrance. The law courts were filled with suits between debtors and creditors.

With paper issues (rural debtors got some relief, but not enough) came appeals to legislatures for stay or mortgage-moratorium laws, laws to scale down mortgages, and laws to abolish imprisonment for debt. Judges who authorized the forfeiture of property because of non-payment of mortgage interest and the jailing of debtors were denounced and threatened. To protect its judges North Carolina shut down its courts altogether.

When agrarians took up arms in western Massachusetts in 1786 and threatened to march against government—this uprising came to be known as Shays' Rebellion—disquietude turned to alarm. Massachusetts, instead of trying to bring relief to those temporarily in distress (they were property owners and not *sans-culottes*), did the reverse: it sought to raise taxes, require specie payments, and encourage foreclosures. Appeals to its General Court (legislature) for paper emissions and stay laws were in vain. The Shaysites moved on the Springfield Arsenal and threatened to converge on Boston. The General Court called on citizens to put down "lawless and violent men," and the Shaysites were quickly disbanded. But, as General Henry Knox wrote to George Washington— these words in one form or another echoed again and again at the meetings of the Constitutional Convention when it met in Philadelphia from May to September, 1787:

> In a word, they [the Shaysites] are determined to annihilate all debts, public and private, and have agrarian laws, which are easily effected by means of unfunded paper money which shall be a tender in all cases whatever.

After the Convention was over James Madison—who more than any other person at Philadelphia was responsible for the particular form taken by the Constitution—in writing to Thomas Jefferson (then in France as America's emissary), put it this way:

> The mutability of the laws of the states is found to be a serious evil. . . . the evils issuing from these sources contributed more to the uneasiness which produced the Convention . . . than those which occurred to our national character and interest from the inadequacy of the Confederation to its immediate objects.

Two other considerations were in the minds of the Philadelphia delegates as they sat down to their work in private sessions. First, the Confederation itself, inadequate as it was, was in danger of falling apart. Thus Washington wrote to Madison in November 1786: "We are fast verging to anarchy and confusion. . . . Thirteen sovereignties pulling against each other, and all tugging at the federal head, will soon bring ruin on the whole." Madison, in February 1787 stated, that if "some very strong props are not applied" the Confederation could not last: no funds were coming into the federal government and no respect was being paid to it. The correspondence of other responsible men of the period, James Monroe of Virginia, Daniel Humphreys of Connecticut, Benjamin Rush of Pennsylvania—neither rumor-mongers nor seeking personal or class advantage in writing to their friends—reported that there were discussions in many places of the dismemberment of the Confederation and the creation of independent leagues. Thus Benjamin Rush wrote to his English friend, Richard Price, in October 1786:

> Some of our enlightened men who begin to despair of a more complete union of the states in Congress have secretly proposed an Eastern, Middle, and Southern Confederacy, to be united by an alliance offensive and defensive. These Confederacies, they say, will be united by nature, by interest, and by manners, and consequently they will be safe, agreeable, and durable.

Second was the growing insecurity of the "United States in Congress" *vis à vis* its greater and more aggressive neighbors. There had been some gains in international relations between 1782 and 1787: commercial treaties had been written with France, the Netherlands, Sweden, Prussia, and Morocco, but Britain had refused to do so and had kept its West Indian ports almost entirely closed to American commerce. Worse still, taking its stand on the Treaty of 1783 (the American states were to stop their harassment of loyalists and to facilitate the payment of prewar private debts, but were not doing so), Britain kept its garrisons in the western posts, stopped American shipping on the Great Lakes, stationed its customs officers in American territory, and stirred up the Indians.

In the southwest, Spain was even more aggressive. Refusing to accept the northern boundary of Florida as agreed on in the Treaty of Paris, it held on to Natchez on the Mississippi's eastern bank and then closed the river's mouth to American ships and commerce. In 1785 Congress instructed John Jay, then its foreign minister, to negotiate a commercial treaty with Spain. He came back with half a loaf: in return for a commercial treaty, he agreed to the closing of the Mississippi for 25 or 30 years. A bitter storm blew up in the country: the mercantile East and North, seeking to expand their trade with Spain, the Canaries, and the Spanish Caribbean, were in favor; the South, looking to the southwest for its economic growth, was opposed. The treaty received seven votes in the Congress and therefore failed; the regional hostilities that had emerged and the general frustration over the weakness of the country in trying to bargain with Spain contributed to the sense of helplessness.

THE WORK OF THE CONSTITUTIONAL CONVENTION

The broad intentions and general accomplishments of the makers of the Constitution are well known. Because there were among them few spokesmen for the leveling interests that had become so prominent in many of the states, it is silly to argue that they spoke for the opposite pole—for men of large property, for speculators in loan-office certificates and state debts, and for dealers in soldier land-warrants and public lands. At Philadelphia there was no conspiracy, tacit or overt, no counter-revolution ("Thermidor" is the fancy word), no subverting of the principles of liberty to which the Declaration of Independence had pledged the United States. The survival of the Republic was really the issue, and if the men of Philadelphia were more or less politically conservative (Alexander Hamilton more, James Madison somewhat less) it was because the feeling was common that only from such a general position could stability and economic advance be assured. There was agreement (not unanimous; of the 55 delegates who attended with some regularity, only 34 signed the final document and some did so with reservations) that what Robert Morris and Alexander Hamilton had been saying all along at the Confederation Congress was correct: that only a strong union, an "energetic" (opponents were to say "coercive") central government to check the states in their headlong career could prevent disintegration and establish a United States of America.

Disregarding its instructions, the Convention did not revise the Articles of Confederation; it replaced them. It reported back to Congress and the several legislatures only formally, asking for the approval of what it had done by specially elected state conventions. The new Constitutioin was ratified after only nine of the states in convention had approved, instead of all, as the Articles of Confederation required for amendments.

There was one issue that had to be settled first—how were the small states to be protected from being overwhelmed by the big ones? In consequence, a compromise had to be worked out, and this was the reconciliation of the Virginia Plan speaking for the big states with the New Jersey Plan speaking for the small ones. (The former, incidentally, was so broad and thorough that it really provided the frame of government on which the Constitution was built.) The Convention sat from May 25 to September 17. The Virginia Plan was presented on May 29 and debated from May 30 to June 13. The New Jersey Plan was presented on June 15 and debated from June 19 to July 26. As a result of these deliberations, 23 resolutions were approved and submitted to a committee on detail. These resolutions included the compromise to safeguard the position of the small states alluded to: equal representation in the senate; amendments requiring concurrence of both Houses of Congress by two-thirds votes and ratification by three-fourths of the states; the choice of President by the electoral vote of the states rather than by popular vote. The draft of the committee on detail was then examined and discussed, and the draft drawn up by the committee on style (which wrote the Constitution as we know it) was submitted to similar scrutiny. On September 15 the Constitution was agreed on and signed two days later "by the unanimous consent of the states present." (Rhode Island never sent delegates; New York had only one signer among its three delegates—Alexander Hamilton.)

The Constitution established a federal system with, presumably, a tripartite division of equal powers; but it made possible an "energetic" one and, when a strong hand was at the helm in the Presidency or in time of crisis, there were powers (real or implied) that could be used to make the central government and the Executive the seat of authority. This was demonstrated almost at once, from 1789 to 1795, when Alexander Hamilton, as Secretary of the Treasury, laid out the principles, with Washington's agreement, on the basis of which government could innovate and even participate positively, particularly in economic affairs, to "establish justice, insure domestic tranquility, provide for the common defense, and promote the general welfare." (At another time and in other circumstances so did Abraham Lincoln and Franklin D. Roosevelt; and in our own time so did John F. Kennedy and Lyndon B. Johnson.)

An observation in passing. I have said "participate" and not "direct." There is a world of difference between the two concepts. (The case of a central bank is one in point. Minority shares in the capital of Hamilton's First Bank of the United States could be and were acquired by the government, but even these could be sold, as under Jefferson they were. Britain's central bank, today, the Bank of England, is owned entirely and managed by the government.) Mercantilism, as has been pointed out, in the interests of ensuring and maintaining the political and national power of the state, directed the whole economy of the nation. To this extent Hamilton was no mercantilist, as has too frequently been charged, for rather than abhorring "a dead stock called plenty" he knew how necessary it was to stimulate its formation. He sought—by the use of fiscal powers (the funding and servicing of the public debt) and, hopefully, by monetary ones (through the creation of the First Bank of the United States as a central bank)—to encourage the development of a free market and free choices and decisions by what he called "the most enlightened friends of good government"; that is, men of affairs, businessmen, who would take risks, embark on new enterprises, invest and form capital, and thus widen the opportunities for employment and the creation of welfare.

When state policy has other goals which are more social than economic—full employment, a more equitable distribution of the national income, the expansion of the public sector—participation can drift into direction or *dirigisme*. Once wage and price controls (if the halting of inflation becomes so stubborn that political pressures must be yielded to) and, as a counterbalance, ceilings on profits are installed, then neo-mercantilism is taking over. To this extent some of the economic advisers of President Johnson and those who were expressing open hostility to the "gradualist" program of President Nixon—J. K. Galbraith * was a characteristic example—were closer to the alleged Alexander Hamilton than the real one.

To resume: These were the economic powers that were vested in the Congress in the new federal government created by the Constitution. (However, the President could, and did, give to the Congress "information on the State of the Union" and recommended whatever legislation he might "judge necessary and expedient.") The Congress was to have the right to levy and collect taxes, duties, and excises in order "to pay the debts and provide for the common defense and general welfare of the United States." It could borrow money. It could regulate foreign and interstate commerce. It could establish a uniform law on bankruptcies (and thus protect property from what Madison called "the mutability of the laws of the states.") It could coin money and regulate its value and that of foreign coins. It could establish post offices and build post roads. It could write laws for the granting of patents and copyrights "for a limited time." It had the power "to dispose of and make all needful rules and regulations respecting the territory or other property belonging to the United States," and it could admit new states. The states could not disregard treaties made by the United States (with the advice and consent of the Senate), which were to be "the supreme law of the land." The judicial power of the United States was to "extend to all cases, in law and equity, arising under this Constitution, the laws of the United States, and treaties made . . . under their authority."

The wings of the states were clipped; the dangers of "mutability" were carefully analyzed and forestalled. States could not coin money; they could not issue bills of credit, nor make anything but gold and silver legal tender; and they could not impair the obligation of contracts (i.e., pass stay laws or mortgage-moratorium laws). States could not, without the

* See his demand for wage and price controls, in *The Wall Street Journal,* September 2, 1969.

consent of Congress, impose duties on imports or exports, and the prohibition and exception applied to duties on tonnage. They could enter
into interstate compacts, but again the consent of Congress was required.

THE HAMILTONIAN PROGRAM

George Washington was inaugurated the first President of the United
States on April 30, 1789, and proceeded to organize the Executive branch
by naming his formal advisers as heads of departments (the Constitution
did not use the term "Cabinet" as such). For these posts he picked four:
Alexander Hamilton Secretary of the Treasury, Henry Knox Secretary of
War, Thomas Jefferson Secretary of State (he was not to return from
France until March 2, 1790), and Edmund Randolph Attorney General.
Even before Alexander Hamilton was prepared to present his program to
the Congress (it had two axes, one to establish the "faith and credit of the
United States" and the other to "justify and preserve the confidence of
the most enlightened friends of good government") it proceeded to give
the new government a revenue.*

On July 4, 1789, President Washington signed a bill which in effect
enacted the impost of 1783. What was passed was tariff legislation to supply the government with a revenue but which contained mildly protective
features. The law incorporated both specific and ad valorem duties on
more than 30 kinds of commodities; ad valorem duties ran from 5 to 10
per cent; the average rate of duties was 8½ per cent. Iron was to pay 7½
per cent, linens, woolens, and cotton fabrics, 5 per cent, and glassware,
10 per cent. Certain enumerated raw materials—cotton, wool, hides—were
on a free list and all other articles not specified were to pay 5 per cent.
The law included tonnage duties, but at the same time gave American
ships definite advantages. Foreign ships could not engage in the fisheries
and coastwise trade. A tonnage tax of 50 cents a ton was placed on goods
entering American ports in foreign vessels, but those carried in ships that
were native built and owned received a drawback of 10 per cent.

What Hamilton was thinking about when the time came to propose
his program has already been stated. It was to be presented in a series of
reports to Congress on the public credit, the excise, the chartering of a
national bank, the creation of a mint, and the stimulation of manufactures in an economy of balanced growth. All but the last were enacted

_____

* A full discussion of the Hamiltonian program, in modern economic terms, will
be found in Louis M. Hacker, *Alexander Hamilton in the American Tradition*, 1957.

much along the lines he had set out. How did Hamilton view the role of government? It was to innovate, it was to invigorate, and in limited measure it was to assist and participate. The "incitement and patronage of government," he called it. Such notions inform all the reports. In 1801 he put it succinctly: "In matters of industry, human enterprise ought, doubtless, to be left free in the main; not fettered by too much regulation; but practical politicians know that it may be beneficially stimulated by prudent aids and encouragements on the part of government. . . ."

In 1791, in the *Report on Manufactures,* he had flown higher. He was suggesting that Congress, to encourage "infant manufacture" in the United States, should impose protective duties but also, and preferably, pay bounties, premiums, and awards to stimulate innovation. Then, he went on to say (using Adam Smith's language; the whole statement leans heavily on *The Wealth of Nations*):

> If the system of perfect liberty were the prevailing system of nations, the arguments which dissuade a country, in the predicament of the United States, from the zealous pursuit of manufactures, would doubtless have great force. It will not be affirmed that they might not be permitted, with few exceptions, to serve as a rule of national conduct. In such a state of things, each country would have the full benefit of its peculiar advantages to compensate for its deficiencies or disadvantages.

On January 14, 1790—Congress had requested such a statement on September 21, 1789—Hamilton submitted his first great public document, the *Report on the Public Credit.* In it he called for the recognition of all elements of the debt—foreign, domestic, and state. He asked for the payment of the defaulted interest on the first two. He proposed refunding through new public issues carrying a maximum 6 per cent coupon. He requested that specific revenues (receipts from duties on imports and tonnage and new excises) be earmarked for interest payments, that debt retirement come from a sinking fund also from earmarked revenues, and that machinery be set up to engage in open-market operations to prevent the securities from declining in value. By his calculations the total came to $77,124,464, of which the foreign debt (with arrears of interest) was $11,710,379, the domestic debt (with arrears of interest) $40,414,085, and the state debt $25,000,000.

Why assume and refund entire? Notably in view of the fact that a good part of both the domestic and state debts was no longer the property of the original holders (speculators had bought up the certificates of the Continental Congress and the issues of the states at heavy discounts), whereas some states had worked hard to extinguish their debts and others had not. To Hamilton, as a nationalist, the answers were simple. (They were not to his opponents, who resisted strenuously the assumption of the state debts.) The debts had been incurred to finance the war for independence. It was imperative that the good faith, and therefore the credit and honor, of the new government be established at once. "States, like individuals," said Hamilton, "who observe their engagements, are respected and trusted; while the reverse is the fate of those who pursue an opposite course."

A country and a people, for public purposes and to initiate private promotions, must be prepared to borrow, particularly a country like the United States which "is possessed of little active wealth, or . . . little monied capital." Borrow from whom? From "the most enlightened friends of good government." Such "friends" were to be found both at home and abroad. Hamilton's willingness to place no obstacles in the way of foreign investments in the United States is another important example of how far he had moved away from mercantilist ideas. Why get their good will? He went on to say:

> To justify and preserve their confidence; to promote the increasing respectability of the American name; to answer the calls of justice; to restore landed property to its due value; to furnish new resources both to agriculture and commerce; to cement more closely the union of the states; to add to their security against foreign attacks; to establish public order on the basis of an upright and liberal policy . . .

such were the ends to be secured from a support of the public credit. In addition, a funded debt would augment the money supply, and to this argument, in his plan for a national bank, he came back later in greater detail, and with a sophisticated knowledge of money unusual for his time.

This he presented in his second public paper, the *Report on a National Bank,* which he laid before Congress on December 14, 1790. In a thoughtful, closely reasoned, knowledgeable document—reinforced by his familiarity with the history and functions of the Bank of England and his study (often using word for word, as he was to do in the case of his *Report on Manufactures*) of *The Wealth of Nations*—he sought to educate the Congress and his fellow countrymen on the role of money and banking, if you will, in a developing economy. First, a national bank—government contributing to its capital with minority representation on its board of directors, but not manipulating it—would facilitate the governmental operations by providing for its normal needs and also rendering extraordinary aid in time of emergency. Second, it would, as far as private enterprise was concerned, help mightily in "the augmentation of the active or productive capital of the country," that is, its money supply. Then it would assist agriculture, trade, and industry by stimulating credit and making money easier. It would help in attracting foreign capital to the United States. In conjunction with government it would play an important part in regularizing the country's money supply and therefore the orderly flow of credit.

Some of Hamilton's observations about money show how closely he had studied and familiarized himself with a subject of perennial interest to Americans and, by the same token, regularly misunderstood by so many of them well into the twentieth century. Banks should have the right of note issues, of course, but more important, for adding to and controlling the supply of money, was their role in the creation of deposits. Thus he said:

> Every loan which a bank makes is, in its shape a credit given to the borrower on its books, the amount of which it stands ready to pay. . . . But in a greater number of cases, no actual payment is made in either. The borrower frequently by check or order transfers his credit to some other person. . . . And in this manner the credit keeps on circulating, performing in every stage the office of money.

Government obligations, the funded debt, was what we recognize today as "near money"—assuming proper debt management, that is, a sinking fund for its extinguishment and funds to allow open-market operations. Thus more "active and productive capital" would be created (the phrase is Adam Smith's); that is, liquidity would be increased while the narrow fluctuation in government bonds would make them sound security for bank loans as they added to the money supply.

Further, he recognized the part played by the velocity of money in determining prices and the volume of trade. In 1780, when writing to Robert Morris to propose the creation of a national bank, he pointed out the reasons for the depreciation of the Continental currency. Its quantity kept on rising; the inability of the Congress to redeem its own paper led to a more rapid circulation. This paper moved into the channels of trade, and, because goods were scarce, prices rose and the decline in the real value of money inevitably set in. Given confidence in government, however, even if the quantity of money grew and its velocity stayed constant or rose (Hamilton called this "money's circulation"), the increase in the volume of goods produced or traded in would be greater than the increase in prices.

As for the organization of a national bank, it should be chartered by the Congress for 20 years. It should have branches. It should not lend on land (thus threatening its liquidity). It should be under private direction, but with governmental right of inspection. It should have a capitalization of $10 million, to which the federal government would be permitted to subscribe up to $2 million. (How ambitious Hamilton was may be noted from the fact that the state banks then in existence, in Philadelphia, New York, and Boston, had among them a combined capital of $2 million.) Subscriptions to the capital were to be one-fourth in specie and the other three-fourths in the government's new 6 per cent bonds. The bank's liabilities (excluding deposits) were not to exceed its capital. The bank was to deal only in bills of exchange, gold and silver bullion, and goods pledged for loans; 6 per cent was to be the maximum interest rate on its loans and discounts. The bills and notes it issued by writing up deposits were to be payable on demand in gold and silver coin, and they were to be legal tender in all payments to the United States. It was to be a bank of first resort with its own customers, but it was as well to be a bankers' bank which would handle the notes of the state-chartered banks (and, if it saw fit, restricting their circulation), in this way performing the important function of a central bank by the regularization of the money supply.

A bill much on these lines was introduced in the Senate on December 23, 1790, and was passed in a month with only perfunctory debate. In the House it had harder sledding. Madison, who led the opposition (largely made up of southern representatives) raised the question of constitutionality. Finally, in February 1791 the bill passed but Washington withheld his signature—he was troubled by the debate in the House—and asked for extended opinions from his Secretary of the Treasury (Hamilton), his Secretary of State (Jefferson), and his Attorney General (Randolph). Randolph and Jefferson advised a veto on the grounds of constitutionality; Hamilton advised signing. Washington followed Hamilton and on February 25, 1791 approved the creation of the First Bank of the United States. A great precedent had been set: the federal government could create corporations; it was to do so again in chartering the Union Pacific Railroad in 1862. In large numbers, corporations with federal charters were an important device employed by the New Deal in its effort to stimulate recovery.

What was there in Hamilton's argument that persuaded Washington? It was based on the theory of "implied powers" necessary to give government the means by which it could carry out its functions. The nature and objects of government were these:

> The means by which national exigencies are to be provided for, national inconveniences obviated, national prosperity promoted, are of such infinite variety, extent, and complexity, that there must of necessity be great latitude of discretion in the selection and application of these means.

Within such general outlines the American government has been able to function, to acquire new territory, to make possible the building of the western railroads into still unsettled regions, to protect agriculture, and to pass social legislation. The Supreme Court has recognized again and again the pertinency of Hamilton's doctrine of implied powers not only to permit the First Bank to function but to allow the government to regulate corporations and put on the statute books laws of the widest general consequences.

This is what Hamilton had to say about "implied powers" and the Constitution:

> It is not denied that there are *implied,* as well as *express powers,* and the *former* are as effectually delegated as the *latter.* . . . Then it follows, that as the power of erecting a corporation may as well be *implied* as any other thing, it may as well be employed as an *instrument* or *means* of carrying into execution any of the specified powers, as any other *instrument* or *means* whatever. . . . [Thus a corporation may be erected by Congress] in relation to the collection of taxes, or to the trade with foreign countries, or to the trade between the states, or with the Indian tribes; because it is within the province of the federal government to *regulate* these objects, and because it is incident to a general *sovereign* or *legislative* power to *regulate* a thing, to employ all the means which relate to its regulation to the best and greatest advantage. (Italics original.)

The stock of the Bank of the United States was quickly subscribed, and it was able to open its main office in Philadelphia in December 1791. In time, eight branches were set up in New York, Boston, Baltimore, Washington, Norfolk, Charleston, Savannah, and New Orleans. The Bank established friendly relations with state-chartered banks, extending credit to them and handling their notes. As Hamilton had anticipated, it watched over their note issues and as early as the 1790s, in order to check the speculative issues of the state banks—and to limit their money supply—restricted the note circulation by calling for specie payments. The Bank serviced the government's needs. It lent the Treasury the $2 million to make possible the government's subscription. It lent when emergencies arose, so that at the end of 1795 total long-term loans outstanding were in excess of $6 million. This was going too far, of course; the Bank's services to trade and commerce were being severely limited, as was its ability to handle the Treasury's short-term needs. The Bank therefore requested that the loans already due be taken up. During 1796–1797 the government sold a portion of its Bank stock to reduce its obligations; in 1802 the remainder was disposed of in London (due to Jefferson's continued hostility to the Bank). The government gained from its relations with the Bank in another and interesting way. It received more than $1 million in dividends and almost another in premiums from the sale of its stock.

The *Report on Manufactures,* submitted to Congress on December

5, 1791, calling as it did for high protective duties and for bounties to entrepreneurs prepared to launch an "infant manufacture," did not lead to legislation. It is of continuing and fascinating interest to us today, however, for it is a text on how a developing country, as the United States was in the first decade of its history, goes about the business, with government assistance, of pulling itself up by its bootstraps.

Industrial production, manufactures employing machinery, is the key to growth. This is so because successful manufacture is based on the division of labor, resulting in reduction in costs, and increase in output. The use of machinery stimulates all these processes. "May it not, therefore, be fairly inferred [Hamilton wrote] that those occupations which give greatest scope to the use of this auxiliary, contribute most to the general stock of industrious effort, and, in consequence, to the general product of industry?"

Industry (manufactures) adds to a country's labor force; that is, it makes possible the expansion of human capital. The sources of labor would be these: immigrants, women, and children. Hamilton places particular stress on the first. Immigration of workers would be stimulated because in the United States wages are higher; and for entrepreneurs raw material costs are lower. Both would be relieved of "the chief part of the taxes, burdens, and restraints which they endure in the Old World."

Industry, rather than harming agriculture, would strengthen its role in the economy. To use a modern locution, balanced growth would result; for agriculture, instead of depending on uncertain and inconstant foreign markets to dispose of surpluses, would find an expanding and steady domestic market on its own doorstep. Hamilton ties the whole together in this fashion:

> The foregoing considerations seem sufficient to establish, as general propositions, that it is in the interests of nations to diversify the industrious pursuits of the individuals who compose them; that the establishment of manufactures is calculated not only to increase the general stock of useful and productive labor, [and, in the same connection, he says elsewhere "to an augmentation of revenue and capital"] but even to improve the state of agriculture in particular,—certainly to advance the interests of those who are engaged in it.

The establishment of manufactures would go hand in hand with a program for what we call today the development of the country's infrastructure. Like Adam Smith (he quotes him verbatim but does not name him), Hamilton is prepared to concede that the building of roads and canals and the improvement of navigable rivers is a legitimate function of central government. Such internal improvements lower costs of carriage and widen markets, and, he says (the words are Smith's), "Good roads, canals, and navigable rivers, by diminishing the expense of carriage, put the remote parts of a country more nearly upon a level with those in the neighborhood of the town."

Finally, manufactures in America would attract foreign aid, in this case not from government, as is so today, but from private capital. Foreign capital can be counted on for investment purposes as "an augmentation of real wealth." Capital transfers will occur because there is "a deficiency of employment" at home at the same time that rates of interest and profits in America are higher. He goes on:

> Both these causes operate to produce a transfer of foreign capital to the United States. It is certain, that various objects in this country hold out advantages, which are with difficulty to be equalled elsewhere; and under the increasingly favorable impressions which are entertained of our government, the attractions will become more and more strong. These impressions will prove a rich mine of prosperity to the country, if they are confirmed and strengthened by the progress of our affairs. And, to secure this advantage, little more is now necessary than to foster industry, and cultivate order and tranquility at home and abroad.

Hamilton sought to allay his countrymen's fears of a spreading foreign influence. Hostility to foreign capital he calls an "unreasonable jealousy." Then this:

> Instead of being viewed as a rival, it ought to be considered as a most valuable auxiliary, conducing to put in motion a greater quantity of productive labor, and a greater portion of useful enterprise, than could exist without it. It is at least evident that . . . every farthing of foreign capital which is laid out in internal meliorations, and in industrial establishments, of a permanent nature, is a precious acquisition.

Two other aspects of the Hamiltonian domestic program must be mentioned briefly, the establishment of a mint and the imposition of excises to supplement the revenues coming from import duties, tonnage taxes, and the sale of public lands. The Mint Act of 1792, based on Hamilton's proposals, provided that both gold and silver coins be minted by the government at the ratio of 15 to 1, which were the existing bullion values in Great Britain and Holland, the countries with which the United States largely traded. (The standard silver dollar was somewhat lighter than the Spanish piece of eight.) Foreign coins continued to circulate widely in the United States until the 1850s, when the discovery of gold in California gave the country its own metallic resources. Now they were all tied to the American dollar, thus preventing the United States from being at the mercy of foreign coinages, which, as Hamilton said in his

Report, could "change with the changes in the regulation of a foreign sovereign." It should be noted that as American balances of payments improved and foreign coins flowed into the United States some of them were reminted so that American coins did appear—the totals were about $2 million in 1800 and about $8 million in 1809.

Congress yielded reluctantly to Hamilton's request for additions to the country's revenues and passed a series of excise laws. In March 1791 it added to the imposts of 1789 taxes on domestic spirits, rum and whiskey, and on domestic stills. This created an uproar and let in 1794 to the Whiskey Rebellion in western Pennsylvania—and mutterings in all those other areas in which small grains were being converted into whiskey as an article of commerce. Resistance to the collection of the new taxes quickly vanished when Washington assembled the militia of the disaffected states (Virginia, Maryland, Pennsylvania, and New Jersey) and an armed force marched on Pittsburgh. Nevertheless, the tax on whiskey did not produce all of the required revenues, so that in 1794 additional excises were imposed on carriages, the sale of foreign liquors, the manufacture of snuff, and the refining of sugar and on auction sales. The upshot was that out of a total of $13 million in ordinary receipts in 1801 $1.6 million came from internal revenues.

THE ECONOMIC RESULTS OF A FOREIGN POLICY OF NEUTRALITY

Successful foreign policy can have equally significant effects on work and wealth; in short, the energizing of the economy of a young and developing country such as the United States in the first decade and a half of its history. Here is a characteristic example of the futility of a purely economic interpretation of events. D. C. North sees as the turning point in America's sudden rise in the years 1790–1807 (to North this is the magical period of America's "take-off" to sudden and sustained growth) the great expansion of American shipping and the increasing prominence of the country's export and re-export trades. All this was happening when general war broke out in Europe between the two great coalitions headed by France and Great Britain, starting in 1793 and continuing with only brief intervals of peace until Napoleon's final defeat in 1815. (North stops in 1807 when Jefferson imposed his disastrous embargo on American trade with Great Britain.)

Disregarding completely the consequences of fiscal and monetary management—funding and the creation of a national bank—North also disregards the basis on which American merchants, shipbuilders, and shipowners could flourish; that is, the establishment of American neutrality when great European powers were locked in a life and death struggle.

The point I am making is that the adoption of neutrality by the United States was a conscious choice, made by George Washington and implemented by Alexander Hamilton over the bitter opposition of Jefferson and his friends. Neutrality meant these two things: the repudiation of the treaties with France and the disavowal of all entangling alliances and a political and commercial settlement with Great Britain so that American foreign trade could continue, occasionally harassed, it is true, by British fleets (searches on the high seas and the impressment of American seamen) but more often under the protection of their guns.

Under the leadership of the Jacobins—which established a reign of terror and a republican dictatorship at home and whipped up popular sentiment to obtain a *levée en masse*—France was committed to making herself and her Revolution secure by taking the offensive against her enemies. She looked for the United States for active support in the war against Britain and Holland because of sentimental ties, claims of gratitude for earlier aid, and the bonds of alliance and amity. France had two treaties with America, both drawn up in 1778. One was a treaty of alliance which guaranteed the territorial integrity of both countries "forever against all powers." The other was a treaty of amity and commerce which, among other things, permitted each country to use the ports of the other for the anchorage of warships, outfitting privateers, and granting a haven to their prizes.

When France sent its minister, Edmund Genêt, in effect to cash these checks—by openly seeking and obtaining support for his country among the so-called secret Democratic Societies; by sending out armed privateers from American ports; by meddling in domestic politics, and by courting the help of Jefferson and his followers—the United States teetered on the edge of war. Washington acted swiftly, and in so doing denounced the French alliance. A declaration of neutrality by the President (without congressional consultation) was issued on April 22, 1793. Jefferson was still (until the end of 1793) Secretary of State; he was a friend of France, indeed, an admirer of the Jacobins, and Genêt had his confidence. He continued to hesitate as Genêt's overt acts clearly indicated he meant to embroil the United States in the European war. Jefferson had to accede to the request for Genêt's recall, but he had become so hostile to everything Hamilton, with Washington's support, stood for that he had to quit the Cabinet, thus ending its disunion. The outcome was that the risk of involvement in Europe was spiked, once and for all.

Now was the time to push for a settlement with Spain, at war with France. In 1794 Thomas Pinckney was sent to Madrid, and in October 1795 a treaty was finally written, the United States obtaining everything it had failed to get earlier. The American southern boundary was fixed at the thirty-first parallel; each country promised not to meddle with Indian relations in the other, and both were to share in the free navigation of the Mississippi. Americans were given the right of deposit at New Orleans for three years; thereafter either New Orleans or "an equivalent establishment" was to be made available to American ships and merchants "without paying any other duty than a fair price for the hire of the stores."

To come to an understanding with Britain was more difficult. None of the problems and difficulties left suspended by the Treaty of 1783 had been resolved: the western posts, disordered Indian affairs, the collection of prewar debts owed to British merchants, the counterclaim of the United States that British troops had carried off some 3,000 Negro slaves and freed them, and the unsettled northern boundary, which involved the headwaters of the Mississippi and therefore the river's navigation. Nor had Britain signed a commercial treaty with the United States. The result was that American merchants and ships were suffering from discriminatory treatment in British ports all over the world and, with the war waging, were at the mercy of British fleets hunting for contraband and British deserters.

The pro-French sentiment that had been whipped up by the Democratic Societies (and the Jeffersonian Republicans) was equally anti-British. Congress heard talk of reprisals against British investors in the United States and the establishment of nonintercourse with Britain commercially. (This would have been fatal to the young America, for 90 per cent of American imports came from Britain, with the duties they paid, whereas 60 per cent of all the goods carried between the two nations was in American bottoms—in 1800, this had become 95 per cent.) Only by a hair's breadth did nonintercourse fail. In April 1794 the House carried such a bill; in the Senate the vote was tied but the bill was lost because Vice-President Adams voted against it. Madison, Jefferson's chief lieutenant, continued to press for the same result by the introduction of a joint resolution. This also was defeated, and it was in such a climate of bitter acrimony and division that Washington sent Chief Justice John Jay to London in May 1794 to negotiate directly with the British Secretary of State for Foreign Affairs. Hamilton drew up Jay's instructions; he was as much responsible as Jay for the treaty that was written; and on his head as well descended the obloquy that greeted Jay when he brought back less than a whole loaf.

Nevertheless, the Jay Treaty, with all its shortcomings, ensured peace and recognized the existence of American nationality and its continuance to survive commercially as a neutral. (Tacitly, for Britain, commanding the seas, did not surrender its right to define contraband and therefore to searches and seizures). Surely Admiral Mahan * was right when he characterized Jay's work as an event of "epochal significance." Hamilton, writing in defense of the treaty, said with a command of the dangers confronting the United States Jefferson could not understand (he called it an "execrable thing"), for survival at this point was touch and go,

> Few nations can have stronger inducements than the United States to cultivate peace. Their infant state in general, their want of a marine [navy] in particular, to protect their commerce, would render war, in an extreme degree, a calamity. It would not only arrest our rapid progress to strength and prosperity, but would probably throw us back into a state of debility and impoverishment, from which it would require years to emerge.

The Jay Treaty, a treaty of "amity and commerce," extended to American trade full reciprocal rights in the British European territories and its East Indian ports. It created the peaceful machinery of joint commissions to settle the debt claims of British merchants against Americans and the claims of American merchants for unlawful searches and seizures on the high seas. It called for the evacuation of the British western ports by June 1, 1796, provided for reciprocal trading privileges for Americans and British in the northwestern territories of both countries; and for another joint commission to settle the northern boundary and establish the source of the Mississippi. (On this last the boundary and the origins of the Mississippi were favorable to the United States.) On open trade with its West Indian islands the British would not yield. American vessels of limited tonnage could bring American wares into the islands—a gain; they could not take out or re-export the island's sugar, molasses, cocoa, or cotton—a loss. Over bitter opposition Washington (and Hamilton) prevailed, and the Jay Treaty was ratified by the Senate in June, 1795.

It was in this turmoil that Washington issued his Farewell Address on September 19, 1796. He besought his fellow Americans to stay out of Europe's quarrels; he was pleading not so much for isolation as for the integrity and independence of the Republic. The Address said, in part:

> Against the insidious wiles of foreign influence . . . the jealousy of a free people ought to be *constantly* awake; since history and experience prove that foreign influence is one of the most baneful foes of Republican government. . . .

* A. T. Mahan, *Sea Power and Its Relation to the War of 1812*, 1895.

The great rule of conduct for us, in regard to foreign nations, is in extending our commercial relations, to have with them as little *political* connection as possible. So far as we have already formed engagements let them be fulfilled with perfect good faith.—Here let us stop." (Italics original.)

Thus domestic and foreign policy—funding, a revenue, a national bank in one part and neutrality as war raged in the other—underwrote and ensured survival and the beginnings of economic growth and prosperity. The tonnage of American ships in the foreign trade increased from 123,893 tons in 1789 to 981,019 tons in 1810. Exports grew from $19 million in 1790 to $94 million in 1801. (After the Jay treaty re-exports —the produce of foreign lands that American ships were permitted to transport to Europe—steadily mounted so that by 1801 they were worth fully half the total of the export trade.) Earnings of American ships, in consequence, increased enormously—from $5.9 million in 1790 to $31 million in 1801. Together, exports and re-exports almost equalled the value of American imports in 1790 ($29 million) and exceeded them in 1801 ($111.4 million). The fact is there was every evidence of a favorable balance of payments, for in the years 1790–1801 the United States was able to pay off $2.5 million on the principal of the federal foreign debt and $15 to $20 million was sent abroad to meet interest and profits on federal bonds and investments in American companies held by Europeans. Other evidence of this turn in American fortunes were the following: sterling exchange during the greater part of this period was selling at a discount in New York and Philadelphia; foreign specie flowed into the country to double the circulation from $9 million in 1790 to probably as much as $20 million in 1801.

Hamilton's expectations that foreign investments would take place in the United States were fully realized. As of June 30, 1803 (the estimates are those of Samuel Blodget's *Economica,* published in 1806), the American capital balance sheet was, in part, as follows: federal debt stood at $81.3 million, of which $43.7, or 53 per cent, was held abroad; the stocks of American corporations (banks, insurance companies, and turnpike and canal companies) were worth $48.4 million, of which $15.9 million, or 33 per cent, was owned by foreigners; the Bank of the United States (included in the above) was capitalized at $10 million ($6.2 million, or 62 per cent, was in foreign portfolios). So good was American credit that when Jefferson came to buy the Louisiana Territory from France (she had obtained it from Spain) a purchase price of $15 million was fixed, with $3.7 million going to American claimants against France for her war on American shipping between 1796 and 1800. The balance, $11.3 million, was raised by issuing 6 per cent bonds, which were snapped up in European money markets (the British took $9.2 million, the French, $1.3 million, and the Dutch, $500,000).

Similiarly, American capital eagerly embarked on promotions, many of which were made possible by the issuance of company charters by state legislative action. During the 1780s only 33 charters had been granted; in the 1790s there were 295. As a result, by 1800 there were 34 banks in the United States, of which 27 were established after 1789, and 33 marine and fire insurance companies, of which 30 were created after 1789. Other private corporations obtaining approval—and most of them were actually set up—were inland navigation (including canals), turnpike and toll bridge companies, water supply and dock companies, and manufacturing and mining companies. The last represented a tiny minority—only eight manufacturing companies were incorporated.

Looking back on this era, the Earl of Liverpool told the English House of Lords in 1820 that "America [had] increased in *wealth,* in *commerce,* in *arts* [industry], in *population,* in *strength* more rapidly than any nation [had] ever before increased in the history of the world." (Italics original.)

Was this the "sudden and sustained" growth that hastened the industrialization of the United States? This conclusion is highly doubtful. The economy and the labor force in 1800 continued to be largely agricultural. Thus Stanley Lebergott * puts the labor force at 1,850,000, of which the self-employed numbered 1,190,000 (57 per cent), slaves, 490,000 (31 per cent), and wage earners, 170,000 (12 per cent). Among the last Lebergott estimated those in manufactures, as we know it, factory workers wholly dependent on their wage labor, at not more than 21,000. Another 80,000 were "mechanical artisans," men with skilled crafts who worked in grist and flour mills or in "bespoke" (custom) trades or home "manufactures" as joiners, blacksmiths, shoemakers, boat builders, and the like. To the question whether there was an ante-bellum Industrial Revolution we must now turn.

* In Seymour Harris, Ed., *American Economic History,* 1961.

IV

THE ANTE-BELLUM YEARS

DOUBTS ABOUT THE INDUSTRIAL REVOLUTION APPEARING BEFORE THE CIVIL WAR

Did the American Industrial Revolution take place in the years before the Civil War? With the so-called "take off" occurring, variously, before the 1830s, in the 1830s, between 1843 and 1860, and some time between 1830 and 1860, did the United States start on its career of steady, self-sustained growth? To put it in econometric terms, was there a fairly sharp break somewhere in the period in the trend of real national product per head? From then on did a continuous secular advance follow as more and more capital and workers moved into industrial production and national capital and product markets appeared?

As a result of the conjectures, and efforts at proof, of a sizable company of econometric historians, this is the present-day canon: by 1860 the United States was already an industrialized nation; the Civil War temporarily stopped its progress, and from 1865 on the American economy continued along the lines clearly laid out before war had broken out.

The learned analysts do not, however, agree on the timing, the initiating circumstances, or the processes by which this extraordinary phenomenon took place. In fact they end by canceling one another out; so much so that the only consequence of these complex explanations (and bickerings) is a healthy dubiety that the Industrial Revolution really did happen when they say it did. A variety of reasons may be offered.

First, generally before 1840 statistics that would make possible an acceptable examination of the course of the GNP are nonexistent. Simon Kuznets, who in fact initiated the technique of GNP analysis and continues to make many fruitful and imaginative comments on its role in the national economy, will not start before 1869 because of the inadequacy and unrealiability of the data.

Second, all of the econometric historians completely neglect the part that the mores of the ante-bellum period played to forward or retard the Industrial Revolution: the attitudes toward capitalist accumulation and investment, the appearance of the key figures (innovators-entrepreneurs), the public policy of government, and the position of the South and slavery in the whole drama.

Because these commentators—some of whom we shall pass in review —do not prove their cases by their econometric reconstructions, and because their analyses are wholly economic and deterministic, I remain unconvinced. Therefore, my position is that industrialization did have beginnings in the ante-bellum period but only with respect to light industry (textiles, shoes, and clocks); there was no national market of capital or products; the entrepreneur (who was no innovator in the Schumpeterian sense) was usually a merchant and not an industrialist; and it is doubtful that real GNP per head made impressive advances (partly because the contributions of technology and education were still too slight). Most important; the mores of the time did not favor the broad acceptance of the capitalist processes (this was true of the North as well as the South), with the result that innovators-entrepreneurs did not find a congenial climate in which their risky ventures could flourish. If to this we add the absence of a positive public policy to aid such ventures it is imperative to say that all the stars were unfavorable in their courses.

It was not until the Civil War had been fought and won, slavery terminated and the political power of the South crushed that there emerged a united nation, committed to the creation of both mores and public policy in which industrial capitalism could thrive. The Industrial Revolution in America, in other words, with all of its consequences of the growth and expansion of heavy industry, an industrialized labor force, an efficient agriculture, and steady rise in the real GNP per head, "took off" after 1865.

EFFORTS TO PROVE IT DID BY THE ECONOMETRIC HISTORIANS

The speculations and studies of the econometric historians, a characteristic Schumpeterian "swarm," start around 1960. It was in 1959, when he appeared before the Joint Economic Committee of the 86th Congress (published as *Historical and Comparative Rates of Production, Productivity and Prices*, p. 278), that Raymond Goldsmith began the procession by throwing out the thought—he admitted it was no more than a guess:

> There must have occurred a fairly sharp break in the trend of real national product per head sometime before 1839. . . . I would hazard the guess . . . that the break occurred not very long before 1839 and that it reflects both the transition of the United States from a predominantly agricultural to a more and more industrial country and the advent of the railroads.

Rostow * sought to create a theoretical model for a developing economy. He set up a series of stages (no harm in this; Marx, Werner Sombart, and, more recently, Simon Kuznets have also done so) through which a society evolves. Rostow proposed five such periods: a traditional, a preindustrial in which the preconditions for further advance were appearing, a "take-off" into the industrial, followed by a mature age, and then one of high mass consumption. (Some nations have skipped one or the other of these stages; the United States, for example, never went through the first; many developing countries today are trying to leap from the first to the third; and Rostow recognizes this.)

Rostow concentrates on the "take-off," which is presumably to be characterized by continued self-sustained growth and rising real GNP per head. It is the period of "decisive," "rapid," "radical" structural change, as a result of which growth inevitably (automatically?) follows. In his schema he notes as the conditions for the leap from preindustrialism to industrialism: (a) a rise in the capital-output ratio (investment as a proportion of the national income) from 5 per cent or less to over 10 per cent; (b) the development of one or more substantial manufacturing sectors with a high rate of growth; (c) the existence or immediate emergence of "a political, social and institutional framework which exploits the impulses to expansion." (Elsewhere he speaks of the rise of innovators-entrepreneurs, but, unlike Schumpeter, does not make clear that they are part of the initiating factors; one assumes, then, that they emerge in the "institutional" framework after conditions (a) and (b) have first appeared successfully.)

Using this theoretical equipment, Rostow comes to the conclusion (pp. 38 and 39) that the "take-off" in the United States took place dur-'ing 1843–1860 and says why in the following passage:

> The American take-off is here viewed as the upshot of two different periods of expansion; the first, that of the 1840s marked by railway and

* W. W. Rostow, *The Stages of Economic Growth*, 1960.

manufacturing development, mainly confined to the East—this occurred while the South and West digested the extensive agricultural expansion of the previous decade; the second the great railway push into the Middle West during the 1850s *marked by a heavy inflow of foreign capital.* By the opening of the Civil War the American economy of North and West, *with real momentum in its heavy industry sector,* is judged to have taken-off. (Italics added.)

Rostow has not wanted for critics; thus Simon Kuznets has said simply and finally: "Unless I have completely misunderstood Professor Rostow's definition of 'take-off' and its statistical characteristics, I can only conclude the available evidence lends no support to Professor Rostow's suggestion." His fellow historians are more severe. Fogel, Fishlow, and North, in the works mentioned in Chapter I, submit Rostow's hypotheses and proof to elaborate examination and conclude with its complete rejection. Fogel and North declare flatly that Rostow's analysis is not grounded in theory (we shall see that the same strictures in one degree or another apply to them as well); Fishlow—who is a more careful worker, incidentally, and less inclined to shoot the moon—refuses to enter into the "theoretical" debate, although he does not take Rostow seriously.

North makes much of the fact that no sudden increase in capital formation took place and that regarding a heavy inflow of capital from Europe during the "take-off" years quite the reverse occurred. The foreign borrowings of the 1850s constituted a much smaller proportion of the national product than had those of the 1830s. North pooh-poohs industrialization as the magical ingredient that starts the whole world rapidly spinning. (Perforce he must, because his own theory is based on a rapid expansion of the export sector.) He denies that the nascent railroads played a part of any importance in the growth of wheat and cotton production and the movement of these crops into foreign markets. (In both cases transportation was largely by water—canal and/or river.)

Fogel is the complete econometrician and, using his own and Robert E. Gallman's reconstructions (sectoral distributions of the shares of value added in commodity production; more of Gallman later), he denies that 1843–1860 were years of decisive change. Looking at cotton, textiles, and iron in detail, but including also a miscellany of other industries, he comes to the conclusion that if we are seeking a real reference date for the inauguration of the Industrial Revolution it is to be found in the decade of the 1820s. He admits that his data are crude, but having said this, asseverates boldly:

> However, there does seem to be a prima facie case for the view that the third decade of the nineteenth century was one in which the shift toward

manufacturing approached the rate that prevailed during Rostow's "take-off" years.

More than this, Rostow's span of less than two decades when an explosion presumably took place is no more (and possibly less) unequivocally the right one than other such short spans. Fogel goes on:

> Instead, the data [he called them "crude"] suggest a process of more or less continuous increase in the absolute and relative size of manufacturing extending from 1820—a good argument can be made for viewing 1807 as the starting date. . . .

There was, therefore, no Industrial Revolution in the sense of sudden, discontinuous growth. Finally Fogel rejects the Rostovian thesis of the significant influence of railroad construction and operation (the "primary growth sector") on a group of industries supplying it—the so-called backward linkages. He examines coal, iron, machinery, transportation equipment, and lumber, and concludes that the value added in manufacturing the goods consumed by lthe railroads in 1859 was "probably less than . . . 3.94 per cent of the figure for all manufacturing."

Fishlow's book devotes 60 pages to these backward linkages of the ante-bellum railroad industry, and although he shies away from putting a price tag on them he is willing to make a number of tentative observations which, because of their very caution, cancel out the categorical claims and counterclaims of Rostow and Fogel. Fishlow says:

> . . . the impressive historical contributions of these investments [in the railroads] may well reside in their dual function as significant suppliers *and* demanders, with the latter emerging first.
>
> The specific form of railroad requirements, at least, reinforces this conjecture. Not that the ante-bellum period was the scene of their principal triumphs. Only the production of rolling stock took root immediately. Rails continued to be imported through the major part of the boom of the early 1850s, and railroad consumption of coal was modest before the war. . . . By the last part of the prewar period railroad consumption took off a goodly amount of total domestic iron production. . . . More of the output of the nation's coal mines found its way to the railroad sector than any other. Machine shops and skilled employment multiplied at an increasing pace.

It is North * who is the most consistent and the most unyielding of the econometric historians. His position is this: the reasons for and the methods of growth should be the only concerns of the economic historian; the methodology is the examination of statistical data and the use of mathematical reconstruction when these data are only fragmentary and disparate. There follows the isolation of a few independent variables—

* D. C. North, *The Economic Growth of the United States, 1790–1860*, 1961.

wholly endogenous, by the way—and their employment to test a limited number of hypotheses. These form and inform a model which, presumably, is to have general application.

Thus theory is the firm underpinning of what may become—it does with North—a complex, architectonic structure. Theory, says Fogel, North's leading coadjutor, will help to "measure that which was previously deemed unmeasurable." And again, econometrics is the tool with which to test and establish "the logical and empirical validity of the theories on which their measurements are based." Guided by such touchstones, economic history, then, is a science with built-in predictability.

It should be noted, therefore, that North, and Fogel like him, is a determinist (as Marx was; it is no accident that North had studied Marx closely). By the same token Marx called his historical analysis and the application of *his* model to the future "scientific socialism." Only the economic processes will furnish clues to what North is seeking—that is to say, growth. Exogenous factors—wars, revolutions, the plans and schemes of political leaders and their impacts on other nations—are irrelevant. Everything else—public policies, the attitudes and decisions of individuals, and institutions such as the law, the churches, banking, and workingmen's organizations—is what Marx called the "superstructure," mirrored reflections, with no independent life of their own, of the "relations of production."

North states his over-all theory in this way in the preface of his book:

> This study is based on the proposition that United States growth was the evolution of a market economy where the behavior of prices of goods, services and productive factors was the major element in any explanation of economic change. Institutional and political policies have certainly been influential. . . . But they have modified rather than replaced the underlying forces of a market economy. [Later, he includes the innovators-entrepreneurs and their acceptance and leadership among the "institutional policies"; they do not constitute an independent, initiating force.]

All this is familiar enough, historically, in terms of American experiences (indeed, we have seen that a market economy was a characteristic of American development in the early days of the colonial period) and in the static theory of classical and neoclassical economics, in which factor products and resource allocations operating in a free market inevitably produce equilibriums. The processes are timeless, and, at a given point, changeless.

But North's is a dynamic theory; and he introduces a single major variable with an ancillary one to account for the "growth" in his title.

These are the success of the export sector of an American exploitative industry (cotton), the characteristics of this export industry, and the extraregional disposition of the income received from the export sector. The export industry originated and grew in the South with the opening up of the Southwest to cotton and the expansion of the cotton textile industry (more particularly in England, less so in the United States). Because the South (in North's view) concentrated on a monoculture (cotton) and the income generated there was disposed of elsewhere, the ancillary theory accounts for the progress of the rest of the United States; this is the theory of linkages, first fully developed by Hirschman.*

With the South almost entirely dependent on cotton, it looked to the Northwest, using the Mississippi Valley system as the means of transport, to feed it (wheat, wheat flour, and meat animals) and furnish it with its work animals (mules, oxen, and horses) and its tobacco and whiskey; this was a backward linkage. From the profits the Northwest presumably made its investments in banking and canals and was able to afford to specialize in an "investment in human capital," that is, education. Similarly, the capital produced by the cotton industry flowed into the Northeast (to pay for goods and services and as an investment): this was a forward linkage. The consequence was the industrialization of the New England and Middle Atlantic states, the growth of their banking institutions, and their ability to improve their transportation facilities (first canals, then railroads) and to take flyers in the construction of middle-western and far-western railroads.

This nexus of the cotton-export industry, the linkages that occurred, and the accelerating influence on the whole economy of the United States, which resulted in a long-term rate of growth of aggregate product per head, first appeared in the early ante-bellum period, although North at different times uses different dates. In his book it seems to have begun around 1830. In *Growth and Welfare in the American Past, A New Economic History*, 1966, it took place "between 1815 and 1860." In his article, "Industrialization in the United States" † he gives part III of his essay the title "The Era of Industrialization, 1820–60." (It should be noted, in passing, that neither by 1815 nor by 1820 had the cotton-export industry become important.)

But to quote North (from his book):

> An expanding external market [cotton] has provided the means for an increase in the size of the domestic market, growth in money income, and

* A. O. Hirschman, *The Strategy of Economic Development*, 1958.
† D. C. North, *The Cambridge Economic History of Europe*, Vol. VI, Part II, 1965.

the spread of specialization and the division of labor. Under the favorable conditions outlined below [with respect to the disposition of income from the export sector], it set in motion a chain of consequences leading to sustained growth.

It turns out that North's is not a general theory equally applicable in time and place; it is a special theory having relevance only to the cotton-producing South and only for a specific time. For a brief continuous period, say 1830–1860, North attempts to prove mathematically—and it may be true—that cotton exports enjoyed favorable terms of trade; that is, prices for cotton sent out of the region were relatively higher than the prices the South had to pay for its imports. Suppose that a commodity export has unfavorable terms of trade, as in Cuba and Brazil (they exported sugar) during the very years North has under review. Despite the heavy exports of these two countries, neither linkage effects developed nor sustained growth into industrialization appeared. The same thing occurred in Argentina after the 1890s: the appearance of a great export industry (wheat), unfavorable terms of trade, no linkages, and no sustained growth.

It appears that favorable terms of trade—a special case—is at the heart of North's general theory. His hypothesis, then, cannot be converted into a universal empirical law; and if the linkage effects are challenged, or fail to appear—as I shall indicate immediately—the theory cannot explain causatively the sustained growth (if, indeed, any occurred) of the American economy before the Civil War.

It should be observed that cotton exports constituted only 42.3 per cent of the total value of American exports in 1820, 50.8 per cent in 1830, 57.1 per cent in 1840, 53.3 per cent in 1850, and 60.8 per cent in 1860. The rest consisted of a miscellany of commodities that filled the holds of the American ships engaged in trading voyages. These ships, particularly during the 1830s and 1840s, ranged all over the world and because they did not sail on schedule, they moved in and out of ports, buying and selling, in Caribbean waters, up and down the coasts of South America, and in the China and Southeast Asia trades.

Departing from New England seaports but also from New York and Philadelphia, the "Chinamen" first took off for the northwest Canada coast with trade goods and picked up otter skins in exchange; thence to the Sandwich (Hawaiian) Islands, where they acquired sandlewood; and so out to the China coast to sell their furs and wood for tea, silks, pepper, porcelains, and fine cottons. Similar trading voyages—with ships and crew gone for as long as three years—moved in and out of the islands and the mainlands of the South China Sea as far westward as the Gulf of Siam, the Strait of Malacca, and the Bay of Bengal. Here is where the New England merchants and sailors made their profits: to build their lovely white wooden houses in every Massachusetts, Rhode Island, and Connecticut port town; to invest their gains in the cotton and woolen textile mills of Rhode Island, Massachusetts and Maine; to set up land companies or syndicates to buy huge tracts in the public domain in the Southwest and Northwest; to finance the railroad construction and the merchant-banks of New England; and to open the copper mines of Michigan, to provide the capital for the southern Michigan railroads, and a sizable part of the Illinois Central Railroad.

The merchants of New York and Philadelphia traded in similar fashion, with their foci the Caribbean and Europe; in this instance they were assisted in their activities by English merchant-bankers whose commercial credits to Americans in the 1830s reached as much as $100 mililon annually.

These merchants were the typical American businessmen, and when Freeman Hunt collected from his magazine in 1856 a series of biographies of some of America's successful businessmen, he called his two volumes *Lives of American Merchants*. And this is what Hunt wrote in the Preface of his first volume:

> It is trade that is converting the whole continent into a cultivated field, and bending its ends together with the iron bands of the railroad.
> If commerce be thus preeminently the characteristic of the country and of the age, it is fit that the Lives of the Merchants should be written and read.

The subjects of the *Lives* are these merchants. They were the sons of merchants, had been apprenticed to merchants, or, as immigrant boys, had started by buying and selling a part of a newly arrived cargo and so had become merchants. Many had cut their eyeteeth by going out on ships as sailors or supercargoes or by setting up as factors in distant ports. Most of them continued as merchants at the same time that they engaged in private banking or helped to promote and finance a local canal company, railroad, or insurance company. Some—after making their fortunes as merchants—moved wholly into other pursuits: banking (Stephen Girard), real estate and urban property development (John Jacob Astor), cotton textile manufacture (Patrick Tracy Jackson), woolen manufacture (William Lawrence), and midwestern railroad development (John Murray Forbes, the builder of the Michigan Central and the Chicago, Burlington and Quincy). Next to none of these men had anything to do with the cotton trade or benefited from the income it generated. The forward linkages with the Northeast are nonexistent.

Before we examine the backward linkages with the Northwest a

.word about British investments in the South (an exogenous factor and therefore with no place in North's model). Between 1824 and 1840 southern and southwestern states issued $52.8 million in bonds (most of which were bought in Britain) to help in the establishment of state-chartered or public banks.

Fishlow submits North's contention of a linkage between the South and the Northwest (i.e., the flow of northwestern foodstuffs to the South because the South, devoting itself to a monoculture, was incapable of feeding itself) to a rigorous examination and ends by denying its valid-ity. The South was self-sufficient in regard to its foodstuffs and, equally, in regard to its work animals. (Indeed, southern corn, as measured by value of product, was more important than southern cotton.) North, like other econometric historians discussing slavery, misses the class structure of the southern society and its economy. At the outbreak of the Civil War not much more than one-fourth of the white families of the South owned slaves; the greater proportion of the rest were yeomen farmers engaged in general farming and in growing wheat, corn, oats, and hay and in producing swine, cattle, and work animals. The surplus crops they took to market were for the most part sold regionally. This was particularly true of the work animals, cattle, and sheep of Kentucky, Tennessee, and Missouri which were moved to other southern states.

TABLE 5

PRODUCTION OF CORN, WHEAT, OATS, AND SWINE,
1839–1859

	1839	1849	1859
Corn			
United States	378	592	838
Total South	252	349	436
Wheat			
United States	85	101	173
Total South	30	28	50
Oats			
United States	123	147	173
Total South	43	50	32
Swine			
United States	26	30	34
Total South	16	21	21

Source. L. C. Gray, *History of Agriculture in the United States to 1860*, (1933), Vol. 2, pp. 1040, 1042.

Table 5 shows the production of corn, wheat, and oats and the number of swine in the United States and the southern states during the period 1839–1859. By southern states is meant the 11 seceding states and the four border states (Kentucky, Delaware, Maryland and Missouri). Figures are in millions of bushels for the crops and millions of units for the swine.

What of the receipt of agricultural goods at New Orleans? Do they represent northwestern crops? If so (a large part of the produce originated in northern Louisiana, Arkansas, and Missouri), how much was consumed in the South?

Fishlow comes to a number of conclusions. For the period of almost four decades (1823–1860), "Western products, and therefore western foodstuffs, made up less than half of the New Orleans receipts." "A second noteworthy result is the *absolute* decline in western shipments in the 1850s." Again, "Receipts of western produce at New Orleans were not entirely consumed but were also re-exported either to foreign or coastwise ports." Fishlow ends in this fashion:

> These new consumption data permit us now to re-examine the West-South trade with respect to three basic characteristics: its absolute magnitude vis-à-vis other inter-regional trade, the relative importance of the exports to the West, and the relative importance of the imports to the South. First, we can conclude rather assuredly that the trade relatively was quite small. [Second,] the $18 million consumption of foodstuffs in 1858–1861 . . . is only a third of the exchange between the West and the East, and for that matter, a smaller proportion of the shipments from the North to the South. . . . It therefore does not appear that southern demands for foodstuffs were an important mechanism by which increasing exports of staples from the South transmitted a dynamic impulse to the West. [Third,] If relatively unimportant to the West, the imports were minute compared with production of foodstuffs within the South itself. [And Fishlow cites the figures given in Table 5.]

THE ECONOMETRIC HISTORIANS
DISAGREE AMONG THEMSELVES

Gallman *—throwing a smaller net than his fellow-econometricians and staying away from any claims to a theory of growth or "take-off"—is much more satisfying and, by the same token, implicitly, highly critical of the claims of Rostow and North. His article "Commodity Output in the United States" sets out to do the following things.

Starting with 1839—he is dubious of the value of earlier data—

* Robert E. Gallman, in Studies in Income and Wealth, *Trends in the American Economy in the Nineteenth Century*, National Bureau, 1960.

Gallman examines by quinquennial periods only the commodity-producing industries, agriculture, mining, manufacturing and construction, and attempts to measure the value they added rather than the income they generated. He does this in both current and constant prices (the latter, obviously, with all the shortcomings of such index figures).

Tables 6 and 7 are two of Gallman's key tables:

TABLE 6

PERCENTAGE DISTRIBUTION OF VALUE ADDED
IN COMMODITY PRODUCTION, 1839–1859

Year	Agriculture	Mining	Manufacturing	Construction (Variant A)
1839	72	1	17	10
1844	69	1	21	9
1849	60	1	30	10
1854	57	1	29	13
1859	56	1	32	11

Source. Gallman, *op. cit.,* p. 26.

TABLE 7

ABSOLUTE INCREASES IN MANUFACTURING'S SHARE
OF VALUE ADDED IN COMMODITY PRODUCTION,
1839–1899

Quinquennium	Increase in Manufacturing Share
1839–1844	3.7
1844–1849	8.4
1849–1854	−0.3
1854–1859	2.8
1859–1864	—
1864–1869	—
1869–1874	6.4
1874–1879	−2.4
1879–1884	7.0
1884–1889	4.0
1889–1894	5.4
1894–1899	−0.1

Source. Fogel, *op. cit.,* p. 21, calculated from Gallman,
op. cit., pp. 43ff.

It is apparent, from Table 6, that the share of the manufacturing sector grew in the ante-bellum period; but it grew more rapidly in the years before Rostow's "take-off" than it did during them.

Table 7 not only makes Rostow's claims but those of North as well highly improbable. In the 12 quinquennia in Gallman's calculations the manufacturing share increased by three points or more in six: one (1839–1844) preceded Rostow's "revolution" and only one (1844–1849) lay within it; the other four followed the Civil War years and their advance was checked only by the appearance of sharp depression (1874–1879 and 1894–1899). The Industrial Revolution, in short, really took place in the post-Civil War period and not before it.

The continued progress of manufacturing and mining and the decline of agriculture is even more sharply pointed up by the developments after 1869. Gallman's calculations are shown in Table 8.

TABLE 8

PERCENTAGE DISTRIBUTION OF VALUE ADDED IN
COMMODITY PRODUCTION, 1869–1899

Year	Agriculture	Mining	Manufacturing	Construction (Variant A)
1869	53	2	33	12
1874	46	2	39	12
1879	49	3	37	11
1884	41	3	44	12
1889	37	4	48	11
1894	32	4	53	11
1899	33	5	53	9

Source. Gallman, op. cit., p. 26.

Stanley Lebergott's analysis of the labor force leads us to draw similar conclusions (Table 9). In 1800 the proportion of agricultural workers among those gainfully employed was 83.5 per cent; it dropped to 64 per cent in 1840, and to 53.0 per cent in 1870 and 37.5 per cent in 1900. Those in manufacturing, the handicrafts, and "bespoke" trades (undoubtedly largely the last two) made up 5.4 per cent in 1800 and 18.8 per cent in 1840. In 1870 the proportion of workers in manufacturing was 20.5 per cent and in 1900, 28.2 per cent. (By this time the handicrafts were playing a minor role.) Over the century the absolute decline in workers in water transport and the great increase in those in the trades, professions, mining, and "all other" (including construction and

TABLE 9

GAINFUL WORKERS IN THE UNITED STATES

1800–1900

(In thousands)

Type of Employment	1800	1840	1870	1900
Total	1,850	5,590	12,925	29,073
Agriculture	1,545	3,590	6,850	10,912
Manufacturing (including the hand trades)	100	1,050	2,643	7,199
Water transport	55	120	90	78
Trade	25	170	878	3,085
Professional services	25	90	342	1,181
Mining	3	20	187	695
All other	97	570	1,935	5,923

Source. "The Pattern of Employment Since 1800" in S. E. Harris, Ed., *American Economic History,* 1961, p. 182.

railroading) can be observed. In short, from 1840 to 1900 the proportion of agricultural workers in the total labor force *declined* 40 per cent whereas that of the nonagricultural workers *increased* 80.0 per cent.

THE ANTICAPITALIST SPIRIT OF THE NORTHERN INTELLECTUALS

In contemplating the ante-bellum period and in searching for reasons why the economic progress of the United States did not make more rapid strides forward than it did, we are confronted by the negativism, nay, hostility, toward the economic processes of the middle-class intellectuals, North and South—the clergy, the publicists, the men of letters.

In the North, notably in New England—but the so-called revolt against materialism in the three decades of the 1830s, 1840s, and 1850s had its votaries far and wide—there was a sudden retreat and, for many, a withdrawal from the world of reality. One group, the most influential, that of the transcendentalists, following Ralph Waldo Emerson, Henry David Thoreau, and Theodore Parker, proclaimed the supremacy of the individual who, freeing himself from the huckstering of the market-place and automatic loyalty to political authority, the state, was to find his true self in a mystical, pantheistic union with the "Over-Soul."

In 1842, in the essay "The Transcendentalist," Emerson declared why he was parting company with what he regarded as the reigning materialism of his time; idealism was the wave of the future. He said:

> The materialist insists on facts, on history, on the force of circumstances and the animal wants of man; the idealist on the power of Thought and Will, on inspiration, on miracle, on individual culture. [In the essay 'Man and the Reformer' he indicated what he meant by the last in this way: "a man should have a farm or mechanical craft for his culture."]

Emerson could not come any closer than the following when he tried to say what the idealist was. He

> . . . does not respect labor, or the products of labor, namely property, otherwise than as a manifold symbol, illustrating with wonderful fidelity of details the laws of being; he does not respect government, except as far as it reiterates the law of his mind; nor the church, nor charities, nor arts, for themselves; but hears, as at a vast distance, what they say, as if his consciousness would speak to him through a pantomimic scene. His thought—that is the universe.

As for the ultimate reality of nature, the "Over-Soul," Emerson fumbled in this fashion:

> Within man is the soul of the whole, the wise silence; the universal beauty, to which every part and parcel is equally related; the eternal One.

He knew what he meant by his withdrawal, by his refusal to enter the lists, to fight for the "reform" he was always talking about, and to free man from his chains of inequality, poverty, vice, and ugliness. When he was asked to join Brook Farm, he held off—as he did from everything else—justifying himself with this observation in his *Journal* (October 17, 1840):

> I have not yet conquered my own house. It irks and repents me. Shall I raise the siege of this hencoop, and march baffled away to the pretended siege of Babylon? It seems to me that so to do were to dodge the problem I am set to solve, and to hide my impotency in the thick of a crowd.

To W. H. Channing, that gentle and wise Unitarian who called on Emerson to enlist in the Abolition crusade, Emerson's reply was that he had other slaves to free, the slaves of ignorance, superstition, and fear. In his *Ode Inscribed to W. H. Channing,* he sought once more to explain in his characteristically oblique fashion:

> Though loathe to grieve
> The evil time's sole patriot,
> I cannot leave
> My honied thought
> For the priest's cant,
> Or statesman's rant.

Of what Boston and its masters in State Street were up to, the so-called Hunkers of the Whig party, Emerson was clear and direct and nasty. V. L. Parrington, in applauding him, said of Emerson:

> He was at one with Jefferson in preferring an agrarian to an industrial order. Manchester economics—the doctrine of the economic man, of the iron law of wages, and other obscenities of the school—he quite frankly loathed.

Parrington quoted with approval from this remark in Emerson's *Journal* (written in 1839 when he was 36):

> A question which well deserves examination now is the Danger of Commerce. This invasion of Nature by Trade with its Money, its Credit, it steam, its Railroad, threatens to upset the balance of man, and establish a new, universal Monarchy more tyrannical than Babylon or Rome.

Thoreau refused to be circumspect or to take refuge in Emerson's cloudy mysticism. He called on his fellow men to stop "pawing him with their dirty institutions." He retired to his hut at Walden Pond because he despised what the world about him was doing—engaged in making goods and making money, turning to machines to drive out the handicrafts; he would live in nature where his individualism and therefore his spirit had free rein.

If mechanization was evil, public authority was even worse. Thus in "Civil Disobedience," written in 1849, when Thoreau was 32, he defied organized society, yet daring it to cast him out:

> I simply wish to refuse allegiance to the State, to withdraw and stand aloof from it effectually. . . . In fact, I quietly declare war with the State, after my fashion, though I will still make use and get what advantage of her I can, as is usual in such cases.

Churches, organized religion, were among the man-made institutions Emerson and Thoreau would have no truck with. Theodore Parker was a Bostonian minister and remained one all his life. Transcendentalism gave him all the answers, not only in his search for the divinity of man in God but equally in revealing the purpose of politics. Thus in his essay "Transcendentalism" (written in 1876, after a long life of battling for his conception of righteousness; he had come to his Congregational pulpit in 1846), he said:

In politics, transcendentalism starts not from experience alone, but from consciousness; not merely from human history, but also from human nature. It does not so much quote precedents, contingent facts of experience, as ideas, necessary facts of consciousness. . . . It appeals to a natural justice, natural right; absolute justice, absolute right. Now the source and original of this justice and right it finds in God—the conscience of God; the channel through which we receive this justice and right is our own moral sense, our conscience, which is our consciousness of the conscience of God.

This conscience in politics and in ethics transcends experience. . . . [and] it anticipates history; and the ideal justice of conscience is juster than the empirical and contingent justice actually exercised at Washington or at Athens. . . . In transcendental politics the question of expediency is always subordinate to the question of natural right. . . .

Armed with this sword, Parker proclaimed the Church militant. In his installation sermon in 1846, he announced the roles of his church and himself:

A Christian church should be the means of reforming the world, of forming it after the pattern of Christian ideas. It should therefore bring up the sentiments of the time, the ideas of the times, and the actions of the times, to judge them by the universal standard. We expect the sins of commerce to be winked at in the streets; the sins of the state to be applauded on election day and in Congress, or on the Fourth of July; we are used to hear them called the righteousness of the nation. You expect them to be tried by passion, which looks only to immediate results and partial ends. Here they are to be measured by Conscience and Reason, which looks to permanent results and universal ends. . . .

It was the business of Parker and his church, of Congregationalism and Protestantism, to declare war on slavery, on war itself, and on poverty and the rich who were the oppressors of the poor. Parker went on:

If the church were to waste less time in building its palaces of theological speculation, palaces mainly of straw, and based upon chaff, it would surely have more time to use in the practical good works of the day.

Thus, secure in his dedication, Parker entered every fray, championed every humanitarian cause, instructed and scolded every public figure, but remained outside and above the battle himself.

Parker was moved and turned indignant when he saw women and children working in factories; the best he could do, however, was express his distaste for "the institution of money—the master of all the rest." He hated slavery and agitated always against it; for the efforts of northern Whigs and Democrats to arrive at an accommodation with the South—time was on their side; the industrialization Parker and the rest condemned would end by compelling the South to surrender its "peculiar institution"—he had no use. Parker looked forward to war as the only way out—the very means of resort to arms that in another breath he was so quick to condemn. Commager,* his biographer, admits:

> He preached the inevitable conflicts, he talked of appealing from the parchment of the Constitution to the parchment on the head of a drum, he struck fine gestures and assured his friends that he bought no more books— he needed his money for cannon.

Therefore Parker in 1851 said of both political parties:

> The dollar is the germinal dot of the Whig party; its motive is pecuniary . . . it sneers at the poor; at the many; has a contempt for the people. It legislates against the poor, for the rich. . . . Everything must yield to money. . . .
> The Democratic party appeals to the brute will of the majority, right or wrong, it knows no Higher Law. . . . The Whig party inaugurates the Money got; the Democrat inaugurates the Desire to get money.

Schlesinger † properly expressed his impatience when he looked at Emerson, Thoreau and Parker:

> For the typical transcendentalist the flinching from politics perhaps expressed a failure they were seeking to erect into a virtue. The exigencies of responsibility were exhausting; much better to demand perfection and indignantly reject the half loaf, than wear out body and spirit in vain grapplings with overmastering reality.

It was Lydia Maria Child, reformer, abolitionist, popular and well-to-do journalist who summed up the contempt for her age that was so much part and parcel of transcendentalism. In her *Letters from New York* (1843) she wrote:

> In Wall Street, and elsewhere, Mammon, as usual, coolly calculates his chance of extracting a penny from war, pestilence, and famine; and Commerce, with her loaded drays, and jaded skeletons of horses, is busy as ever fulfilling the "World's contract with the Devil.". . . I have often anathematized the spirit of Trade, which reigns triumphant, not only in 'Change, but in our halls of legislation, and even in our churches . . . I sometimes ask whether the Age of Commerce is better than the Age of War? Whether our "merchant princes" are a great advance upon feudal chieftains? Whether it is better for the many to be prostrated by force, or devoured by cunning?

The other group that fled were the Utopians, who meant to live outside society entirely in self-sufficing communities. The spokesmen, the soothsayers, were middle-class intellectuals, too, but this time they

---

* Henry Steele Commager, *Theodore Parker, Yankee Reformer*, 1936.
† Arthur M. Schlesinger, Jr., *The Age of Jackson*, 1945.

addressed themselves to the workers—and led them astray for two decades. Workers, proclaimed the Utopians, would escape from Manchesterism and the iron law of wages by forming communities of their own and engaging in farming and the handicrafts. There was only the vaguest kind of notion how such activities would fit into a market economy. It was hoped that benevolently inclined capitalists would come to their assistance and would provide the needed funds to establish the producers' cooperatives that would sustain the colonies in their new Canaan.

The transcendentalists had gone to Germany for their inspiration, to Kant, Schelling, Fichte, and the other German philosophical idealists; the American Utopians turned for their guidance to the Englishman Robert Owen and to the Frenchmen Count Claude de Saint-Simon, Pierre-Joseph Proudhon, and above all to Charles Fourier.

Robert Owen, the wealthy New Lanark (Scotland) textile manufacturer, had turned out to be a model employer, and had then flown high into the empyrean in his *A New View of Society* in which he expounded the thesis that self-sustaining cooperative units would metamorphose industrial capitalism and spare the workers endemic unemployment. Well-wishing, wealthy men (Saint-Simon in France was making his appeal to the same group) would start the communities off, and the operating financial engine would be provided by so-called "labor-exchange" banks. Labor exchanges would be established in which commodities, their value based on labor costs, would be traded for "labor notes"; these in turn were to be used to acquire other kinds of goods similarly deposited. What if goods did not move and surpluses piled up in the exchanges? There would be suspended in circulation accumulating "labor notes" whose values obviously were bound to depreciate. Owen set up such an "Equitable Labor Exchange" in London in 1832; it quickly failed. Nevertheless the idea kept popping up; in 1848 in Paris Louis Blanc had a somewhat similar notion, and probably the Sub–Treasuries of the Farmer Alliances in the United States went back to the same Utopian source.

Meanwhile in 1824 Owen himself took the plunge. He bought out for $150,000 the Rappite Community, founded by a religious group, in Harmony, Indiana, and he set up the New Harmony Community with his 23-year old son William (soon replaced by his older brother Robert Dale Owen) in charge. A varied host descended on the new Utopia: well-intentioned but unskilled men and women, sharpers, the lazy and ineffectual, and some really distinguished people with sound ideas about education and agronomy. But the scheme could not work—it ate up the greater part of Owens' fortune—and by 1828 Owen was ready to cry quits. Similar Owenite colonies, nevertheless, bloomed and as quickly faded away in other parts of the country: the Yellow Springs Community in Ohio, the Franklin Community of Haverstraw, New York, the community in Nashoba, Tennessee, founded by the redoubtable Frances Wright, which was to combine cooperation with the emancipation of the Negro. (100 to 150 Negro slaves were to be purchased, manumitted, and allowed to work a plantation on a cooperative basis, thus paying off their purchase price.) "The Wright Plan for the Gradual Abolition of Slavery in the United States Without Danger of Loss to the Citizens of the South" started out with five slaves; when the colony was abandoned in 1830, it had only 30 Negroes, whom Frances Wright moved to Haiti on land she had purchased.

Most influential of all was Charles Fourier and his "scientism," who had "discovered" a new social psychology and new principles of efficient and happy labor. (Albert Brisbane popularized Fourier's teachings in his *Social Destiny of Man,* 1840, and obtained the support of and a good deal of free publicity from two of New York's influential newspapers—Horace Greeley's *Tribune* and Parke Godwin's *Post.*) Fourier's psychology was based on what he called the human "passions," from which he spun out broad theories of social behavior and, using both, formulated systems of education and societal arrangements through which men would be free and contented in their daily pursuits. The social unit for the new society was to be the so-called Phalanstery, in which work would be "attractive," waste eliminated, and labor discord charmed away. The members of a Phalanstery were to divide themselves into groups and series, and all were to find useful work conforming to their particular "passions." There was a place for small children: Fourier, a bachelor who loved cats and hated children, saw that youngsters liked to mess around in dirt. Such a "passion" had its usefulness; children were to be organized as Little Hordes to clean streets and sewers and spread manure.

This kind of pretentious silliness attracted the attention of a band of lofty, middle-class New England transcendentalists who in 1841 established their famous Brook Farm outside Boston. Initially Brook Farm was a community, with a good school, based on a "system of brotherly cooperation" in place of "selfish competition." It got nowhere. (Hawthorne, who visited what he called the "pic-nic," saw why. The good women did not like to serve as "chamber-maids to the cows.") In 1844 the Brook Farmers turned to Fourier for inspiration, divided themselves into groups and series, and struggled as agriculturists and educators until the building that was to house all the business of the Phalanstery burned down.

Brook Farm itself was finished in 1847 but its influence was pervasive, in part as a result of the launching of *The Harbinger,* a journal for the dissemination of Fourier's ideas and for attacks on "the exploitations of trade and commerce," to which, among others, Henry James (the elder), John Greenleaf Whittier, and James Russell Lowell contributed. There were other Phalansteries, as many as 40 or 50, but none survived beyond the 1850s.

The land reformers constituted still another company. Their inspiration came from the Englishman George Henry Evans, who migrated to America and began at once to broadcast his message of equal property for all. Evans' ideas underwent a number of transformations. At first he preached the necessity for destroying industrialism and replacing it with "rural republican townships," in which land would be held only by the cultivators themselves in an inalienable tenure; industrial production, on the basis of the handicrafts entirely, would be wholly for use. In time, however, Evans was compelled to bow before the inevitable: his program came to stand simply for free lands from the public domain for all actual settlers.

Evans found a patron in Horace Greeley, who threw open the columns of his New York *Tribune* to the Englishman's strange and somewhat hysterical notions. Evans talked of getting rid of the "hoary iniquities of Norman land pirates" and subduing capitalism by pulling away its chief prop—feudal landholding! The escape for the worker (who had no funds) was free entry into the public lands, for then, said Evans, "Tens of thousands who are now languishing in hopeless poverty, will find a certain and speedy independence." It is difficult to understand what Horace Greeley—high tariff protectionist and foe of trade unionism—was doing in this gallery. In any event, the only outcome of Evans's preachments was their absorption in the form of Homesteadism by the new Republican party; and it was in the Republican party, too that Greeley found a sheltering harbor.

Still another program for broad social amelioration—it was to help workers to get away from "wage slavery" by permitting them to set up their own little shops—was linked with currency reform, that will-o'-the wisp that Americans of good intentions pursued so assiduously and so unsuccessfully right into the 1930s. This was the scheme of Edward Kellogg, a New York merchant, who, because of his own reverses, began to cast about for the reasons for the existence of an unequal society and his own misfortunes. In 1848 he published his *Labour and Other Capital* which took its basic notions from the Ricardian socialists and from John Law, the colonial land banks, Robert Owen, and Pierre-Joseph Proudhon. Labor was the source of all value, but labor was robbed of the fruits of its toil because production, for its financing, paid an interest rate in excess of the labor cost of the banking business. The physical wealth of the country, said Kellogg, was growing at the rate of

1¼ per cent a year; but money, the "representation of wealth," on the other hand, was increasing at an annual rate of 12 per cent. If money's interest could be kept at around 1 per cent, then, as Kellogg said in the subtitle of his book, the rights of both labor and capital would be secured and the wrongs of both eradicated, "without infringing the rights of property" and at the same time giving labor its "just reward."

How to do it? By using government, said Kellogg. And he declared:

> . . . if excessive interest rates deprived labor of its just reward and diverted its savings to the capitalists, and if accumulation by interest is a necessary function of money delegated to it by law, the evil lies in existing monetary laws and can be remedied only by legislation.

The Kellogg proposal ran as follows. The federal government was to issue paper legal-tender currency to individuals on real-estate security (obviously, for the workers, as skilled artisans and mechanics, this also meant their shops and tools) at an interest rate uniform throughout the nation, a rate that reflected labor's "natural power of production." This rate was to be 1.1 per cent. To keep the rate around 1 per cent the currency was to be made "interconvertible" with government bonds, the government changing the currency into bonds if the interest rate fell below 1 per cent and the bonds back into currency if the rate went up.

Nothing came of Kelloggism; yet the same notion bobbed up in 1864, when the short-lived National Labor Union adopted a modified version based on Alexander Campbell's pamphlet "The True Greenback, or the Way to Pay the National Debt Without Taxes and Emancipate Labor." Now the enemy, instead of the "trade and commerce" of the New England Hunkers, was "the money monopoly, the parent of all monopolies—the very root and essence of slavery"; but this hope for haven in a Utopia based on floods of government paper money ended as all the others had.

THE ANTICAPITALISM OF THE SLAVE SOUTH

There were equally persuasive voices raised in the South to attack capitalism; they were louder and more strident, for the survival of slavery, the South's "peculiar institution," was at stake. The South did not want for literate defenders; by the same token they knew where the North's jugular vein was and how to strike at it. This was the system of *laissez-faire* of Adam Smith and Ricardo, one that produced a free-marketplace in which capitalism could flourish but whose victims were the wage-driven workers, beset by poverty and insecurity, of the industrializing North. The trouble with the defense was that it became an ideology to which, whether they liked it or not, virtually all southerners found it necessary to conform. The upshot was, the South was anti-capitalist, so that the processes of accumulation, investment, diversification of enterprise, and the widening of a southern market—because all of these processes were under a cloud—were held back until a war had to be fought and slavery torn up root and branch.

In this large company * of intelligent but committed southerners there were the Virginians Thomas Roderick Dew (1802–1846), who knew his Smith and Ricardo and lectured on them but who could use them nonetheless to make a case for slavery; N. Beverley Tucker (? –1851), whom Joseph Dorfman calls "The Thomas Carlyle of the South," and who, combining Burke and Carlyle, saw "order and freedom," linking slavery and *noblesse oblige,* the basis of a flourishing civilization; and George Frederick Holmes (1820–1897), historical sociologist (a close student of Comte) who ended in the same place—rejecting Locke, Smith, and the utilitarians (they succeeded only in "the canonization of the existing order of human development") and extolling slavery because the long stretch of history had proved it true and just.

The southerner who went farthest and who was read most widely was that other Virginian George Fitzhugh (1806–1881). He had studied his Locke and Smith and followed closely the arguments of the European Utopians; he admired the English "Tory Socialists" of Disraeli and Young England and was at one with them in condemning the blighting influences (on England and America) of the Manchester economics and the practices of the Manchester (and New England) mill owners. His two books, *Sociology for the South; or the Failure of Free Society* (1854) and *Cannibals All; or, Slaves Without Masters* (1857) closed southern, but also northern, ranks. It was impossible, in the face of Fitzhugh's slashing, clever, often telling attacks—his contempt for capitalism and all its fruits; his avowal that northern wage-earners were the real slaves with no "masters" to show any humanity; his demonstration that in southern slavery all the hopes and yearnings of the Utopians were being realized: here was the real socialism—for any reconciliation among men of good will, north and south, to take place.

Man's modern fall began with the espousal of Lockian natural rights, enshrined in the Declaration of Independence and the Virginia Bill of Rights.

As a result of Locke and the philosophers of the Enlightenment:

* The reader is referred to Joseph Dorfman's *The Economic Mind in American Civilization,* Vol. 2, 1946, for his excellent and precise analysis of the thinking and writings of ante-bellum southern intellectuals. I have leaned heavily on him.

The human mind became extremely presumptuous and undertook to form governments on exact philosophical principles just as men make clocks, watches, or mills. They confounded the moral with the physical world, and this was not strange, because they had begun to doubt whether there was any other than a physical world.

It was absurd to hold that men were born "physically, morally, or intellectually equal," for their "natural inequalities beget inequalities of rights." "It would be far nearer the truth to say 'that some were born with saddles on their backs, and others booted and spurred to rid them,'—and the riding does them good." The real devil of the piece, however, was Adam Smith; the "free society" his free trade was to produce was a snare and a delusion whose victims made up the greater part of mankind. Said Fitzhugh of Adam Smith in his first book:

> There was another and much larger world, whose misfortunes, under his system, were to make the fortunes of his friends and his country. A part of that world . . . was at his door, they were the unemployed poor, the weak in mind or body, the simple and unsuspicious, the prodigal, the dissipated, the improvident and the vicious. *Laissez-faire* and *pas trop gouverner* suited them not at all; one portion of them needed support and protection; the other, much and rigorous government. Still they were fine subjects out of which the astute and designing, the provident and avaricious, the cunning, the prudent and the industrious might make fortunes in the field of free competition.

The "free society" was based on the "selfish virtues": "self promotion, self-elevation." In it "every man is taught that it is his first duty to change and better his pecuniary situation."

And this of Locke's natural rights and the social contract:

> We believe no heresy in moral science has been more pregnant of mischief than this theory of Locke. . . . [The reverse is the case.] Man is born a member of society, and does not form society. . . . He and society are congenital. Society is the being—he one of the members of that being. He has no rights whatever as opposed to the interests of society; and that society may very properly make any use of him that will redound to the public good.

And of capital and labor:

> All great enterprises owe their success to association of capital and labor. . . . The dissociation of labor and disintegration of society, which liberty and free competition occasion, is especially injurious to the poorer class; for besides the labor necessary to support the family, the poor man is burdened with the care of finding a home, and procuring employment, and attending to all domestic wants and concerns. Slavery retrieves our slaves of these cares altogether, and slavery is a form, and the very best form, of socialism.

Fitzhugh had harsh things to say about the Utopians, Fourier in particular; he noted how "in the free state of America, too, Socialism and every other heresy that can be invoked to make war on existing institutions, prevail to an alarming extent." Toward the end he let fly with his heaviest charge against Manchesterism, English and northern style:

> But far the worst feature of modern civilization, which is the civilization of free society, remains to be exposed. Whilst labor-saving processes have probably lessened by one-half, in the last century, the amount of work needed for comfortable support, the free laborer is compelled by capital and competition to work more than he ever did before and is less comfortable. The organization of society cheats him of his earnings, and those earnings go to swell the vulgar pomp and pageantry of the ignorant millionaires, who are the only great of the present day.

In *Cannibals All* Fitzhugh continued to range widely, drawing on Marx (he showed his familiarity with the dialectic) and on Thomas Carlyle, notably his "The Present Age" from *Latter-Day Pamphlets* (1850); both were used to train his big guns on the northern capitalists, who were "this vampire capitalist class." They were "the moral Cannibals." Fitzhugh pointed out that Carlyle had subtitled his *Latter-Day Pamphlets,* "The Failure of Society," whereas his own carried the same import; it was "Slaves Without Masters."

As for Marx, in his Preface, he says:

> My chief aim has been to show that *labor makes values and not exploits and accumulates them;* and hence to deduce that the unrestricted exploitation of so-called free society, is more oppressive to the laborer than domestic slavery. (Italics original.)

He begins the body of his book with the following:

> We are all, North and South, engaged in the White Slave Trade, and he who succeeds best, is esteemed most respectable. It is far more cruel than the Black Slave Trade, because it exacts more of its slaves, and neither protects nor governs them.

Because of the labor theory of value, he says to the North:

> You, with the command over labor which your capital gives you are a slave owner—a master without the obligations of a master. They who work for you, who create your income, are slaves, without the rights of slaves. Slaves without a master.

What neater summary of the dialectical process than this of the emergence and consequences of industrial capitalism?

> We contend that it was the origin of the capitalist and moneyed interest government, destined finally to swallow up all other powers in the State, and to bring about the most selfish, exacting and unfeeling class despotism.

Fitzhugh goes back again and again to the ambivalence of the North: The espousal by its intellectuals of Fourier socialism; they are joined by

> Infidels, Skeptics, Millerites, Mormons, Agrarians, Spiritual Rappers, Wakemanites, Free Negroes and Bloomers, [who] disturb the peace of society, threaten the security of property, offend the public sense of decency, assail religion, and invoke anarchy.

As for its businessmen, they are blindly led by "Adam Smith, Say, Ricardo & Co." He foresaw bitter struggle in the North as it "oscillates between Radicalism and Conservatism," with this observation:

> It is falsely said, that revolutions never go backwards. They always go backwards, and generally farther back than where they started. The Social Revolution now going on at the North, must some day go backwards.

Toward the end, he offered this advice:

> A word at parting to northern Conservatives. A like danger threatens North and South, proceeding from the same source. Abolitionism is maturing what Political Economy began. With inexorable sequence "Let Alone" [*laissez-faire*] is made to usher in No Government. North and South our danger is the same. . . . "Let Alone" must be repudiated, if we would have any government. . . . You of the North need not institute negro slavery; far less reduce white man to the state of negro slavery. But the masses require more of protection, and the masses and philosophers equally require more of control.

The irony was, it was too late for any *modus operandi* to be worked out; Stephen A. Douglas's failure proved this. As for Fitzhugh's impact, as Joseph Dorfman so justly says:

> . . . he had done such a good job in condemning free society in the name of slavery that the only alternative was to root out slavery if free society was to be maintained.

V

THE STRUCTURE OF THE
ANTE-BELLUM ECONOMY (I)

THE EXPANSION OF THE CONTINENTAL DOMAIN
AND THE LAND LAWS

There can be no doubt that significant changes were occurring in the northern ante-bellum economy. The land under cultivation increased enormously, thanks to the expansion of the public domain. Regional markets, one of which was the important inter-regional West–East, grew rapidly because of advances in transportation—in roads, rivers, canals, the railroads. One industry, cotton textiles, which had become mechanized and operated on a factory basis, was stimulating a forward linkage, the development of machine-tools manufacture. Credit resources—in the appearance and growth of state banking—added to the money supply and led to the inauguration of new ventures, some only speculative but many that made possible investment in hard goods and therefore capital creation. Foreign funds flowed into the country to help in short-term financing of foreign trade, and, more important, in long-term public improvements. Immigration, particularly the great burst of newcomers who arrived during the 11 years 1846–1857 (almost 3.5 million), both because of the push out of Europe and the pull of employment opportunities in the United States, added to the labor supply, for the first arrivals were preponderantly males between the ages of 15 and 45 years.

Education was increasing with the advance of the common (public) school and the beginning of technical instruction.

All were important, but still constituted only what Rostow has called the preconditions for the "take-off." The relative number of the labor force in agriculture declined, it is true, but it is doubtful that it showed a significant advance in man-hour productivity—at any rate, before the late 1850s. A small increase occurred in the labor force in manufacturing (and the hand trades), most of which was not industrialized. A national market for credit and goods and services did not yet exist. The leap forward, the process of self-sustained growth of the whole American economy—which led to impressive upward movements in real per capita GNP—awaited the termination of the Civil War, when federal government policy, the end of slavery, and a broad and general acceptance of the processes of accumulation and investment created a favorable climate in which entrepreneurship and innovation could flourish. Then the "take-off" did occur.

By purchase, conquest, and treaty, from 1803 to 1853, the United States was able to spread across the whole continent from the Atlantic to the Pacific and from the Gulf of Mexico to the forty-ninth parallel. Most of this new land lay in the public domain and was available for easy and quick settlement by grant, purchase, or squatting (subsequently converted into purchase) on lands owned by the federal government or by the states and already surveyed. Available credit facilities furthered the advance.

The Louisiana Purchase in 1803 (roughly the Mississippi-Missouri river system) totaled 827,000 square miles; the Florida Purchase, which took place in 1819, added 72,000 square miles; Texas became a Republic by breaking away from Mexico in 1836 and was annexed in 1845, thus furnishing another 390,000 square miles; a treaty with Great Britain in 1846, which settled the Oregon dispute, fixed the northern boundary along the forty-ninth parallel from Lake of the Woods in northern Minnesota to Puget Sound and added almost 300,000 square miles to American territory; the war against Mexico in 1848 gave the United States California and the vast New Mexico Territory, with more than 529,000 square miles; and the Gadsden Purchase in 1853, a total of 29,600 square miles, placed the southern border where it stands today.

The result was a continental area of at least 3 million square miles, of which 1.4 billion acres (72 per cent) was in the public domain and almost three-quarters of it in public hands (federal and state) until 1862. The broad lines of disposal—a survey established a section of one square mile (640 acres) as the unit of measurement—had been laid out by the Land Ordinances of 1785 and 1787, as we have seen. Two policies emerged: the federal government was to use the lands as grants to further desirable public projects (to reward veterans of wars, as bounties for enlistment, and to encourage internal improvements); and for quick and cheap sale to obtain revenue and further settlement.

Veterans, including those of the Indian wars, were granted soldier warrants to public land which they could use or sell, and bounties were offered for recruitment in the war with Mexico. Some 60 million acres were given away in this fashion and most of the soldiers sold their warrants for 50 to 80 cents an acre—usually to land companies.

Land was given to the states for the building of canals, wagon roads, railroads, the improvement of rivers and harbors, and swampland drainage. It was also granted for the furtherance of education (public schools, the Morrill Land-Grant College Act of 1862). Beginning in 1862 and continuing for a decade, the Congress itself voted huge tracts from the public domain to hasten the building of western trunk railways in advance of settlement.

These basic principles were laid down by congressional legislation in a series of land acts between 1796 and 1862: land was to be sold for cash (but with partial credit from 1796 to 1820, thereafter strictly for cash); there were to be unrestricted sales (after 1820 the auction system was used); there were to be no barriers to land transfers and sales were to be in small units to get farmers to buy. The law of 1796 fixed the minimum unit of sale at 640 acres and the price at $2 an acre. In 1800 the minimum unit was lowered to 320 acres, in 1804, to 160 acres, in 1820, to 80 acres at $1.25 an acre, and in 1832, to 40 acres. For $50 a settler could acquire a tract of land large enough for a farm—if it was in the prairie country of the Middle West. But he needed more cash than that to transport himself and his possessions, erect a dwelling, fence, plow his fields, and feed his family and livestock while producing his first crop—as we shall see.

If the potential settler was not able to buy he went in as a squatter into the tracts already surveyed, and set up with his fellows a "protective association" to prevent others (usually land companies) from bidding in land that had already been improved but not legally held. Congress, however, quick to protect squatter rights, passed regularly in the 1830s special pre-emption laws for those already settled and a general pre-emption law in 1841 to ensure fair treatment for those who were to continue to "enter" as squatters. This act fixed the pre-emption price at $1.25 an acre; and from 1862 to 1891 farmers could establish themselves under the Homestead Act (getting 160 acres for nothing if an improvement was erected in five years) or commute the homestead into a pre-emption at $1.25 an acre. They could also obtain, as a pre-emption, another 160 acres at the $1.25 price. Less desirable land, which had been passed over by the settlers, was put under the Graduation Act in 1854; this provided for regular reductions in price, if land remained undisposed of for 30 years, until it could be had for as little as 12.5 cents an acre.

THE MOVEMENT INTO THE
NORTHWEST AND THE SOUTHWEST

Movement into the public lands synchronized with upturns in the business cycle and not the reverse. (Reformers kept on arguing—and so did historians who followed the lead of Frederick Jackson Turner—that the West was a "safety valve"; when times were out of joint, the urban unemployed and farmers on poor lands in the East could take off for the new territories and start life anew. Economists proved it was not so.) There were four great pushes westward, all during good years when cash was in hand to finance the journey and bank credit was available for land mortgages.

The first wholesale advance westward took place immediately after the Revolution was over and resulted in the admission of Kentucky (1792) and Tennessee (1796) as states. The second came at the turn of the century into the Northwest Territory, and in 1803 Ohio joined the Union. The third occurred during 1810–1830, and here the movement was into the Southwest (to grow cotton) and the Northwest (to grow wheat and corn and raise livestock); the result was the creation of the states of Louisiana (1812), Indiana (1816), Mississippi (1817), Illinois (1818), Alabama (1819), and Missouri (1821). The fourth begun in the late 1830s but was stopped by the depression of 1837–1843. It was resumed in the late 1840s and early 1850s, with the consequent admission into the Union of Arkansas (1836), Michigan (1837), Texas (1845), Iowa (1846), Wisconsin (1848), California (1852), and Minnesota (1858). By 1860 12 million people out of the country's 31 million were to be found in the American West; the Northwest had grown from 50,000 in 1800 to 7.6 million in 1860, and the Southwest from 335,000 in the earlier year to 4.7 million in the later.

Land speculation—a characteristic of the period of merchant capitalism in which the United States then was—tempted promoters to acquire large tracts of land and hold them for the next rush of settlers. Sometimes they lost; sometimes they gained. According to Gates,* there

* P. W. Gates, "Land Policy and Tenancy in the Prairie States," *The Journal of Economic History*, May 1941.

were four such speculative waves in the ante-bellum period. The first stretched from the close of the Revolution to the turn of the century. (It was during this time that Robert Morris controlled 6 million acres and ended in a debtor's prison.) The second, during 1815–1819, ended in depression, in part brought on by the financing of such purchases by state banks and the federal credit system. The third reached a peak during 1834–1837, but the absence of the restraining hand of the Second Bank of the United States and consequently the heavy involvement of state banks once again acted as a contributing factor to the depression that thereafter set in. The fourth occurred during 1853–1857; here federal land policy—the Graduation Land Act, the generous swampland grants to the states, railway land grants (to the builders of the Illinois Central, the Mobile and Ohio, and some 45 other railroads, totaling in all about 22 million acres), and military bounties and warrants—precipitated another surge by men with funds and credit who sought easy money; the recession of 1857–1859 following it will be noted.

Incorporated companies were formed or groups of capitalists pooled their own resources. An outstanding example of the former was the American Land Co., organized by New York and Boston businessmen in 1835, who capitalized it at $1 million and obtained 80 per cent of it in a year. They "entered" prairie lands of the Northwest and the new cotton lands of the Southwest, acquiring (and selling) as much as 350,000 acres up to the Civil War. Eastern capitalists (from Connecticut, Philadelphia, and New York) found the Northwest particularly attractive and there are records of huge holdings of prairie country totaling 220,000 acres (by a group headed by H. L. Ellsworth of Connecticut) and 124,000 acres (by a group made up of men from Connecticut, Brooklyn, Philadelphia, and Illinois). In the middle 1840s and 1850s eastern and middle western syndicates "entered" similar large domains in the rich farming country of Indiana, Illinois, Kansas, and Iowa. In the last, according to Gates, in less than 10 years more than 20 million acres were "entered," the larger part acquired by speculators.

Cole * gives receipts from public land sales for five southern states (Alabama, Arkansas, Florida, Louisiana and Mississippi) and seven western states (Illinois, Indiana, Iowa, Michigan, Missouri, Ohio, and Wisconsin). Those listed in Table 10 are for the boom years.

It has been said that capital and agricultureal skills were needed to become a western farmer; this was even more true of the cotton growers of the Southwest who, in addition to land purchase, had to move or buy their slaves. Some calculations follow of costs made by western farmers

* A. H. Cole, "Cyclical and Sectional Variations in the Sale of Public Lands, 1816–1860," *Review of Economic Statistics*, January 1927.

TABLE 10

RECEIPTS FROM PUBLIC LAND SALES, 1815–1857

(THOUSANDS OF DOLLARS)

Year	Southern States	Western States
1815	$ 332	$ 2,078
1816	899	2,741
1817	2016	3,068
1818	9063	4,556
1819	4441	4,540
—	—	—
1834	3256	2,807
1835	7159	9,007
1836	7170	17,765
—	—	—
1853	1023	3,970
1854	1363	9,771
1855	927	9,215
1856	685	3,453
1857	808	1,895

themselves. The first were those of a man in Wisconsin who set up in 1843 to grow winter wheat (part of the costs undoubtedly represent labor time):

300 acres at $1.25	$375.00
Fencing	300.00
Breaking the sod	525.00
Seed	281.25
Sowing and harrowing	300.00
Harvesting	375.00
Transportation, house, food, etc.	840,00
Total	$2996.25

The second were those of an Illinois farmer, also in 1843, whose cost figures represented only the building and equipping of his house, the cost of his land and its initial plowing, and the stocking of the farm. Transportation, subsistence, and value of labor in making a crop were not included.

The house and furnishings	$ 439.77½
The farm, breaking, live stock	1,277.60
Total	$1,717.37½

Even under the Homestead act, with free land, there were quite sizable out-of-pocket expenditures. The following is an early estimate; because it leaves out breaking, for which professional plowers were usually hired, it is assumed that the homesteader performed all his own labor.

Cost of transportation	$100.00
Two oxen	100.00
One wagon	100.00
Subsistence until the first crop was gathered	90.00
Farming implements	150.00
Seed for the first crop	100.00
One cow	50.00
Total	$690.00

THE LABOR FORCE, URBANIZATION, AND THE PARTICULAR ROLE OF AGRICULTURE

The relative proportion of the whole labor force in agriculture continued to decline; this was particularly so during the decades 1840–1860, but in those 20 years there was an increase of more than 100 per cent in the free-labor working population. (The slaves in the working population multiplied 60 per cent.) It should be borne in mind, however, that most of the urban communities of the period were still preindustrial—their expanding populations were largely engaged in trade and commerce in the old port communities of the eastern seaboard and in the new river, lake, and canal towns or in the building and servicing of the canals and railroads that expanded so much in the same 20 years. Lebergott * gives estimates of the workers in agriculture and manufactures (Tables 11 and 12). It will be seen that the "industrial" population was still quite small up to 1860; by 1870 it really had leaped ahead.

From 1850 to 1860 the total agricultural working population increased 31.3 per cent in manufactures, 25 per cent; but from 1860 to 1870 the farm labor force grew only 15.3 per cent, whereas in manufactures it rose 61.4 per cent. Table 13 lists figures for urbanization; that is, the number of communities, their population, and per cent of total in places of 2500 or more.

* Stanley Lebergott, "Labor Force and Employment," in *Output, Employment, and Productivity*, National Bureau of Economic Research, Studies in Income and Wealth, Vol. 30, 1966.

TABLE 11

LABOR FORCE, 1800–1870 (IN THOUSANDS)

Year	Total	Agriculture	Manufactures
1800	1,900	1400	75 (1810)
1840	5,660	3570	500
1850	8,250	4520	1200
1860	11,110	5880	1530
1870	12,930	6790	2470

The "large" American cities (population of 100,000 or more) in 1850 were commercial rather than industrial: these were New York, Baltimore, Boston, Charleston, New Orleans (which were seaports), Cincinnati, St. Louis, Pittsburgh, Louisville (which were river towns), and Chicago and Buffalo (which were lake towns).

It was not until the last quarter of the nineteenth century that many of the earlier "large" cities, notably New York, Philadelphia, St. Louis, Pittsburgh, Chicago, and Buffalo, also became significant industrial centers, and these new ones emerged: Providence and Fall River (seaports), Memphis (a river town), Cleveland, Detroit, Milwaukee, Toledo (lake ports), and—made or largely developed by the new form of transportation, the railroad—Minneapolis, Rochester, Kansas City, Omaha, Indianapolis, Denver, Columbus, Worcester, Syracuse, New Haven, Paterson, Los Angeles, and Scranton. In the last group they were truly and wholly industrial cities, whose destinies and fortunes were linked with one of the great attributes of the industrial age—specialization of function. Thus, when one thought of Minneapolis, it was in connection with flour-milling, of Kansas City, meat-packing, of New Haven, clockmaking, and of Paterson, silk mills.

TABLE 12

PERCENTAGE DISTRIBUTION OF LABOR FORCE, 1800–1870 . .

| Year | Total | Agriculture | | | Nonagriculture | |
		Free	Slave	Total	Total	Manufactures
1800	100.0	72.1	27.9	73.7	26.3	2.8 (1810)
1840	100.0	73.8	26.2	63.1	36.9	8.8
1850	100.0	76.1	23.9	54.8	45.2	14.5
1860	100.0	78.9	21.1	52.9	47.1	13.8
1870	100.0			52.5	47.5	19.1

TABLE 13

URBAN POPULATION, 1800–1870 (IN THOUSANDS)

Year	No. of Places	Urban Population	Per Cent of Total Population
1800	33	322.4	6.7
1840	131	1,845.1	10.7
1850	236	3,543.7	15.3
1860	392	6,216.5	19.8
1870	663	9,902.4	25.7

The census of 1860 pointed up the notion presented here: that "large" cities were not yet, to any significant degree, associated with manufactures. The figures in Table 14 give the proportion of the laboring population engaged in manufactures.

TABLE 14

PROPORTION OF LABOR POPULATION ENGAGED IN MANUFACTURES, 1860
(PER CENT)

Newark	26.2	Baltimore	8.0
Providence	20.0	Buffalo	6.9
Cincinnati	18.3	St. Louis	5.8
Philadelphia	17.5	Chicago	4.9
Boston	10.8	New Orleans	3.0
New York	9.5	San Francisco	2.6

What of increasing productivity of American farms as a reason for the relative contraction of the agricultural labor force? This is to be doubted; at any rate, it is the conclusion of two agricultural authorities, Towne and Rasmussen,* who are prepared to assume constant per capita rates of output or consumption during 1800–1840 and probably also in the 1840s. During this half century agricultural technology and productivity remained more or less static. "Dynamic developments" were not to appear until after 1850 and more particularly after 1860. They do not question that preparations for these developments in research, experiments, and education did emerge during the first half of the nineteenth

* M. W. Towne and W. O. Rasmussen, "Farm Gross Product and Gross Investment in the Nineteenth Century," in *Trends in the American Economy in the Nineteenth Century*, National Bureau of Economic Research, Studies in Income and Wealth, Vol. 24, 1960.

century, but the appearance of better and heavier plows, threshers, corn planters and corn cultivators, mechanical reapers, the greater use of fertilizer, and improved livestock became common after 1860, rather than before. Said the authors:

> The effects of this new technology were not to be felt until after the Civil War. No substantial rise in demand for grain products had occurred and farmers generally felt no strong incentive to buy machines that would increase output.

In Table 15 it is clear that Gross Farm Product per farm worker did not increase until 1860 and did not rise sharply until 1870. (It was prepared by Towne and Rasmussen.)

TABLE 15
GROSS FARM PRODUCT [a] 1800–1870 (IN 1910–1914 DOLLARS)

	1800	1840	1850	1860	1870
Gross Farm Product (millions)	$362.0	$1222.0	$1536.0	$2156.0	$2597.0
Farm population (millions)	4.3	12.3	15.8	20.1	22.4
Farm workers (millions)	1.1	3.7	4.9	6.2	6.8
GFP per farm worker	$292.0	$ 311.0	$ 294.0	$ 332.0	$ 362.0

[a] The Gross Farm Product includes the sales of farm commodities, the value of farm products consumed, and the value of home manufactures and of improvements made on farms.

Farm investment in implements and machinery, in constant dollars, jumped from $11 million a year during 1845–1855 to $23 million a year during 1855–1865 and to $54 million a year during 1865–1875.

The first important technological breakthrough came in the case of the plow. An improved plow, in which the moldboard, share, and landside were made of cast steel—the work of John Deere of Grand Detour and then Moline, Illinois, in the late 1840s—was able to break the tough sod of the prairies for the planting of wheat. (But even with its use two plowings were necessary, so that putting in an acre of wheat in Michigan around 1847 still required 20 man-hours of labor.) It was John Oliver's plow, coming in 1868—he used chilled iron (a soft-center steel), which was more durable and cheaper—that overcame all the difficulties of breaking the soil in the Middle West. In the early 1870s the sulky plow (a riding implement with one bottom) and the sulky gang plow (with a number of bottoms) appeared. Riding machines made the horse important; the mechanical revolution in agriculture was as much associated with the horse, and therefore with the growth of hay, as it was with the improved plow and the mechanical reaper.

The second breakthrough was the mechanical horse-drawn reaper, the inventions of Obed Hussey in 1833 and Cyrus H. McCormick in 1834. McCormick, a Virginian, moved his manufacturing plant to Chicago in 1847, and his aggressive and imaginative merchandizing methods popularized and spread wide the use of the reaper in the growth of wheat. He manufactured instead of licensing as Hussey did; he advertised; he sold at a fixed price, guaranteed his machines, and trained his agents to give instruction in maintenance and repairs; and he sold on credit.

By 1858 there were 70,000 mowing and reaping machines in the United States, but the great leap forward did not take place until during the Civil War as a result of the expansion of exports. The United States began to feed England; American wheat exports shot up from 3 million bushels in 1859 to 31 million in 1861 and 37 million, 36 million, and 24 million in 1862, 1863, and 1864, respectively. By 1865 there were some 250,000 mowing and reaping machines in use in the country. Improvements in the reaper (now called the harvester)—to increase productivity—came in the late 1860s and the 1870s: a man stationed on a platform was able to bind the cut grain by hand; then came a mechanical wire-binder and finally a twine-binder, which was cheaper and safer. But it was not until the 1890s that the combine, which joined the harvester and thresher in a single operation right on the field, completed the mechanical revolution as far as wheat was concerned.

The increase in productivity by the 1890s was sensational. Although in the 1830s (and also into the late 1840s) putting a crop in—plowing and sowing—required 15 to 20 man-hours per acre, in the 1890s, on the large farms of North Dakota and California, the man-hour labor time had been reduced to three hours. As for securing it—reaping, binding, shocking, and threshing—the man-hour time per acre fell from 50 to about 6 hours.

The westward movement of wheat-growing before the Civil War is shown in Table 16 by crop yields for the leading states. It will be observed that the four middle-western states were responsible for 29 per cent of the total crop in 1839 and for 42 per cent in 1859.

WHO WAS RESPONSIBLE FOR THE CREATION OF TRANSPORTATION FACILITIES

All of these achievements in agriculture would have been impossible without significant changes and improvements in transportation: for

TABLE 16

WHEAT GROWING BEFORE THE CIVIL WAR, 1839–1859

(IN MILLIONS OF BUSHELS)

	1839	1849	1859
Ohio	16.6	14.8	15.1
Pennsylvania	13.2	15.4	13.0
New York	12.3	13.1	8.7
Virginia	10.1	11.2	13.1
Illinois	3.3	9.4	23.8
Indiana	4.1	6.2	16.8
Wisconsin	—	4.3	15.7
Rest of the United States	25.2	26.1	66.9
Total United States	84.8	100.5	173.1

carriage by road, river, canal, and finally railroad made possible the flow of passengers and goods, the widening of regional markets, and, more particularly, the linking of East and West so that eastern (and European) capital moved westward, as western farm products moved eastward to help feed the East and, starting in 1860, Great Britain.

The history of transportation development in the ante-bellum period cannot be separated from the key role of public promotions, and it is exactly at this point that Douglass North's analysis of the forward and backward linkages, appearing out of the growth of the export sector, falls apart. Except for private financing of early local turnpikes, some canals, and initial (and also local) railroad construction in the Northeast, by far the greater part of canal and a very considerable part of railroad building were made possible only because capital for them was furnished by the states and to a lesser degree by cities and the federal government. This was so, first, because of the absence of a national capital market; that is, the inability of private enterprise to command the savings of individuals and the resources of financial institutions (banks, insurance companies) for such large ventures.

Second, and here we are indebted to the pioneering work of Goodrich,* much of the canal and railroad building was "premature": they were laid out in unsettled country; they were therefore risky ventures with immediate returns on investment impossible and sizable losses probable. Public authority had to step into the breach, and its intervention took a variety of forms.

* Carter Goodrich, *Government Promotion of American Canals and Railroads, 1800–1890*, 1960.

The federal government directly financed the building of the National Road (as we shall see) and contributed small sums for the construction of some canals. It financed indirectly on an even larger scale by land grants to the states wagon roads and canals and the building of the great Illinois Central Railroad and the Mobile and Ohio Railroad with which it was joined. (This last method was utilized to make possible the laying down of the western trunk railroads after the Civil War.)

The states participated much more fully. They furnished the funds directly—through bond issues—for building most of the canals, and they helped in early railroad construction by financing directly, by the purchase of securities, or by guaranteeing privately floated bond issues.

Municipalities made contributions to or bought the securities of large numbers of early railroad companies; they also gave land for rights of way and town lots for railroad depots, roundhouses, and repair shops. All this added up to a very large sum. The funds for state ownership or state aid came from the willingness of the English money market to buy state bond issues because of the confidence in the faith and credit of the United States and because of the hope for large capital gains if the ventures turned out successfully.

If Albert Gallatin, President Jefferson's great Secretary of the Treasury, had had his way, the federal government would have assumed largely, if not entirely, the planning and costs of the internal improvements of the country. At the behest of the Senate in 1808 Gallatin submitted a masterly plan that would have bound together, North and South and East and West, by roads and canals, the already widely dispersing American people.

His program required federal support, for these were national objectives he was advocating, whose benefits should "diffuse and increase the national wealth in a very general way." Gallatin put his finger unerringly on the reason why federal intervention was necessary.

> The great demand for capital in the United States, and the extent of territory compared with the population, are, it is believed, the true causes which prevent new undertakings, and render those already accomplished less profitable than had been expected.

He also stressed the economic and political benefits of such intervention:

> The inconveniences, complaints, and perhaps dangers, which may result from a vast extent of territory, can no otherwise be radically removed or prevented than by opening speedy and easy communications through all its parts. Good roads and canals will shorten distances, facilitate commercial and personal intercourse, and unite, by a still more intimate community of

interests, the most remote quarters of the United States. No other single operation, within the power of government, can more effectually tend to strengthen and perpetuate that Union which secures external independence, domestic peace, and internal liberty. . . .

To achieve these broad purposes, Gallatin's program required $20 million to be distributed as follows:

I. From *north* to *south,* paralleling the seacoast:

1. Canals opening an inland navigation for sea vessels from Massachusetts to North Carolina and across all the principal capes (to cost $3 million)
2. A turnpike from Maine to Georgia (to cost $4.8 million)

II. From *east* to *west,* penetrating the Appalachian barrier (by linking the upper waters of four western rivers with four Atlantic rivers):

1. To improve the navigation of the four Atlantic rivers, including canals paralleling them (to cost $1.5 million)
2. To build roads from these four rivers across the mountains to the four corresponding western rivers (to cost $2.8 million). The four pairs of rivers were these:

   The Allegheny and the Susquehanna or the Juniata (Pennsylvania)
   The Monongahela and the Potomac (Maryland)
   The Kanawha and the James (Virginia)
   The Tennessee and the Santee or the Savannah (North Carolina, South Carolina, Georgia)

3. Other minor projects (to cost $500,000)

III. In a *northern* and *northwestardly* direction to link the Atlantic seacoast and the Great Lakes and the St. Lawrence:

1. Connecting the Hudson River with Lake Champlain (to cost $800,000)
2. Connecting the Hudson River with Lake Ontario by canal (to cost $2.2 million)
3. Canal around the falls and rapids of Niagara, opening up the Great Lakes (to cost $1 million)

IV. Other local projects (to cost $3.4 million).

Gallatin could not get Congress's ear because the country was in difficulties brought on by Jefferson's Embargo and because the southern leaders were already beginning to move toward a narrow states' rights interpretation of the Constitution. In the presidency of John Quincy Adams some effort had been made to pick up a few of the pieces: land grants were made to Ohio, Indiana, and Illinois to aid in road and canal building, the country's first river and harbor bill was passed, and the federal government was authorized to subscribe a total of about $2 million to the stock of four canal companies.

President Jackson dashed all hopes that these were beginnings, for his veto of the Maysville Road bill (1830) on states'-rights grounds—the federal government was to subscribe $150,000 to the stock of a turnpike to be built wholly in Kentucky—put an end to the dream (until 1916) that the United States itself would finance the building of roads by appropriations. These were the decisions that emerged from Jackson's hostility to the expansion of federal power and its participation in enterprises that Jackson felt were properly the functions of the states and of private capital.

1. It was not the business of the federal government to lay out a comprehensive plan for a system of national highways. (River and harbor improvement was something else again: this was part of the national defense.)

2. The federal government was to refrain from building revenue-producing public works.

3. It could not construct roads and canals on which tolls were to be collected.

4. It was not to subscribe to the stock of state or private companies.

From then on the larger part of the burden, in the ante-bellum period, fell upon the states. The development of transportation facilities followed these lines.

TURNPIKES, RIVER TRANSPORTATION, AND CANALS

Turnpikes

As soon as the Republic was established toll turnpike companies appeared, financed by private capital, and because they were successful they stimulated others. The first, chartered in Pennsylvania, was built from Philadelphia to Lancaster, a distance of 66 miles, at a cost of $500,000. Within the next 30 years some 32 chartered companies in Pennsylvania put down 2200 miles of road. In New England there were 180 such companies by 1810, and in New York 137 companies by 1811. Here a combined capital of $7.5 million was responsible for 1400 miles of highway. It cost about $10 per 100 miles to move freight by wagon on these toll roads; passengers in stage coaches paid 6 cents a mile.

In 1806 Congress, encouraged by these enterprises and their results, authorized the construction of a national turnpike, which came to be called the National Road; it was to be free of tolls, and it was to be pushed westward, first across the Appalachian mountains and then over the prairies, starting at Cumberland on the Potomac River. The first leg, begun in 1811 and finished in 1818, ran to Wheeling in western Virginia, a distance of 130 miles. It was then extended to Zanesville, Columbus, and Springfield, Ohio, to Richmond, Indianapolis, and Terre Haute, Indiana, and finally to Vandalia, Illinois's original capital, which it reached in the 1850s. The total length of the National Road was 834 miles and it cost $7 million in build. In time, because of the need for maintenance and replacement, the various parts of the road were turned over to the states, which then began to charge tolls. Large numbers of migrants walked or rode in their Conestoga wagons over it; it was the first and the cheapest way by which the rich prairie states were settled and brought under the plow.

River Transportation

Simultaneously the steamboat, notably on the Ohio and the Mississippi, made possible not only the movement of passengers but, even more important, heavy freight up river. Like the Conestoga wagon, the riverboat was a typical example of American ingenuity. The first appeared in 1815; it was built on a keelboat with engines, boiler, and saloons added. Its draft necessarily had to be light because of the shoals, bars, and shifting channels in the rivers; at the most, it required 12 feet or two fathoms of water (hence "mark twain"). The pilots of these light and swift craft became the kings of the rivers—Mark Twain was one of them—highly skilled in navigating in the dangerous and ever-changing waters. The boats were constructed of wood and side-wheel paddles were added. They were built cheaply ($35,000-$40,000 for the great "showboats") because they frequently caught fire. The competition was keen; they were raced and sparks from the engines ignited cargoes or superstructures. Large ones could accommodate 100 to 300 passengers, as well as cargoes of cotton, wheat, flour, tobacco, and livestock.

By the outbreak of the Civil War there were as many as 900 craft on the Ohio (steamboats, but also slower moving barges and flatboats); more than 100,000 passengers a year were carried by them and as much as $140 million in goods. On the Mississippi as many as 1000 steamboats (as against 60 in 1819) brought $185 million in produce down to New Orleans annually. They cut the travel time from Pittsburgh to New Orleans from 100 to 30 days.

Canals

The canals came next. They were constructed to run east and west (the Erie Canal, to link the Hudson River along the Mohawk Valley with Lake Erie); north and south (the Ohio canals to connect Lake Erie with the Ohio River); or for special purposes to bring a particular commodity (anthracite coal in Pennsylvania and New Jersey) to the seaboard.

The great era of canal construction started with the success of the Erie Canal (there had been earlier and smaller ones in Virginia and New England, usually around the falls of rivers). It set a pattern in another way: it was publicly financed by state bond issues, which were sold abroad. This was the point at which foreign capital began to flow into the United States on a significant scale. The advantage of the canal was simply this: it could move slow freight in barges (at little cost to operate) much more cheaply than the turnpikes. The cost per ton-mile for the carriage of freight from Buffalo to New York in 1817 by wagon was 19 cents, over the Erie Canal in 1860 it was 8 cents. A horse, walking on a towpath, could drag a load 50 times heavier through water than it could on land over a road. The disadvantage, however, was serious: canals could be kept open only about six months in the year.

The Erie Canal, started in 1817 and finished in 1825, ran 363 miles and cost $7 million because construction included the building of locks as well as the grading of towpaths and the cutting of a wide but shallow ditch (it was 30 feet wide and 4 feet deep and could accommodate 30-ton barges).

The tolls collected on the Erie Canal exceeded the interest charges on the state's indebtedness even before it was finished. Because of the heavy traffic moving from West to East and the low freight charges, tolls brought in $8.5 million during its first nine years.

In consequence, the desire (and craze) for quick canal construction which swept over the whole country involved many states in heavy indebtedness. Some were profitable, many not, because they were located in regions in which the freights did not bear the costs or in which railroads quickly entered to furnish superior facilities. By 1860 there were 4250 miles of canal at a total investment of almost $195 million (of which about 70 per cent was publicly financed.) Table 17 is the regional breakdown, in millions of dollars by source of financing.

TABLE 17

INVESTMENT IN CANALS

	United States	Northeast	West	South
Total	$194.6	$141.3	$33.5	$19.7
State	121.1	88.8	29.8	2.5
Private	73.5	52.5	3.8	17.2

Source. H. Jerome Cranmer, "Canal Investment, 1815–1860" in Studies in Income and Wealth, National Bureau of Economic Research, Vol. 24, 1960, pp. 555–556.

TABLE 18

COSTS OF LARGER CANALS

Canal	State	Cost in Millions
Erie	New York	$ 7.1
Genesee Valley	New York	5.6
Black River	New York	3.2
Oswego	New York	2.5
Chenango	New York	2.3
Champlain	New York	.9
Mainline [a]	Pennsylvania	16.5
Five lateral canals	Pennsylvania	15.0
Delaware Division	Pennsylvania	1.5
Miami and Erie	Ohio	5.9
Ohio	Ohio	4.2
Wabash	Indiana	6.3
Illinois and Michigan	Illinois	6.6
Chesapeake and Ohio [b]	Maryland	11.0
James and Kanawha	Virginia	10.4

[a] Including rail connections.

[b] Run by a private company with the stock owned by Maryland, Virginia, and the United States government.

Some of the larger canals and their costs are given in Table 18.

How the Erie Canal linked the West and the East is indicated by the figures in Table 19. They are for thousands of tons of goods, moving to and from Buffalo and tidewater.

Because the canals were made possible almost entirely by state funds, state indebtedness shot up sharply. (State financing was used for canal construction but also to assist early railroads and to help furnish the capital for state-chartered banks.) In 1820 total state debts stood at $12.8 million; by 1840, in excess of $200 million. The overbuilding of the canals and the depression following 1837 hit many states hard and during 1840–1844, for the first time in American history, states defaulted on interest payments and some even repudiated their debts. (There was one other time, and this was after the Civil War, when eight southern states repudiated Reconstruction debts.) The states defaulting interest were Maryland, Illinois, Indiana, Michigan, Mississippi, Louisiana, Arkansas, Florida, and Pennsylvania. Those that repudiated were Mississippi, Arkansas, Florida, and Michigan (in part). The consequences in European money markets were dire: confidence in American credit was badly shaken, investment funds were stopped dead, and not until the late 1850s did a slight trickle recommence to flow (and this was into the privately organized and operated Illinois Central Railroad).

A word about profitability. Roger L. Ransom (in a paper read before the American Economic Association in 1963) was prepared to say that only five state-financed canals were "probably successful": the Erie, Champlain, and Oswego of New York, the Ohio of Ohio, and the Delaware Division of Pennsylvania; these had cost $16.2 million. The rest,

TABLE 19

TRAFFIC MOVING ON THE ERIE CANAL

Year	Tonnage from New York		Tonnage from Western States to New York
	Total	to the Western States	
1836	364.9	38.9	54.3
1841	308.3	31.0	224.1
1846	600.4	58.3	506.8
1851	462.9	331.9 [a]	1045.8
1860	379.0	119.7	1896.9

[a] 1854.

listed in Table 18 (and a few smaller ones not included), were "probably not successful"; they had cost $86.4 million.

Ransom had engaged in an econometric exercise to establish "success" or "want to success" and ended up with a Scottish verdict—not proven. To quote him: "While I have conveyed my personal skepticism concerning the contribution of the canals to growth, I would be the first to admit that such a judgment remains to be confirmed (or refuted) by further research." That is to say, Ransom did not question the "social benefits" or the "external economies" the canals brought to the United States during their heyday, that is, up to about 1850. A good deal of the productive land of the West that came under cultivation was directly due to the canals with not only an increase in the food supply (wheat, corn, hogs) but the forward linkage of the stimulation of the agricultural implements industry. Many new towns appeared on the canals, originally to serve the needs of the bargemen; in them appeared industries not all necessarily associated with the canals, and they continued to flourish. Land values, both rural and urban went up, thus broadening the tax base from which public services were able to expand. Finally, the West was linked with the East, a fact of the utmost political (as well as economic) importance, for the West moved into opposition to the slave institution and with the East began to challenge the power of the slave owners.

To put the question narrowly, as Ransom and other econometricians do, could the $195 million that the canals cost have been spent more efficiently and with more than regional benefits? is a futile and pointless exercise in what has come to be called "counterfactual" analysis. The canals suffered from technological obsolescence because of the coming of the railroads, it is true, but that fact in itself is a sign and a consequence of growth.

THE ROLE OF PUBLIC FINANCING AND RAILROAD BUILDING

Before discussing the ante-bellum railroads, we might pause to look broadly at the extent to which the state promotions went in underwriting publicly constructed improvements or in participation in what Goodrich calls "mixed enterprises." (Goodrich's analysis is followed here.)

By 1860 in the 33 states in the Union some $425 million was committed in cash or credit to further public works, of which the states were responsible for $300 million and local governments for around $125 million. Among the states 60 per cent came from those facing the Appalachian barrier (New York, Pennsylvania, Maryland, Virginia, North Carolina, South Carolina, Georgia), with New York and Virginia alone committed to $70 million and $50 million, respectively. City involvements were frequently very large; in fact Portland, Maine, Louisville, Kentucky, and Mobile, Alabama, spent more than their own state governments. Baltimore backed heavily the construction of the Baltimore and Ohio Railroad, buying its stock, making loans, and guaranteeing its bonds to the extent of $13 million.

The financing was of various kinds. Goodrich describes it:

> Money could be spent directly on a public work, or aid might be granted to a corporation under various terms and conditions—subscription to stock, loan, guarantee of interest or principal or both of the company's obligations, or simply an outright donation.

The early railroads obtained large assistance. New York helped in the construction of the New York and Erie. Massachusetts aided similarly in the building of the Western Railroad and the Boston and Maine (so that Boston could reach the Hudson River and the Erie Canal). Michigan itself started laying down the Michigan Central and the Michigan Southern.

When the bubble of public promotions was pricked, as a result of the unhappy consequences of the depression of 1837–1843, there was a "revulsion of sentiment," to use Goodrich's phrase. In the 1840s and again in the 1850s states, in their constitutions and by legislative enactment, ordered a stop to public outlays for further canal construction and building and for loans to private corporations. New York's constitution did so in 1846; Pennsylvania ended state help in 1857 and disposed of all its enterprises at a considerable loss; Maryland quit in 1842; Ohio in its 1851 constitution forbade both state and local aid to private companies and ordered the sale or lease of the public works it had itself financed; in 1846 Michigan sold its railroads (at a loss) and its constitution in 1850 put a stop to further involvements. So it went across the country. A resumption of interest in public help (but never public construction) to the railroads in the West occurred after the Civil War; this we shall examine later.

It was not until 1835 that the railroad technological pattern took shape in the United States: steam locomotives fired by wood (later, anthracite coal) were to haul cars for passengers and freight, using flanged wheels on tracks covered with iron over fixed roadbeds. The railroads grew slowly for almost a decade and a half. Early roads, in settled areas, were financed privately and as a matter of community pride or regional competition among cities: they were built as feeders to waterways, to reach a lakeport, canal, or a well-constructed turnpike. In New England, for example, they ran north and south in the beginning, many in order to get to Long Island Sound; and as late as 1850 the average length of the New England lines was only 36 miles. The short road from New Haven to Boston came much later; it was not until 1847 that New Haven and Boston were joined by rail. Right through the 1830s canals were regarded as a superior form of transportation.

In 1830 there were only 23 miles of line; in 1840, 2808 miles (as against 3326 miles of canal); in 1850, 8929 (as against 3700 miles of canal). From 1850 to 1855 the miles of track doubled, and in the next five years doubled again, so that by 1860 mileage totaled 30,626. What was the cost of construction? The figures offered by contemporaries are highly dubious. Careful calculations made by G. R. Taylor put their value (this includes preliminary costs, rolling stock, later grading) as follows: 1850, $260.7 million; 1855, $654.8 million; 1860, $1,178.0 million. In the last year the capital debt of the whole railroad network of the country was about $900 million.

In the decade of the 1850s the new construction took place largely in the Middle Atlantic, middle-western and southern states, but by 1860 short lines were already running west of the Mississippi River into Iowa and Missouri, and a little building had already been started in California and Oregon. Trunk systems had appeared with the New York and Erie and the Baltimore and Ohio Railroads. The Illinois Central and the Ohio and Mobile joined the Great Lakes and the Gulf (more on this later). In 1853 nine small companies between Albany and Buffalo were combined to form the New York Central. The Pennsylvania, running from Philadelphia to Harrisburg, was pushing across the Alleghenies to reach Pittsburgh before the decade was over; and it was with this western division that the fortunes and rise of Andrew Carnegie were joined, for he became its superintendent in 1859. And by leasing and by establishing communities of interest with middle-western railroads, by 1860 the Erie, the Baltimore and Ohio, the New York Central and the Pennsylvania were coming into Chicago. Chicago saw ten different lines entering the city and, with 20 branch and feeder lines, was reaching 4000 miles.

Poor's *Manual* (the great railroad authority) gives these figures of railroad mileage regionally (see Table 20).

These evidences of growth are impressive; yet it could scarcely be claimed that in 1860 or, in fact, in 1865 even the eastern United States had an integrated or an efficient railway system. It is true, to the enthusiast, and Fishlow * is one, there seemed to be what he calls an "articu-

* See Albert Fishlow, *American Railways and the Transformation of the Ante-Bellum Economy*, 1965.

TABLE 20

RAILROAD MILEAGE, 1840–1860

	1840	1850	1860
New England states	517	2507	3,699
Middle Atlantic states	1566	3105	6,321
Middle Western states	89	1276	9,583
Iowa and Missouri			1,472
Southern states	636	2036	9,535
California and Oregon			23
Total	2808	8929	30,626

lated national network." It was possible to travel from New York to Chicago or St. Louis or Dubuque, Iowa, by an all-rail route, but not on a single trunk line to carry through traffic. In the South there had been a good deal of building in the late 1850s, but its railroads fed the ocean and gulf ports rather than running east and west or north and south and even here water transportation continued to be the preferred, and cheaper, form of carriage.

One could ride by rail from Memphis to Savannah or Charleston, about 750 miles; the journey, however, took 58 hours. From Memphis to Richmond, about the same distance, the time was 52 hours. The gaps were great: there was no connection between eastern Tennessee or eastern Kentucky and Ohio and none from New Orleans to Mobile; there was no through line from New Orleans to Washington, and it took three and one-half days to go from New Orleans to New York by rail. The South was unable to reach the Middle West or the Northwest by railroad until 1859, when the Illinois Central joined the Mobile and Ohio.

THE BUILDING OF THE ILLINOIS CENTRAL AND MOBILE AND OHIO RAILROADS

In 1850 the federal government was prevailed on to grant 3.7 million acres from the public domain to the three states of Illinois, Mississippi, and Alabama. This was for the construction of two railroads: one (the Illinois Central) to run from LaSalle on the Illinois and Michigan Canal—with branches to Chicago and Dubuque—southward to Cairo; the other (the Mobile and Ohio) to connect with it through

Alabama, Mississippi, Tennessee, and Kentucky, northward at the Ohio River.

The Illinois Central was financed almost entirely from bond issues, most of them against the land grants. Capital was raised in Boston, New York, London, and Hamburg. London merchant-bankers (but not the Rothschilds or Baring Brothers) had taken the lion's share of the bonds so that the railroad, when it was finished in 1857, was really owned abroad, for $12 million of its bonds and 80,000 shares of its stock were in foreign portfolios. The road was 700 miles long and by that token the greatest single system in the country; it cost $16.5 million to build and another $7 million were spent for its equipment. The Mobile and Ohio's share—totaling 483 miles—was not completed until just before the Civil War. (It really reached Columbus, Kentucky, a river town a few miles south of the mouth of the Ohio River.) The financing of its construction came from the states involved by means of grants or loans.

A further word about where railroading stood in 1860. Fishlow, despite his enthusiasm, is compelled to admit that the railroads had not yet bound the country together or furnished a giant push to its economic growth. Thus he writes:

> What the railroads did not do before the Civil War was to forge a national market. The primitive state of physical integration not only prevented it, but probably also testifies to its unimportance. There were too few economies of scale in production or distribution, to be reaped from direct rail contact. . . . This was still a period before interchange of parts was universal, before standard products were marketed, before the full effects of industrialization were apparent, let alone realized.

In addition, before the Civil War, there were no important bridges over wide rivers. The diversity of guages made costly and slow the cross-country shipment of freight. Wooden bridges (more often ferries), iron rails, light locomotives, small-capacity cars, and manual braking and coupling kept down the speed and volume of freight movements—and costs were high. As late as 1860 all the New York canals carried more freight tonnage than the two Erie and New York Central systems. What were still to come were the great western railroads, the use of cheaper bituminous coal, and technological innovations—in steel rails, heavier and more efficient locomotives, larger cars of steel, the safety coupler, automatic air brakes, and iron bridges to span the Hudson, Ohio, Mississippi, and Missouri Rivers.

VI

THE STRUCTURE OF THE
ANTE-BELLUM ECONOMY (II)

Because, from the beginnings of settlement, Americans have been brought up in a capitalist world, it is perfectly natural that they should be thinking and talking of money. They were buying and selling in a market; they were borrowing and lending; they were saving and investing. Many were speculating (and usually losing); some were creating capital goods (and usually gaining from long-term capital appreciation). For all these things they needed money, for exchange purposes, to represent value, and as a basis of credit, whether the ventures they engaged in were socially unproductive (as in speculating) or socially useful (to finance trading voyages or to start a new transportation facility or a new manufacturing enterprise).

Money, most businessmen knew, was more than coin made of gold and silver; money was also created by commercial banks, either by issuing bank notes or by writing up deposits. The latter were liabilities; and against them, to maintain their solvency, banks had to possess capital assets and (it came to be understood by the 1830s) a reserve of coin (although it was not until the 1850s that bankers agreed on what was to be a "safe" fractional reserve).

Thus organized, and in a measure protected, banks were in a position to expand or contract the money supply as business needs grew or became sluggish—ideally, at any rate, because individual banks could not assume this role by themselves, for they might be overzealous, overcautious, or mistaken in their judgments, or their capital assets (for want of proper state supervision) might not be what they seemed.

Hence the important part played by a central bank—initially the First Bank of the United States, later the Second Bank—in trying to regulate the whole nation's money supply and ensure stability of prices by seeking to curb exuberance (in time of boom) and encourage optimism (in time of recession). The early American central banks did not have a full armory of weapons to do so, as the Federal Reserve System did later. The early central bank could operate only in a narrow field (I am talking more particularly of the Second Bank under Nicholas Biddle). In regard to control over inflationary tendencies of commercial banks, the central bank could call for specie redemption of bank notes and thus keep their issues down, and it could raise the discount rate for bills being used in domestic exchange. In regard to the stimulation of business, the central bank could lend, and it did, to commercial banks and it could create deposits for private businessmen through its own many branches. Because it kept a sizable amount of specie as reserve against its own bank notes (much larger than the commercial banks did) and thus in a real sense protected the country's credit against a specie drain from abroad in periods of contraction, the central bank provided another stabilizing influence.

With the Second Bank gone in 1836, there followed, particularly in the Northwest and South, an era of unregulated (or wildcat) banking—but this, curiously, did not lead to an enormous increase in the money supply. The best indication is that American interest rates were not abnormal, whereas American commodity prices, taking the whole period 1800–1860, fell by nearly 50 per cent— a phenomenon that was occurring generally in Europe. Because the greater part of American economic activity was tied to world markets—we bought a large part of our finished goods abroad and sold most of our greatest export, cotton, also abroad—this was to be expected and therefore did not reflect an inadequacy in the American money supply.

As Gurley and Shaw * point out, the growth of the American money supply continued amazingly stable over the whole period 1799–1958 (except, of course, for war years). The average annual rate of increase was in the narrow range of 5 to 6 per cent, and in the period we are

* J. G. Gurley and E. S. Shaw, "Money," in S. E. Harris, Ed., *American Economic History*, 1961.

considering, a bit more than 5 per cent. Before we look at the amount of the money supply available to Americans during 1799–1859 a few other general observations are in order.

The commercial banks we have been referring to were created by state charter and up to 1838 by special legislative enactment, so that banking activity was closely limited. Those that appeared after the Revolution and for the most part the first two decades of the nineteenth century were sound and conservatively run, for their capital was as a rule paid up, and in specie as well, and the loans and discounts they made, against security and for short terms, were the basis of their note issue.

As banks began to spread, after the recession of 1818–1819, notably in the South and Northwest, and with many states themselves either forming state banks or subscribing to the capital stock of private banks, the integrity of the bank promoters and managers of the earlier period disappeared. Legislatures stopped requiring that capital be paid up in specie or in fact be paid up entirely, so that a good deal of sharp practice ensued, the most common being that subscribers paid for their stock by their own notes. The result was banking fell into disrepute and the hostility that developed toward the Second Bank in part arose out of suspicion of all banks. This was in the 1830s, a whole decade before wildcat banks became common. The upshot was that workers were hard-money men, and when talk arose about the expansion of the money supply to help them out, as we saw in the case of Edward Kellogg, the demand was made for a public currency, issued by the federal government and without the intervention of banks.

All this was occurring as commercial banks kept on growing, issuing larger and larger amounts of bank notes, but also expanding their deposits. In fact, during the 1850s the latter kept on inching up on the former, and by 1855 deposits exceeded notes and constituted the larger part of the money supply. In 1791 there were five banks; in 1800, 28; in 1811, 117; in 1818, 338; in 1837, 729; in 1850, 824; in 1855, 1307; and in 1860, 1562.

According J. J. Knox's very good *History of Banking in the United States,* 1900, the ratios of deposits to notes for a selected number of years are given in Table 21.

What of metallic currency? The Coinage Act of 1792, which established the Mint Alexander Hamilton had called for, fixed the silver-gold mint ratio at 15 to 1, the prevailing market ratio at that time. Before long, however, the market price of silver dropped, so that the ratio became 15½ to 1 and then moved toward 16 to 1; the consequence was that silver was overvalued at the Mint and it drove gold out of circulation.

TABLE 21

MONEY BEFORE THE CIVIL WAR: DEPOSITS AND NOTES

Year	Deposits [a]	Notes [a]
1840	$ 75.2	$107.0
1843	56.2	58.6
1845	88.0	89.6
1850	109.6	131.4
1855	190.4	187.0
1857	230.7	214.8
1858	186.0	155.2
1859	259.6	193.3
1860	253.8	207.1

[a] In millions of dollars.

Gold was hoarded, used for the payment of foreign balances, or shipped abroad to buy silver (which was cheaper in France and Great Britain) and returned to the United States to be minted at a higher value. The United States was thus virtually on a silver standard until 1834, when the mint ratio was put at a fraction above 16 to 1 (which this time overvalued gold, so that gold drove out silver). This was rectified in 1837, when the mint ratio was fixed at 16 to 1, but only temporarily, for the market price of silver went up once more in the early 1850s, and even minor coins were being melted down to be taken to the mint. Thus gold

TABLE 22

NOMINAL AND REAL MONEY SUPPLY, 1799–1859 (IN MILLIONS OF DOLLARS)

Year June	Nominal Money Supply (1)	Demand Deposits (2)	Currency Outside banks (3)	Real Money Supply (4)	Real Money Supply per Capita in Dollars (5)
1799	30	—	—	30	5.80
1819	80	—	—	90	9.60
1839	240	90	150	290	17.40
1849	270	90	180	450	19.90
1859	580	260	320	950	31.00

Source. Gurley and Shaw, op. cit., p. 105.

and silver seesawed up and down until the discovery of gold in California in 1849. A larger part of the gold mined was used to pay American balances abroad because of the decline in earnings by American ships and the high interest charges owed to foreigners on their investments in the United States. Nevertheless, during the 1850s the Mint was responsible for something like $400 million in gold coins and thus relieved the shortage of specie in the country. (More of gold exports later.)

We can now present the estimates of the money supply made by Gurley and Shaw, referred to above (see Table 22). The nominal money supply (column 1) consists of the demand deposits of commercial banks (column 2) plus currency outside banks—made up of bank notes and specie (column 3). The real money supply (column 4) is the nominal money deflated by the Bureau of Labor Statistics wholesale price index (1926 = 100). The real money supply per capita (column 5) is obtained by dividing the real money by the total population.

THE NATURE OF THE BANKING SYSTEM

Private, or unincorporated banks, which issued notes, were quite common in the United States up to 1820, but because many of them engaged in purely speculative activities and failed easily they were in large part responsible for the hostility toward banking that was so common in the 1820s and 1830s. The result was that state legislatures began to prohibit them. The field was now left open to the private incorporated banks, which state legislatures authorized, usually by special enactment. Generally, the capital necessary to launch such an institution was to be raised by private subscription; in the early years, however, state governments sought, or found it necessary, to participate and in the charters reserved the right to buy the banks' stock. In some ten states (they were usually in the South and Northwest) so much stock was owned by the government that legislatures appointed bank directors.

Such banks were to engage primarily in the extension of short-term mercantile credit by issuing notes and writing up deposits. Those in the larger cities also engaged in the business of selling domestic bills of exchange (representing goods in transit) on which they received 6 to 8 per cent interest and discounting such bills as well for their own customers at rates of 1 to 2 per cent. State charters also included provisions for the granting of long-term credit (so-called accommodation paper). Thus the Pennsylvania legislature, and it was only one among many states, in 1814 and again in 1826 stipulated that all banks had to make

such loans at 6 per cent to farmers, mechanics and manufacturers up to
20 per cent of their paid-in capital. In addition, southern states, harking
back to the Colonial experiences, set up their own real-estate banks,
Louisiana being an outstanding example. In all, three such public banks
were created, financed from bond issues and sold largely in England.
Florida, Arkansas, and Mississippi were other states to do so.

These were not the only state-owned banks. By 1837 state-owned
banks, engaged in regular commercial business, were to be found in the
eight states of Tennessee, Kentucky, Arkansas, Georgia, Illinois, Vermont,
South Carolina, and Alabama; Ohio and Indiana joined them in the
1840s. It will be observed that these banks appeared in regions in which
private savings were still small and therefore incapable of providing
the necessary capital to launch such enterprises. (On the other hand,
representing the still prevailing suspicion of banks and bankers, state
constitutions as late as 1860 barred the chartering of banks in Texas,
California, and Oregon.)

Banks were looked on as public-service corporations and were expected to perform all sorts of functions in the common interest as the
price they had to pay for their charters. The support of public education
was the most frequently undertaken. Banks were ordered to pay bonuses
into state or city educational funds and their capital-stock was frequently
taxed for the same purpose. Similarly, state-owned banks in Kentucky
and Tennessee set aside part of their profits for the establishment of
schools.

It was not uncommon for bank charters to require the financing,
in whole or in part, of a particular kind of social-overhead capital. Thus
the Manhattan Company of New York was to lay out a water-supply
system; the Dry Dock Bank of the same city was to build wharfs; the
New Orleans Light and Banking Company was to install gas lights; and
other banks were to engage in the insurance business. In the 1830s South
Carolina, Georgia, Mississippi, and Louisiana authorized the establishment of 16 banking and railroad companies; their purpose is clear from
their titles.

Along the same lines, and to push internal improvements, banks were
called on either to invest part of their capital in turnpike and railroad
companies and state bonds (issued to build canals and railroads) or to
extend long-term loans to states at interest rates fixed by statute. In
consequence a good deal of the domestic capital needed to construct
the early transportation facilities of the country came from banking
institutions.

In the 1830s and 1840s banking began to escape from these hobbles
and to take on many of the aspects of the functions we associate with it

today. New York took a tentative step in this direction in 1829 and then a sounder and permanent one in 1838. Its legislature established a Safety-Fund System in the earlier year under which all the banks in the state, when their charters were coming up for renewal or when new ones were being granted, were to participate in a state-wide fund to protect all note issues and to accept the supervision of state authorities.

The Safety Fund was to be made up of bank contributions based on the capitalization of the individual banks, starting with one-half of 1 per cent of the capital the first year until 3 per cent had been paid up. The Fund was to be invested and the participating banks were to share in the dividends. After their assets had been disposed of banks that had failed were to have their remaining liabilities—notes first, but deposits as well—met from the Safety Fund. Periodic and careful examinations under the direction of three commissioners in the office of the State Treasurer were to be made at least every three months and on the spot if alleged irregularities were charged against a bank by three other banks.

The Safety-Fund idea was not powerful enough to withstand depression, and in the years following 1837 its assets could not meet all the claims of noteholders and depositors. Because the state was compelled to come up with almost $1 million to supplement the Fund, it turned to the creation of what came to be known as "free banking." Such a law was passed by the New York Legislature in 1838 and its example was followed by at least half the states in the Union in the 1840s and 1850s.

"Free banking" meant release from legislative restrictions and also from the imposition on banks of special purposes to serve public or social needs. Under the New York law any group of persons could start a bank without further ado if they satisfied the following requirements: deposit with the newly created state comptroller of the currency bonds of the United States, those of the state of New York, and those of other approved states, against which the comptroller would issue to the bank an equal amount of bank notes; or alternatively, deposit mortgages on New York land (worth at least twice the amount of the mortgages), against which the comptroller would issue to the bank notes at half the value of the mortgages thus put up for security. The comptroller had the authority to sell these securities to satisfy noteholders if on demand they were not paid in specie. As a further safeguard banks were called on to keep in their vaults a specie reserve of 12½ per cent against their note liabilities.

New York took a step backward in 1840 when it gave up the fractional reserve requirements, but other states went ahead on these lines in addition to establishing "free banking" so that by the 1840s the notion of a legal reserve demanded of banks, this time to cover deposits as well as notes, began to appear on statute books. In 1842 Louisiana was the first state to do so; here the stipulation was that banks (there were only five in the state with central offices in New Orleans and branches throughout the rest of the commonwealth, hence supervision was easy) were to hold a specie reserve of 33⅓ per cent against note and deposit liabilities. One further development: country banks, maintaining deposits in central cities (Boston, New York, Baltimore, and Philadelphia were the outstanding ones) began to regard such idle funds as part of their reserves, a sound enough notion if, in time of emergency, the big city banks released these reserve deposits. In the recession of 1857 New York City banks did not do so, however, and thus the effects of the business downturn were prolonged.

THE SECOND BANK OF THE UNITED STATES

Reference, in passing, has been made to some of the consequences of central banking in the United States. We must now look more closely at the activities of the Second Bank of the United States. In 1816, after a lapse of five years, following the termination of the First Bank's charter, Congress authorized the creation of the Second Bank, again for 20 years. Its characteristics were much like those of the First Bank, except that they were now drawn larger in scale. Capitalization was to be $35 million, with one-fifth subscribed by the federal government. One-fourth of the private capital furnished was to be in specie and the rest in specie or government bonds. It could establish as many branches as it pleased (it ended with 26). Notes could be issued up to the total of its capital (in 1830 they reached $16 million and in 1836, $23 million). Loans to the federal government were limited to $500,000 and to any state, to $50,000. It could act as a government depository and as its fiscal agent; the government, on its part, pledged itself to accept as legal tender only specie, the Bank's notes, Treasury notes, and the notes of state banks. As in the case of the First Bank, the Bank could engage in private business, make loans and discounts and sell and discount foreign and domestic bills of exchange.

The first seven years of the Bank's record were unimpressive; this was particularly so during the boom preceding and the hard times that set in during the recession of 1819. Nicholas Biddle, wealthy Philadelphian, without previous banking experience except as a government director but highly knowledgeable in finance, came to its presidency in 1823, and from then on the Bank became a power in the land. Biddle

established it as a central bank. Equally impressive were the expansion
of its activities and its influence on the country's money supply and the
ways in which it facilitated the flow of goods inter-regionally.

Hammond * thus pays tribute to Biddle's achievement: the Bank,
under him, developed "a rounded and complete central banking function." And he goes on to say:

> It regulated the supply of money; restrained the expansion of bank
> credit; governed the exchanges; safeguarded the investment market; pro-
> tected the money market from the disturbing force of Treasury operations
> and of payments on balance, interregional and international, and facilitated
> Treasury operation vis à vis the rest of the economy. It was in train to be-
> come the sole bank of issue and repository of the country's specie reserves. . . .
> Moreover the Bank performed these functions deliberately and avowedly—
> with a consciousness of quasi-governmental responsibility and of the need
> to subordinate profit and private interest to that responsibility.

There can be no doubt that in greater rather than lesser measure
this was so. By encouraging its southern and western branches to issue
their own notes, the Bank began to play, particularly in the South, a
preponderant role in the commercial activity of the two regions. Its large
dealings in domestic exchange (these rose from $1.9 million in 1823 to
$5 million in 1828 and to $17 million in 1832) facilitated the inter-
regional flow of funds and commercial transactions. With its branches
in important commercial centers, it provided a convenient clearing
system for the country. Ever watchful of the integrity of the money supply, it held over state banks the threat of demanding specie payments
for their notes and in return helped to eliminate the discounting of these
notes when offered in places distant from home offices, whereas the government looked to it to certify the notes of state banks as acceptable for
government payments. As a consequence, the Bank prospered. Between
1823 and 1828 its investments increased from $41.8 million to $51 million; between 1828 and 1832 its loans and discounts increased by $15.7
million, and it was paying an annual dividend of 27 per cent.

Willburn † indicates how closely meshed the Bank's branches were
with southern business needs. Table 23 shows the Bank's circulation (as
of April 4, 1832), compared with the total circulation of all state banks
(as of 1834 or 1835).

Thus Willburn found, when she examined state bank memorials
to Congress in 1832, that in the South and West the Second Bank's assist-

---

* Bray Hammond, *Banks and Politics in America from the Revolution to the
Civil War*, 1957.
† J. A. Willburn, *Biddle's Bank. The Crucial Years*, 1967.

TABLE 23

BANK CIRCULATION IN THE SOUTH, 1830s [a]

States	Bank Circulation	Total Circulation of State Banks	Bank Circulation as Per Cent of State Bank Circulation
Virginia	$1091.1	$5598.4	20%
North Carolina	887.7	955.9	93
South Carolina	1003.7	2150.3	50
Georgia	1317.1	3694.3	35
Alabama	1276.3	2054.5	52
Louisiana	3566.6	5114.1	70
Mississippi	794.1	1510.4	53
Missouri	395.7	—	—
Tennessee	1609.9	1520.9	106

Source. Willburn, op. cit., p. 49.
[a] Figures in thousands of dollars.

ance to business had been warmly welcomed. These testified to the Bank's readiness to lend to southern planters and merchants and to make available, at favorable rates, domestic and foreign bills of exchange. Willburn quotes the Commercial Bank of Cincinnati, in which city the Second Bank had a branch:

> Bills of exchange then, drawn on all Atlantic cities and Europe, can be disposed of so easily as to promote the spirit of enterprise, encourage competition, and secure to the Western traders and local planters the highest prices for their products.

Van Fenstermaker * is not so sure of the high-mindedness of the Second Bank when it helped to expand and contract the money supply. He points out:

> . . . between 1830 and 1837 the money and credit supply continued to increase faster than real production (except for the period 1833–34). Wholesale prices rose, imports increased, and land speculation became prominent.

It is Van Fenstermaker's opinion that the "Bank contributed heavily to a rise in prices in 1830, to a recession in 1833–34, and to inflation again in 1834–36." It did so for "political reasons"; that is, it was prompted by fear that with Jackson's election in 1828 it would not be rechartered;

* J. Van Fenstermaker, Development of American Commercial Banking: 1782–1837, 1965.

hence its efforts to obtain supporters in the business community at large and in Congress.

To call such activities "political" is to put a narrow construction on the term; the Bank had every right to struggle for its life on the one hand, and on the other, if its efforts were unsuccessful, to prepare for liquidation. As for its part in helping to bring on the inflation and then the depression of 1837–1843, Van Fenstermaker does not exonerate Jackson. The states, fearful of the threat to the Bank on which they counted so heavily, rushed into the breach and chartered more banks, which issued notes and wrote up deposits to increase the money supply. The panic of 1837 was given a mighty push by London; monetary contraction here, the fall in the price of cotton, and the resulting drop in American bills of exchange led to an outflow of American gold and illiquidity in American banks. Suspension of specie payments in the United States was a consequence, but it could not forestall bank failures.

In any event, Jackson from 1829 on—a foe of banking generally and of the Bank in particular—was determined that the charter would not be renewed. To forestall him, and to throw the whole Bank question into the political arena—both parties were already preparing for the presidential election of 1832—Biddle's Whig friends introduced a bill for rechartering in Congress in that year. It passed the Senate by a vote of 28–20 and the House by 107–85. Professor Willburn's analysis indicates that the Bank was heavily supported (more than 50 per cent) by members of Congress from Massachusetts, Rhode Island, Connecticut, New Jersey, Pennsylvania, Delaware and Maryland and by others from Ohio, Kentucky, Indiana, Illinois, Missouri, and Louisiana. Voting more than 50 per cent against were members from Maine, New Hampshire, and New York, plus support from Virginia, North Carolina, South Carolina, Georgia, Alabama, Tennessee, and Mississippi. Congress could not muster the needed two-thirds to over-ride the veto, and the Bank became the issue in the ensuing campaign with Henry Clay as the Whig candidate; Clay lost and the Bank was doomed.

In his veto message and in the campaign President Jackson and his supporters rang all the changes, from the solemn claim of unconstitutionality to open appeals to class passion and narrow national interest. The Bank was the "money monster" (oppressing agrarians and workers); it was the spokesman for the "aristocracy" (and the state banks of the small towns and countryside had to dance to the tune piped from Chestnut Street, Philadelphia, the Bank's central office); it stood for "wealth," "privilege," and "monopoly." It was tied to international finance, as its large number of foreign shareholders demonstrated.

Did the congressional vote and the Bank memorials to Congress support these charges? Clearly, the East (wealth, privilege, monopoly power) was not aligned against the South and West (agrarian, small town, victim of the machinations of Chestnut Street). There is no doubt that the furor was stirred up in large measure in New York; in part, because New York City bankers were jealous of Chestnut Street and restive under the restraints the Bank imposed on free enterprise and speculation; but in greater part because of the expert political skills displayed by the Albany Regency (headed by Martin Van Buren) in manipulating the New York Assembly and the New York congressional delegation—all to make certain that New York would vote Democratic in the 1832 election.

Hammond stresses the rivalry between Wall Street and Chestnut Street, and he is right. Thus he answered the contention of Parrington and Schlesinger that the attack on and the repudiation of the Bank represented a rising of the "white masses" (the poor farmers and the workers) against the monopoly Money Power. The Bank, like King Canute, and just as ineffectively, was trying to sweep back a mighty tide. Says Hammond:

> The Bank of the United States was an important restraint and corrective, but to suppose that it could maintain itself in the teeth of the overwhelming inflationary tide established in the Jacksonian age and dominant over the American economy ever since, is illusory. . . . It may therefore be recognized for what it was and not as the agrarian reform it has been made out to be. The federal Bank was not destroyed by champions of the helpless contending against the money power, but by a rising and popular interest that found the Bank doubly offensive for being both vested and regulatory— Wall Street, the State banks and speculative borrowers dressing up for the occasion in the rags of the poor and parading with outcries against oppression by the aristocratic Mr. Biddle's hydra of corruption, whose nest they aspired to occupy themselves.

Professor Willburn must be listened to as well. In looking at the voting in the New York Assembly, she finds powerful support for the Bank from western counties and New York City itself, but Van Buren's hold on the New York legislature and the state's congressional delegation could not be shaken. As a result of Van Buren's masterly handling of the 1832 campaign, there is much merit in Professor Willburn's contention that the issue, as the voters saw it, was not the Bank as much as it was Jackson himself.

THE RESULTS OF THE END OF THE BANK

The consequences were both good and bad, although the bad undoubtedly outweighed the good. New York, now free of Philadelphia, was able

to experiment with its Safety Fund and "free banking." Jackson withdrew
the federal deposits and state banks increased vastly in number (doubling
from 1837 to 1860), as did their augmentation of the money supply. The
expanding credit—for new money was created, notably in the Northwest—stimulated production and trade, but it also lent itself easily to get-
rich-quick schemes and to speculation. "Free banking" was responsible for
the appearance of "wildcat" banks (more of this later) and the disorder-
ing of the paper currency of the country.

The effort to put the country on a hard-money basis (the Specie
Circular of 1836, which demanded that all payments for public lands
be made in coin or in obligations of the United States, is an example)
led to the determination to establish an Independent Treasury. Under
this plan—a law was adopted in 1840, repealed in 1841, and passed again
in 1846—government funds were to be segregated from the banking
system and immobilized. All monies due the Treasury were to be paid
only in gold and silver and were to be kept in the Treasury's vaults or
in subtreasuries set up in a number of cities. The officials of the Treasury,
said the act, were "to keep safely, without loaning, using, depositing in
banks, or exchanging for other funds than as allowed by this act, all the
public money collected by them . . . till the same is ordered . . . to be
transferred or paid out." The law remained on the statute books until
the Federal Reserve System was established in 1914. The law could not
work, of course. With surpluses in the Treasury (this was so during the
1850s and the 1870s and 1880s), banks were in danger of being drained
of their specie reserves. When pressures were on the country's economy
to help in the financing of crop harvesting and movements, or banks were
threatened by runs, the Treasury's help was needed. Not only had the
law to be by-passed, but in fact the Treasury had to develop central-
banking functions in limited part to maintain some sort of balance lest
the country be at the constant mercy of short, sharp cycles of expanding
and contracting credit.

The demise of the Bank and the adoption of "free banking" in many
of the states in the South and the West led to an era of monetary confusion. This was caused by the "wildcat" banks on which were imposed
no real requirements for adequate capitalization, the maintenance of
specie reserves, note redemption, and supervision by state authorities;
in fact, many of them were simply agencies for note issue. Said a contemporary:

> In the West, the people have suffered for years from the issues of almost
> every State in the Union, much of which is irredeemable, so insecure and so
> unpopular as to be known by opprobrious names [after the figures on the
> notes or their size, or the colors in which they were printed]. . . . There the

frequently worthless issues of the State of Maine, the shinplasters of Michigan, the wildcats of Georgia, of Canada, and Pennsylvania, the red dogs of Indiana and Nebraska . . . and the not-to-be forgotten stumptails of Illinois and Wisconsin are mixed indiscriminately with the par currency of New York and Boston.

These free banks monetized state debts (usually the bonds of southern states which sold at discounts of 10 to 20 per cent), issued bank notes against them, and made redemption—even if it could have been achieved —difficult or impossible by opening their offices in inaccessible places. The panic of 1857 took a heavy toll of them. Bray Hammond's severity about this kind of banking is justified. Said he: "The results of this Jacksonian revolution were obvious in monetary inflation, in speculation, in wasted labor, in business failures, in abandonment of an efficient means of credit control, and in corruption of a sound monetary system." It was to put an end to such ignorance, indifference, or irresponsibility of state legislatures and officials that the National Banking Act was passed in 1863 and amended in 1865.

THE BALANCE OF PAYMENTS

An analysis of the American ante-bellum balance of payments confirms a number of observations already made here: that the United States was still largely a trading nation (buying more than it was selling and buying manufactured goods); that unfavorable balances of trade, up to the 1850s, were met from the freight earnings of American ships and the sale of many of them in foreign ports; that a good part of the short-term financing of American commerce came from the credits extended by English merchant-banking (this began long before cotton exports became important); and that, when American shipping and its net earnings began to decline, the discovery and export of California gold as a commodity—one of those exogenous influences North and the other econometric historians have distainfully dismissed—kept American international payments in balance.

We have two estimates of the American balance of payments and both are used. The first was made in 1919 by Bullock, Williams, and Tucker * and this is employed for the years 1789 to 1849 because they reflect secular swings in the economy. The second was drawn up by North † and is employed for the 1850s.

* C. J. Bullock, J. H. Williams, and R. S. Tucker, "The Balance of Trade of the United States," *The Review of Economic Statistics*, Vol. I, 1919.
† Douglass North, "The United States Balance of Payments, 1790–1860," National Bureau of Economics, Studies in Income and Wealth, 1960.

The first period analyzed by Bullock, Williams, and Tucker covered the years 1789–1820. It showed an excess of imports (including merchandize and specie) of $512 million, which, with $200 million interest on the public debt, earnings due foreigners on investments in the United States, and short-term credits extended to American merchants came to a debit of $700 million. This was more than offset by the earnings of the American merchant marine, the sale of ships abroad, and the duties retained on re-exported goods (sizable from 1789 to 1807); our authors estimated this sum as high as $800 million. The soundness of the economy—and the confidence Europeans had in it—is evidenced by the following: the increase in the specie in the country (from $7 million in 1791 to more than $20 million in 1821), London exchange selling at a discount in the United States for much of the period, the reduction of the foreign debt, and the repayment of foreign capital invested in the first Bank of the United States.

The second period spanned the years 1821–1837, again characterized by an excess of imports of merchandize ($215 million) and specie ($37 million). Interest due and other earnings of foreigners constituted an additional debit of $60 million. Immigrants brought capital with them of about $11 million, but this was offset by the same amount in expenditures by American tourists abroad. The net earnings of American ships and their sale in foreign ports came to $214 million; the difference between credits and debits was more than counterbalanced by fresh capital investments of Europeans—the estimate for this item was $125 million; in addition there was a reinvestment of old capital (largely in the paid-up public debt) of something like $50 million. Foreign confidence continued high—the amount of specie in the country increased during these years—but the onset of depression in 1837 left unsettled balances that were reflected in sterling exchange selling at a premium in the United States.

In the third period, 1838–1849, merchandize movements were almost in balance. Bullock, Williams, and Tucker estimate an excess of exports of $34 million; North an excess of imports of $4.8 million. More specie entered the country than left it (due to famine conditions in Ireland and the sudden stepping up of grain purchases from the United States). Interest payments on foreign holdings came to $114 million and an additional $100 million (North's estimate) was either repudiated or returned to Europe. Although immigrants brought in $75 million, there were tourist expenditures abroad of $85 million and immigrant remittances of $15 million. Net freight earnings and the sale of ships totaled only $214 million (in part because of the fall in rates in the Atlantic traffic, in greater part because of heavy competition in the Southeast Asia trade

and the superiority of English iron steamships to American wooden sail-
ing vessels). Nevertheless, American shipping earnings paid the interest
due foreigners, and, despite depression in the greater part of the period,
international payments were in balance.

The 1850s (with a return of prosperity that lasted until 1857) saw
a continuance of an unfavorable trade balance and a sharp and permanent decline in American shipping earnings. At the same time the United
States was attracting and welcoming long-term foreign investments
(largely for railroad building), although the inflow was not so heavy
as it had been in the 1830s. The discovery of California gold and the
shipment of most of it overseas paid for interest earned by foreigners
and the import surpluses. Heavy immigration during the decade produced capital, but immigrant remittances and American tourist expenditures balanced out this gain. These credit and debit factors kept the
American international account on an even keel.

For the years 1850–1860 imports exceeded exports by $505.8 million,
interest and dividend payments came to $219.4 million, and the net
earnings of ships and the sale of ships and other current items (immigrant funds offset by immigrant remittances and American tourist expenditures) came to only $116.5 million. On the other hand, the specie
net balance was enormous—about $420 million dollars, out of the total
California gold production of $630 million. These are North's calcula-
tions (Table 24).

TABLE 24

EXPORTS AND IMPORTS OF SPECIE, 1850–1860

Year	Specie Exports [a]	Specie Imports [a]
1850	7,523	4,629
1851	29,466	5,453
1852	42,674	5,505
1853	27,487	4,201
1854	41,197	6,759
1855	56,247	3,660
1856	45,746	4,207
1857	69,137	12,462
1858	52,633	19,274
1859	63,887	7,434
1860	66,546	8,550

Source. North, op. cit., p. 605.

[a] In thousands of dollars.

North's efforts to estimate the capital, or funds, immigrants brought into the United States are praiseworthy and indicate that immigrants (including the Irish) were not exactly destitute; quite the reverse. For the 16 years 1845–1860 these funds totaled more than $300 million, against immigrant remittances in the same years of about $90 million.

How great were foreign investments in the United States over the period 1800–1860? There are guesses—some good ones by contemporaries and later historians, others merely off-hand opinions. North has gathered together a number and these are presented in Table 25 for selective years for what they are worth.

TABLE 25
FOREIGN INVESTMENTS IN THE UNITED STATES, 1803–1857

	Long-term [a]	Short-term [a]	Total
1803	$ 52	$ 23	$ 75
1839	200	85	285
1843	197	28	225
1853	225	155	380
1857	250	150	400

Source. North, *op. cit.,* p. 623.

[a] In millions of dollars.

FOREIGN TRADE, SHIPPING, AND THE ROLE OF FOREIGN MERCHANT-BANKERS

The domination of American exports by cotton began in the 1820s. In 1811 the total value of exports was $45 million, of which cotton represented $10 million; in 1821 cotton's share of the $45 million was $20 million, and by 1860 with exports worth $319 million, cotton stood for $192 million. Other exports of importance were leaf tobacco, wheat and flour, and cotton manufactures. Nevertheless they were small. In 1860, for example, the exports of leaf tobacco came to $16 million, wheat and flour, $20 million, cotton manufactures, $11 million, and meat products— a newcomer—$14 million. By 1879, however, cotton's supremacy was over, for in that year the combined value of wheat, wheat flour, and meat products came to $262 million, against cotton's $162 million.

Imports in the ante-bellum period were a mixed bag in which finished manufactured goods exceeded foodstuffs (coffee, tea, sugar). In 1860, when the total imports added up to $354 million, finished manufactured goods accounted for $172 million (wool manufactures, $43 million, cotton manufactures, $33 million, and iron and steel manufactures, $26 million).

The decline of the American merchant marine is evidenced by these figures. In 1826, when American shipping was still at its height and American ships were trading all over the world—piling up those great mercantile fortunes—92.5 per cent of the country's foreign trade entered and cleared its ports in American bottoms. In 1860 the proportion had dropped to 66.5 per cent. The reasons were the following: Americans were falling behind in the Southeast Asian trades because of the stiffer competition they were meeting from British ships—the East India Company's monopoly was being terminated. Of greater importance were the waning American wood industries and the superiority of British technology (assisted by government subsidies for construction and operation). In the 1850s the British iron boats with screw propellers and compound engines appeared in large numbers, they were cheaper, faster, and safer to run—and even the magnificent American clipper ships of the 1850s could not stand up to them. The wooden clippers, designed and built in New York and New England yards—great long ships, narrow in the beam, with heavy complements of sail, constructed for speed and not payloads—represented an effort to recapture leadership in the China trade. They were able to cut the run from New York to Canton from 150 days to 84 days, but they were too expensive to operate (because of the large crews they had to carry) and had only a brief decade of glory in the trade with California, where the cost of goods was not so important as the speed of delivery.

The role of Anglo-American and English merchant banking (unincorporated companies, or partnerships, which did not issue bank notes and to this extent were unlike commercial banks) in the financing of American commerce requires a further word. W. and J. Brown Co., which originated in Baltimore, established English connections. So did George Peabody, who started in Massachusetts, transferred to Baltimore, where he made a large fortune (he left $8.5 million), and then in 1837 founded a London banking house. His partner was another transplanted American merchant, Junius Spencer Morgan of Hartford, who organized Morgan, Grenfell and Co. in 1854. It was in this office that J. Pierpont Morgan, the elder Morgan's son, cut his eyeteeth in the investment banking business. Their great English rivals were Baring Brothers and Co. and the English branch of Rothschild and Sons (it was August Belmont, a German, who moved to America to become their resident representative). There were lesser merchant-bankers, some of whom failed in the depression of 1837 to be succeeded by others, who were in and out of American financing, along with their other interests all over the world, for London was the great international money market.

These merchant-bankers performed a variety of functions. They bought and sold commodities on their own account; they acted as agents for foreign correspondents, buying and selling for them and charging a commission for their services; they were factors—advancing short and middle-term credit to domestic and foreign customers who fabricated primary products into semiprocessed or finished manufactures; they accepted drafts in exchange for their services or bills drawn on England and also dealt in foreign exchange, discounting bills on whatever bankers they were drawn; finally—and this loomed larger and larger among their activities—they financed (and made a market for) long-term securities of governments and private corporations.

Because a national credit market was still nonexistent in the United States, Americans turned to London for these services. Until the emergence of similar bankers in New York in the 1850s, London bankers handled (and financed) the American cotton crop. They not only made funds available for American imports from England, but for the purchase as well of iron from Sweden, wines and silks from France and Spain, linen and opium from Italy and the Levant, sugar, wool, and hides from Latin America, and tea, coffee, spices, fine cottons, and chinaware from the Far East. They accepted, in payment, drafts (charging a commission of 1 to 2 per cent), or up to three months' bills of exchange (for European purchases) and bills up to one year (for Far Eastern goods); the latter they discounted at rates prevailing in the money market.

It was to these bankers (now in the capacity of investment houses) that borrowers of long-term funds turned. The American states, when they embarked on their programs of public improvements in the 1830s, and the American railroad companies, when they started building on a large scale in the 1850s, sold their bonds—at discounts—to these bankers, who in turn moved them into private portfolios and maintained a market for the securities. At the end of the Civil War Andrew Carnegie laid the basis of a fortune—with which he could go into steel manufacture—by acting as an agent for American bridge and railroad companies and placing their bonds with London (and German) banks.

This short-term mercantile financing loomed large in the American balance of payments, representing as much as one-third and sometimes as much as one-half the total foreign American indebtedness; similarly, the earnings of foreign bankers (commissions, interest) made sizable additions to the interest foreign investors obtained from the United States for the American securities they held.

New York bankers (and factors) moved into the cotton trade significantly in the 1850s. New York became the apex of what Albion * called the "cotton triangle." Early cotton shipments had begun by being sent to New York and from there transshipped to Liverpool and Havre. By the middle of the 1850s most of the South's cotton crop was putting out for Europe directly from Charleston, Savannah, Mobile, and New Orleans; the ships carrying the cotton brought back freights and immigrants to New York and then returned to the South with cargoes or in ballast. Because the trade pivoted on New York, New York merchant-bankers and factors financed the cotton planters (and many of the domestic American cotton mills that purchased the raw cotton) and sold their cotton abroad and at home by sample and on the basis of bills of lading. They also financed the southern purchase of European and American wares (dry goods, hardware, and wet goods) by southern merchants who came to New York with their families in the summertime —and went on (also financed by their merchant-bankers) to Saratoga Springs and Newport for their holidays.

Southerners were not unaware and resentful of their dependence on New York. De Bow's Review again and again tried to encourage southerners to cut the nexus: by diversification, the use of regional funds for financing the South's own merchants, and bypassing New York by the stimulation of direct trade between southern and European ports. New York was a southern creation, said the Review, in exasperation (because its efforts were unavailing): "Southern liberality has done its utmost to feed and pamper that monster city." The ties between the South and New York were badly stretched as a result of the panic of 1857 and the following recession when New York bankers refused or were unable to buy the sterling bills with which Liverpool had paid for the 1857 cotton crops. Cotton, which went on the market initially at 16½ cents a pound ended by being dumped at 10 cents in New Orleans. Southerners claimed that New York's failure to stand by cost them $35 to $50 million that year. Nevertheless the uneasy alliance continued, and when Ft. Sumter was fired on there was talk in New York—abetted by some of the bankers and merchants—that the city, too, ought to secede from the Union and set itself up as a "free port."

* R. S. Albion, The Rise of New York Port, 1939.

VII

THE PROCESSES OF
INDUSTRIALIZATION BEFORE
THE CIVIL WAR

THE DOMINANCE OF THE MERCHANT-CAPITALIST

We have already seen how Paul A. David has taken issue with his fellow
econometric historians by casting doubts on the existence of any accelerated growth in the real per capita Gross Domestic Product of the United
States before the Civil War. There was, it is true, a sizable shift of the
labor force out of agriculture, which fell from 82.6 per cent of the total
in 1800 to 53.2 per cent in 1860, and most of it took place during
1820–1850.* Did this mean greater productivity per farm worker because
of mechanization (and there is doubt on this point) or the transfer of
staple production from less fertile lands to the more fertile (cotton to the
Southwest, cereals to the Northwest)? Did the movement of workers into
nonfarm pursuits, including factory labor, mean a significant change in
the structure of the American economy?

If this had happened—and if a changeover from primary production
(largely agriculture) to secondary production (manufacturing plus public
utilities and construction) had occurred—then the leap forward should
have been in real per capita GDP. Such has been historical experience.

---

* The proportions are somewhat different from those of Lebergott, cited earlier.
This is so because David corrects Lebergott's estimates.

As Nicholas Kaldor has said (in his Cambridge Inaugural Lecture, "Causes of the Slow Rate of Economic Growth of the United Kingdom," 1966):

> It is the rate of growth of manufacturing production (together with the ancillary activities of public utilities and construction) which is likely to exert a dominating influence on the overall rate of economic growth: partly on account of its influence on the rate of growth of productivity in the industrial sector itself, and partly also because it will tend, indirectly, to raise the rate of productivity growth in other sectors. . . . And of course it is true more generally that industrialization accelerates the rate of technological change throughout the economy.

This did not take place in the United States, as David has pointed out. To quote David again:

> Instead, it appears more reasonable to maintain that no significant acceleration of the secular trend in real GDP per capita took place within the period of our national history that preceded the Civil War. The evidence points to average annual rates of increase close to 1.3 per cent . . . over the whole time span between 1790 and 1860. . . .
>
> After the Civil War, however, long-term rates of growth per capita real product between years of peak activity were higher than this, being closer to 1.8 per cent per annum. . . .

As a result, David is forced to the conclusion that we are confronted by "something of a paradox, if not a bitter dilemma." Would not paradox or dilemma be resolved if the following conclusions were accepted? First, that the shift of the labor force out of agriculture or primary production did not necessarily mean a transfer into manufactures or secondary production. Second, that a good, possibly even larger, part of the increased proportion of workers in "manufactures" was in reality still in non-industrial production—household, cottage, "bespoke" trades, in which productivity continued low. Third, that the greater part of the nonfarm workers were in the tertiary sector—services that included transportation, distribution, domestic work, and clerical activities—in which productivity also was low. In short, a merchant-capitalist economy, which is largely what the ante-bellum America was (rather than industrial-capitalist), will require as many workers in the tertiary sector as a country that has gone through its industrial revolution. Finally, the technological improvements that H. J. Habbakuk (see below) reports he found in cotton textiles and in a handful of other industries in the ante-bellum period did not lead to a significant development of the iron and machine-tools industries; in short, broadly, there were no forward and backward linkages with manufacturing on a large scale.

Therefore this final observation: industrialization, when it comes in full, as it did in Great Britain in the last quarter of the eighteenth century and the first quarter of the nineteenth, permeates every aspect of the economy and is an excellent demonstration of the concept of balanced growth. When industrialization appears in limited degree, as it did in the United States before the Civil War—and when a national capital market, a national transportation system, and a national market for goods and services did not exist—then self-sustained, steady growth was still to emerge.

Tryon * argues that production in the home—and this meant handicrafts and the use of crude tools—and the transfer to shop and factory were generally completed before the close of the third decade of the nineteenth century. This did not mean that cottage or domestic manufacture or the putting-out system did not linger on, indeed flourish, in many industries. The differences between cottage and industrial manufacture are great.

At the heart of the first was the merchant-capitalist; at the second, the industrial-capitalist. In the domestic system production took place in the home (the use of the term "cottage" is significant—this was a country pursuit) in which the artisan was frequently a farmer who also furnished his own equipment: a workbench and tools (as in the making of shoes or broomstraw or hats), a loom (as in the weaving of wool or linen), a frame for the manufacture of hosiery and other knit goods, or an outbuilding (for slaughtering meat animals). In the manufacture of iron products the so-called iron plantations played a large role in the industry right through the Civil War; the cottagers were as often as not farmers or farm workers at the same time that they labored at country forges and furnaces. In most instances an intermediary, the merchant-capitalist, furnished the raw materials and semi-processed goods, paid the independent artisan for his services, and moved the product of the cottage into the market. The merchant-capitalist had no capital investment in the manufacturing.

The "bespoke" trades were not far distant from cottage production, except that they took place in urban shops. These were largely hand (as opposed to machine) production and they turned goods out on order: silverware and plate, furniture, men's clothing and shoes, carriages, carpets, and other household necessities or luxuries. In all such cases the producer or artisan was not a wage laborer primarily.

Industrial manufacture means these things: the investment of capital in plant and equipment by the industrial capitalist: rationalization

* R. M. Tryon, *Household Manufactures in the United States, 1640–1860*, 1917.

of production under the factory system—standardization of product, factory discipline, specialization of function (Adam Smith's "division of labor"), regular hours, supervision and a steady pace of work, for which wages are paid on an hourly basis. The conversion of the worker from an independent artisan or part-time farmer into a wage laborer thus takes place, and the divorce of the worker from the ownership of the means of production is complete. With rationalization, division of labor, and technology, the productivity per worker must rise.

Clark * thus describes this earlier (cottage or domestic) organization of production:

> Early yarn mills distributed beams of warp and filling to country weavers to be made into cloth. . . . Large vans circulated through New England and the Central States, leaving at farmhouses along the way bundles of straw plait to be sewed into hats and bonnets, and boot and shoe uppers to be closed and bound. Before the war [Civil War] knitting machines made the legs and feet of stockings separately and many country workers were employed to piece them together. The making of garments was less an urban occupation than at present, and farmers' wives and daughters sewed and finished goods for city merchants.

In talking of woolens, Clark declares that as late as 1840 hand weavers "formed an important fraction of the industrial population of New York and Philadelphia." Cole † goes even further; he is authority for the belief that not until the 1870s did domestic manufacture in woolens become a negligible factor in the industry. In an article written in 1932 on carpet manufacture, which flourished in Philadelphia, he has this to say:

> . . . as late as 1860 we find published a complete description of the system as it existed in 1857. . . . Work was "distributed among a large number of workers" who were dependent upon the "manufacturers" for directing the industry. The "individual manufacturers," who numbered about 100, furnished employment to at least 1500 hand and loom weavers. . . . Seemingly, the relationship between employer and workers was that common to the putting-out system. The weavers owned their loom and tackle, and the employer furnished the material. . . .

The same observations are in order for boots and shoes. The "manufacturer" engaged in a mixed operation. He employed a few journeymen on a piecework basis in a central shop to prepare the leather; they also cut the soles and uppers. This material was delivered to cottagers—in New England they had built ten-footers, or "ells," onto their farm homes, in which they did the sewing and nailing. The "manufacturer" furnished

---

* V. S. Clark, *History of Manufactures in the United States, 1607–1860*, 1916.
† A. H. Cole, *The American Wool Manufacture*, 1926.

the leather, binding, thread, and nails; the cottagers, the cobbler's bench and tools. The semiprocessed leather and the finished boots and shoes were delivered and collected by carriers who received a percentage of the cottagers' pay.

Automatic machinery for cutting and rolling the leather, pegging the soles, and finally sewing on the uppers, did not appear until well into the 1840s. But the cottagers remained on, says Clark:

> . . . [the installation of machinery] required capital and their maximum economy was derived from continuous operation. . . . Ultimately [the machinery was assembled] in factory buildings. The result was not accomplished, however, until power was applied to shoe machinery, a development postponed until the outbreak of the Civil War.

Hazard * confirms all this. The "factory stage" of production did not appear until 1855. In fact, commenting on the 1860 Census, which called itself "Report on Boot and Shoe Manufacture," and discussing the number of establishments in New England, Professor Hazard remarks: "Most of these were probably central shops. Only a few of them could be termed factories in the modern sense." It was the Civil War that finally pushed the domestic system out. Says Professor Hazard:

> The large order of shoes for the Union armies, added to the scarcity of labor . . . were additional important factors in urging the use of machinery in general, and in encouraging the trial of the McKay machine. During the war, the practicality of the McKay machine run by steam power was demonstrated, and it was widely adopted during the late sixties.

The same analysis is applicable to the food industries, which, in value of product, led all the "manufacturing" activities of ante-bellum America. In all likelihood flour milling, baking, brewing, and meat slaughtering and packing were the last of the industries to quit the cottage-and-mill stage for the factory stage. Originally they were household industries; they moved into the cottage system when local and limited regional markets began to appear. The role of the merchant-capitalist in meat packing was characteristic. He was called a "packer," but the term was used loosely in the 1840s and 1850s to include commission men, provision dealers, drovers, commercial farmers, and even stock raisers. Despite the existence of a number of packing centers in the West—Cincinnati (the "Porkopolis" of the 1840s), Louisville, Milwaukee, St. Louis, and, later, Chicago—a large number of the animals slaughtered and packed were handled by country butchers and at small rural and

---

* Blanche Evans Hazard, *The Organization of the Boot and Shoe Industry in Massachusetts Before 1875*, 1921.

temporary plants. Indeed, in the 1850s technical journals found it neces-sary to quote prices for something like 233 different packing points scattered over nine states of the Middle West. Once again, the paucity of capital markets (and therefore high interest rates) and integrated trans-portation systems made the "packer" really a commission merchant in-stead of a manufacturer in the modern sense; for it was he who moved up and down the countryside, picking up animals, curing hogs, packing provisions, and selling them for the accounts of his farmer-butcher suppliers.

The needs of the Union army for large quantities anl regularity of supply—for example, shoes, clothing, and blankets—forced the rational-ization of meat production that characterizes the factory system. Financed by government contracts, a group of innovators was transformed over-night from country butchers and commission men into packers in the industrial sense. They set up their own stockyards (near receiving points), created a cash market (with daily quotations) for animals, and in fac-tories—using assembly-line techniques for the first time in America, thus achieving the economies of a division of labor—slaughtered, packed meat, and erected plants for the utilization of waste products (converted into lard, tallow, soap, glue, fertilizer, dressed bristles, and prussiate of potash). It was no accident that the men who obtained Union army contracts— Philip D. Armour, Jacob Dold, and Nelson Morris—were to emerge by 1865 (when the Chicago Union stockyards were established) as the pack-ers of industrial capitalism. It is to be noted, however, that one of the aspects of rationalization—continuous operation—did not emerge in meat packing until about 1869 and was brought about by the introduction of ice cooling, which made slaughtering, curing, and packing a year-round instead of a seasonal (summertime) business.

THE DIFFERENT CASES OF
IRON AND COTTON TEXTILES

In the case of iron the tale is a mixed one. The manufacturing of iron was more fully developed in the East, where there was some evidence of integration of furnaces, forges, and mills. Nevins,* in his careful study of the early industry, reported the existence, up to the Civil War, of only six companies that combined all the processes of smelting, puddling, and shaping iron, and three of them were to be found in eastern Pennsyl-vania, two in New Jersey, and one in Maryland. That is to say, the

* Allan Nevins, *Abram S. Hewitt: With Some Account of Peter Cooper*, 1935.

making of pig-iron was a separate and distinct activity and usually carried on in the country at small blast furnaces. Castings, wrought iron, and finished iron (e.g., for wire) were the products of other manufacturers. The most successful of these integrated plants was the Trenton Iron Works of New Jersey (run by Hewitt and his brother-in-law Edward Cooper). Created in the 1840s with a capitalization of $1 million and outstanding bonds of $287,000, it owned its own iron mines in Ner Jersey, operated three blast furnaces (with an annual production of 25,000 tons of pig iron), turned its billets into rails, beams, and rods out of the wrought iron it made itself in its own reverberatory furnaces, and operated a wire mill. For power it used water mills (and not steam); for fuel, the more expensive anthracite coal (and not bituminous). Only three similar, fairly large companies appeared in the 1850s—the Cambria Iron Works at Johnstown, Pa., in 1853, the Jones & Laughlin Co. Ltd., at Pittsburgh, in the same year, and the Bethlehem Iron Co., at Bethlehem, Pa., in 1860.

All sought to make wrought-iron rails, as did some smaller plants, but despite the continued existence of high tariffs—which at times reached as high as 100 per cent in ad valorem duties—domestic requirements were met largely by importations from England. Not only was British iron cheaper but the English were able to help finance American purchases. During the height of the railroad boom of 1850–1855 American production of iron rails was 438,000 gross tons, whereas imports totaled 1,287,000 gross tons.

Pittsburgh did not emerge as the center of the industry until the Civil War broke out. In 1850 14 rolling mills in the region consumed 59,000 tons of pig (the country's total production was 563,000 gross tons); in 1857 the number of mills had increased to 21 and the consumption of pig, to 132,600 gross tons (the country's total production was 712,600). Hunter,[*] in a pioneering study, put his finger on an important reason for the backwardness of the industry: the high interest rate for new capital. In fact, it was not until 1859 that the manufacturers of heavy and finished iron began to erect their blast furnaces to free themselves from their dependence on the uncertain supply of the country plants. There was an even more important reason and that was the weakness of the demand factor. Says Hunter:

> . . . [The year 1859 marked] the transition between two essentially different phases in the development of iron manufacturing in this country and at Pittsburgh. Of the period just closed it may be said that the manu-

[*] L. C. Hunter, "Influence of the Market Upon Techniques in the Iron Industry in Western Pennsylvania to 1860," *Journal of Economic and Business History*, Vol. 1 1929.

facture of iron was controlled and conditioned by the needs and requirements of a pioneer agricultural population, which were met to a large
extent by the forges and rolling mills without the mediation of finished iron
products. The principal function of the manufacturer of wrought iron was
to supply the country iron workers, blacksmiths by profession or necessity,
with bar iron to be shaped to meet the needs of farmer, wagoner and mill
owner. . . . The demand for iron came increasingly from industries engaged
in the production of finished iron goods and the machinery of industry and
commerce. . . . The agricultural era gave way to what might be termed the
industrial era.

How primitive the country iron establishment remained as late as
the Civil War may be seen from this account written by Thaddeus
Stevens on July 11, 1863, of the losses he suffered when the Confederate
army swept northward toward Gettysburg, as it engulfed his works near
Chambersburg in south-central Pennsylvania:

> They then seized my bacon (about 4,000 lbs.), molasses and other con-
> tents of the store. . . . On Friday, they burned the furnace, saw-mill, two
> forges and rocking mill. . . .
> They even hauled off my bar iron, being as they said convenient for
> shoeing horses, and wagons about $4,000 worth. . . . My grass (about 80 tons)
> they destroyed; and broke in the windows of the dwelling-houses where the
> workmen lived. . . .

It is not difficult to reconstruct the picture. Stevens, in conjunction
with a group of farms, ran a sawmill and an ironworks. His workmen, in
addition to being employed making iron, undoubtedly labored on the
farms as well, for the 80 tons of hay destroyed was a sizable quantity. The
whole establishment was located in the country; for the workers' dwelling
houses on Stevens' property and the "store" and its contents are to be
noted: the large amount of bacon and the molasses, the usual stock in
trade of the truck-payment system, is also typical. It is not difficult to
draw the conclusion that Thaddeus Stevens, as an iron master, had
closer links with the cottage-and-mill system of production of seventeenth-
century England than with the industrial Pittsburgh of the 1870s.

Temin,* pursuing a somewhat different analysis, does not essentially
disagree with Hunter. He is seeking to explain why the United States
was so slow to use coke, made of bituminous, as the fuel in manufacturing iron (as England was), instead of charcoal or anthracite. Says Temin:

> The reason why coke was not adopted in the 1840s in contrast to the
> adoption of anthracite was because the iron made with anthracite was of
> substantially better quality. . . . and the price of coke was not sufficiently

---

* Peter Temin, *Iron and Steel in Nineteenth-Century America*, 1964.

low to offset this factor. The barrier to the spread of mineral-fuel technology to the West was not the different character of demand in the West, it was the different supply conditions in the West. . . . The lack of raw materials was remedied in the 1850s and later years by the exploitation of the Connellsville coke region, leading to the elimination of the price differential between anthracite and coke pig iron. The new price structure encouraged the use of coke, and its production expanded rapidly in the years following the Civil War.

It should be noted that Temin telescopes his dates. George Harvey, the biographer of Henry Clay Frick (who became "king" of Connellsville) records the fact that there were only four coking ovens in the country in 1850 and had been increased to only 21 in 1860 and 25 in 1870. Frick did not begin to buy bituminous coal lands until 1871 and by 1873 had built only 50 coke plants. Indeed, it was not until 1875 that bituminous coal and coke, as the basic fuel in the production of pig iron, caught up with anthracite and not until 1883 that coke made up more than one-half of the total fuel employed. The figures are from Temin. (See Table 26.)

In one manufacturing area industrialization—the establishment of the factory system and mechanization of production—did occur and this was in the making of cotton textiles. Even here development was slow because the initial appearance of the cotton industry was linked with cottage production, which lingered on—in Rhode Island, Connecticut, southern Massachusetts, and Philadelphia—until the 1830s. This so-called Rhode Island system had its inception when Samuel Slater, who had worked in the Arkwright factories in England, was induced to migrate

TABLE 26

PRODUCTION OF PIG IRON BY DIFFERENT FUELS

Year	Total Production (1000 Gross Tons)	Fuel Used (Percentages)		
		Bituminous Coal and Coke	Mixed Anthracite and Coke	Charcoal
1859	751	10	56	34
1869	1711	29	51	20
1875	2024	42	40	18
1879	2742	47	41	12
1883	4596	52	37	11

Source. Temin, op. cit., pp. 266, 268.

to the United States. Financed by the Rhode Island mercantile firm of
Almy and Brown, Slater set up a small textile mill at Pawtucket in 1791
to manufacture spun yarn, duplicating from memory the English machines. The weaving of cotton cloth had been carried on by cottagers in
their own homes on a putting-out basis. Children did the spinning; payment was in truck, and capital consisted of the original financing and
reinvested small profits. According to Ware,* Rhode Island plants in
the 1830s were capitalized at not much more than $30,000. The same
kind of organization existed in Philadelphia, New England's principal
rival, where for a long time production continued to take place in small
hand-weaving shops with yarn furnished by merchant-manufacturers.

The breakthrough took place in 1813, when a power loom, designed
by Francis C. Lowell, a Bostonian, made its appearance (water power, not
steam, was used) at Lowell and Waltham and then at Lawrence and
Manchester. Spinning and weaving were integrated for the first time and
the factory system was fully installed. The Waltham Company, financed
by a group of Boston merchants, started with $300,000 paid-in-capital
which was doubled in less than a decade. Lowell, which became the center of the factory industry, was the seat of plants capitalized from
$600,000 to $1,000,000. Power production, rationalization, the wage system, and cost-accounting procedures were responsible for rapid growth.
Whereas in 1831 there were 1.2 million spindles in the country, by 1860
the number had grown to 5.2 million and the value of the product from
$32 million to $115 million. In 1860, by value added ($54.6 million), the
manufacture of cotton goods led the country's industries.

Douglas North thinks the backward linkages, particularly those of
the manufacture of textile machinery in the United States, were important. The Waltham plant also had its own machine shop and from then
on moved into the manufacture of other kinds of machinery, stationary
engines, and machine tools. North quotes Gibb †:

> . . . the manufacture of textile machinery evolved from the local trade
> sporadically practiced by many small shops to an industry characterized by a
> few large shops and an increasing number of smaller more specialized shops
> all of which were beginning to compete vigorously for business on a national
> scale.

Gibb (full of enthusiasm over this development, probably over-enthusi-
astic) goes on to say: "The part played by the textile machinery industry
in fostering American metalworking skills in the early nineteenth century
was a crucial one."

* Caroline Ware, *The Early New England Cotton Manufacture*, 1931.
† George S. Gibb, *The Saco-Lowell Shops. Textile Machinery Building in New England, 1813–1849*, 1950.

WAS THERE A DISTINCTIVE AMERICAN TECHNOLOGY?

Gibb and North are not the only ones to be persuaded that American technology had an early start; so is Habakkuk,* the English historian, in his fascinating theoretical analysis which unfortunately does not stand up under close scrutiny. Following the leads given him by a number of English observers in the 1850s, who commented favorably on American machines, Habakkuk is convinced that technology in the United States had to appear for the following reasons. The cost of labor was high because the entry of farmers into the lands of the Middle West was easy and cheap, and mechanization and improved productivity in agriculture made farming profitable. The pull of the land was felt particularly by America's (potentially) unskilled labor for those who went into the Middle West were eastern farmers and not workers; therefore the dearth of unskilled laborers—that is to say, the inelasticity of American, compared with British labor—forced up the price. (Habakkuk says money wages were at least 30 per cent higher in the United States, but the data are fragmentary and untrustworthy.) Thus the American entrepreneur —assuming that capital was available—was forced to replace labor with machines. The appearance of a machine-tools industry, which made possible the turning out of interchangeable parts, was a simultaneous phenomenon.

Machine-tools developed from early arms manufacture with which Eli Whitney and Simeon North were associated; and also from the needs of woodworking manufacture and the manufacture of locks, clocks and watches, New England industries as well. Habakkuk says that "the system of interchangeable parts" was "an autonomous invention." If this were so, there would have been a distinct American technology as much rising out of peculiar American conditions plus—said the English visitors of the 1850s—the better technical education of American workers and the extent of the American market. It wasn't so, for American technology was not unlike British technology—the ideas developed in Britain flowed across the ocean to be followed by English machines after the relaxation of the Acts of Trade and Navigation against their exportation in the 1840s.

Another important reason why an American technology, or, in fact, seriously competing American machinery and machine-tools industries, did not appear before the Civil War, was the dearness of capital in the

---

* H. J. Habakkuk, *American and British Technology in the Nineteenth Century,* 1962.

United States. Temin * points this out. Short-term interest rates for commercial paper in New England averaged 10.6 per cent annually in the 1830s, 8 per cent in the 1840s, and 8.5 per cent in the 1850s. (The rates for accommodation loans would have been higher.) This being so, for less capital had to be used, American machines were built more flimsily and became obsolescent more quickly. Habakkuk is aware of the makeshift character of the American machines, but he attributes this to the fact that the American entrepreneurs hastened obsolescence—they ran their machines faster and for longer hours, not only getting more work out of them but making possible their replacement sooner by better machines. Says Habakkuk:

> American manufacturers were readier than the English to scrap existing equipment and replace it by new, and they therefore had more opportunities of taking advantage of technical progress and acquiring know-how.

If Habakkuk is right, then American machines, embodying a superior technology, would have captured the American market and competed with English machines in world markets. They did not do so, and for this reason and the others cited, Temin is prepared to dismiss Habakkuk's general argument and its specific applications. And I agree.

WAS THE AMERICAN WORKER BETTER EDUCATED?

The English visitors of the 1850s made much of the "energy and education" of the American workers, in partial explanation of the high level of American technology. The American commitment to education was widely commented on and early reformers (city workingmen's parties among them) sought the expansion of the common school (financed by public authority) and the creation of workers' education programs (with the help of private philanthropy). The common school, teaching at the elementary level, got under way when the Massachusetts legislature in 1827 authorized local districts to support their schools from taxation. In 1834 a permanent state board of education was established; in this body, as its secretary, Horace Mann—the most eloquent proponent of free, universal, public education—had a forum and a platform, for his reports were read all over the land. Education would have social and moral accomplishments, and, with an amazing prescience that anticipated modern-day economists who emphasize the part played by "human capital" in growth, Mann predicted that such education would act

* Peter Temin, "Labor Scarcity and the Problem of American Industrial Efficiency in the 1850s," *The Journal of Economic History,* September 1966.

. . . as the grand agent for the development or augmentation of natural resources: [it was] more powerful in the production and gainful employment of the total wealth of the country than all the other things mentioned in the works of the political economists.

By 1860, in the North at any rate, the battle for the common school had been won; a majority of the states had provided for public education through the elementary grades. It was estimated that in 1850, in a total of 23.2 million whites, 3.6 million children and young people were enrolled in all types of educational institutions and that 3.4 million attended those publicly supported. There was still a long road to travel before all of Mann's hopes were to be implemented by these later devices —compulsory attendance, the lengthening of the school year and the school-leaving age, the inclusion of the secondary school in the common-school program, and the formal training of teachers in publicly financed "normal" schools.

The great leap forward in the exploration of these desiderata took place in the 35 years from the end of the Civil War to the turn of the century; consensuses among educationists were arrived at and formal responsibility by public authority accepted. Still another half-century had to go by, however, before state legislatures and municipal bodies (with citizens voting bond issues for capital improvements) were ready to furnish the necessary funds to accomplish such a grand design. (This does not mean that illiteracy did not exist among whites and tragically in greater numbers among blacks, to whom education was not made available.)

What may we conclude in the light of the claims made by the English visitors of the superiority of the American workingman because of his greater literacy? Granted the wide interest in education in the United States, it is impossible to prove (or refute) the point; in any event, it is unnecessary, for American technology was not that far ahead, if, indeed, it was abreast of British technology in the first half of the nineteenth century.

The same observation is in order with respect to workingmen's education in vocational and technical skills. There was a good deal of talk about this in the United States, but so there was in Britain, and it may very well be that America followed eagerly the discussions and experiments going on across the sea (in Switzerland first, then in England) and imitated rather than initiated.*

---

* What follows is largely based on the excellent (and only discussion we have) work of Charles Alpheus Bennett, *History of Manual and Industrial Education Up to 1870*, 1926.

The "manual labor" movement, which appeared in the United States around 1825, was much discussed for a decade with great enthusiasm and then cut down to size. It gained its inspiration from the ideas of Philip Emmanuel von Fellenberg, a Swiss, and Johann Heinrich Pestalozzi, another Swiss (but both inspired by Rousseau.) It was Fellenberg who in 1807, in conjunction with Pestalozzi, established a boarding academy at Hofwyl, near Berne, where instruction in agriculture and the manual arts (along with a classical curriculum as well as a "modern" one in the sciences and mathematics) was to be furnished the children of the well-to-do. Thought was also given to the less privileged, and a farm-and-trade school was set up at which students could work off the costs of their instruction, board, and lodging.

It was the latter feature of Fellenberg's scheme that Americans seized on: instruction and work for poor boys of the middle class; theological seminaries led the way, the first being Andover in 1826, whose success encouraged other similar efforts. The idea then percolated down to private secondary schools; the Maine Wesleyan Seminary (really an academy) ran a farm and "mechanical shop" in which chair making, cabinet work, and the construction of tools took place along with an academic curriculum.

Private philanthropy was inspired also by the Fellenberg experiment, but here the interest was in the "poor"—those who had strayed and fallen foul of the law (industrial reform schools were established for them) and the children of workers who had been orphaned (in their case, manual labor schools). One pioneer school was the Farm and Trade School of Boston, founded in 1814. Girard College (an academy) made possible by the munificent gift of $2 million left in the will of the great Philadelphia merchant Stephen Girard for the education of "white male orphans" was outstanding. Opening in 1848, Girard College offered, in addition to academic subjects, instruction in carpentry, typesetting, printing, book binding, photography, and electrotyping. Bennett records a large number of orphan schools in the United States in 1850. New York alone had six.

New York philanthropists were pioneers in opening a House of Refuge for juvenile offenders on Randall's Island in 1824, at which boys and girls, many younger than 14 years, were taught academic subjects for three hours and also put to work, presumably to learn a trade. Similar schools appeared in Philadelphia and Boston. The laudable intentions of the well-meaning, however, were not realized. A report made to the New York legislature in 1867 pointed out that the accent in these "industrial reformatories" had shifted from preparation for a trade to keeping the children busy—to train them in the habits of industry, said the governors and matrons of the schools. All of this came to nothing—along with so many of the other noble "reform" ideas of the high-flying transcendentalists of the period.

Workers' education—mechanics' institutes—was something else again. This movement started in England to give instruction to the "laboring classes"—in chemistry, mechanics, geometry, farriery, architecture, and mechanical and architectural drawing. Bennett ran down such a school in England as early as 1800. Doctor George Birkbeck put such schools on their feet when he founded the London Mechanics Institute in 1824, with a sound course of study. The idea spread throughout England and Scotland, and by 1841 (says Bennett) there were 216 of these establishments in Great Britain at which 25,000 student-workers were enrolled. Two things emerged from Birkbeck's efforts: technical colleges (academies) for full-time day students; and night colleges (at the university level) for workers who were willing to carry on an academic curriculum after a day's labor. The London Mechanics' Institute became Birkbeck College, formally affiliated with London University, to give instruction at night and, more important, offer examinations and grant external degrees on the basis of home study (correspondence courses).

American schemes never attained the ambitious proportions of the Birkbeck program. They did, however, have a wide reach, having in mind that attendance was voluntary and that a good deal of the lecturing to "mechanics and artisans" was bound to become popular in content and unsystematic in structure. The first American prototype was the General Society of Mechanics and Tradesmen of New York which, in 1820, opened a library for apprentices and established a "mechanics school." The Franklin Institute of Philadelphia, founded in 1824, had a library and provided lectures on scientific subjects. A similar society, set up in Boston in 1827, had as its object "mutual instruction in the sciences as connected with the mechanic arts." (The word "mutual" is to be noted; much of American adult education, unlike the British, took on this characteristic. As recently as the 1950s adults formed together in small reading circles with their own leaders to study "Great Books" and, presumably, to "learn" from conversation.)

From these beginnings developed the Lyceum Movement, first propounded by Josiah Holbrook, a Yale graduate, in the late 1820s. His plan, known as "The American Lyceum of Science and the Arts," was designed to give popular instruction to adults in "useful and practical knowledge" and called for the creation of local societies to be linked into a national federation. Holbrook founded the first lyceum in 1826; by 1832 there were as many as 1000 groups scattered over the country. Annual national conventions were held to bind them together in a common purpose. The

movement spread overseas and became just as popular in England as in
the United States. Holbrook himself manufactured scientific apparatus
for the lyceums and edited *Scientific Tracts*, a journal whose title high-
lighted the true emphasis of the movement.

The Lyceums organized lectures and sponsored study groups, but
instruction was to be "principally by discussion and conversation." The
members were to get their own books and furnish apparatus and collections of minerals or "other articles of natural or artificial production."
According to Holbrook, the societies were to hold meetings

> for the purpose of investigating and discussing subjects of knowledge, and
> may choose for discussion any branch of Natural Philosophy such as Me-
> chanics, Hydrolics, Pneumatics, Optics, Chemistry, Mineralogy, Botany, the
> Mathematics, History, Geography, Astronomy, Agriculture, Morals, Do-
> mestic or Political Economy, or any other subject of useful information.

The Lyceums, as such, went the way of other such movements—
their life span was short—but their influence was not to be underesti-
mated. They (and their successors—the Chatauqua movement toward the
end of the century was one form; private correspondence schools in the
"mechanical arts" was another) showed the great interest of American
adults in continuing education in science and more particularly in applied science. Out of them grew formal programs of education (for
young people, however, and as full-time day students) in engineering,
agriculture, and mechanics. In other words, private engineering schools
and the land-grant colleges, popularly known as A. and M. colleges, were
among the consequences of this interest and activity in "investigating and
discussing subjects of useful knowledge."

One observation, in passing, to tie all this in with the presumed
superiority of the American worker and a unique American technology.
These things were going on in Britain and in the United States simultaneously, ideas to stimulate them appearing in one country or the other
but with imitation quickly following. To this extent the workingmen of
both countries thought much the same and set up similar programs,
whether they were mechanics' institutes, libraries, scientific collections,
or Lyceums.

At one point the United States went ahead—and this must be considered an important factor in American technological superiority over
Britain in the *second* half of the nineteenth century—in the establishment of engineering (really applied science) schools beyond the secondary
level. It was here that the great difference between Britain and America
emerged. Britain sought to train its engineers by the apprenticeship
method (with the inevitable restriction of entry); the United States, by

formal education in schools which, after 1862 with the creation of the land-grant colleges, received public financial support. The first American engineering program was introduced at the United States Military Academy at West Point in 1817; the second (though short-lived) at the Gardiner (Maine) Lyceum in 1823, which started as a manual-labor school and, like the mechanics' institutes, offered short-term courses in the applied sciences. It also established a full-time scientific and technical school with a three-year curriculum that included mathematics, mechanics, chemistry, agricultural chemistry, civil engineering, and architecture. Gardiner shut down in 1833 when the state legislature withdrew its support; but the Rensselaer Polytechnic Institute of Troy, New York, founded in 1824 by private philanthropy, survived.

Rensselaer, which started modestly enough, sought to teach in the popular and familiar language of the day "the sons and daughters of farmers and mechanics" "the application of science to the common purposes of life." In 1835 Rensselaer set up a department of "mathematical arts" to give instruction in engineering and technology and it was soon graduating civil engineers. Liberal arts colleges watched these experiments closely and then installed science curriculums of their own—again America was far ahead of Britain: Union College in 1845, Yale (the Sheffield Scientific School) in 1847, Harvard (the Lawrence Scientific School) in the same year, and Dartmouth (the Chandler Scientific School) in 1852, followed by the University of Michigan. By the outbreak of the Civil War 600 civil engineers had been graduated; Rensselaer was responsible for 318 and West Point, for 200. Departments in mechanical engineering were to follow as soon as the war was over.

There is no doubt that the inspiration for the land-grant colleges came from this earlier interest (fed by the Lyceums) in agricultural and mechanical education. The idea of federal support of "industrial universities" originated in Illinois, the progenitor being J. B. Turner, the president of the Illinois State Teacher's Institute. In 1850 he delivered an address called "A State University for Industrial Classes," which he repeated a number of times to large audiences and which was taken up widely by farmers' organizations, agricultural journals, and many newspapers. Turner concerned himself with "the educational needs of the industrial classes of society," differentiating them from the professional (i.e., middle) classes. Instruction was to be for "thinking laborers" and should include

> all those studies and sciences, of whatever sort, which tend to throw light upon any art or employment which any student may desire to master, or upon any duty he may be called to perform, or which may tend to secure his moral, civil, social, and industrial perfection as a man.

The idea of using federal land grants to found such "universities" came from the Illinois legislature in 1854, which so memorialized Congress. These notions were the origin of Congressman Justin S. Morrill's measure, which he introduced in 1857. His first bill passed the lower house but failed in the Senate. His second, in 1859, carried in both houses but was vetoed by President Buchanan. His third was passed in 1862 and signed by President Lincoln. Thus the famous A. and M. colleges ("to teach such branches of learning as are related to agriculture and the mechanic arts") were born. Michigan (1857) and Pennsylvania (1859) did not wait for Congress to act. Illinois, under the Morrill Act, named its institution significantly the "Illinois Industrial University," later to become the University of Illinois. In time these A. and M. colleges were to be found in almost all the states; some (and not only in the South) established separate ones for Negroes. These schools turned out more engineers than agronomists; in fact, engineering education in the United States in the fourth quarter of the nineteenth century was being conducted largely in these state institutions made possible by the rich bounty of the federal land grants.

VIII

THE SOUTHERN PLANTATION ECONOMY

WAS THE SOUTHERN SLAVE SYSTEM A PROFITABLE ONE?

In June 1905 Ulrich B. Phillips, a highly reputable southern historian, published in *The Political Science Quarterly* his article "The Economic Cost of Slaveholding in the Cotton Belt" and opened a debate that has continued for more than 60 years. Presenting two schedules of figures— the price of prime field hands compared with the average New York price of upland cotton—he came to the conclusion that slave ownership was unprofitable and that the plantation system, with which it was linked, was doomed. Slaves were being overcapitalized, as evidenced by the meteoric rise in slave prices, slave labor was inefficient (because of the inherent incapacity of the Negroes), and the additional costs of maintaining all Negroes when they were unproductive—the very young, the sick and incapacitated, the aged—contributed to the same conclusion. The ante-bellum southern planters were hoist with their own petard: having expanded into the rich lands of the Gulf and Delta states and the Southwest to grow the single staple cotton almost exclusively, and of necessity using slaves in the plantation system for this purpose, they were the alleged beneficiaries but in reality the victims of a society they had created. Because, held Phillips, the Negroes were inferior and needed supervision of the minutest kind in their labor and care when they were young, incapacitated, or old, the South had to defend its "peculiar institution" and fight for its expansion. In effect, it did not know what else to do with the four million blacks (largely slaves, to be found almost entirely in the South) to which the Negroes had grown by 1860.

Phillips pointed to these facts to make his case:

The average New York price of upland cotton during 1795–1805 was 30 cents a pound and by the 1850s had fallen to 11 cents. The average price of a prime field hand (male between 18 and 30 years of age) had been $450 in 1800 and had risen to $1800 by 1860. In 1800 a prime field hand was worth in the market about 1500 pounds of cotton; in 1845, 12,000 pounds; and in 1860, 15,000 to 18,000 pounds.

And said Phillips:

> . . . the ten-fold or twelve-fold multiplication of the price of slaves, when quoted in terms of the product of their labor [i.e., ginned cotton], was too great to be explained except by reference to the severe competition of the planters in selling cotton and in buying slaves. Their system of capitalized labor was out of place in the modern competitive world. . . . In other words, when capital and labor were combined, as in the American slaveholding system, there was an irresistible tendency to overvalue and overcapitalize slave labor, and to carry it to the point where the financial equilibrium was unsafe, and any crisis threatened complete bankruptcy.

The capital fund (its inelasticity) was in effect immobilized in slave ownership. Phillips went on:

> Circulating capital was at once converted into fixed capital; while for their annual supplies of food, implements and luxuries, the planters continued to rely upon their credit with the local merchants, and the local merchants to rely upon their credit with northern merchant-bankers.

The plantation system (I had called it *planter capitalism* as early as 1940 in my *Triumph of American Capitalism*) produced a great staple, cotton (and to a lesser extent sugar, rice, and hemp), for the world market. Except for corn (as feed for its work animals, mules and oxen, and as the basis of the slave diet), the South was dependent on local suppliers or the West for its wheat and beef and on other markets for its livestock, work animals, and implements. It therefore had to pay heavily for credit and its purchases. It should be noted, further, that the ratio of prices paid to prices received was dropping adversely, for during the 1850s, when the price of cotton remained around 11 cents a pound, wholesale prices rose 34 per cent from 1851 to 1857 and at an annual average of 18.4 per cent from 1851 to 1860.

Said Phillips further:

Negro slave labor was expensive not so much because it was unwilling as because it was overcapitalized and inelastic. The Negro of himself, by reason of his inherited inaptitude, was inefficient as a self-directing laborer in civilized society. . . . to make him play a valuable part in it, strict guidance and supervision were essential. Without the plantation system, the mass of the Negroes would have been an unbearable burden on America. . . . the Negro slave was a Negro first, last and always, and a slave incidentally.

Phillips agreed that these factors contributed to the drop in the price of cotton by the 1850s: costs were lower because of improvements in cultivating, ginning, and marketing. (He might have added the drop in oceanic freight rates to Liverpool, the world's primary market for cotton, and the increase in competitive growing areas outside the United States, so that Liverpool was handling, and the Lancashire cotton mills had available for spinning, a good deal more ginned cotton than the American supply alone.)

These factors contributed to the rise in slave prices: better supervision of the work of slaves on plantations under the overseer and gang-labor system; the bidding up of slave prices, and the greater use of slaves in Virginia because the revival of tobacco growing and manufacture in that state, beginning in the 1840s, diminished the number of Negroes that could be sold into the Lower South. (He might have added increased demand for skilled slaves or artisans who were rented out usually on the hire system, in construction, factory work—tobacco, cotton textiles, and iron—and in the handicrafts as masons, blacksmiths, carpenters, and the like.) In short, the plantation South was confronted by inelasticity of supply and elasticity of demand. Phillips gave these figures for slave hire in middle Georgia: 1800, $100 a year; 1816, $110; 1833, $140; 1860, $150, and in Virginia, 1860, $225. Skilled artisans in 1860 were commanding $500–$600. Hired slaves, particularly in the cities, were given cash bonuses and often incentive payments for good performance, so much so that not a few Negroes were able to buy their manumission out of their savings. (A matter of great embarrassment to the South, incidentally, for it disproved the contention of the defenders of slavery that the Negroes were inferior and could work only at simple tasks and, at that, under the strictest discipline.)

Phillips—unfriendly as he was to the Negroes as Negroes, yet aware of the damage slavery had done to the South—ended almost on a note of Götterdämmerung:

Cotton and slavery were peculiar to the South, and their requirements were often in conflict with the interests and ideas prevailing in other parts of the United States. [Elsewhere Phillips had also said, "slavery was an obstacle to all progress" in the South as well.] As that conflict of interests and sentiments was accentuated, it became apparent that the South was in a congressional minority, likely at any time to be over-ridden by a northern majority. Ruin was threatening the vested interests and the social order in the South; and the force of circumstances drove the southern politicians into the policy of resistance. To the leaders in the South, with their ever-present view of the possibility of Negro uprisings, the regulations of slavery seemed essential for safety and prosperity. And when they found themselves about to become powerless to check any legislation hostile to the established order in the South, they adopted the policy of secession, seeking, as they saw it, the lesser of the evils confronting them. . . . To be rid of the capitalization of labor as a part of the slaveholding system was a great requisite for the material progress of the South.

This is magnificent; for Phillips was not talking of profitability alone, with cotton growing as a business, but of the viability of the whole South as a way of life, a morality, a politics, a psychology. This is what Marx meant by historical materialism: that the relations of production created their own superstructure and the habits of thought and conduct reflected these relations and inevitably defended them.

These things Conrad and Meyer,* then at Harvard University, did not understand—as they still did not as late as 1967. Using all the elegant (and frequently untrustworthy) devices of contemporary econometric methodology and reconstruction, and with Keynes as their guide, they set out to prove both the profitability of slavery and, in fact, the viability of the southern economy.

They explained their method in this fashion. Slavery was to be analyzed in terms of two production functions having to do largely with the growth of cotton: the first related to the inputs of Negro slaves, that is, their value and the materials required to maintain them; the second to the inputs of the "intermediate good," that is, the breeding of slave labor by child-bearing Negro females. Then their hypothesis: slavery was "an efficient, maintainable form of economic organization," and this was to be tested in the following Keynesian terms:

. . . by putting appropriate values on the variables in the production functions and computing the rate of return over cost, the stream of income over the lifetime of the slave. This rate of return, the marginal efficiency of slave capital, must, in turn, be shown to be at least equal to the rate of interest currently available in the American capital markets.

The refinements of calculation (and guessing) need not be entered into here. Enough to say that a good deal of bickering ensued—most of

* Alfred H. Conrad and John R. Meyer, "Economics of Slavery in the Ante-Bellum South," *The Journal of Political Economy,* April and October 1958.

it really inconsequential—among other econometricians who rushed into the fray. In any case, Conrad and Meyer assumed that they had proved their hypothesis in little and in the large:

1. Slavery was about as remunerative as alternate employments to which slave capital could have been invested.

2. Although great planters made "large or excessive" returns, small planters did not suffer.

3. Slavery was profitable to the whole South because of the efficiency of regional specialization (the rich regions grew the staples, the poor bred and sold their surplus Negroes.)

4. "General sharing in the prosperity" of the South was guaranteed if proper marketing mechanisms existed (and the authors were satisfied they were) for the breeding and movement of slaves "on the poorest land" (i.e., the Old South) to the best (i.e., the Lower South). The selling states were Virginia, Maryland, Delaware, South Carolina, Missouri, Kentucky, and the District of Columbia. The buying states were Georgia, Alabama, Mississippi, Florida, Louisiana, and Texas. Conrad and Meyer were not sure of Arkansas, North Carolina, and Tennessee.

5. Slavery, in the immediate ante-bellum years was therefore an economically viable institution in virtually all areas of the South.

And this grand conclusion:

The slave-plantation system produced not only a viable economy in the whole South but it was capable of fostering growth and development. Conrad and Meyer must be quoted in full, for what they ended in saying inevitably followed from their methodology and theory (and their limitations):

> The available productive surplus from slavery might have been used for economic development or, as in totalitarian regimes in this century, for militarism. In spite of this good omen for development, southern investment and industrialization lagged. It is hard to explain this except on the social ground that entrepreneurship could not take root in the South or on the economic ground that the South did not really own the system but merely operated it. Furthermore, the American experience clearly suggests that slavery is not, from the strict economic standpoint, a deterrent to industrial development and that its elimination may take more than the workings of "inexorable economic forces." Although profitability cannot be offered as a sufficient guaranty of the continuity of southern slavery, the converse argument that slavery must have destroyed itself can no longer rest upon allegations of unprofitability or upon assumptions about the impossibility of maintaining and allocating a slave labor force.

THE SLAVE SOUTH NOT A VIABLE SYSTEM

The Achilles heel in the Conrad and Meyer analysis—that the slave-plantation system was a viable one and therefore conducive to economic development—was struck at at once by one economist (Douglas Dowd) and two historians (Eugene D. Genovese and H. D. Woodman). Of course, these three critics had been anticipated in a general sense by Phillips and Gray.* Gray had examined in the greatest detail every aspect of the southern ante-bellum economy; one has to read Gray first before embarking on any speculations about the South. Gray himself ended flatly with this judgment:

> Although slavery was profitable from an individual point of view and for certain uses conferred a competitive superiority as compared with free labor, its ultimate influence upon the economic well-being of the South was pernicious.

Gray in his concluding observations reviewed what he had said earlier in his first volume in extenso: that the tendency of the commercial plantations to stress maximum current money income was not conducive to wealth accumulation; that the plantation economy had involved the neglect of the soil; that the whole system stimulated extravagance in the planting class, of necessity, for consumptive living was an evidence of status and racial superiority; and that the slave-plantation system concentrated the greater part of the money income of the South in the hands of a small class. In consequence "a large proportion of the remaining white population were pushed into isolated regions where they pursued a largely self-sufficing economy." White immigration had been discouraged, and the sparseness of the free population made it difficult to develop roads, schools, and churches. White artisans were under an especial disability because of the "social stigma" associated with human labor. Gray's final two sentences were these:

> Slavery . . . retarded the development of the compensating conditions [of expansion]—immigration and industrial diversification—which in the North alleviated the "growing pains" of agricultural expansion. Hence we have the near-paradox of an economic institution competitively effective under certain conditions, but essentially regressive in its influence on the socio-economic evolution of the section where it prevailed.

One notes the phrase "socio-economic evolution," for by this is meant the modern-day concept "economic development" (which Conrad

* L. C. Gray, *History of Agriculture in the Southern United States to 1860*, 1933, 2 vols.

and Meyer had to use to prove viability). The quote a typical definition,*

> . . . at the most general level, "economic development" may be defined as a sustained secular improvement in material well-being, which we may consider to be reflected in an increasing flow of goods and services. Perhaps, as an aside, it should be noted that while the *definition* of economic development is cast in material terms, the *study* of this subject is concerned with those changes—social, cultural, political, as well as economic—which contribute to or impede material progress. [Italics original.]

It is this idea of socio-economic evolution, as the key to development, that the more percipient critics of Conrad and Meyer have stressed.†

Douglas Dowd was the first to challenge Conrad and Meyer when they read their paper at a conference in September 1957. Dowd knew why entrepreneurship (and "the basic elements of capitalist society") had not taken root in the South, if Conrad and Meyer, as they admitted, did not. Said he:

> If profits were made from the slave system, it was at a price; the domination of southern society by the slave issue. This in turn meant the suppression of that kind of social rationality which has been, for better or for worse, associated with the development of industrial capitalism.

Slavery was a deterrent to economic development, even assuming its profitability. Dowd went on:

> A society where wealth is derived from plantation economy does not tend, as does an industrial society, to push its prosperity down through all the layers of the population. . . . [It is compelled to develop an ideology] to buttress that which was materially inimical to the well-being of the mass of the people. That is, an irrational ideology had to dominate the mind of

---

* Bernard Okun and R. W. Richardson, *Studies in Economic Development*, 1961.
† The recent discussion has its *vade mecum* in S. L. Engerman's "The Effects of Slavery Upon the Southern Economy: A Recent Debate," in *Explorations in Entrepreneurial History: Second Series*, (Winter 1967). Engerman, a Conrad-Meyer partisan, reviews all the literature. Other places in which discussants have had their say are in Alfred H. Conrad and John R. Meyer, *The Economics of Slavery*, 1964; H. D. Woodman, Ed., *Slavery and the Southern Economy*, 1966, and his article "The Profitability of Slavery: A Historical Perennial" in *J. Southern Hist.* (August 1963); E. D. Genovese, *The Political Economy of Slavery*, 1965, which contains all his articles; and "Slavery as an Obstacle to Economic Growth in the United States: A Panel Discussion," *J. Econ. Hist.* (December 1967). I say, in little, much the same as Genovese says in "The New Revolution in Economic History," *Explorations in Entrepreneurial History: Second Series*, (Spring 1966). See also my *Triumph of American Capitalism*, 1940.

the South . . . or the Old South would be destroyed by internal and external pressures.

In December 1967, as reported in *The Journal of Economic History,* Dowd was even clearer in his rejection of viability and development as achievements of the slave-plantation as an economy and a way of life. Said Dowd, distinguishing between growth (quantitative change) and development (qualitative change), as the terms are currently being used by economists:

> It is of course reasonably obvious that in any functioning social system, slave or otherwise, there will be incomes that are high at the top and decrease as one moves to the bottom of the social scale; and that power will be roughly proportionate to income and wealth. What is less obvious are the costs of a given system—costs in terms of alternatives foregone, as well as the social and human costs of the existent reality.
>
> For the South, it surely was good business sense that led planters to emphasize cotton cultivation, slaveholding, and slave-breeding; and good business sense was also good economic sense, if the short run and the interests of those in power are taken as guiding criteria. But when we speak of economic development it is not business sense or economic sense for the short run as viewed by those in power that are, or should be, taken as the appropriate referents for judgment; for then we are speaking not only of structural realities and changes in the economy, but also of far reaching social and political structures and changes. . . .
>
> To say that slavery was profitable and yet it inhibited economic development is not to say that slavery but that slave society in the United States in the nineteenth century, during and after its existence, inhibited economic development. But this is to say something else: both before and after emancipation, social, economic, and political power in the South was held by those who had helped to create, and fought to maintain, slavery. . . . For the South to develop economically, it was essential—and it is essential—either for a social upheaval within the South to take place and/or for steady pressures, positive and negative, to be introduced from "outside." Power—its sources and uses—has to be changed, that is, its possessors have to be changed.

H. D. Woodman, a historian, said essentially the same thing, although in less sophisticated fashion. He rallied to the support of Phillips, who, he said properly, had not talked only of profitability but of the destructive consequences of a way of life—of a polity, society, and economy. So did Genovese, who knew his Marx and his Keynes and used both to undermine the crude determinism of Conrad and Meyer. Genovese ranged widely over the whole ante-bellum southern scene, discussing with confidence and proof a score and more evidences of the failures of the southern planters to create a viable system. They could not maintain the fertility of their lands. They could not breed an efficient livestock. Southern slave labor, perforce, resulted in low productivity because, among other things, the inadequate diets fed the slaves resulted in malnutrition, protein hunger, and low vitality. The nonslaveholding whites were at their mercy: if they raised some cotton, they had to accept the charges of the planter for ginning and his price for the sale of the crop; if they raised nonstaples (corn, wheat, hogs, cattle, work animals), their market was the nearby planter and not that of an urban center. Says Genovese: "Thus the paternalism of the planters toward their slaves was reinforced by the semipaternal relationship between the planters and their neighbors." No wonder the so-called yeoman farmers were "politically, economically, and socially backward."

This is what Genovese had to say about the slave-owning class:

> The planters commanded southern politics and set the tone of social life. Theirs was an aristocratic, antibourgeois spirit with values and mores emphasizing family and status, a strong code of honor, and aspirations to luxury, ease, and accomplishment. . . . Slavery established the basis of the planter's position and power. It measured his affluence, marked his status, and supplied leisure for social graces and aristocratic duties.

These were the economic consequences:

> A low level of capital accumulation, the planter's high propensity to consume luxuries, a shortage of liquid capital aggravated by the steady drain of funds out of the region, the low productivity of slave labor, the need to concentrate on a few staples, the anti-industrial, anti-urban ideology of the dominant planters, the reduction of southern banking, industry, and commerce to the position of auxiliaries of the plantation economy—these are familiar.

In Keynesian terms, the low level of demand—caused by the skewed income distribution and the virtual impoverishment of the great majority of the nonslaveholding whites—was an outstanding reason for the retardation of economic growth. No internal market could develop and, in consequence, no proper transportation system, no diversification of agriculture, nor the creation of a broad base of local industries, trade, and services. In Marshallian terms, the external economies of urbanization and industrialization were not available to the slave-plantation South.

Two further comments may be made concerning the Conrad and Meyer analysis, one particular, the other general.

First, it was not true, as they assumed, that their second production function—the breeding and sale of slaves—had complete market mobility.

One should note that the internal movement by sale of Negroes reached its high point in the 1830s, declined sharply in the 1840s and in the 1850s was less than it had been two decades before. Further, not only were there social reasons (distaste of the domestic slave trade) for this but there were economic ones (the growing expansion of the hire system and the use of Negroes as artisans and for labor in railroad construction, mining, lumbering, and textile mills and tobacco factories). The hire system as well as the demands of the Lower South for more plantation hands bid up the price of Negroes. Therefore it was no accident that, beginning in 1854, in every southern commercial convention, there should appear a demand for the reopening of the African slave trade (which had been outlawed in 1808).*

Second, the southern world had all the characteristics of a Marxian model of a pyramidal class society—and not the simple one of slave users and slave breeders conjured up by Conrad and Meyer. At the peak was the tiny ruling elite, the large planters; the middle stratum was made up of yeoman farmers who owned a few Negroes or were entirely nonslaveholding; and at the bottom were the completely dispossessed, the Negro slaves and the "poor whites." H. R. Helper, a North Carolinian, in his *Impending Crisis of the South,* 1857, saw this clearly. Of the nonslaveholders (the great majority of southern whites) who were as much as the victims of the class system as the Negroes, Helper said: "Never were the poorer classes of a people, and these classes so largely in the majority . . . so basely duped, so adroitly swindled, or so damnably outraged." The Civil War Radical Republicans were also aware of these conditions. Not only do Conrad and Meyer show no grasp of the character of the southern white society and the antagonisms that had developed within it, they even—in an effort to account for the failure of the South to "develop"—adopt the highly dubious Leninist thesis "that the South did not really own the system but merely operated it."

THE SOUTHERN CLASS SOCIETY

The invention of the cotton gin in 1793 made possible the commercial growth of cotton as a staple crop, but it was not until the Peace of Ghent (1814), which ended the second war with Britain, that the movement of planters and slaves into the Lower South began on a mass scale. The constantly expanding demand in England for cotton, the fertility of the

* I discuss this in great detail, indeed, the first historian to have done so, in *Triumph of American Capitalism,* 1940.

regions around the Gulf and in the Mississippi Delta, the availability of slave labor for the simple task of plowing, chopping, and picking (thus furnishing almost year-round employment) gave a great spurt to the settlement of the Lower South—and the domestic trade in slaves. Congress formally prohibited the African importation of Negroes in 1808; in 1820 it declared engagement in this unholy business an act of piracy. Yet it is estimated that 270,000 Negroes were smuggled into the country during 1808–1860. However, the Lower South's supply came from the domestic trade—the surpluses of Negroes of the Old South and the border states which were sold to planters in South Carolina, Georgia, Alabama, Mississippi, Tennessee, Louisiana, and Texas. Between 1820 and 1860, according to Gray, who quotes W. H. Collins writing in 1904, 742,000 Negroes were transferred in this fashion.

In consequence, the cotton crop doubled from 1815 (209,000 bales) to 1822, doubled again by 1826, and once more between 1830 and 1837. In 1859 the crop was 4.5 million bales (of 450 pounds each). In 1801 almost all of the crop had been raised in the Old South—in upper South Carolina, central Georgia, Virginia, and North Carolina. In 1826 more than one-half the crop was still grown there, but by 1859 the proportion had fallen to less than one-fourth and Mississippi alone was growing more than the entire older region. In 1859 the crop in Mississippi was 1.2 million bales, in Alabama, 1 million, in Louisiana, 777,000, in Georgia, 701,000, in Texas, 431,000, in Arkansas, 367,000, in South Carolina, 353,000, in Tennessee, 296,000, in North Carolina, 146,000, and in Virginia, 12,000.

The penetration of cotton is shown by the proportion of the slaves to the total population in some districts of high growth. (See Table 27. The figures are L. C. Gray's.)

TABLE 27

DISTRICTS OF HIGH COTTON GROWTH IN THE SOUTH AND SLAVES,
1820–1860

	1820	1860
Central Alabama	46.4%	66.4%
Yazoo Delta, Mississippi	—	89.2%
Alluvial cotton parishes, Louisiana	68.1%	86.2%
Alluvial cotton counties, Arkansas	12.1%	66.2%
Red River Valley, Arkansas	21.4%	43.2%

The cotton kingdom, along with the lesser ones of sugar, rice, to-bacco, and hemp, became a slave kingdom as well. While the rest of the country was ridding itself of its bondsmen (only 18 Negro slaves were recorded in the Northeast), the South in 1860 had 3.95 million slaves. For the section as a whole about one out of every three inhabitants was a Negro slave; in the Lower South the proportion was 45 per cent.

According to the Census of 1860, in the South (the eleven seceding states and the four border states) only 383,635 white families (one-fourth of the total white population) owned the 3.95 million Negro slaves. How great the concentration was may be had from the figures in Table 28. The plantation lords owned 50 slaves or more; the middle-sized planters between 20 and 50. These were the well-to-do members of the southern aristocracy. Between them they constituted 12 per cent of the owners and possessed 52 per cent of the slaves. Those who owned nine or fewer slaves were largely general farmers who also raised some of the planta-tion crops; they made up 72 per cent of the owners but possessed only 25 per cent of the slaves. (See Table 28.)

TABLE 28

DISTRIBUTION OF SLAVES BY CONCENTRATION OF OWNERSHIP, 1860
(In thousands)

No. of Slaves Held	No. of Holders	Per cent of All Holders	No. of Persons in Holding Families	Per cent of White Popula-tion in Families	No. of Slaves Held	Per cent of Total Slaves
50 and over	10.7	3.0	—	—	827.0	21.0
20 and over	46.3	12.1	231.4	2.9	2,055.9	52.0
10–19	61.7	16.1	308.4	3.9	895.4	23.0
5–9	89.4	23.3	447.1	5.6	995.5	25.0
1–4	186.3	48.5	931.3	11.8		
Totals	383.6	100.0	1,938.2	24.2	3,946.8	100.0

Source. B. B. Kendrick and A. M. Arnett, *The South Looks at its Past*, 1935, p. 42.

What of the southern yeomanry who presumably constituted the south's middle class, owning no slaves or only a handful and making up at least 75 per cent of the South's white population? They were general farmers: some lived in the neighborhoods of the planters (as here defined) and raised a small amount of cotton, and also hay, corn, wheat, hogs, cattle, and vegetables, for which they found local markets. The larger number, however, because of the paucity of towns (and therefore banks) and the absence of interior means of communication—roads and rail-roads—were for the most part self-sufficing farmers who either owned or rented or who were squatters on public land. They produced some cash crops—cattle being the most important—and occasionally brought them to market. It is Gray's estimate that as many as 40 per cent of the nonslaveholding whites were not property holders.

There is sharp disagreement among historians about their status. Professor Owsley * of Vanderbilt University and a group of his students, by examining the census schedules or reporting sheets in a number of selected southern regions, came to these conclusions. That these "very considerable" middle-class farmers enjoyed economic and social well-being in the South; that ownership of land and slaves was well distributed among them; that sizable numbers of them, who started out by being nonslaveholders, were able to move upward and become owners, and that the soil they tilled was comparable in quality to that of their richer, slave-owning neighbors. Finally, in the 1850s all strata among the white farmers, particularly those at the lower levels, were prospering and expanding.

All this has been rejected by Linden † who went over the same ground as the Vanderbilt group (sections in Alabama, Louisiana, and Mississippi) and found their methods faulty and some of their assump-tions highly dubious. He doubted, for example, that those nonslave-holders who presumably lived among the planters had lands of equal quality: the census takers, he found, were not careful in recording the exact locations of all those they were reporting. The same was true of property ownership. Linden says:

> From that questionable proposition [that property holding was "well distributed"] the authors have drawn fallacious statistical inferences, in-validly bridging the specific and the general. Indisputably, a significant section of the ante-bellum population consisted of small and medium-sized property holders, but in the areas studied their relative numerical importance is somewhat less than the authors suggest, and their share of the section's operating income was considerably less than their numbers warranted. The large plantation holder, as in the orthodox view, controlled excessive pro-portions of the labor and land wealth.

At the bottom of the white social scale were the "poor whites," the denizens of "Tobacco Road" of modern parlance. How many they were

* F. L. Owsley, *Plain Folk of the Old South*, 1949.
† Fabian Linden, "Economic Democracy in the Slave South: An Appraisal of Some Recent Views," *Journal of Negro History*, April 1946.

there is no means of telling. Kendrick and Arnett * declare that they
made up a "decided minority" of the nonslaveholders, yet they admit that
"the poor whites" and the yeoman farmers "shaded imperceptibly together." According to these authors, the "poor whites" lived largely in the
infertile lands of the coastal plain, but many undoubtedly were to be
found in the pine barrens and sand hills into which they drifted when
the more fertile areas (the "black belts" and "delta regions") were taken
over by commercial planters. These were the impoverished of the white
South, who owned no land or land virtually uncultivable, produced
nothing for cash, the victims, say Kendrick and Arnett, "of poverty and
poor soil but more especially, it seems, of malaria and hookworm." These
were the "clay eaters"—dirt was actually eaten because the ravishes of
hookworm and inadequate diet did lead to a craving for clay. In any
event, all the nonslaveholding whites, of course, were not "poor whites,"
but poverty was much more widespread among the whites than modern-
day defenders of the ante-bellum South would like to have us believe.
There can be no doubt that these people, along with the Negroes, were
the victims of the slave system—not only because of the concentration of
wealth and income in the hands of a few but as much because the South
spent so little on its infrastructure, i.e., its interior means of transportation, education, health, and other social services.

THE SOUTH A POLICE STATE

The South also took on all the characteristics of a police state. On the
large plantations, under the supervision of white overseers, elaborate
police regulations for the slaves were drawn up and enforced. Says Gray:
"stealing, lying, adultery, fornication, profane language, fighting, and
quarreling" were punished—usually with the lash. There were curfew
hours for bedtime, and Negroes could not leave the plantation without
written permission. They could not marry off the plantation. Negro
preachers were not allowed, and Negroes could not trade, traffic, or bar-
ter, nor could they raise livestock.

The law, as enacted into statutes by legislatures and enforced by
the courts had a different kind of code for the blacks. This code included
the following: trading with slaves was prohibited; they could not own
domestic animals (occasional exceptions were made of cats and dogs);
persons trying to educate Negroes were to be fined; and it was unlawful
for more than five male slaves to congregate. The whites, particularly in

* B. B. Kendrick and A. M. Arnett, *The South Looks at Its Past*, 1935.

the lower South, lived in fear of slave uprisings and the burnings and murder that accompanied them. (There were many more such occurrences than the South was ready to admit.) To be on guard both the slaveowning and nonslaveholding whites served in a patrol system to preserve peace and order. All males, eligible for military duty, were called on to join these patrols, which were made up of detachments of three to five armed men who moved around on horseback and took regular turns of duty.

DuBois,* the Negro sociologist, thus summed up the legal position of the slaves:

> Slaves were not considered men. They had no right of petition. They were "devisable like any other chattel." They could own nothing; they could make no contracts; they could hold no property, nor traffic in property; they could not hire out; they could not legally marry nor constitute families; they could not control their children; they could not appeal from their master; they could be punished at will. They could not testify in court; they could be imprisoned by their owners, and the criminal offense of assault and battery could not be committed on the person of a slave. . . . A slave could not sue his master; had no right to redemption; no right to education or religion; a promise made to a slave by his master had no force nor validity. Children followed the condition of the slave mother. The slave could have no access to the judiciary. A slave might be condemned to death for striking any white person.

In the light of these observations, and a careful examination of the mores of a sharply unequal class society, to argue on the basis of an econometric reconstruction that the ante-bellum South was a viable system capable of "economic development" is to do the discipline of economics a grave injustice.

* W. E. B. DuBois, *Black Reconstruction in America,* 1935.

IX

THE TRIUMPH OF INDUSTRIAL CAPITALISM*

THE TAKE-OFF IN THE POST-CIVIL WAR PERIOD

The Civil War blew across the United States, dispelling the miasmas that had hung over it for an entire generation. It freed the Negroes and in the process destroyed the slave-plantation system as a way of life and a *Weltanschauung*. The anticapitalism of the South (and of the northern intellectuals as well) was suddenly gone. Now North and South were finally united under a common banner and the Republican and Democratic parties were committed (except on matters of detail) to a single program: nothing was to stand in the way of the quick industrialization of the United States. Two things facilitated the process. The first was the active role of government, which on the one hand assisted the opening up of broad new avenues for economic growth and development and on the other consciously refrained from interfering with the innovator-entrepreneurs who emerged to take advantage of them. The second was the radically changed mores of the time, which, rather than rejecting, assented to and approved the ways and means by which industrialization was to be achieved—private and unequal accumulation, the acceptance

* The materials discussed in this chapter and in the two following, are treated in greater detail in L. M. Hacker, *The World of Andrew Carnegie, 1865–1901*, 1968. For a contrary view, arguing the limited impact of the Civil War, see D. T. Gilchrist and W. D. Lewis. Ed., *Economic Changes in the Civil War Era*, 1965.

of the rough (and harsh) judgments of the market place, and the writing of a rule of law which equated freedom of contract with liberty.

In the midst of war itself, so swiftly did the Republicans, now in control of all three branches of government as a result of secession and the departure from Washington of the spokesmen for the southern slaveocracy, move, that the grand design at once took shape. Mercantile, as well as planter, capitalism was pushed into the lumber room of history and public policy; industrial capitalism alone was to guide the actions and thinking of the country. The Homestead Act opened up the vast areas of the West (and the South after the war) to free or easy settlement and permitted the quick exploitaion of the natural resources of timber, stone, coal, and other minerals. The chartering of the Union Pacific Railroad (and other trunk lines), with help from free grants of land and federal loans, made possible the spanning of the continent to the Pacific— and the creation of a national market. High tariff walls were erected behind which infant industries could grow and thrive—thus making possible the harmony of interests and balanced growth that Alexander Hamilton, Henry Clay, and the economist Henry C. Carey had advocated. The country's doors were thrown open to the immigrants of Europe to take up farms in the public domain and to furnish that large, young, and eager working force so necessary for the development of heavy industry. A national bank act was passed to establish federal control over banking to expand and regularize the money supply. With the war over, the states followed to assist in railroad construction and to create new kinds of banking agencies.

How did the federal and state governments help entrepreneurship by not interfering? They did not encumber the profits of individuals and companies with a heavy burden of taxation; they did not seek or direct enterprise by regulations and controls, presumably in the public interest; there were no codes (for good or ill) of social legislation—no broad and sweeping commitments to health, safety, and education. An unequal society emerged. The risk takers, if they were successful, became wealthy but they plowed back their gains into new ventures—expanding the economy and also building a large part of the country's infrastructure with their contributions to colleges and universities, hospitals, health centers, and family organization societies. The less favored, the farmers and workers, bore the greater share of taxation and the mischances of a market economy with wide business-cycle swings; the first because their prices were tied to world production, the second because the toll of unemployment was heavy in periods of recession and depression. Yet profits were not the result of exploitation, for if farmer income was low farm wealth increased enormously, with current earnings being deferred; and

TABLE 29

DECADAL RATES OF GROWTH OF GNP BY SELECTED COUNTRIES, 1869–1913

Country	Period	GNP (%)	GNP (per Capita) (%)	Population (%)
United States	1869–1878 to 1904–1913	56.0	27.5	22.3
United Kingdom	1860–1869 to 1905–1914	25.0	12.5	11.1
France	1841–1850 to 1901–1910	18.6	16.3	1.9
Germany	1860–1869 to 1905–1914	35.6	21.6	11.5
Canada	1870–1879 to 1905–1914	47.1	24.7	17.8
Japan	1878–1887 to 1903–1912	49.2	33.7	11.6

Source. S. S. Kuznets, *Economic Development and Social Change,* October 1956, p. 13.

as for the workers real wages grew impressively, and both skilled and un-skilled benefited from the steady rise in productivity made possible by the capital inputs of profits and savings converted into investment.

Three sets of figures, in little, demonstrate the progress and accomplishments of the industrial revolution in the brief period from the end of the Civil War to the outbreak of World War I. Table 29, the work of Simon Kuznets, gives percentage increases per *decade* from 1869 to 1913 for the Gross National Product and for the GNP in constant dollars and compares American performance with other industrial and industrializing nations. Table 30, the work of Raymond W. Goldsmith, lists *annual* rates of growth, again in constant dollars, for the United States.

TABLE 30

ANNUAL RATES OF GROWTH OF GNP, UNITED STATES, 1869–1913

Period	Population (%)	GNP (%)	GNP (per Capita) (%)	Consumption (%)	Consumption per Full Consumer (%)
1869–1898	2.17	4.32	2.11	4.75	2.33
1869–1913	2.03	4.24	2.16	4.49	2.26

Source. U.S. Congress Hearings before the Joint Economic Committee, 86th Congress, 1st Session, Part 2 "Historical and Comparative Rates of Production, Productivity, and Prices," 1959.

TABLE 31

PRODUCTION OF RAW MATERIALS, UNITED STATES, 1860–1900

Commodity	1860 (Millions)	1900 (Millions)	Increase (%)
Anthracite coal (short tons)	11.0	57.4	422
Bituminous coal (short tons)	9.0	212.3	2260
Crude petroleum (barrels)	0.5	45.8	9060
Pig iron (short tons)	0.9	15.4	1600
Crude steel (long tons)	0.01	10.2	10,190
Wheat (bushels)	173.1	559.3	223
Wheat exported (bushels)	4.0	102.0	2700
Corn (bushels)	838.8	2662.0	217
Cotton (bales)	3.8	10.1	170

Source. U.S. Department of Commerce, *Historical Statistics of the United States,* 1960, *passim.*

Table 31 presents some figures of increases in the production of raw materials, on which economic growth was based so heavily, for the years 1860 and 1900; during these 40 years the country's population increased 140 per cent.

THE MORES AND ENTREPRENEURSHIP

I have talked of mores; the brilliant analysis of this conception of how a society acts was the work of William Graham Sumner. Sumner, who became engrossed in the study of cultural and comparative anthropology in the 1890s, published a number of short pieces in preparation for his great book *Folkways,* which appeared in 1907. Sumner, in describing how a society achieves stability, started with its "folkways"—the customary or habitual manner devised by a people for living together. As it evolved to reach the stage of conscious reflection, as it worked out a theory of "societal welfare" with an ethics and a law, the "folkways" changed at a higher level and became "mores." The mores were the rules of conduct that determined right and wrong, and, as Sumner said, "the standards of good and right are in the mores." The mores served a particular time and a particular place. He had this to say about "rights" themselves in a short essay written about 1900.

It is certainly far wiser to think of rights as a rule of the game of social competition which are current here and now. They are not absolute. They are not antecedent to civilization. They are a product of civilization, or of the art of living. . . . they must be enjoyed under existing circumstances, that is, subject to limitations of tradition, custom, and fact. To be real they must be recognized in laws and provided for by institutions, but a great many of them, being inchoate, unsettled, partial, and limited, are still in the mores, and therefore vague and in need of further study and completion by courts and legislatures. This further work will be largely guided by the mores as to cognate matters, and by the conceptions of right and social welfare which the mores produce.

One cannot understand (or judge) the mores of the post-Civil War period in terms of our present-day standards of individual, corporate, and social behavior and in the process reject Sumner's notion of "welfare" because it meant only material well being and therefore underwrote inequality, exploitation, and the defenselessness of the weak in the presence of the strong.

These were the conceptions of societal welfare, of the mores of that time and in that place of the United States from 1865 to 1900. These mores—articulated by the country's spokesmen, its economists, spiritual leaders, trade-unionists, writers on public affairs and the law, legislatures, and courts—gave approval to acquisition, unequal wealth, the competitiveness and ruthlessness of the age's innovator-entrepreneurs. Sumner had said in the folkways, and also in the mores, "Whatever is, is right." It was in this climate of assent, that the innovator-entrepreneurs of the time were able to rise and flourish.

The theory of innovation as the root cause of economic development had been set out brilliantly in 1911 by Joseph A. Schumpeter, a young Viennese economist. In an effort to account for the interruptions by business cycles in the circular flow of economic activity he saw the intrusion of entrepreneurs as innovators who, appearing in "swarms," started new kinds of business ventures or used new methods in the old ones. A static economic world had become dynamic, and change meant improvement, progress, and "development" as long as the innovators had free rein (or the approval of society; thus Schumpeter and Sumner are linked).

The innovators are new men: they are interlopers or adventurers— businessmen, in short (Schumpeter called them "captains of industry") who were able to start a whole new economic round that had linkage effects with other parts of the economy. The capital for these undertakings? It came initially from men of means (who were silent partners), more frequently from commercial banks, and, if the fresh enterprises started off well, from "the entrepreneurial profits" which were plowed back into further investment of plant, machinery, necessary raw materials, and the exploitation of markets. The supplier of capital was the risk taker, and the entrepreneur became risk taker when earnings were converted into further capital inputs.

Schumpeter entered into a series of fascinating psychological and social speculations about the characteristics and habits of these "new men." They had to be ready to back their hunches, to challenge habit, customary use and wont, and be strong enough to disregard the resistance of their fellows and face up to ostracism, physical obstruction, and even personal attack.

Their motives were not hedonistic; among their outstanding qualities was a willingness to avoid conspicuous consumption and, more particularly, leisure. Because they started out humbly, they were interested in social recognition and social distinction; power meant that, and not the desire to create dynasties or "families" with entrenched privilege and surviving by prescription. The will to conquer, said Schumpeter, was represented by "the impulse to fight, to prove oneself superior to others, to succeed for the sake, not of the fruits of success, but of success itself." Perhaps most important of all, the entrepreneurs were creators who worked hard and imaginatively because of the pleasure to be derived from accomplishment. Said Schumpeter: "Our type seeks out difficulties, changes in order to change, delights in ventures. This group of motives is the most distinctly anti-hedonist" of them all.

This perceptive analysis of the habits of the innovator—granted, as we do, that the prevailing mores were prepared to look on entrepreneurship and the entrepreneur as just and right—helps to explain the emergence, acceptance, and triumph of that extraordinary company of captains of industry of the post-Civil War years. To name but a few: Jay Gould and J. J. Hill in railroading; Andrew Carnegie and Henry C. Frick in iron and steel; John D. Rockefeller in oil refining and transportation; Cyrus H. McCormick in agricultural implements; George Westinghouse, Thomas Edison and Frank J. Sprague in electrical equipment; J. P. Morgan and Jacob H. Schiff in investment banking; Philip Armour and Gustavus F. Swift in meat packing; and William Clark of the Singer Sewing Machine Company in marketing.

BINDING THE UNION TOGETHER

It was not until 1877 that the South was restored to its "normal relations" in the Union, and because this was so, the Radical Republicans, who had seized control of Congress and who had been forcing Lincoln to see the War as they did, gained only a partial victory. The Radical Republicans were Jacobins in a double sense: they sought a recasting of American society economically (and therefore they pushed the program of government intervention to speed the processes of industrialization in which new, lesser men would have a chance to rise); but they were also egalitarians socially and politically—the southern seceding states were to pay a heavy price before being readmitted as equal commonwealths. The Radical Republicans had been abolitionists and they carried this moral commitment into their plans for reconstruction. The freed Negroes and the white yeoman farmers were to be given every assistance: lands (from the public domain and confiscated estates), a more equitable tax system, public education (on a nonsegregated basis) and public welfare programs, and the reapportionment of voting districts for the Congress and state legislatures. All this to effect a social revolution in the South, shift the loci of power, and link the South and North together in a common purpose (under the leadership, of course, of the Republican party).

The economic side of this plan, except for a single detail that points up the lower middle class (and therefore Jacobin) character of the Radical Republicans, was won. They wanted both high tariffs and soft (preferably public) money; the latter device would free them of dependence on banks (which they distrusted and which, they believed, were more disposed to favor merchants in the export trade and therefore were deflationary) and give them an expansion of the money supply so that ample credits would permit the financing of industries the high tariff walls now assured. Soft money lost out to hard money when the United States returned to the gold standard in 1879.

A greater defeat was the abandonment of Radical Reconstruction. In part, this followed the disappearance of Radicals from both houses of Congress in the immediate postwar years, in part from war weariness. The high ethical resolves, the demands for political and social equality and equal economic opportunity, and the necessity for policing the southern states: these goals required a consecration, a single-mindedness on the part of a whole people, that was too much to expect after victory in the field. The North, in consequence, began to pull out of the "conquered provinces"—its soldiers and federal marshals. The Force Acts of 1870 and 187., to protect the civil rights of Negroes, fell into desuetude and the North made its retirement complete in 1877 as a result of a political bargain. President Rutherford B. Hayes' dubious election was validated; in return, federal troops from the last of the occupied southern states— South Carolina, Louisiana, Florida—were recalled. The Negroes and southern white masses were abandoned, and the curtain was rung down on what turned out to be the second act of a great drama; the third is being played out today.

Curiously, "redemption" in the South did not mean the restoration of the power of the old ante-bellum ruling class. Those who took over politically and economically, the so-called southern "Redeemers," were the founders of the New South and they accepted with alacrity the processes and ideas emanating from the North by which the South was to be restored by the espousal of a capitalist program: the rebuilding and expansion of southern railways to open up the South's backcountry, the exploitation of the region's great natural resources of timber, coal, and iron, the creation of new national and state banks and the establishment of local industries, particularly cotton-textile and tobacco manufactures and the building of new towns as mercantile and industrial centers. Northern and British capital were eager to assist, but new southern bankers with new ideas could stimulate the growth of local capital as well. This last is important, for it gives the lie to the contention that the New South was a "colonial" dependency of foreign financial interests who invested in the region only to expatriate their profits. Southern entrepreneurs plowed back earnings into improvements and fresh ventures. Thus the Tennessee Coal, Iron and Railway Co. (southern-led and in good part southern-financed) was not satisfied with mining coal and iron but created out of profits a great industrial complex in Alabama and Tennessee, with Birmingham-Chattanooga as its base. It erected steel furnaces and mills and pioneered (with Carnegie in the North) in the making of open-hearth steel. Tobacco-manufacture, also by southern men and capital, was modernized, the work of leaders like R. J. Reynolds and James Duke, and it was Duke who moved earnings into the beginnings of southern electric power and light. Cotton-textile mills and spindles, also financed by southern capital, grew impressively, so that from 1880 to 1900 the number of spindles in the four outstanding textile states of North Carolina, South Carolina, Georgia, and Alabama increased from 423,000 to 3,792,000 and capital invested, from $17.4 to $124.6 million.

Again, however, there was industrialization without "development," for southern leaders, the "Redeemers" and their successors, the spokesmen for the "white masses," refused to carry out the land and educational reforms that lay at the heart of Radical Reconstruction. Southern agriculture, using black and white share croppers, of whom the crop-lien system and store financing took a heavy toll, was based on the misuse and abuse of a dependent and ignorant rural population always living in poverty. There were no significant changes in well being, no impressive rises in real income, and therefore no indigenous small industries and services which are the mark of an advancing lower middle-class population. Because education and other social services were not pushed, no improvement in "human capital" took place. The demagogic leaders of the "white masses," who rose to power in the 1880s and 1890s, consciously moved in the opposite direction, for they politically disfranchised the Negroes and constantly sustained the fires of race hatred and fear by keeping their followers ignorant, prejudiced, and dependent. A characteristic example of growth without "development."

THE PUBLIC POLICIES OF GOVERNMENT

The Absence of Taxation

By *not* taxing enterprise and entrepreneurs public authority—the federal government and the states, counties, and cities—contributed mightily to risk-taking ventures. Well into the first decade of the twentieth century tax systems were frankly inequitable, the greater part of the burden—and even then it was light—being borne by the consumers (which meant largely the workers) generally and by the farmers both as producers and consumers. I have said that taxes were not onerous, and this was so because public programs, whether for the initiation of enterprise, the creation of infrastructures, the financing of social-service programs, or for the building up and maintenance of a defense establishment, were virtually nonexistent. These figures, in the light of contemporary heavy involvements by public authority in the four general areas mentioned above, are no less than startling. At the end of the nineteenth century federal taxes absorbed only about 3 per cent of the national income ($6.64 per capita) and all the state, county, and municipal taxes, another 6 per cent ($13.28 per capita).

The federal tax system, after the Civil War taxes were dismantled, was based on consumption—tariff duties and excises. State, county, and municipality systems were based on real property ownership: in the rural areas, on farm property and farm equipment; in the cities, on real estate, the tax being carried largely by dwellings. In consequence taxation was regressive, for the larger proportion of the population—farmers and workers—those with small incomes, bore the tax load. On the other hand, companies and corporations (on their plants, equipment, patents, as well as land and earnings) and large income receivers and large estates got off scot free or paid so little that accumulation, risk taking, and investment were hardly affected.

The federal government, to finance the Civil War, was forced to push taxation into many avenues, for high tariffs, presumably to augment the revenue, and the issuance of greenbacks and sale of short-term Treasury notes were scarcely enough. Indeed, greenbacks and Treasury notes, by increasing the money supply, accelerated inflation to an alarming degree. Congress therefore was compelled to turn to income, inheritance and business taxes as well as to an expansion of excise taxes. Beginning with the Revenue Act of 1862 and continuing in subsequent acts, a mildly progressive income tax on individuals and a small inheritance tax were imposed; there were also taxes on bank capital and deposits and on checks and business documents. There were taxes on the gross receipts of some kinds of corporations (largely having to do with transportation) and excises on a limited group of manufactured goods (which, of course, were shifted to the consumers). During the war, it should be noted, workers paid more than the farmers and whereas real wages dropped agricultural income rose.

Despite all this busyness, profits were not cut and inflation remained unchecked; for Civil War tariff duties brought in only $305.3 million, the excises $292 million, and income taxes $55 million. The war costs were borne by interest-bearing bonds and notes ($2.5 billion) and greenbacks ($450 million). As soon as the war was over Congress began to dismantle this jerry-built structure, most of which was pulled down in less than a decade. The inheritance tax and levies on sales and gross receipts went in 1871, personal income tax, in 1872, and manufacturers' excises even earlier, during 1866–1868. A remnant—taxes on banks and banking and extra levies on tobacco—went in 1883. In 1885 federal receipts consisted only of customs ($182 million) and internal revenues, largely from alcohol and tobacco ($112 million).

In the states, counties, and municipalities extraordinary wartime taxes also were quickly abandoned; what remained were the general property taxes that produced most of the modest revenues sought. Some states went through the motions of imposing small taxes on railroads, banks, and other corporations (but not on manufacturing and mining companies); a handful had inheritance taxes but none had a tax on income. Tax reformers, largely academic, who raised their heads in the 1880s and 1890s were particularly harsh with the general property tax and also advocated an income tax. The leading proponent was E. R. A. Seligman of Columbia University. He called the general property tax "iniquitous" because of its inability to reach personal property and because it fell heavily on agriculture. Said Seligman: "The farmer bears not only his share, but those of other classes of society."

The idea of an income tax was taken up by agrarians and other reformers in the late 1880s and adopted by the Democratic party in 1894, when it tacked an income-tax provision on its tariff act of that year. It took the Supreme Court only one year to declare the law unconstitutional. The United States had to wait until the ratification of the Sixteenth Amendment in 1913 before this form of revenue—as well as a device, through progressive rates, that would provide social control of income— was made available. The states, in the first decade of the twentieth century, under the lead of reforming governors, also began to experiment with taxes on corporations and on the franchises of public utility com- panies. Thus enterprise and entrepreneurs in the post-Civil War years had their cake and could eat it too: next-to-no taxes, plus direct govern- ment aid in a number of areas. We must now look at the latter.

Tariffs

The role of the tariff in American fiscal affairs has been explored and discussed often enough. It is common knowledge that an effort by Congress to encourage domestic industrial growth through protection, starting in 1816, was abortive because of the abandonment of the program by southern leaders and the Democratic party. The result was that at the beginning of the Civil War the average *ad valorem* rate on dutiable goods stood at only 18.8 per cent. This trend the Republican party was committed to reverse, and using wartime fiscal needs as an excuse the Civil War Congresses set to work to raise duties. In the space of three years, from 1861 to 1864, the average rate was pushed up from 25 to 47 per cent.

Protectionism continued first on the agenda of public policy through the rest of the century; the interesting point is that in this both parties concurred and only tariff tinkering and not tariff revision took place in the brief interludes in which the Democrats controlled the Congress. The history of 1892–1894 is instructive. In these years the Democrats had gained possession of both the Congress and the Presidency, and President Cleveland was determined to carry out his party-platform's mandate. The Wilson bill, originating in the House, sought to reduce rates generally and sharply; in the Senate Democrats joined with Republicans, some 600 amendments were introduced, and Wilson's work was undone. Cleve- land, in high dudgeon, refused to sign; the Wilson Tariff Act became law nonetheless, but in three years, in 1897, it was superceded by the Dingley Tariff, which turned out to be the highest in American annals, the average rate being put at 52 per cent. The two pet schedules—wool and woolen goods and iron and steel products—played an important role in encouraging the domestic production of wool and the exploration for iron resources at the same time that they furthered industrialization in both areas.

What of the pure theory of foreign trade? Did tariffs artificially stimulate price increases, limit American production to a domestic market, and end only in high profits without the necessity for innovation? Professor Frank W. Taussig, a leading American proponent of free trade, in examining the impact of tariffs on the iron and steel industry, was compelled to admit that the Hamiltonian program of protection for "infant manufacture" had really worked. Taussig's studies indicated that during the years 1870–1895 American imports of pig iron and steel continued high and the domestic price, as a rule, was the foreign price plus the duty; but while duties were being reduced domestic prices were falling even more sharply, so much so that by 1895 American prices for both pig iron and steel were lower than those of Britain and the United States was competing in world markets. The reason was plain and the one Hamilton had anticipated: profits had moved into investment and therefore innovation. Taussig admitted this, albeit grudgingly. Said he: "The object of protection to young industries—the ultimate fall in price to the foreign level—seems to have been attained." Perhaps the steel industry would have grown without protection (how, if the British had had a free market for their goods in the United States?); but, acknowledged Taussig,

> . . . not so soon or on so great a scale. With a lower scale of iron prices, profits would have been lower, and possibly the progress of investment, the exploitation of the natural resources, even the advance of technical arts would have been less keen and unremitting.

Aid to Railroads

As early as 1845 Congress began to talk of constructing Pacific trunk lines that would link the Mississippi-Missouri rivers with the West Coast and in the process unite the whole country politically, make possible the settlement of the empty (except for roaming Indian tribes) western plains, and create a national market. Southern spokesmen in Congress raised all manner of objections: if a trunk system were to be built, it should move through the Southwest and have no federal financing. To preserve the integrity of the southern states its construction and capital should be provided by them. These obstructive tactics were successful and it was not until 1862, when all southern legislators had left Washington, that Congress was able to move. It then chartered the Union Pacific Railroad to lay down a line from Omaha, Nebraska, to the western boundary of Utah. This was to be joined by another line—the Central Pacific Railroad, a California corporation—which was to start from

Sacramento and build eastward until the two railroads were joined. All this needed help, and it took a characteristic form which Congress itself had developed to aid the states in their public improvements—generous grants of land from the public domain, but with a difference: in the case of the Union Pacific and Central Pacific loans were to be made on first mortgages as construction was completed, leg by leg, and in 1864 subordinated to second mortgages. The total federal loan came to $65 million, of which the two pioneer roads received the lion's share. Federal intervention accomplished another purpose: the enabling statute fixed the railroad gauge at 4 feet, 8½ inches, and this in time became the "standard" gauge for all the railroads in the country.

Land grants to railroads by a generous Congress continued until 1871; by then some 70 railroads, the beneficiaries of Congressional largess, had received 155.5 million acres, contingent on actual construction, of course. On this basis some 131.3 million acres were patented; this came to about one-tenth of the whole public domain, and it has been calculated that 18,738 miles of road were made possible. It should be kept in mind that more than the federal government rushed to help: states contributed 49 million acres of their own public lands, and they, as well as counties and towns, bought or guaranteed railroad bonds and assisted in the construction of railroad yards and terminals. Perhaps of even greater importance was their failure or inability to tax the railroads or, positively, to offer them tax forgiveness or postponement.

What was the federal assistance worth? In 1884 the Democratic party estimated the land given away at $2 an acre, or $360 million. In 1944 a federal agency put the net proceeds of the sales of federal and state land grants, to December 31, 1941, at $434.8 million and the value of the lands still retained at $60.7 million. Thus average price was only $3.38 an acre. Why so little? This was so because the land-grant railroads for obvious reasons sold their lands as quickly as possible: to encourage settlers and therefore the growth of marketable products (loans were on very generous terms, with foreclosures infrequent); and to obtain revenues with which to service the land-grant bonds the railroads had to issue to help finance construction. The general assumption that great land empires were built up by the Union Pacific, Northern Pacific, Santa Fe, and Southern Pacific simply was not true. The federal government, it would seem, got the better of the bargain. In 1898 the original loans made, around $63 million, were repaid with accrued interest of $104.7 million. The government was able to sell the alternate sections it reserved to itself within the land-grant belts at $2.50 an acre instead of the $1.25 for pre-emption lands. The grants had stipulated that the railroads were to carry the mails and government property and troops at less than going rates, and

these savings turned out to be very sizable. In 1945 a federal agency estimated that they came to twice as much as the railroads had obtained
from selling their lands. The result was that in 1947 Congress ended
federal special privileges.

To put a total on all the direct forms of assistance from all the public
authorities participating requires guessing: perhaps from the very beginning of railroad construction in the 1830s until the whole network
was completed in the early 1890s, and not including the purchase of securities, as much as $1.5 billion. It is impossible to estimate the public
revenues foregone because of laxity of tax practices or tax forgiveness.
On the other side of the ledger were the social and economic gains to the
United States. A vast territory was united to form a single nation which
was never troubled by the regionalism and separatism so common in
European politics. A national market was achieved. The role the railroads
played in the capital formation of the period was immense, as were the
forward and backward linkages and the external economies they created.
In the 1870s railroad construction alone was responsible for 20 per cent
of the country's gross capital formation, 15 per cent in the 1880s, and
still as much as 7.5 per cent in the 1890s. To this must be added the great
effects on the railroad suppliers—the iron and steel industries, the manufacturers of locomotives and cars, and those who built bridges and cul-
verts—and the external economies resulting from the opening up of
backcountries to settlement and the creation of new towns. One guesses:
the capital formation involved in all these enterprises and others of a
similar nature must have been at least as great as the initial railroad
outlays, whereas the value of their goods and services as their contribution
to the Gross National Product, and therefore the country's growth, was
equally enormous. There is no question that the railroad industry led all
the rest among the nation's economic enterprises and that public help,
in its many and various ways, was the key factor.

Assistance from the Public Domain

American land policy from the beginning, had one grand purpose
and that was the transfer of the public domain into private hands as
quickly as possible. It was hoped and assumed that in the process the
public revenues would be augmented; but at the same time, as the basis
of the stability of the Republic, settlement would be hastened by independent small farmers who were to be given every encouragement (but
not financial assistance) to enter and patent their titles. The pre-emption
law of 1841 subordinated the first to the second, and the Homestead Act
of 1862 added the capstone to the structure. Now a quarter section was

to be acquired for nothing by bona fide settlers and the family holding could be augmented by the purchase, at the pre-emption price of $1.25 an acre, of another quarter section.

The Homestead Law arose out of the clamor of the reformers of the 1830s and 1840s, who looked on the public lands as a safety-valve: family farms, granted by the government, would permit workers being absorbed into the industrial processes of the growing factory system, losing their independence as self-employed skilled artisans, and threatened with insecurity and unemployment still to remain free men. Because the dangers of land concentration always threatened (and this cry was raised in the 1830s for public sales put no maximum limits on purchase), land reform was also linked with transfer to workers transformed into farmers on the basis of inalienable tenure. These notions were characteristic of the Utopianism of the time, and no serious thought was given to the fact that commercial agriculture required skills (which industrial workers did not necessarily possess) as well as capital to move and settle on the lands thus to be acquired from the public largess.

In the 1850s the discussions came closer to reality. A Homestead Act, free grants of the public domain for family farms, but without inalienable tenure, was taken up by the new Republican party not to rescue impoverished workers, however, so much as to hasten the processes of industrialization. A high protective tariff would be one aspect of the program; the other, land settlement on a grand scale, would widen the domestic market for the manufactured goods the tariffs were to encourage. The political implications could not be ignored: filling out the western prairies and plains would strengthen the alliance between the West and the East and make forever impossible the penetration of slavery into the region north of the line fixed by the Missouri Compromise of 1820.

The idealistic strain in the advocacy and conduct of the egalitarian Radical Republicans must not be lost sight of, however. Thus George W. Julian, Congressman from Indiana (in the words of his daughter, speaking for him) stated:

> Should it [the Homestead bill] become a law, the poor white laborers of the South as well as the North would flock to the territories, where labor would be respectable, our democratic theory of equality would be put in practice, closely associated communities could be established as well as a system of common schools offering to all equal educational opportunities.

Homesteadism was pressed in Congress and a bill was passed in 1860 only to be vetoed by the Democratic President James Buchanan; but secession gave the Republicans their opportunity. The Homestead Law of 1862 fell far short of the expectations of the dreamers. It did not provide for inalienability; it did not recast the existing and complicated land system; the right of commutation of homesteads into pre-emptions encouraged fraud (by the use of dummy entrymen) and the building up of large properties by land companies. No credit machinery was set up; the only concession made to the reformers was that homesteads were to be exempt from attachment for debt.

The Homestead Act was a disappointment in one particular: between 1860 and 1900 fewer than one-sixth of the new farms were the result of free entries, perhaps even considerably fewer because of the ease with which land companies obtained properties by false entries and commutation. Fred A. Shannon's guess was that not many more than 400,000 families, representing a population of some 2,000,000, obtained free land and kept it. In the same 40 years the farming population of the north central, south central, and western states and territories increased by more than 8,000,000, or approximately 1.6 million families; that is to say, the great majority of the western farmers bought, through the pre-emption system, from land companies, the railroads, or the states themselves. With purchase often went credit—at any rate, many land-grant railroads offered easy terms; and with the erection of an improvement and the planting of a cash crop mortgage loans were available from a great variety of sources.

In another sense the Homestead Act was a great success, for it was an important reason why immigrants with farming skills were attracted to the United States. The push out of Europe was real: too many farmers in Great Britain, Scandinavia, and Germany were the victims of landlordism, and the hope of becoming owners of land in fee simple instead of forever remaining tenants captured the imagination of hundreds of thousands. So they came to settle in that tier of North and South Central states running from Minnesota down to Texas. Later, the filling out of the public lands and the appearance of a highly productive agriculture generated a movement in reverse: for the sons and daughters of native-born farmers took off for the cities to augment a growing labor supply (the immigrants were the chief source) that an expanding industrialization and its linked service industries required.

The land policy of quick disposal into private hands was applied as well to the opening up of timber and mineral lands for development, exploration, exploitation. Here were opportunities for profit but also for increasing production of wood, lead, copper, coal, iron, and petroleum. In 1864 the pre-emption of coal lands was made the subject of a general law; the same idea was extended to all minerals in 1866 and again in 1870 and 1872. Over this period the Public Land Office had the authority to sell coal lands at $10 to $20 an acre and other mineral lands at $2.50 to $5. The Timber Culture Act of 1873 gave homesteaders, and others, title to quarter-sections if they agreed to plant trees. The Desert Land Act of 1877 gave away whole sections on condition that irrigation be employed. The Timber Cutting Act of 1878 allowed settlers and miners to cut timber on public lands free of charge, and the Timber and Stone Act of the same year authorized the sale of quarter-sections at $2.50 an acre if the Public Land Office decided that such lands were unfit for cultivation.

To aid in the process of rapid and successful exploitation Congress in 1879 created the Geological Survey to examine and classify the public lands and make public "their geological structure, mineral resources and products." Many states set up similar agencies, but it was not until 1891 that some effort at restraint began to appear. In that year the Pre-emption and Timber Culture acts were repealed and limits were placed on the number of entries under the Desert Land Act; also a Forest Reserve Act was passed which permitted the President to close timber areas to settlers and establish them as national parks. Real concern for the conservation of the country's natural resources did not emerge, however, until the presidency of Theodore Roosevelt. Granted the profligacy of congressional programs in opening up the public lands for exploration and development and the frauds that occurred, in part because of the inadequacy of supervisory machinery, the consequences of speeding up industrialization were there for all to see. The index of physical production in mining (10 metals plus coal and petroleum) showed a fivefold increase between 1879 and 1900. From 1860 to 1897 coal production was multiplied 14 times and pig iron, 11 times. From 1876 to 1896, barrels of petroleum pumped up increased sevenfold, and from 1869 to 1899 the number of board feet of lumber sawed increased threefold.

Expanding the Labor Force

The industrial labor force was not the work of government, of course but government did create an environment and a policy that encouraged its growth. Its greatest impact in this connection was on immigration. Immigration brought young people of working age, the greatest number of whom were males; some had skills, some had not, but all could be inducted into a labor force that grew larger, proportionately, than the total population itself. The figures that follow are illuminating.

Between 1860 and 1900 the population of the United States increased 140 per cent. In that same span of years the civilian population of working age (15 years and over) grew 170 per cent, the male population within those years, 190 per cent. The growth in population on farms in the same 40 years was only 70 per cent, in urban communities, 300 per cent—and by the same token the industrial labor force exploded, whereas the farm labor force increased only modestly. This curious shape of the American population was largely the work of immigration. One set of figures alone tells the story. From 1840 (when immigration began on a large scale) to 1930 (when it virtually ceased) the population of native American stock grew from 14.2 to 82.7 million, a sixfold increase; but that of foreign stock (foreign-born and native born of foreign or mixed parentage) expanded from 3 million to more than 40 million, or 13 times the original number. By 1930 one-third of the country's total population was of foreign stock.

Immigrants came for economic reasons (the "pull" of job opportunities in the United States); economic and social conditions in Europe (the "push" of unequal opportunities for work, plus all kinds of social, religious, and political disabilities); the propaganda of railroad, steamship, and land companies, that sought workers, passengers, and buyers of farms; and positive encouragement by the American government to make entry into the United States easy.

The "pull" of the United States was significant because its greatest effects were to be felt during those upturns in the American business cycle in which the construction industries (railroads, housing, and public utilities) needed large numbers of unskilled male laborers. The "push" out of Europe took place for a great variety of reasons, mostly economic: population growth, declining opportunities for farm workers, and the elimination of the skilled handicrafts by machine production but also the social, religious, and political disadvantages under which minorities suffered.

There were four great movements of immigrants out of Europe, most of whom set out for America, and each coincided with an upswing in the long investment cycle (and construction) in the United States. They occurred, roughly, in these decadal periods: 1844–1854 (2,870,000); 1863–1873 (2,915,000); 1878–1888 (4,401,000); and 1898–1909 (6,804,634). In two particulars the fourth movement was unlike the earlier three. The origin of the immigrants changed; now they came almost entirely from southern, central, and eastern Europe (the so-called "New Immigration"), whereas earlier they had come from the British Isles, Germany, and Scandinavia (the so-called "Old Immigration"). The "New Immigrants" were less likely to be the skilled workers that the "Old Immigrants" had been.

The Republican party was pledged to a federal immigration policy, and this it fulfilled in 1864 when the law passed by Congress was called "An Act to Encourage Immigration." This legislation set up an Office of

Commissioner of Immigration in Washington and provided for a superintendent of immigration at the port of New York, thus placing the regulation of entry and the supervision of steamship companies for the safety
and comfort of their passengers under federal authority. Immigrants
could come under contract; contractors (who presumably paid transportation costs) were permitted a year's lien on wages and attachments on
property. An important function of the Commissioner of Immigration
was the wide publicity he was to give the law by circularizing all of
America's consular agents overseas who were to spread word of the ease
of entry, the protections afforded, and the free land available under the
Homestead Act. Federal control of immigration, against the authority
claimed by the states to regulate their ports, was upheld by the Supreme
Court.

The contract-labor provisions probably did not encourage too many
immigrants: letters home from previous arrivals telling of the jobs available and the satisfactory working conditions, but, most important, containing immigrant remittances and steamship tickets (proving that wages
in the United States made savings possible), were far more significant.
Nevertheless, American labor raised a hue and cry, the Knights of Labor,
in particular, demanding repeal. The law was modified in 1868, again
in 1883, and finally repealed in 1891. Congress stood steadfastly against
proposals to pass selective legislation, that is, to limit entry to those of
"Nordic" stock. A small number of specified classes of undesirables—
those likely to become public charges, anarchists, the diseased and insane
—were to be barred, and a modest head tax of 50 cents was imposed on
the newly arrived. On one point Congress did yield, when it passed
literacy-test requirements, but presidential vetoes staved them off until
1917, when President Wilson was over-ridden by Congress. It was to the
credit of the American Federation of Labor that it refused to join the
clamor of Boston's Back Bay (fussing over "purity" of stock) and the so-
called "sociologists" (who demonstrated to their own satisfaction that
poverty and crime were the result of too many immigrants coming into
too many cities), as the advocates of selection and restriction. An AFL
resolution of 1897 said:

> Further restrictive measures would close the door of our great country
> to a great many honest, intelligent, progressive workmen who should become
> true and ardent trade unionists. . . . Trade unions, on account of their pro-
> gressive tendencies, should be the last bodies of American citizens who advo-
> cate the turning away of fugitives from European oppression, either political
> or industrial.

It was not until the end of World War I that the AFL changed its
mind and supported quota laws.

The "New Immigration" went into the hard, manual labor jobs but was readily trained for the automatic processes that American technology made increasingly possible (in iron and steel, mining, glass making, meat packing, and the manufacture of clothing). Two things resulted: native-born American workers and the sons and daughters of the Old Immigrants were able to move up into skilled occupations and supervisory jobs, whereas those who continued to come from northern Europe in the first decade of the twentieth century (and they still made up 30 per cent of the total) were technicians, metallurgists, chemists, and tool designers. The latter proved these things: that automation required more rather than fewer skills and that the brain drain out of Europe was not a modern-day phenomenon.

The Immigration Commission, established in 1907 because of the many unfriendly and false things being charged about the newcomers, caught in its report all of the things I have said above. America's industrial advance was closely linked with an expanding labor force to which all kinds, skilled and unskilled, contributed. The Commission, therefore, did not recommend restriction.

The Social and Economic Consequences of Immigration

It would be idle and fatuous to gild the lily: the New World to which so many millions of immigrants thronged was no utopia. Most of them collected in large cities in which slums quickly developed (in part because new housing and rapid transit were not able to keep up with urban population increases, in part because of the absence or laxity of public inspection and supervision, and in part because of exploitation). In consequence, there were sweat shops, child labor, and heavy death rates among the young. In smaller communities, where the mining and metal industries were to be found, there were company towns; and always, in times of business recession, there were unemployment and want; along with hostility toward the newcomer and social and job discrimination. The Irish were openly resented by native-born Americans, but they, in turn, turned against the Italians, the Poles, and the Jews. Every immigrant child in large American cities was brought up amid and trained in the art of street warfare. The realities of American politics, however, worked out a truce, for immigrants could quickly become naturalized and vote; before too long their spokesmen were recognized and elected to municipal councils, state legislatures, and judicial benches.

What was the impact of all this on wages? Despite the weakness of trade unions, real wages in America climbed during this period of speeded-up industrialization; thus, increases in real wages were synchronous with the rise in productivity based on both capital and labor inputs. Two careful analyses, made under the direction of the National Bureau of Economic Research, demonstrate these increases.* Long found that real wages in manufacturing rose 50 per cent in 30 years (1860–1890); Rees found that real wages, also in manufacturing, in the 24 years from 1890 to 1914, at the peak of the "New Immigration," went up 40 per cent. The wages of skilled workers, however, rose faster than those of the unskilled. Here the failures of trade unionism showed themselves, for trade-union negotiations on an industry-wide basis today tend to narrow differentials because gains are across-the-board. One study bears this out.† Coombs may be compared with Rees (using Rees's cost-of-living index as the basis for calculating real wages for both). According to Rees, the real hourly wages for *all* workers in manufacturing went up 40 per cent from 1890 to 1914. According to Coombs, the real hourly wages of the *unskilled* rose 11 per cent in the same period. Rees found increases of 17 per cent for *all* workers from 1890 to 1900 and 15 per cent from 1901 to 1914. Coombs reported a rise of 8 per cent for the *unskilled* from 1890 to 1900 and only 2 per cent from 1901 to 1914. If there was any worker exploitation (having in mind the balance between wages and productivity) it was not that of the skilled, who possibly got more than their share, whereas the unskilled got less. In any event, the growing American economy was able to absorb all the immigrants of working age into its labor force, and this steady availability plus the profitability of industry (which it did not have to share with government) by 1900 made the United States the leading manufacturing nation in the world.

* C. D. Long, *Wages and Earnings in the United States, 1860–1890*, 1960, and Albert Rees, *Real Wages in Manufacturing, 1890–1914*, 1961.

† Whitney Coombs, *The Wages of the Unskilled in Manufacturing in the United States, 1890–1924*, 1926.

X

THE SUPPORTS OF INDUSTRIAL CAPITALISM

From many quarters voices were raised to justify, explicitly and implicitly, the processes of entrepreneurship and the work of the innovator-entrepreneurs. From Protestant pulpits and from academic economists, publicists, educators, lawbook writers, law courts, and trade-union leaders came ideas that were being shaped to form the mores of the time. The consequence was that unequal property ownership, private accumulation, and the leadership of captains of industry were deemed just and right, and because of them societal welfare was hastened. It will be observed that all this has nothing to do with what today is called Social Darwinism: that, largely the work of Herbert Spencer and based on a simplistic analysis of Darwin's struggle for existence and the survival of the fittest, the emergence of the entrepreneur followed much the same pattern through which the evolution of the species had gone. Spencer was accepted in the United States because he put in terms of broad principles what the mores had already demonstrated; and when a man like Andrew Carnegie, for example, quoted Spencer it was only because Spencer was explaining why and how Carnegie had achieved his success.

I have said that the Protestant clergy and the professional economists played an important part in making acceptable the mores of the time. It is interesting to observe that right through the 1880s churchman and economist were frequently one and the same person; that is to say, the search for a providential intelligence at work took those trained in theological seminaries into an examination of the laws by which social arrangements were effected. This note was struck again and again by the Reverend Francis Wayland, later professor of moral philosophy and president of Brown University, whose *The Elements of Political Economy*, first published in 1837, was studied widely in editions revised by himself and the Reverend Aaron L. Chapin right into the 1880s; by Arthur Latham Perry, a minister's son and a professor of Williams College, whose *Elements of Political Economy*, first printed in 1865, ran into 22 editions; by the Reverend Francis Bowen, professor of natural religion, moral philosophy, and civil polity at Harvard College, whose *American Political Economy* came out in a new edition in 1870; and by Amasa Walker, this time a successful businessman turned lecturer in economics at Oberlin and Amherst, whose *Science of Wealth* was rewritten in 1866 and used in colleges throughout the 1870s.

Providential intelligence was at work everywhere. Property, said Wayland, was founded on the "will of God, as made known to us by *natural conscience,* by *general consequences,* and by *revelation.*" (Italics original.) Perry saw on all sides "the footsteps of providential intelligence." Walker, in the same vein, noted "how perfectly the laws of wealth accord with those moral and social laws which appertain to the higher nature and aspirations of man." Those who labored were fulfilling "an established law of our being," according to Wayland. And he went on:

> The results which our Creator has attached to idleness are all to be considered as punishements. . . . And, on the other hand, God has assigned to industry rich and abundant rewards.

Walker pointed up the specific applications of such a rule. (He drew on the French economist Frédéric Bastiat, as did Perry and Bowen. Bastiat expounded Ricardo with a difference: his dictum that "the good of each tends to the good of all, as the good of all tends to the good of each," made it possible to see labor and capital working together to achieve a higher purpose.)

Thus Walker:

> The union of capital and labor will be most effective when each is sure of its just reward. If the rights of man as a holder of property are sacred, and the rights of labor equally so, the greatest motive to production can be secured. If otherwise, the creation of wealth will be restricted. Men will not work or save unless sure of their reward.

Thus Perry:

> The presence of capital anywhere constitutes a demand for labor. The more capital there is anywhere, the stronger the demand for labor; and capital therefore is the poor man's best friend. . . . They come of necessity into a relation of mutual dependence, which God has ordained and which, though man may temporarily disturb it, he can never overthrow.

And, thus Bowen, tying all the loose ends together:

> Society is a complex and delicate machine, the real Author and Governor of which is divine. . . . Men cannot interfere with His work without marring it. The attempts of legislators to turn the industry of society in one direction or another, out of its natural and self-chosen channels. . . . to increase or diminish the supply of the market, to establish a maximum of price, to keep specie in the country—are almost invariably productive of harm. *Laissez-faire;* "these things regulate themselves," in common phrase, which means, of course, that God regulates them by his general laws, which means in the long run, work to good.

It followed that Walker, Perry, and Bowen rejected the Ricardian theory of rent and the Malthusian theory of population on which it was based. According to them, Malthus and Ricardo expounded a special case and not a general law; their "gloomy views" described Britain's society in which landlordism flourished and a caste system was the inevitable consequence. Classical economics had to do with a static world in which wages found their level at subsistence and the profits of enterprise moved toward zero; because arable lands were limited, the landlord was the only one to benefit. Not so in the United States, notably in "the great valley of the Mississippi." Here was the dynamic factor in America. The presence of rich, abundant, cheap lands, the production of foodstuffs for home consumption "in the amplest manner" and for export overseas made possible the maintenance in the United States of an open society. Work and wealth went together, and here frugality and saving had their social as well as economic rewards. The proof, said Bowen, was to be found in "the *mobility* of society, or the ease and frequency with which the members of it change their respective social positions." An important factor in this regard was education, said these American economists. By thrift and work but also continuing education Americans could escape the fall into the Malthusian pit.

These ideas were propounded from Protestant pulpits, in church periodicals and the success manuals of the time, which frequently were written by Protestant clergymen. The way to salvation, to the company of God's elect, was in the cultivation of the Protestant rules of sobriety, thrift, and most particularly of work, that is, a devotion to a calling. In this way men could overcome Original Sin and achieve a Christian life. It is a mistake to assume that the Protestantism of the second half of the nineteenth century was the stern Calvinism of the early Puritans who looked to a majestic and fierce Creator, the "Monarch God," as their only support and comfort because life was harsh and beset by all sorts of perils. Evangelical Christianity—which was what most Protestants began to accept—offered more hope. Indeed, all could enter the company of the saints and not the predestined elect alone because the Diety had become a God of Love and Service, working through Jesus. It was this kind of Christianity the Congregationalist Henry Ward Beecher preached, and his influence spread far beyond the walls of his Brooklyn Plymouth Church. Grace was possible through both work and service, and these the individual could achieve. Therefore one accepted the rough world of the time—private property and unlimited accumulation, individual and competitive striving, success because of personal devotion to work, and sobriety and failure because of want of it; but the Christian, first having acquired self-descipline, built into this a commitment of personal responsibility to society and his fellowmen. The Christian, taught Beecher, started out with Jesus and accepted the stewardship Jesus had proclaimed.

Three things emerged from the belief in this this-worldly accomplishment. First, the man in business, attaining worldly success, could be a good Christian if he acknowledged the stewardship of membership in the community of his fellowmen. William Lawrence, Episcopal Bishop of Massachusetts, cut from much the same cloth as Beecher, declared as late at 1901 that "material prosperity is favorable to morality." This showed itself by using a part of one's wealth for good works: erecting chapels among the poor, maintaining family-organization and child-care societies, and supporting schools for Negroes in the south and colleges that made scholarships available to children of the less fortunate.

Second, the man wholly preoccupied with his personal quest for salvation was the true Christian. (Not, as the Protestant churches were to say later, an involvement in man's inhumanity to man, injustice, the absence of opportunity for the socially and economically deprived; not the assumption of public responsibility for those who fell behind in the race for success.) When material well-being crowned his efforts, he knew he had won, for his wealth was a sign of divine approval. Those who faltered and failed in the struggle with Original Sin also got their just desserts in poverty and unemployment.

Third, all this was confirmed by the new Darwinian doctrine expounded by Herbert Spencer. Beecher saw at once how evolution, particularly Spencer's "Survival of the Fittest," fitted into his evangelical Christianity. Here he was followed by most Protestant divines. Evolution held out the promise of constant improvement—for the free individual, for the race. Beecher put it thus:

> The more the world advanced, the more rapidly it could advance; and the glory of the blossom and the fruit lies before us yet, and it will come, not according to the speed of the ages gone by, but according to the acceleration which belongs in the nature of things, to the advanced stages of growth.

Here was the same optimistic note of the promise of America that the economists were sounding.

THE CONTRIBUTIONS OF THE PUBLICISTS

The same set of notions was enunciated by a group of publicists who spread their message in speeches, lectures, and articles that were printed widely in newspapers and popular journals. The leaders of this company were David A. Wells, Edward Atkinson, and William Graham Sumner. Wells was the government expert in fiscal matters who had become a successful businessman; Atkinson, a highly competent New England textile manufacturer, devoted himself largely to the industrial character and needs of the United States; Sumner, initially an Episcopalian minister turned professor of political and social science at Yale, threw a wider net. He discussed theoretical and applied questions and in preliminary articles began to lay out the conceptions that were to go into his later and famous *Folkways*.

All three had this in common: they were suspicious of government intrusion in the self-regulating operations of the market. Wells and Atkinson put their opposition to tariffs, cheap money, "inquisitorial, vexatious, and unnecessarily multiple taxes" in terms of the lessons they had learned from Adam Smith and the later Frédéric Bastiat and Jerome Blanqui. Sumner was *sui generis,* an American original, who initially, because of his theological training, had sought final causes and then turned scientist, in the process discarding metaphysics and ethics. He was an Aristotelian and not a Platonist, guided broadly by Smith, Hume, and Locke, and not by Hegel. Because he was interested in the "science of society," he had saturated himself in Buckle and Spencer and knew his St. Simon, the Simonians, and Comte; yet he went his own way. He followed the French rather than the English in one particular: industry linked with technology was the basis of progress and societal welfare; but the French were neutral in regard to the source of authority and power;

he, on the other hand, had firm convictions (and here he was in accord with Spencer) about statism.

This is the shape taken by his "science of society," firmly grounded in technology. Said he:

> It [industrial organization] creates the conditions of our existence, sets the limits of our social activity, regulates the bonds of our social relations, determines our conceptions of good and evil, suggests our life philosophy, molds our inherited political institutions, and reforms the oldest customs, like marriage and property.

The doers and shakers were "intelligent men," at this pass in Americal development, the captains of industry. Any interference by the state—tariffs, monetary tinkering, excessive taxation, the Single Tax, or socialism—threw a monkey wrench into the processes by which society was evolving. Sumner's acute essay, *What Social Classes Owe to Each Other,* ended in this fashion:

> Instead of endeavoring to redistribute the acquisitions which have been made between the existing classes, our aim should be to *increase, multiply,* and *extend the chances.* Such is the work of civilization. Every old error or abuse which is removed opens new chances of development to all the new energy of society. Every improvement in education, science, art, or government expands the chances of man on earth. (Italics original.)

The enemies, in consequence, were dogmatism, *dirigisme,* statism; these were the foes of liberty. In an article written in 1889 Sumner set forth his faith. Liberty grew out of the experiences of men in the use of civil institutions and could flourish only under law, the final authority and the greatest of the arrangements men made to live together. "These facts go to constitute a status," said he, "the status of a free man in a modern jural state."

THE CONTRIBUTIONS OF THE
LAW WRITERS AND THE COURTS

As a result of the writings of a number of lawyers and, following them, the decisions of state and federal courts, a legal climate that imposed limits on public authority was created to ensure this freedom in another respect; that is, liberty of contract. The state courts explored the conception quickly; it was not until the late 1880s, however, that the doctrine was embodied into federal law and there it stayed as late as 1937.

The architects of the notion that there were restraints that state legislatures and courts had to accept were three whose treatises were widely used in law schools, conned by lawyers, and cited by judges: Thomas W. Cooley of Michigan, lawyer and state judge; Christopher G. Tiedeman of Missouri, lawyer and law-school professor; and John F. Dillon of Iowa, lawyer and state judge.* These were western men; so much for the idea that the experiences of the frontier naturally disposed its sons to question authority.

All three sought and found the sources for limitations on the powers of states and municipalities in regard to persons and property. It is unnecessary here to explicate the basic assumptions from which Cooley, who was the theoretician of the group, started. Enough for us to note the rules he adduced from them and which became the law, as expounded by the courts. First, because the powers, notably the police powers, of public authority were limited by due process (guaranteed in the Fifth and Fourteenth Amendments of the Constitution), it was up to the courts to ensure "substantive due process"; that is to say, it was their duty to examine the substance of legislation and to intervene when property rights were being threatened. This meant that statutes and administrative rulings were unconstitutional when they interfered with the rights of property (the power of the owner to full liberty of choice and action) and the relations between business and labor regarding working conditions, hours, wages, and the like. Second, partial legislation, what Cooley called "class" legislation, which affected or benefited only a portion of the community, was equally under the ban. Third, from these laws followed the notion of "liberty of contract," which Cooley proclaimed in this wise in 1884: "This is the right essential to government, essential to society, essential to the acquisition of property, and to domestic relations." Fourth, there were limitations on the fiscal powers of the state; that is, unless taxes, appropriations, and borrowing had a "public purpose," they could be challenged in the courts. Tiedeman rang the changes on the limitations on police power and expanded broadly the rule of "liberty of contract" and Dillon acted similarly on the powers of tax and borrow. Thus the canon was filled out.

The state courts heard at once and so acted, citing as authority Cooley, Dillon, and Tiedeman, all three as text writers, the first two also as judges of the supreme courts of their states. The powers to tax, ap-

---

* Their initial works—there were many others—were the following: Cooley, *A Treatise on the Constitutional Limitations which Rest Upon the Legislative Powers of the States of the American Union* (1868); Tiedeman, *A Treatise on the Limitations of the Police Power of the States* (1886); Dillon, *Treatise on the Law of Municipal Corporations* (1872). See Hacker, *The World of Andrew Carnegie, 1865–1901,* 1968 for a full exposition of the law expounded and the responses of the state and federal courts.

propriate, and borrow were sharply cut back. Of what? Of attempts on the part of state legislatures to employ public moneys to assist enterprise, come to the relief of the distressed, and even to grant scholarships to worthy students. Said the highest court of Missouri in 1898 in connection with the last:

> Paternalism, whether state or federal . . . is the assumption by the government of a quasi-fatherly relation to the citizen and his family, involving excessive governmental regulation of the private affairs and business methods and interests of the people. . . . In a word it minimizes the citizen and maximizes the government.

The import of this hands-off policy has been mentioned before and should be stressed again: the tight rein held on public fiscal operations and their restriction to the barest necessities—safety, health, and education—gave private enterprise its greatest lift. The earnings of companies, instead of being shared with government, could be plowed back into the expansion of old and the investment in new ventures.

The state courts operated effectively in another sphere, which had to do with welfare legislation, the payment of wages, and the areas in which workers as trade unionists could operate. Hour legislation, even where health was involved, was declared unconstitutional because it interfered with the right to work. A decision along these lines, handed down by New York's highest court in 1885 was widely quoted and accepted in other jurisdictions. Judge Robert Earl, speaking for a unanimous bench, thus defined liberty:

> liberty, in its broadest sense as understood in this country, means. . . the right of one to use his faculties in all lawful ways, to live and work where he will, to earn his livelihood in any lawful calling, and to pursue any lawful trade or avocation. All laws, therefore, which impair or trammel these rights . . . are infringements upon his fundamental rights of liberty which are under constitutional protection.

Similarly declared unconstitutional up and down the land were statutes and ordinances that provided the following: work on city contracts could be performed only by union labor; ordinances fixing the eight-hour day and minimum wages for similar contracts; statutes prohibiting the payment of wages in truck (merchandise) or script; laws preventing companies from selling their products to their employees at higher prices than those prevailing in the market; laws prescribing hour and wage legislation for women, miners, and others engaged in occupations deleterious to health and safety; statutes outlawing "yellow-dog" contracts—under which workers refused to join unions after obtaining employment. In 1892 the Illinois highest court thus defined "liberty of

contract"; workers and employers were as equal in setting conditions of
work as other buyers and sellers negotiating in the market:

> Those who are entitled to exercise the elective franchise are deemed
> equals before the law, and it is not admissible to arbitrarily brand, by
> statute, one class of men, without reference to and wholly irrespective of
> their actual good or bad behavior, as too unscrupulous, and the other as too
> imbecile and weak, to exercise that freedom in contracting which is allowed
> to others.

It is important to bear in mind that the federal courts followed
rather than led; that is to say, in interpreting the Fourteenth Amendment, the Supreme Court started out by giving it a strictly procedural
reading having to do only with the civil rights of Negroes who had been
declared free under the Thirteenth Amendment. When the Court was
called on to pass on state legislation that limited property rights or sought
to regulate public utilities (railroads, warehouses), it found that the
Fourteenth Amendment's "equal protection" and "due process" clauses
had not been breached. This it did up to 1886, when it yielded to the
arguments of Associate Justice Stephen J. Field, whose early dissents were
now accepted and became the law of the land. The "equal protection"
clause was interpreted to include all "persons" mentioned in the amendment, corporate as well as natural, and the "due process" clause was given
a wide substantive reading.

In two leading sets of cases the Supreme Court brushed aside the
insistence of counsel and the claims of its own dissenting justices (Field,
the leader among them) that the Fourteenth Amendment had set up a
new national citizenship. The first was in the so-called *Slaughter-House*
cases of 1873. When in the interest of health the Louisiana legislature
created a slaughter-house monopoly in New Orleans, the argument was
made for companies seeking to establish abattoirs that the Fourteenth
Amendment protected "individual liberty, individual property, and individual security and honor from arbitrary, partial proscriptive, and un-
just legislation of state government." Not so, declared the majority of the
Supreme Court; the Fourteenth Amendment related only to Negro rights.

In 1877, in the *Granger* cases (the important one was *Munn v. Illinois,*
which had to do with a law passed by the Illinois legislature that sought,
among other things, to establish maximum railroad rates and the charges
of grain elevators), the Supreme Court stood by its guns. The "due
process" and "equal protection" clauses of the Fourteenth Amendment
had no relevance. Public authority, said the majority opinion, had always
had the power to regulate businesses affected with a public interest and
grain elevators were such. Field in his dissent held that grain elevators

were not a nuisance (here following Cooley). Therefore all efforts to cur-
tail property rights—these include use and income—violated due process.
The Court brushed these claims aside and reiterated its position when it
had another go at the Louisiana slaughter-house legislation in 1884.

Field now adopted another tack. He confronted the majority of the
Supreme Court with a series of *faits accomplis;* that is, decisions that
followed his reading of the Fourteenth Amendment rather than theirs.
This he was able to do as federal judge of the Ninth Circuit (California)
on which he sat (as did all Supreme Court justices on circuit until 1891).
The first came in 1882 when the Southern Pacific Railroad sought relief
from what it charged were oppressive taxes applied to it alone by San
Mateo County. (The case had come to the Ninth Circuit on appeal from
the California state courts.) Field found for the railroad, using all the
constitutional arguments he had employed in his dissenting opinions
and the additional one of "unequal and partial legislation" (again following Cooley). A similar finding was handed down against Santa Clara
County in 1883 by the same court. Said Field, in his 1882 decision, in
which he invoked the Fourteenth Amendment and both the "equal protection" and "due process" clauses:

> All the guarantees and safeguards of the Constitution for the protection
> of property possessed by individuals may, therefore, be invoked for the
> protection of the property of corporators. [Field here was equating "corpo-
> rators," who were "natural persons" with the corporation itself.] And as no
> discriminatory and partial legislation, imposing unequal burdens upon the
> property of individuals, would be valid under the Fourteenth Amendment,
> so no legislation imposing unequal burdens upon the property of corpora-
> tions can be maintained.

The *San Mateo* case came before the Supreme Court in 1882 and the
Santa Clara case, in 1886. In 1882 Roscoe Conkling, a leading Republican politician and recently resigned Senator from New York, appeared
for the Southern Pacific and presented a curious and sensational argument. He had been a member of the House in 1866 and a member of
the Congressional Joint Committee of Fifteen which drew up the Fourteenth Amendment. Conkling said the Committee—as its Journal pur-
portedly showed—had used the ambiguous term "person" rather than
"citizen" in the first article, for it meant to protect the rights of corporate property (and not alone the Negro freedmen) under the "due-
process" and "equal-protection" clauses. Whether Conkling's innuendoes
about the intent of Congress were listened to seriously by the Court we
do not know. The fact is that the Supreme Court gave in without a
struggle, for in 1886, after having heard the pleading in the *Santa Clara*

case, the Court in a unanimous oral opinion refused to upset Field's rulings in the Ninth Circuit by stating that all the justices understood that corporations were "persons" within the "equal protection" clause of the Fourteenth Amendment.

Thus the first wall was erected. In a series of decisions over the next 15 years the Supreme Court put up others, so that before the century ended all property, corporate as well as personal, and the rights of the individual to "freedom of contract" were assured these safeguards under the Fourteenth Amendment. Due process, with a substantive reading, was guaranteed. (This meant judicial review of state legislation and the findings of administrative agencies.) All persons were to have complete equality in the choice of a trade or calling and of acquiring, holding, and selling property. (The *Slaughter-House* cases were jettisoned.) The fixing of railroad rates, under the guise of regulation, by state boards established by legislation had to conform to requirements of reasonableness; the federal courts had the power of investigation to ascertain this and were to be guided by due process. (So the *Granger* cases were abandoned.) The Earl decision in the New York Court of Appeals of 1885 against state welfare legislation was taken under the broad cover of federal protection and the Fourteenth Amendment.

The last was the determination in the famous *Lochner* v. *New York* case which reached the Supreme Court in 1905. This time New York's highest court reversed the earlier finding when hearing arguments on a somewhat similar statute.

Said the Supreme Court about welfare laws:

> Statutes of the nature of that under review, limiting the hours in which grown and intelligent men may labor to earn their living, are mere meddlesome interferences with the rights of the individual, and they are not saved from condemnation by the claim that they are passed in the exercise of the police power. . . .

This drew the celebrated dissent of Justice Oliver Wendell Holmes, who had just been appointed to the Court. The people, through their legislatures, in their wisdom or foolishness, could decide under what laws they were to be governed. His own private feelings, as a justice, were irrelevant; his agreement or disagreement with any particular economic theory had "nothing to do with the right of a majority to embody their opinions in law." And Holmes went on:

> The Fourteenth Amendment does not enact Mr. Herbert Spencer's *Social Statics.* . . . A Constitution is not intended to embody a particular economic theory, whether of paternalism and the organic relation of the citizen to the state or of laissez-faire. It is made for people of fundamentally

differing views, and the accident of our finding certain opinions natural and familiar, or novel, and even shocking, ought not to conclude our judgment upon the question whether statutes embodying them conflict with the Constitution of the United States.

This plea for neutralism on Holmes's part was not to prevail. The Supreme Court continued to enunciate the doctrine of "freedom of contract," assuming that it was constitutional law, until 1937. Then, under the threat of packing the Court made by President Franklin D. Roosevelt, the justices beat an orderly retreat. It was Chief Justice Charles E. Hughes who sought to save "due process" as a safeguard of liberty in that year and to preserve the Court from tampering at the hands of the Executive. The Constitution, held the Chief Justice, did not speak of "freedom of contract," nor did it "recognize an absolute and uncontrollable liberty." Said Hughes, rendering the opinion for the Court in the *West Coast Hotel Company* v. *Parish* case:

> The liberty safeguarded is liberty in a social organization which requires the protection of law against the evils which menace the health, safety, morals, and welfare of the people. Liberty under the Constitution is thus necessarily subject to the restraints of due process, and regulation which is reasonable in relation to its subject and is adopted in the interests of the community is due process.

What was the consequence? From one pole the Supreme Court slowly began to swing to the other. "Due process," under the lead of Field, was a limitation on legislative power in every area in which property rights and freedom of individual action were involved. Following Hughes— and notably in the hands of the Warren Court in the 1950s and 1960s— "the due process clause becomes an actual instigation to legislative action of a levelling nature." This was the judgment of Edward S. Corwin, one of America's most respected commentators on constitutional law, writing in 1948. Both readings of the Constitution incorporated concepts with a difference of what is today called the "Positive State"; the earlier to help promote economic growth and development, the later, social or distributive justice (even if growth—and therefore development—had to be braked down).

THE CONTRIBUTIONS OF ORGANIZED LABOR TO THE GROWTH OF CAPITALISM

It is important to have in mind that organized labor, through autonomous national unions made up almost entirely of skilled workers and combined to act cooperatively in the American Federation of Labor, did as much if not more than the other mores of the time to hasten and secure the triumph of industrial capitalism. The national craft unions and the AFL, to do so, fought two countervailing tendencies at work in the ranks of the workers, one utopian, the other socialist, and prevailed successfully against both. By the end of the century they had won to this extent: they were being regarded in many quarters as spokesmen for the American workers committed to the improvement of wages and working conditions and against revolution.

The leaders of the organized workers, on their part, looked on themselves as a second force in American society which accepted private ownership and management of industry but operated through the unions (and not the state) for a larger share of the product, stability in employment, and protection against the insecurities of old age and invalidity. In effect, to use a modern term, coexistence was acquiesced in by both sides and mutual tolerance was the key: labor to recognize that business decisions were entirely the function of capital; capital to recognize labor's sphere through collective bargaining made secure by written contracts. The right to strike peaceably was accepted, and such agreements not only set up wage scales but also established labor's voice in fixing working conditions, the rights of seniority to the job, and control of apprenticeship and therefore entry.

It should not be assumed that amiability ruled in industrial relations in the United States during the years under review. There were bitter strikes attended by violence; sometimes state militias or federal troops were called in and strikes were often lost. Nor were the state and federal courts prepared to put a liberal interpretation on "peaceable" walkouts and demonstrations by workers. The key demand for recognition by trade unions as representative of all the workers in a trade or industry was not generally acceded to. Here I am talking of the more understanding employers who came to see that unionism, as practiced in the United States, was a force for industrial stability. Yet, as we take the long view, we can see that the movement in industrial relations was in the direction of the coexistence I have referred to. This was a state of "becoming" rather than of "being," and it was increasingly so as time went on and the futility of combat—as against discussion and agreement—came to be the rule. The point is that the basis for such an understanding was laid in the 1880s and 1890s.

This significant accomplishment—truce and peaceable coexistence— can be understood fully if the American working class world is contrasted with that of Europe. In America the ideology and tactics of class struggle and independent class and/or political activity were abandoned. These ideas included the whole range of European radical thought. American workers, as a whole, did not accept the romantic utopianism of anarchism (that of Godwin, Proudhon, Tolstoy, and Kropotkin): that self-governing communes, founded on the handicrafts and agriculture but anti-industrial, could be separated from private property and the huckstering of the market place. Nor did they become converts to the "scientific socialism" of Marx and Engels: the acceptance of industrialization but the inevitable dialectical breakdown as well of the capitalist processes, with the consequent capture of power by the workers (led, as Lenin saw later, by the Communist party) and the abolition of private property. Nor to anarchosyndicalism, which was previsioned by Marx's great antagonist Bakunin: class struggle, but with revolutionary unions in the forefront of the fight and the unions (accepting industrialization) the basis for the creation of a nonpropertied, egalitarian society.

In regard to political action they would have no part of intervention by the state by financing the communes (the form American utopianism took), the passage of welfare legislation, or the creation of a labor party that would work for parliamentary reforms and the achievement of socialism by working–class education and victories at the polling places. In sum, American organized labor looked to its achievement of a place as a second force through trade unionism, its weapons the strike and the boycott, and voluntary (rather than state) action to accomplish protection against the insecurities of an industrial society. The end result? An increasingly larger share of the national income without any disturbance of the processes by which it grew.

American utopianism (without anarchistic overtones) appeared twice. The first time was before the Civil War in the 1840s and 1850s, when it was largely influenced by Fourier and was the work of middle-class intellectuals but had little participation by the workers themselves. The second time was in the 1860s under the lead of the short-lived National Labor Union and in the 1870s and 1880s under that of the Knights of Labor, as the dream and hope of the workers alone. The ante-bellum utopianism represented a flight from growing industrialism and the factory system and refuge in self-sufficing and self-contained communities and financing (land, buildings, workshops) by philanthropists. The post-bellum utopianism tried—without success, however—to be more hardheaded. Appealing to all workers, skilled and unskilled, women, and Negroes, the National Labor Union and the Knights of Labor saw the futility of rejecting an industrializing society. The workers were to be organized in "assemblies," they were to agitate for reforms through the political processes, but their independence was to be assured by the creation of producers' cooperatives, presumably with their own funds but actually by government financing.

I have said that the unions of the National Labor Union and the "assemblies" of the Knights of Labor were to be the instrumentalists of social change and amelioration. The unionization was to be one-big-unionism (the "mixed assemblies" of the Knights of Labor opened their doors to all producers—professionals, white-collar workers, and skilled and unskilled laborers) and it played down strikes and boycotts as the weapons of the working class. Industrial disputes were to be settled by discussion and arbitration. Improvement in working conditions was to be accomplished by pressure on the existing legislative processes but more and more by the formation of independent workers' parties which would seek to attain the following: the eight-hour day, the ending of undesirable, competitive immigration (contract labor, the Chinese), mechanics' lien laws, and, most important of all, monetary reform.

Heart's desire, utopianism's grand accomplishment, was to be the producers' cooperatives. The workers (financed by the assemblies of the Knights of Labor) would buy their own mines, erect their own mills and factories, and create their own distributive agencies; thus they would have independence and security but would also produce better and cheaper for the market because their enterprises would be worker-owned and managed and because they were not tied to the wage-and-profit nexus.

Why monetary reform? More money—government-issued, not created by private banks—would make plentiful funds available, at nominal or low interest rates, to help in the financing of the producers' cooperatives. The idea of government money for this purpose had first appeared in the United States in Edward Kellogg's *Labour and Other Capital* (1848). It was taken up again by the National Labor Union in 1868 when that curious and amorphous body virtually adopted as their own a pamphlet, the work of Alexander Campbell, written in 1864 and recast in 1868 and called "The True Greenback, or the Way to Pay the National Debt Without Taxes and Emancipate Labor." The Civil War Greenbacks were to be the only money in circulation and a full legal tender (this would end the money monopoly of the banks). The Civil War debt was to be turned into interconvertible bonds; bonds and Greenbacks were to revolve around an interest rate of 3 per cent (Kellogg had fixed it at 1 per cent) and were to be used as credit for loans secured by mortgage. The Knights of Labor, succeeding the National Labor Union, abandoned Kellogg-Campbell (interconvertibility and public loans) and opted simply for more money: hence its espousal of Greenbackism and later Free Silver and its support of the political parties that raised these banners.

The skilled workers learned quickly enough—sometimes as a result of unhappy experiences, for neither knew anything about the conduct of strikes—to take the measure of the National Labor Union and the Knights of Labor. They combined their locals into national unions, became practiced in the organization of strikes, and used them to get the eight-hour day and higher wages; they eschewed politics and turned a deaf ear to the radicals, largely made up of European immigrants, who talked only of class conflict. The national craft unions grew in numbers and in combined membership but with varying fortunes, until the appearance of the AFL of 1886, which taught them how to weather recession and depression. In the 1850s these national unions had emerged among the printers, stonecutters, hat finishers, iron molders, and machinists. Subsequently they formed similar bodies among the building-trade and railway workers, cigar makers, and coal miners. At the end of the long depression of the 1870s the total number of organized skilled workers was not much more than 50,000, but by the end of the century there were more than a half million, half of them affiliated with the AFL.

European inspired radicalism—Marxian- and Lasallean-style socialism, anarchism, embryo anarchosyndicalism—appeared in the United States in the late 1860s and in the 1870s and 1880s; its influence was minimal. It was not until the first 17 years of the twentieth century that Marxian socialism (following the lead of the evolutionary gradualism of the Germans and Austrians and not the revolutionary preachments of the Russians) and anarchosyndicalism began to penetrate deeply into American trade unionism.

There were two sections of Karl Marx's First International set up in the United States, one made up of Germans the other a ragtag of middle-class intellectuals who expired even before the First International broke up on the rocks of the wrangling of those two implacable antagonists, Marx and Bakunin. Lasallian clubs were formed in the United States in the large cities and penetrated some of the trade unions. (Their inspiration was Ferdinand Lasalle, who had founded the German Workers party and preached the ideas of the peaceful capture of power by parliamentary means; the creation of a powerful centralized state, nationally orientated; and the carrying out of programs of social reform.) As a result of their influence there appeared in the 1870s the Social Democratic party of North America, which then changed to the Workingmen's party, and then to the Socialist Labor party. It succumbed to the usual swan song of American reformism when it joined the Greenback Labor party in the presidential election of 1878. In 1880 the Socialist Labor party split in two; one fragment threw in its lot with Bakunin's anarchistic International Working People's Association and the other continued as a paper organization until Daniel DeLeon—a proto-Bolshevik, the anticipator, perhaps even teacher, of Lenin, who saw a tightly controlled, rigidly disciplined party as the revolutionary vanguard of the working class—took over in 1890.

Anarchism—not simply the philosophical mutualism of Godwin, Proudhon, and their American disciple Stephen Andrews, but mutualism with terror—attracted more followers in the United States. All authority, to the Bakuninists, was suspect—the organized authority of state, church, military, and police—and terror was to be used symbolically against its leaders to disorganize society. (Later on, at the beginning of the twentieth century—this was the contribution of the Frenchman Georges Sorel— the general strike was added as the means by which the workers would capture power.) But there would be no political action and no "authoritarian communism" (thus Bakunin on Marx). The anarchists sought freedom, to be achieved in the creation of independent communes, bound together in a loose federation made up of the workers only, in which all capital—factories, tools, land, and raw materials—would belong to those who created it. These two notions, when combined, spelled anarchosyndicalism, which was fully developed when the Industrial Workers of the World was formed in 1905. When the German Johann Most arrived in the United States in 1882, he brought the message of Bakuninism and the tactic of terror. An American section of the Bakunin International made its appearance in the next year, and it was with this section that a number of workers affiliated themselves in Chicago and captured a handful of trade unions. These were the unions and their leaders who became involved in the Chicago strikes of May 1886, which culminated in the disastrous Haymarket affair. The bomb that was thrown, the shootings and killings that followed, and the hostile court that tried the Chicago anarchists marked the end of the anarchist unions and also precipitated the abrupt decline of the Knights of Labor.

It was against all of these brands of reformism and radicalism that national craft unionism, particularly under the lead of the AFL, turned its face. The Noble Order of the Knights of Labor had appeared in 1869 as a secret society and began to grow when it gave up the mumbo jumbo of fraternalism (largely as a result of the hostility of the Catholic Church). The original intention was the formation of local "assemblies" along craft lines; but, because the Knights were more successful in smaller communities, the "mixed assembly" became typical. The pattern took on this form: all producers—whether farmers or owners of small shops, blue- or white-collar workers or self-employed professionals, whether men or women, white or black—could belong. When resistance to the dilution of the membership occurred, the Knights were willing to create special "mixed assemblies" made up of women or of Negroes exclusively. Local "assemblies" were combined into district "assemblies" which joined to form the General Assembly. A first meeting was held in 1878 at which the tactics of the Knights, if they can be called that, were evolved; in particular, as has been already said, producers' cooperatives and political action—the latter a mixed bag of the popular agitational questions of the day, with the lead being given to monetary reform.

When it came to the crunch—strikes, boycotts, and industrial warfare, as opposed to debate—the Knights faltered. They refused to form local trade assemblies—there were some—into separate district assemblies. They were averse to or incapable of collecting strike funds. When called upon on May 1, 1886, to join the national craft unions in a widespread strike for the eight-hour day, they promised to participate, but its Grand Master Workman, Terence V. Powderly, gave secret orders to stay out. Despite all this fiddle-faddle, the Knights grew to 730,000 (a floating membership, not necessarily paying dues) in 1886; in that fateful year its rapid descent began. The general failures of its producers' cooperatives, the tragic end of the Haymarket, and most important, the hostility of the AFL were the chief causes.

The American Federation of Labor, after a different kind of effort at common action, begun in 1881, had failed, emerged in 1886. In the next decade and a half it worked out and sharpened its doctrinal and tactical schema. Under the leadership of Samuel Gompers—he had been a Knight and had quit; he had been a socialist and had become disillusioned—the AFL concentrated, in Gomper's own phrase, on "unionism pure and simple." The Federation started out with twenty-five national craft unions whose autonomy and therefore, jurisdictional rights were recognized. Open war was declared on the Knights of Labor. The challenge of socialism was met in 1893–1895 and beaten; the AFL, as such, refused to accept any part of a socialist ideology, no matter how mild. It avoided, again as an organization, independent political activity. The legislation it advocated—to be proposed by its friends—was concerned only with labor: laws to overcome the hostility of the courts to strikes and boycotts; the exemption of trade unions from the antitrust laws; the abolition of child labor; the writing of workmen's compensation acts; and minimum wages for women in industry. It fought dual unionism: first formally barring unions affiliated with the Knights of Labor, then those unions that had thrown in their lot with DeLeon's Socialist Labor party. It made mistakes, the leading one being its failure to grapple with the problem of the unskilled, that is, to form industrial unions. (When Negroes sought to enter AFL unions, they were set up in separate locals and denied apprenticeship training.)

The furrow the AFL plowed was thus a straight and narrow one. The aim and purpose of unionism was to be achieved under the wage-and-profit system of industrial capitalism. Organized labor was to take care of its own through voluntarism. Higher wages, better hours, and control of working rules were to be achieved by industrial struggle, collective bargaining, and hopefully the closed shop. Everything else—producers' cooperation, third-party politics, an independent labor (socialist) party, and collaboration with all "the producing classes"—diverted unionism. From what? From equal partnership, as a second force, with capital.

Thus the AFL and its member unions were not opposed to capitalism. On the contrary: this was the peaceable coexistence to which I have referred: Gompers, representing the AFL, was willing to associate himself with the National Civic Federation, formed by a group of industrialists, of which Mark Hanna (coal and iron tycoon of Ohio and a Senator from that state) was the leader and president. The purpose of the Federation was the maintenance of industrial peace, which could best be furthered by trade-union recognition; Gompers became the Federation's vice president. In 1901 Gompers said:

> There is a substantial trend toward agreement between the laborers and the capitalists, employed and employer, for the uninterrupted production and distribution of wealth, and, too, with ethical consideration for the *common interests* of all the people. (Italics original.)

In the same year, in addressing the National Civic Federation, Gompers was able to declare: "There is in our time, if not a harmony of interests . . . yet certainly a community of interests, to the end that industrial peace shall be maintained." To this extent American capitalism knew it had an ally, albeit an uneasy one, that would fight radicalism and dual unionism and neither threaten the processes of the market, private ownership, or the profit system nor make inordinate demands on the state.

THE CONTRIBUTION OF A COMMITMENT
TO EDUCATION

From the very beginnings of the Republic the United States assumed an important obligation: the establishment and maintenance of the common (publicly supported) school. Initially the term applied only to elementary education; after the Civil War it was broadened to include secondary schools. The federal government, normally standing aloof from programs involving social legislation, as we have seen, made an exception here, again using lands from the public domain to encourage the states to push local authorities into assuming the responsibility for establishing and supporting schools. The upshot was that state legislatures assisted with funds and, even more, laid down the rules for school-leaving age, days of school attendance, the furnishing of textbooks, and provision for the establishment of normal schools for teacher training as conditions for the receipt of state aid. The United States, in this respect, moved farther and faster than the countries of Europe. Built on top of this scheme, again with the federal spur of generous land grants, were the state Agricultural and Mechanical Colleges, also publicly supported which continued to branch out into engineering and applied science. Common-school education for larger and larger numbers of boys and girls and technical education for advanced students help to account in great part for the leap forward the United States made in the post-Civil War period. Here, in other words, was what economists call today an investment in human capital as an important element in the stimulation of America's growth and development.

The commitment to the common school carried with it another significant element, thanks to the thinking, writing, and influence of two outstanding educators, Horace Mann and William Torrey Harris, for with it was linked training in habits of work and mastery of a course of intellectually-grounded study, all designed to prepare the youth of America for meaningful participation in the particular world in which it was to live.

Horace Mann was given a platform for his educational ideas when Massachusetts in 1834 established a permanent state board of education to which he was named secretary. In his reports, other writings, and speeches Mann repeated again and again these claims for the common school. A republic could not endure "without well-appointed and efficient means for the universal education of the people." This universal education would ensure social stability. It would be the "great equalizer." It would be "the creator of wealth undreamed of." It would diminish the hostilities between the rich and the poor, for it would create opportunities by which the sons and daughters of the humble could rise. Mann, brought up in the midst of New England transcendentalism, also proclaimed the common-school's moral triumphs: said he, it "would create a more far-seeing intelligence and a purer morality than has ever existed among communities of men." This was the soft, sentimental side; but there was a hard one as well, and here Mann anticipated the modern-day economists, for he also promised that free, universal education would act

> . . . as the grand agent for the development or augmentation of natural resources; [it was] more powerful in the production and gainful employment of the total wealth of the country than all the other things mentioned in the works of the political economists.

By 1860 the United States (always excepting the South) had made giant strides. A majority of the states had provided for common schools. Massachusetts and New York had taken the significant step forward of enacting compulsory attendance laws. Massachusetts, New York, and Pennsylvania had authorized local authorities to establish public secondary schools. Michigan and Wisconsin had created public state universities. In 1850, in a total of 23.2 million whites, 3.6 million children and young people were enrolled in all types of educational institutions and of these 3.4 million were in publicly supported schools.

William Torrey Harris, a professionally trained philosopher, took up where Mann left off. Harris was superintendent of the St. Louis public schools from 1868 to 1880 and U.S. Commissioner of Education from 1889 to 1906. Harris, as a philosopher, was a Hegelian who accepted the upward movement of progress and the assurance of liberty for the individual by the dialectical process of construction and recreation. Change took place without the repudiation of true and tried values. If society was to survive and freedom to be maintained, the individual had to be prepared to play his proper role. He had to have a regulated mind and orderly habits; his instincts had to be brought under the same controls to achieve that free and rational world that was Hegel's hope.

The common school was to be an important instrument here for maintaining the stability of American society (and private property, law, and representative government). The disciplining of minds obtained from study, the mastery of fundamentals (mathematics, geography, literature and art, grammar, and history), plus a classical education as the essential core of the high school curriculum, and the rules of "regularity, punctuality, silence, conformity to order" were the means by which young people were to be trained to take their places in a changing world.

We must keep this in mind as we evaluate Harris' ideas: he was addressing himself largely to the needs of boys and girls in America's big cities, most of whom were of foreign stock. How better to serve them than by emphasis on such a regimen and, so he believed, the achievement of self-respect and acquisition of "the habit of self-control and of obedience to social order" out of which would emerge "a moral sense of conformity to the order necessary for the harmonious action of all"? To youngsters whose parents spoke in alien tongues and who came as the rejected of Europe's institutions of class, privilege, and prescription, here was a great lift of hope: one could build self-respect and acquire a sense of belonging and a sense of community.

The secondary school, during the half century after the Civil War, also received general acceptance, and public authority indicated its obligation for financing. A debate went on before its purposes were agreed on. Was it to be regarded as a "people's college," the institution "which shall level the distinction between the rich and the poor, as far as power and place are concerned" (so said a school man in 1891)? Was it to be a vocational school that would teach the manual arts? Opposing voices (Harris a leader among them) won the day. A Committee of Ten of the National Education Association, headed by Charles W. Eliot, the respected president of Harvard, issued a report in 1893 which was to guide the theory and practice of America's secondary (they came to be called high) schools for almost a half century. The purpose of the high school, said the report, was to give the student "four years of strong and effective mental training." It was therefore not merely a preparatory school for college entrance, and it broke sharply with the European tradition of being wholly based on a classical education.

This was so in two particulars, which followed the reforms Eliot had effected in the course of study at Harvard, thus transforming the meaning of a "liberal-arts" education. Electives were permitted and "modern" subjects were strongly emphasized: The basic curriculum consisted of Latin and Greek, but there were also German, French, and (locally) Spanish. The English language and literature were to be taught. Mathematics was required of all (algebra, geometry, trigonometry). So was history, and this came to mean American and modern European history. The natural and physical sciences were included—biology required of all; a choice of chemistry or physics later. This program shaped itself in practice somewhat as follows in urban high schools: four years of Latin or three of Latin and one of Greek; three years of a modern language; four years of English (theme writing throughout, the study of English and American novels and poems, and always at least two of Shakespeare's plays); three years of mathematics, and an additional year as an elective; and a year each of biology and chemistry or physics. In the last two years electives were permitted in such subjects as descriptive geometry, geology, physical geography, civics, and even additional foreign languages.

For those eager to learn, particularly among the children of foreign stock, this program opened wide many windows: mastery in the structure of the English language (which a knowledge of Latin helped so magnificently) and practice in writing it; introduction to foreign languages and some of their modern literature; and training in mathematics and the rudiments of science. Those whose appetites were whetted could range far, thanks to the supplementation provided by access to public libraries and membership in high school clubs, usually having a subject content, which met after hours.

The Committee of Ten made concessions to the demand for "practical" training as well: a "commercial" or a "scientific" course of study might also be taken. Some high schools had all three tracks, and some gave emphasis to one over the other two. In any event, crossing from one to another was made possible. Thus the Committee of Ten anticipated much of the thinking that is going on today about the high school—the "comprehensive" school and also the "scientific" school (as opposed to manual or vocational education).

All of these efforts were beginnings, and the advances were modest, but the directions laid out were clearly marked and generally accepted. The way was prepared for the great expansion of American public education in the 1950s. Nevertheless, the gains made by the common schools in the post-Civil War period were not inconsiderable. To cite a few. By 1898 the average length of the school year was 143.1 days (compared with 132.1 days in 1870), the average number of days attended by each pupil was 97.8 days (compared with 79.4 days), and the school age population, 15–18 years, enrolled in school was 70.08 per cent for the whole country (compared with 61.45). At the turn of the century, on the average, the country's population was receiving school instruction for five years of 200 days each. The school-leaving age was generally around 14, but working papers were granted if a child had finished elementary school earlier. All this was not very much, as is evidenced by the fact that in 1900 only 6.4 per cent of the 17-year-olds was graduating from high school (it was 2.0 per cent in 1871 but 62.3 per cent in 1956). Naturally, college attendance was even smaller. In 1900 4.01 per cent of the population 18–21 years old was enrolled in institutions of higher learning (it was 1.68 per cent in 1870 but 30.00 per cent in 1956). Nevertheless, without the commitment to universal public education, the United States would not have started so much sooner than the European countries, would not have made the measurable progress it did from 1870 to 1900, and would not have had the proper trails blazed for the great accomplishments of the 1950s and 1960s.

In an earlier chapter mention was made of the interest in technical education in the United States before the Civil War, the appearance of engineering colleges, and the splendid encouragement given to technical education by the passage of the Land-Grant College Act of 1862. There can be no doubt that American leadership in technology—beginning to emerge in the last decades of the nineteenth century, coming to full flower in the first half of the twentieth century, and assuming the role of teacher all over the world in the 1960s (when supplemented by instruction in business management)—owed much to its engineering (and applied science) colleges and universities that sprang up after the Civil War. The privately supported institutions (some independent, some attached to general universities) expanded their courses of study to include every phase of engineering (mechanical, chemical, electrical, mining, as well as civil) and built them on the firm foundation of mathematics and the theoretical sciences; these schools became technical universities at least 50 years before Europe began dreaming of this kind of formal instruction. The Massachusetts Institute of Technology—founded in 1861 but not opened until 1865—sounded the keynote for the expanding technical university when it declared in its prospectus:

> [It was to furnish] systematic training in the applied sciences, which alone can give to the industrial classes a sure mastery over the materials and processes with which they are concerned. Such a training, forming what may be called the intellectual element in production, has, we believe, become indispensable to fit us for successful competition with other nations in the race of industrial activity. . . .

The state A. and M. colleges, thanks to the Morrill Land-Grant Act, began humbly by offering part-time programs to working farm boys and girls (manual training for the men, home economics for the women) but steadily advancing and improving attendance requirements and courses of study. Most stayed at the college (as opposed to university) level before the turn of the century. On the other hand, their emphasis shifted from farming to applied science, in which engineering became the more important; they had many more students because they were free or charged only nominal fees, and they constituted the beginnings of higher education for Negroes in the United States, for separate Negro A. and M. colleges were established in all the southern (and in some northern) states. Before 1900 separate A. and M. colleges already existed in 28 states; in 15 others, in which state universities were well established, the land grants were turned over to them to include the courses required by the Morrill Act. By 1900, it was estimated, there were more than 25,000 students (not all full-time) attending the land-grant A. and M. colleges, two-thirds of whom were enrolled in courses of study in engineering. A fairly good estimate, made in 1900, gave these totals for engineering graduates: before 1870, 866; 1871–1880, 2259; 1881–1890, 3837; 1891–1900, 10,430.

These figures were to expand impressively in the twentieth century, with by far the larger contribution representing publicly supported institutions. Thus the concept of the common school threw a lengthening shadow.

XI

THE PROCESSES OF
INDUSTRIALIZATION AFTER
THE CIVIL WAR

THE CHANGING STRUCTURE OF THE
AMERICAN ECONOMY

To speed the processes of industrialization in the post-Civil War period changes in the structure of the American economy were required. Broadly, these changes may be summarized, first, as the establishment of a national banking system, under the general supervision of the federal government, which made possible a uniform currency and some control over the money in circulation; and perhaps even more important, the imaginative extension of the role of state banks, by which new kinds of credit facilities were created and the money supply further augmented. The consequence was the appearance of an expanding credit market in which all sorts of risky ventures found financial resources available to them; and, because the credit market was becoming increasingly national, interest rates for accommodation loans and short-term commercial needs began to fall. The money supply thus grew with business needs and at prices that were not deemed oppressive by those who sought financing.

The appearance of a national market for goods and services was another significant change. The greatest factor in its creation was the rapid construction of trunk railroads that spanned the continent; wastefully (because competitively) constructed, initially in advance of settlement, overloaded with debt, the Pacific railroads, and those in the Northwest and Southwest that built branches and feeder lines at a frenzied pace, pushed their tracks into virtually every section of the backcountry. This could not have been achieved so swiftly without financing. The federal, state and county governments helped, as we have seen. Foreign financial resources, by the purchase of railroad bonds, rendered yeoman service, but we must not overlook the great part played by the American banks that furnished the funds to start construction, to help in the acquisition of independent lines, and to round out the systems. They, in effect, monetized the railroad bonds, so that a considerable part of the augmented money supply came from this source. An important effect of this kind of financing and construction was that American railroading—and here the United States was unique—was competitively built and operated. This competition forced reductions in costs, the adoption of new technological devices, and the concomitant lowering of rates. The influence of the last factor on the expansion of the national market must be apparent.

The western railroads sought to open up the Great Plains country to commercial farmers and the cultivation of food staples—cereal grains (largely wheat and then corn), beef cattle, and sheep. Wool clips, of course, were not insignificant, nor were the products of the mining and lumbering industries on the western edges of the Plains. The great expansion of wheat growing and cattle raising, because of the widening railroad net, was of particular significance in two connections: ample food supplies were available for the country's exploding labor force concentrated in industrialized towns and cities, and food surpluses constituted a marketable export (more important than cotton), which could be poured into Europe. After 1873 the American balance of trade turned favorable, thanks to these surpluses of wheat and wheat flour, meat products, and live cattle, and these earnings made possible interest payments on foreign investments in the United States. The United States was solvent on international accounts, although a debtor nation until the outbreak of World War I.

Western agriculture responded to these various impetuses—cheap transportation, available mortgage money, and a national and international market—by quick settlement and technological improvements (farm machinery, as far as cereal production was concerned, and improved strains of cattle, hogs, and sheep for livestock growing). The value of farm wealth jumped spectacularly, farm prices fell, and, if realized income lagged, deferred income was built up to account for the well-being of American agriculture in the first two decades of the twentieth century.

The clamor for an increase in the money supply, which rose in the western country in the late 1880s and 1890s, was not a sign of agricultural malaise, as we shall see.

The great contribution of a working force which had grown faster than the country's whole population has already been referred to. This force helped in the industrialization of many of the towns and notably of the larger cities. Urbanization was a consequence of and a contributing factor to growth. New financial institutions made possible the erection of multiple-family housing, the construction of rapid transit, the electrification of urban trolleys, and the public utilities of gas, electricity, and even water by private companies. Public financing by municipalities played a part in the building of bridges and subways, in the improvement of the water supply and the laying out of sewage and garbage-disposal systems, and in the erection of new schools and hospitals; yet by far the greater share of the cities' infrastructure came from private financing. The external economies of urbanization—one of the great ones was the specialization of services that cities make possible—were an indirect consequence of all the forces and factors at work. On all of these aspects of the changing structure some comments are in order here.

MONEY AND BANKING

As late as the 1880s Americans—even many of the economists—were not aware that money was more than currency in circulation. Because demand deposits were not included in their calculations, all sorts of special interest-groups—reformers speaking for the workers, newly arising manufacturers, the farmers of the Plains country, and southern cotton growers—argued that the money supply was inadequate and demanded more. Why so? Evidence cited was the sharp drop in the wholesale prices during 1873–1896—they fell 50 per cent. Farmers in particular were vocal because the mortgage debts they had incurred for land purchases, farm improvements, and the acquisition of machinery and livestock, it seemed to them, had to be paid off in dearer dollars. The fact is, it can be argued, prices declined because increasing productivity, a national market, which was highly competitive, and low railroad and ocean rates all made possible lower costs and therefore lower prices. Examples of the triumphs of greater productivity will be commented on as we go along.

Initially, the proponents of more money advocated the printing of additional federal greenbacks (and, because they distrusted banks, the supression of national bank notes); then they shifted to the free and unlimited coinage of silver at a ratio of 16 to 1 (when the commercial price of silver had already begun to fall). The farmers of the Plains and those of the South—anticipating the support prices of the New Deal's Agricultural Adjustment Act 40 years later—proposed the so-called Sub-Treasury plan under which public agencies, by issuing negotiable certificates of deposit, would lend against segregation from the market of nonperishable agricultural commodities.

The needs of the Civil War—to finance military requirements, to furnish funds for all the suppliers turning out war materiél, uniforms, shoes, blankets, and foodstuffs for the armies—forced an expansion of the money supply. The heavy outflow of gold to pay for imports and the hoarding of gold at home, as confidence in an easy victory disappeared, led to the suspension of specie payments at the end of 1861. The price of gold went up; the premium in gold was as high as 103 in 1864, and at the end of fiscal 1865 was still as high as 57 per cent. At the same time the Treasury and the Congress were reluctant to sell bonds at a discount and to impose heavy taxes on business earnings and operations. All of these considerations led to the decision to emit fiat money, to borrow through Treasury bills and notes, and to create national banks. The last would be empowered to issue bank notes against the purchase and security of war bonds. Three legal-tender acts in 1862 and 1863 authorized the Treasury to put into circulation $450 million in greenbacks and to float $400 million in Treasury notes; both sets of instruments constituted money. The consequence was a rapid inflation in which the consumer price index jumped from 100 in 1860 to 175 in 1865; however, the real wages of workers fell, despite the demands of the war for labor and the pull of the West (where agriculture was prospering).

At first the Republicans in Congress favored this easy-money policy (which went along with the high protective tariffs they enacted). The expansion of the money supply produced more available credit for business ventures, the mounting premium on gold diminished imports, and tariffs encouraged Hamilton's and Carey's "infant manufacture," in turn financed by the public money in circulation that the banks had available. With the war over, the Republicans shifted to a contracted money supply. The desiderata now became the following: legal tenders (greenbacks) were to be reduced and specie payments resumed, thus ensuring price stability. Monetary stability would encourage the return to the United States of foreign investments and at the same time the maintenance of protectionism would be enough to diminish the flow of foreign manufactured goods into the country. Opposition on the part of manufacturers had begun to weaken.

On the other hand, the Democrats and the workers (both had been for hard money and therefore contraction in the Jacksonian period and later) had become expansionists. We have seen the vagaries the workers' parties and organizations followed: the Democrats in the presidential year 1868 accepted the Pendleton Plan—an augmented greenback supply, the abolition of national bank notes, and the exchange of federal bonds for greenbacks.

The Democrats were defeated in 1868 (and the recession of 1866–1868 was over). In 1869 Congress made a fateful decision: the existing volume of greenbacks was to remain untouched, the Treasury was to pay all its obligations—greenbacks and interest-bearing bonds and notes—in coin and specie payments were to be resumed "at the earliest practicable moment." In 1875 (in the midst of prolonged depression) Congress voted to resume specie payments on January 1, 1879: that is, greenbacks, now reduced to $300 million, were to be redeemed at par, in gold or silver, at the discretion of the Treasury. To conciliate those still hankering after expansion, the National Banking Act was amended to excide the limitation on the issue of bank notes ($300 million) which originally had been written into the law. Resumption was carried out without any loss of confidence, for the Treasury had succeeded in accumulating a sizable gold reserve ($135.4 million, constituting 40 per cent of the legal tenders outstanding; at least one-half, held by the national banks, was not in circulation). Further, the American trade balance was now favorable, thanks to the heavy exports of agricultural goods, a good part of which also had been paid for in gold.

If, as has been argued here, there was no stringency of money, how account for the Silver Purchase Acts of 1878 and 1890? In part, they were due to the pressure of silver-mining interests (for the commercial price of silver had been falling), in part to conciliate the workingmen's parties, and in part because of the exigencies of politics. (The Tariff Act of 1890 could not have been passed had not a bargain been made with the congressional representatives of the silver-mining states.)

There was no Crime of 1873 when silver was demonetized. In that year Congress had suspended the minting of silver coins because the commercial price had been going up since 1837 and little silver had been brought to government offices (in 1873 the silver dollar was worth $1.02). With the discovery of new silver lodes in the Far West, however (and the adoption of the monometallic gold standard by European countries) the price of silver began to fall. In 1874 the ratio was 17.94 to 1 (instead of the 16 to 1 the Treasury had been maintaining up to 1873) and then went up to 18.39 to 1.

The Silver Purchase Act of 1878 brought little relief to the silver miners nor did it satisfy the monetary expansionists. The Treasury was authorized to buy and mint $2 million to $4 million silver bullion monthly, making its purchases at the market; against this it could issue silver certificates. During 1878–1890 only 378 million silver dollars (at a cost of $308 million) were presumably added to the money supply, but as much as 65 per cent of the silver coin did not circulate and was retired by the banks to the government sub-treasury offices. The Silver Purchase Act of 1890 did somewhat better, but it was repealed in 1893 at the insistence of President Cleveland, who saw the flow of gold out of the United States (the depression of 1893–1897 had set in) as a want of confidence on the part of Europe in America's monetary management. Under the Act of 1890 the Treasury was to buy 4.5 million ounces of silver monthly and this time issue against them Treasury notes, which, of course, were full legal tender and therefore part of the money supply in circulation. Between 1890 and 1893 $153 million was expended on silver purchases.

It should be noted that the Treasury bought at the market price (around 20 to 1). Hence the demands of the farmer parties and organizations of "unlimited coinage of silver at a rate of 16 to 1." The position on money of the western farmers is discussed later in this chapter. At this point some mention of the National Banking Act of 1863 is required.

The National Banking Act was passed by Congress for these reasons: to give the country a uniform currency to be issued by national banks and regulated by the Treasury (in 1865 state banks were denied, in effect, the right of note issue by being asked to pay an excise tax of 10 per cent); to establish a market for war bonds, for national banks, to emit notes, had to back them with government bonds; and to create a national reserve system. A new office was set up, headed by the Comptroller of the Currency, who was to approve the charters and watch over the performance of the national banks. The original act had other characteristics, some of which were limitations on the expansion of a national banking system. The minimum capitalization was $50,000 (thus preventing their organization in small towns), but banks could not lend on mortgages (and this prevented the financing of farmers and urban housing construction). Neither could they lend in excess of 10 per cent of capital to a single person or company (thus limiting the size of accommodation loans to finance the capital requirements of businessmen). Nor could they have savings departments or widen their activities through branch banking. To issue bank notes national banks were required to deposit with the Treasury government bonds worth not less than $30,000 or not less than one-third of their capitalization; against this amount they could issue notes equal to 90 per cent of the bonds. (It can be seen that when bonds were selling at premiums—as they were once the war was over—it did not pay the banks to issue bank notes.) The total note issue for the country was to be $300 million; this ceiling was removed in 1875, which virtually established free banking. (This had no effect on the increase of money in circulation; quite the reverse, the total for banknote issue began to fall).

The reserve requirements created three kinds of banks. At the bottom of the pyramid were "country" banks; they were to keep in hand, in "lawful" money, 15 per cent of their notes and deposits, but three-fifths of these reserves could be maintained, at interest, in banks of reserve cities, of which 17 were established. These banks, in turn, had to maintain reserves of 25 per cent but could keep one-half of this amount with national banks in New York (and, later, in Chicago and St. Louis). Central reserve banks in these cities were to maintain reserves of 25 per cent. (In 1874, by an amended act, reserves were to be based entirely on deposits.) These limitations were to be noted. There was no flexibility of reserves as credit was expanded or contracted. The temptation was strong for country banks and reserve city banks to keep their funds in New York, and New York banks, on their part, used these funds to finance the call-money market (stock-market purchases). At harvest time, therefore, when country banks needed all their financial resources, only a limited amount of credit was available. (At this point the Treasury learned how to take on some of the functions of a central bank. Beginning in 1903, Treasury monies, and not merely revenue receipts, were placed in depository banks as needed, thus allowing the Treasury to regulate the flow of money and place reserves in strategic cities.)

One hole in the original act was plugged in 1874. There was no provision for central redemption of bank notes and therefore the creation of a floating note supply, not too sensitive to business needs, which could be an inflationary force, threatened. In 1874 the Banking Act of that year (another concession to the contractionists) provided for the redemption of such notes in "lawful" money by the United States Treasurer. To help, banks were called on to deposit 5 per cent of their circulation in "lawful" money, which in turn was to be considered part of their reserves. The step had two consequences: the government in effect guaranteed all the notes in circulation and the deposit-reserve ratio rose.

Thus the national banks were hedged around with all sorts of protective devices, many of which turned out to be limitations on imaginative banking. The way was open for the creation of a new role for state banking: farmers, new manufacturers, small businessmen, and those interested in urban growth and its infrastructure required banks more amenable to development. Because, by the Act of 1865, state banks were in effect barred from issuing notes, legislatures were encouraged to revise and liberalize state banking laws, thus opening fresh vistas for them. More and more through general enabling acts—and no longer by special charter, as had been the case before the Civil War—state banks were permitted to grow in large numbers and expand their operations; also, a new kind of bank—the trust company (which could buy company securities for its portfolios)—made its appearance. These state banks had smaller capitalizations and lower reserves: part of their capitalization did not have to take the form of investment in public securities and they could lend on mortgages and make accommodation loans. It is to be noted further that savings banks, also state chartered, participated in furnishing mortgage credit (as did insurance companies). Between 1875 and 1895 the total assets of savings banks increased from $896 million to $2.2 billion.

Thus new credit facilities were created and the result was an impressive growth in the country's money supply, as more and more of it took the form of bank deposits rather than currency in circulation. By 1897, it was estimated, there were in existence 2700 state banks (almost half of which had capitalizations of $20,000 or less) with a total capitalization of $69.5 million; this is to be compared with the 1116 national banks whose total capitalization was $58.3 million. By 1876—so rapidly did they grow—the deposits of the state banks already exceeded those of the national banks ($1.2 billion against $841.7 million); by 1896 state bank deposits were $3.3 billion and national bank deposits, $2.3 billion.

We can now say something about the monetary resources of the United States, necessary, in part, because of the prolonged agitation for increases in money during the whole period 1865–1896 and because of the stridency the discussion took on at the hands of the Populists and the Bryanists, during 1888–1896. Friedman and Schwartz * furnish an authoritative answer. There was enough money to meet the country's expanding requirements. Of course, there was no knowledgable monetary policy (and, of course, no fiscal policy at all) to help the country avoid recessions and mitigate the length and rigors of depressions. Therefore, state Professor Friedman and Mrs. Schwartz, "The stock of money displays a consistent cyclical behavior closely related to the cyclical behavior of the economy at large."

These authors, in calculating the money supply, use two concepts. The first is "currency held by the public" (gold and silver coin and certificates, Treasury notes of 1890, greenbacks, national bank notes, subsidiary coinage, but excluding currency in bank vaults and in the U.S. Treasury). The second is "seasonably adjusted deposits" (demand and

* Milton Friedman and Anna Jacobson Schwartz, *A Monetary History of the United States, 1867–1960,* 1963.

also time deposits of all commercial banks and deposits of mutual savings banks, but excluding interbank deposits and U.S. government deposits). In 1870, when the total *nominal* money supply (current values) was $1.7 billion, currency in circulation was $510 million or almost 30 per cent. In 1896, when the total *nominal* money supply was $6 billion, the currency in circulation was $832 million, or about 14 per cent. The differences, of course, were in deposits. From 1870 to 1896 currency in circulation increased 63 per cent, whereas deposits increased 322 per cent.

It is useful to convert *nominal* money (current values) into *real* money (deflated by wholesale prices). During 1870–1896 (using 1870 as 100) wholesale prices dropped by 50 per cent; therefore the *real* money supply was double the *nominal* money supply for the latter year. This gives us a convenient device to test roughly the claims of the monetary expansionists that there was not enough money in circulation. (Usually they discussed "money" only in terms of currency, and by the early 1890s they had fixed on the figure of $50 per capita at the target at which they would aim.) I have therefore made these calculations. In 1870 *nominal* money per capita (circulation plus deposits) was $43.20, and so was *real* money. In 1896 (a depression year) *nominal* money per capita was $84.10, but *real* money per capita was $168.10. In 1892, when business was good (and at the height of the Populist agitation), the *nominal* money per capita was $91.00, and the *real* money per capita was $162.70.

AGRICULTURE

It has been generally assumed—and this has entered into all the discussions in the textbooks on the period—that American agriculture was faring badly in the post-Civil War period. How then explain the appearance of farmer organizations and independent farmer parties during the 1870s and again during 1888–1896? Why, in the second period, was the preoccupation of the so-called farmers' alliances and the People's parties they formed almost entirely with money? A number of observations are in order. The Granger Movement of the 1870s was almost entirely a phenomenon of the Middle West; the farmers then were not talking of money but of the iniquities of the railroads and the need for railroad regulation and rate controls by state authorities. This led to the Granger laws, as we have seen. The farmers' alliances began in the Northwest—in the wheat and cattle country of the Great Plains—and in the cotton South, and when People's parties appeared they met with state and national successes only in those two regions. Their manifestoes spoke of "People's

Money—People's land—People's Transportation," but it was the first that really plunged them into national politics and ended with the endorsement of the Democratic party and the Free Silver platform of 1896. The farmers of the East and the Middle Atlantic states were not touched by either of these activities; the Middle-Western farmers were not Populist. In short, special conditions (largely economic in the Northwest, largely political in the South) were responsible for the commotion of which we continue to read so much and whose significance is so overrated.

I am saying, therefore, there was no general agricultural malaise, and, by the same token, that the country's industrial advances were not at the expense of the farmers or workers. As regards the position of the laboring population, comment has already been made. As regards the farmers, it has been pointed out that taxation was inequitable and that they bore the larger share; because, in the Plains country, farmers were compelled to borrow heavily to become owners and acquire machinery and livestock, their immediate incomes were lower than their expectations. Taking two measures—the formation of agricultural capital and the Farm Gross Product—the value of American agriculture increased greatly during the period of the country's rapid industrialization. The owning farmers of the United States reaped their reward when more and more they were able to diversify and serve the domestic market (one of the consequences of diversification). This was so from 1897 to 1922 or 1923, for during this period farm real estate values went up, as did real farm income when measured by the ratio of prices received for agricultural commodities to prices paid. In short, owning farmers were able to cash in on deferred income.

It is instructive to look at agricultural capital formation, and here we have the work of Tostlebe * to give the answers. Between 1870 and 1900, when farm prices were declining (but no more than other prices), agriculture's *real* capital formation proceeded faster than in subsequent years. This was so because farmers got their land cheap or for nothing; railroad rates kept on dropping while the urban market kept on growing, as did the foreign market, and farmers took their profits in undistributed earnings so that they could improve their capital plant. Tostlebe estimates that for 1900–1909 (he has no earlier figures, but the ratio of self-financing probably was higher before 1900) $6.6 billion of the new capital formation came from farm income and savings and $2.7 billion came from loans and bank credit. The consequence was the rise in capital (in constant dollars) per farm worker: from $2900 in 1870 to $4400 in 1920.

* Alvin S. Tostlebe, *Capital in Agriculture: Its Formation and Financing Since 1870*, 1957.

The value of America's farm plant—land, buildings, implements and machinery, work animals and livestock, and crop inventories—increased 104 per cent during the years 1870–1900, compared with 24 per cent for the years 1900–1920 (in constant dollars). Taking the later years of the nineteenth century alone, the rise was 60 per cent in the cotton Southeast, 63 per cent in the Corn Belt, and 1259 per cent in the wheat-growing Great Plains. On a per capita basis for each farm worker the increase in farm physical assets for the United States was 28 per cent; in the Corn Belt it was 23 per cent and in the Great Plains 130 per cent. It is apparent that the Great Plains grew rapidly; there was overexpansion from the end of the Civil War until the last years of the 1880s because of the good weather and rapidly growing markets.

Gross Farm Product (sales, improvements of plant, home manufacture, and consumption) also show the progress of agriculture.* In terms of constant dollars, the increase was from $2.2 billion in 1860 to $5.8 billion in 1900. The greatest advance was in the 1870s, when the increase was 50 per cent; yet it was also 13 per cent in the 1880s and 26 per cent in the 1890s—the decades of Farmers' Alliances organization and activity. The Gross Farm Product per farm worker increased 60 per cent during the same 40 years. From 1860 to 1900 the farm population grew from 20.1 million to 31.2 million, or 55 per cent; the Gross Farm Product increased 164 per cent.

In this steady advance four factors may be singled out. The first was improvement in transportation, opening up the Southwest and Northwest to agricultural settlement, and making possible the reaching of primary markets quickly and cheaply. The second was urbanization and therefore a great domestic market. (More of these two later). The third was the increase in farm exports. The fourth was improvements in farm technology (largely mechanical, although better breeding of beef and dairy cattle, hogs, and sheep was beginning.)

England in 1849 abandoned its Corn Laws and threw open its ports to the importation of foreign foodstuffs. The United States was the first of the new arable and pastoral lands (because of the speed of its railroad revolution) to take advantage of the British and other European markets. (In the early 1890s American agricultural exports began to meet a widening competition in world markets, also as a result of railroad construction and agricultural settlement in other arable and pastoral lands—Canada, Australia, Argentina, South Africa, and the great central and eastern plain of Europe—present-day Bulgaria, Hungary, Rumania, Yugoslavia,

* Marvin W. Towne and Wayne O. Rasmussen, "Gross Farm Product and Gross Investment in the Nineteenth Century," in *Trends in the American Economy in the Nineteenth Century*, National Bureau of Economic Research, 1960.

Poland, and the western Ukraine of Russia. This was one of the reasons why the price of wheat fell sharply in the 1890s. The same was true of cotton because of exports from Russia, India, and Egypt.)

From 1860–1890 in Europe the American farm surpluses (wheat and flour, corn and other animal feeds, pork products, and live beef cattle) pouring in were regarded with wonder; an Austrian, writing in the late 1870s, called it "the greatest economic event of modern times," comparing its impact on Europe with the flow of precious metals out of the Spanish possessions in the sixteenth century and the ensuing price revolution. American farm exports worked both ways. European countries (Britain, the outstanding one) stopped raising their own foodstuffs, which released redundant farm laborers for their own industrial cities and for emigration to the new lands. Farm exports played a large role in converting America's unfavorable trade balance to a favorable one; the first appeared in 1873. From 1852–1856 (annual averages) to 1897–1901 (annual averages) exports of wheat and wheat flour increased from 19 to 197 million bushels; corn and corn meal from 7 to 192.5 million bushels; pork products from 103.9 million to 1.5 billion pounds; beef products from 26 to 357.9 million pounds; cattle from 1400 to 415,500 head.

The effect on the American balance of payments was very important. (Until the 1860s the United States had been paying for its import surpluses by the earnings of its ships and by the gold mined in California; both were gone by 1870). These figures show what happened. For the period 1874–1895 American exports totaled $17.2 billion against imports of $14.7 billion. American imports shifted from manufactured goods to crude materials used in manufacturing. The surplus made possible American payments of freight charges, tourist expenditures, immigrant remittances (partly offset by capital brought in by immigrants), and a goodly portion of the interest earned by foreign investors in the United States. Because this was so, Europe's confidence in the faith and credit of the United States was high (to which a sound currency and a disappearing public debt also contributed). Thus European investments were stepped up—to play a large part in building the western trunk railroads, finance land-mortgage and mining companies, and contribute toward the creation of the public utilities of the American cities.

American farm machinery (notably improved plows and mechanical harvesters, but also harrows, seed drills, corn planters, and threshers) made possible the commercial cultivation of the prairies (with their long grass) and then the Plains (with their short grass). Corn and wheat quickly appeared on the prairies; wheatgrowing on the Plains made it possible for the Middle West and South to shift over to corn-hogs, dairying, and intensive general farming. Until the 1880s the competition among farm-machinery manufacturers was so keen that constant improvements took place in both plows and harvesters, prices fell, and agricultural productivity rose rapidly. Here are the key figures. In constant dollars the value of implements and machinery on farms increased from $300 million in 1870 to $800 million in 1900. Farm-machine prices dropped from an index of 251 in 1870 to 94 in 1900 (100 = 1910–1914), a decline of more than 60 per cent. Agricultural productivity—technology probably contributing more than labor and capital inputs—from 1869 to 1899 increased 40 per cent.

The plow went through this cycle. In the 1840s John Deere of Illinois made and sold a plow whose moldboard, share, and landside were made of cast steel strong enough to break the tough sod of the prairies. In the late 1860s John Oliver, also of Illinois, put on the market a plow of chilled iron (a soft-center steel) which was more durable and cheaper. A few years later the sulky plow (a riding machine with one bottom) and the sulky gang plow (with a number of bottoms) made their appearance. These machines—and the mechanical harvesters—made the horse important, and farmers grew hay (helped by haying machines) as well as small grains.

The mechanical horse-drawn reaper, which cut the small grains, was the invention of Obed Hussey of Ohio in 1833 and of Cyrus H. McCormick of Virginia in 1834. McCormick was the better businessman (he began to manufacture in 1847 in Chicago, unlike Hussey who licensed; he knew how to merchandise by advertising and offering credit and instruction in maintenance and repairs). It was McCormick who was as responsible as anyone for the spread of wheat growing in the North during the Civil War. In 1865, it was estimated, there were 250,000 mowing and reaping machines in use in the United States, compared with about 70,000 in 1858. McCormick was joined by a swarm of innovators, and improvements in the reaper followed fast. The self-rake reaper, which mechanically distributed the cut grain in a swath at the side of the machine, came in 1854. The year 1864 brought the reaper, now turned harvester; it carried a man on a platform who bound the cut grain. A further innovation came in 1874: mechanical binding with wire. A twine-binder, which solved the problem of wire in the grain, made its appearance in 1880.

At this point tinkering ceased and the number of companies began to decline as McCormick's superior selling methods (and undoubtedly others less praiseworthy) began to reduce the cutthroat competition. By 1880 the McCormick company, family owned, was valued at $3.5 million. The mechanical mowing and binding got a further lift when harvester and thresher were combined (hence the term "combine") in the 1890s.

Thus a single operation on the field was made possible, but the machine was heavy and needed many horses to pull it and was usable only on the "bonanza" farms of 4000 to 6000 acres in California and the Red River Valley of North Dakota. The internal combustion engine (which made the tractor possible) and the constant reduction in the size of the combine, so that it was available to family-size farms, of course, came later.

One such bonanza farm in North Dakota in the 1890s supported the following farm equipment: 67 plows (11 were gang plows), 64 harrows, 32 seeders, 6 mowers, 34 self-binding harvesters, 7 steam engines and threshers, 50 wagons, and 125 work animals. The revolution in productivity is evidenced by these figures.* In 1893 a Red River Valley spring-wheat farm required only 8 hours, 46 minutes man-labor time to prepare (plow and drill) and harvest (bind, shock, thresh, and sack) one acre of grain. In 1829–1830 the man-labor time per acre for all these operations in Illinois had been 61 hours, 5 minutes.

Reference, in passing, has been made here to the Great Plains, for it is here that we are to find the explanation for the monetary clamor in the West and the South that reached fever pitch during 1888–1896. The Great Plains start at about the 98th meridian and run up to the edge of the Rockies (including a good part of the states of North and South Dakota, Nebraska, Kansas, the Indian Territory, and Northeast Colorado). East of the meridian, where the prairies lie, the annual rainfall is in excess of 20 inches a year and the summers are long and hot and the nights humid: this is America's corn country, and the greatest agricultural state of them all is Iowa. The Plains follow a different pattern. They are covered with short grass, and the rainfall averages less than 20 inches and shifts unpredictably. Periods of severe drought are followed by heavy cloud bursts, accompanied by violent winds and great shifts in temperature. The light top soil can easily be blown away; hence the dust storms so typical of the region.

Thirty years before the Civil War there was relatively little rain on the Plains, so that the region took on the aspect of a semiarid rather than a dry subhumid zone. To early Americans this vast area from the Missouri River to the foothills of the Rockies came to be known as "the Great American Desert," but the rains came in the 1870s and continued with some regularity until 1887. This was when the great push into the Plains took place. There were four reasons why so many settlers moved from adjacent states (joined by immigrants) into the Dakota Territory and western Kansas and Nebraska.

First, many of the homesteaders (a generic term) were speculators;

* Leo Rogin, *Introduction of Farm Machinery in Its Relation to the Productivity of Labor in the Agriculture of the United States during the Nineteenth Century*, 1931.

they sold out their farms, which had risen in value, in the east and moved westward, for they hoped for similar profits. The farmer's dream was always retirement to a town and income from rent from tenants—frequently sons and sons-in-law—who worked the family property.

Second, the new settlers were wheat growers, and on the Plains—because land was cheap and machines available—farms of two quarter sections entirely in wheat could be run by a single family. What happened in the Dakota Territory was typical. In 1880 its population was 36,000 and its wheat harvest less than three million bushels; in 1885 the population was 152,000 and the wheat crop, 38 million bushels.

Third, railroads came quickly into the Northwest and Southwest—through branch and feeder lines—to crisscross the whole area. They were competitive railroads; rates had to fall, and farmers found within easy reach rail facilities to which to haul and granaries at which to sell their crops. At the same time, railroads carried on an intensive program to bring settlers and purchasers into the large tracts they owned. They established land departments, sent well-informed agents to Europe, donated land for academies, denominational colleges and town sites, and offered easy credit, even taking 10-year mortgages. As examples of how the railroads grew, in the 1880s alone, when the land boom was raging, the railroads of Kansas rose from 3100 to 8800 miles and those of Nebraska from 1600 to 5600. The Dakotas, starting almost from scratch, had 4400 miles in 1888. Kansas with its sparse population and no industry other than agriculture had a railroad mileage in excess of New York's.

Fourth, mortgage money was plentiful and rates were low, this despite all the charges leveled by the Populists against the "Money Power" and its extortionate practices. Land mortgage companies were usually organized in the West itself but obtained their capital by the sale of bonds in the East and in Europe. In central Kansas, before the bubble collapsed, a farmer with well-improved land could get mortgage money for 6 or 7 per cent; the agent's commission added another 2 per cent a year. In southwest Kansas, where the land was not so well developed and remote from the supervision and inspection of the mortgagee, the maximum rate (including commission) was about 11 per cent. Ten years earlier the mortgage rate had been 16 to 17 per cent—12 per cent for the interest, 4 to 5 per cent for the commission. The commission was paid for only three years; if the mortgagor ran into problems, he could refinance or obtain a chattel mortgage on his equipment and livestock from local bankers.

When the rains stopped in 1887—and for the next 10 years only five of them had enough rain for the making of a crop and only two of them for a full crop—disaster fell on the Plains. During 1886–1887, in particular, blizzards decimated the herds of cattle on the open ranges. Farmers (and cattle raisers) in the Dakotas, Kansas, and Nebraska went bankrupt by the tens of thousands, but so also did the land-mortgage companies and the boom towns as well, which had sprung up to provide schools, churches, grain, feed, and coal merchants, and other services. During 1889–1893 in the whole of Kansas 11,122 farms were foreclosed. In 1895 in 15 Kansas counties 75 to 90 per cent of the land was owned by mortgage companies, themselves in receivership.

A final irony; while this was happening on the Great Plains, the world price of wheat (set in Liverpool) fell because of the entry into production of the new arable lands, mentioned above. The same happened to cotton; American acreage in cotton increased from 9.2 million acres in 1870 to 21.9 million acres in 1894; but cotton in the latter year was also being exported from Egypt, India, and Russia.

The reason for the hue and cry in the West and the South now becomes plain. Wheat and cotton growers had overextended themselves; they had borrowed heavily, and when they were unable to produce crops (at the same time that world prices were declining) they sought relief through the emission of more public money. Initially, under the Sub-Treasury plan, it was a particular kind of money and relief (and this made sense); but when they switched to the free and unlimited coinage of silver, it made no sense at all.

The Southern and Northern Alliances both appeared in the 1880s. The Southern Alliance talked money from the start and quickly fell under the influence of a Texan, Dr. C. W. Macune, who unveiled his Sub-Treasury plan. National banks were to be abolished; instead federal Sub-Treasury offices were to be established to accept for deposit non-perishable farm products against which they were to issue negotiable certificates bearing an interest rate of 1 per cent. The Sub-Treasuries were to lend against these legal-tender Treasury notes; at the same time the crops were to be held off the market for a year and then sold at public auction, with charges for storage made against the borrowers. Those who did not negotiate loans and simply held the certificates of deposit could redeem the commodities if prices went up; the same was true for those who paid off their loans to get their certificates back.

Otherwise the Treasury notes remained in circulation, their numbers being constantly increased with each harvest if agricultural prices did not suit the borrowers. Obviously, prices would go down as more and more farmers expanded acreage to take advantage of price supports, accompanied by the government annual sale of the unredeemed surpluses. While this was going on the inflation of the money supply would affect the prices farmers paid, whereas the prices they received for wheat and cotton would be fixed in Liverpool and London unless American surpluses were segregated entirely from world markets. (This last the New Deal tried in the 1930s, with very little success, until price supports were linked with crop limitations.)

As has been said, the Northern Alliance men were cool to the idea until the Sub-Treasury plan was reworked to include government loans by means of the same Treasury notes on real estate. On this basis both groups joined hands, formed the People's party in 1891, and entered the presidential election of 1892. To catch in their net all kinds of dissident interests, the money plank of the Populist platform was expanded: the national banks were to be abolished; the Sub-Treasury plan was endorsed (but criticism of it had caused uncertainty, so there was this reservation, "or some better system"); and Treasury notes were to be issued to pay for public improvements. A demand for free silver was added and here all the stops were pulled—it was the free and unlimited coinage of silver "at the present legal ratio of sixteen to one." Here also appeared the famous formula that became a battle-cry: "We demand that the amount of circulating medium be speedily increased to not less than $50 per capita." In 1896 the Sub-Treasury plan was dropped, for the Populists had succumbed to the magic of free silver. It was to be the universal panacea for all kinds of maladies, including crop surpluses, farm mortgages, untaxed railroad lands, and the iniquities of the tariff-protected interests.

One final observation on this fascinating money question, which so captured the fancy and aroused the indignation of a sizable part of the American people for a whole generation. If there had been a dearth of money, interest rates would have gone up, but the reverse happened. During the 1880s and 1890s interest rates declined steadily not only for long-term government, corporation, and municipal bonds but for short-term commercial paper as well. Thanks to Davis' * calculations, we have some notion, at least as far as national banks were concerned, of what was happening to the commercial paper rate in nonreserve cities.

New York City banks progressively dropped their interest rates for choice commercial (60–90 days) paper from 8.49 per cent during 1850–1859 (10-year average) to 5.14 per cent during 1880–1889 and 4.5 per cent during 1890–1899. As for the South and the Great Plains, Davis' fragmentary data indicate that during the height of the money agitation the interest rate in the smaller nonreserve cities was falling and that the differential between them and eastern cities was narrowing. Taking only nonreserve cities, the rate for the Middle Atlantic states † was 5.80 in

* Lance E. Davis, "The Investment Market, 1870–1918: The Evolution of a National Market," *The Journal of Economic History*, XXX (1965).

† New York, New Jersey, Pennsylvania, Delaware, Maryland, and the District of Columbia.

1888 and 5.48 in 1896; in the southern states * for the same years, 8.57 and 7.68; in the Great Plains states,† 9.83 and 8.90.

THE RAILROADS

There can be no doubt that the railroad industry was the most important of the period not only in terms of the capital formation for which it was responsible but also for its many backward and forward linkages. As regards the former, it gave the greater stimulus to the manufacture of iron and steel and railroad equipment and the production of coal and timber; as regards the latter, the opening up of the Plains country to wheat and cattle, the development of primary markets for agricultural goods, and a national market for the goods and services of the whole growing economy. The railroad industry arrived at this pre-eminence for a number of reasons. Some of them have already been mentioned— the part played by national public policy and the financial assistance rendered by the states, counties, and municipalities; the competitive building and operation of American rails by private companies led by an extraordinary group of innovator-entrepreneurs; the resulting fall because of competition and therefore the need for greater productivity of railroad rates. Greater attention needs to be given as well to these other factors—how the financing of the rails took place and the technology that was developed.

Before the Civil War, despite the impressive railroad building of the 1850s (about 21,000 miles, which brought the total in 1860 to 30,626 miles), an "articulated national network" did not emerge as Fishlow has claimed.‡ Having said this, Fishlow then has second-thoughts and applying proper economic tests, is constrained to admit that the railroads had not yet succeeded in creating a national market. He goes on: "This was still a period before interchange of parts was universal, before standard products were marketed, before the full effects of industrialization were apparent, let alone realized."

He might have added, specifically about the railroads, that not a single technological or managerial innovation had yet appeared: iron bridges across wide rivers, a standard gauge, the substitution of steel for

* Virginia, West Virginia, North Carolina, South Carolina, Georgia, Florida, Alabama, Mississippi, Louisiana, Texas, Arkansas, Kentucky, and Tennessee. New Mexico, and Oklahoma.

† North Dakota, South Dakota, Nebraska, Kansas, Montana, Wyoming, Colorado,

‡ Albert Fishlow, *American Railroads and the Transformation of the Ante-Bellum Economy*, 1965.

iron in rail manufacture, heavier and more efficient locomotives, larger cars, the safety coupler, and automatic air brakes. These improvements were to come with the great western railroads and the integrated trunk railroad systems of the East and South.

Three great railroad construction booms added vastly to the country's roads and completed the program of building. The first lasted from 1866 to 1873 (about 30,000 miles built), the second from 1879 to 1883 (about 40,000 miles), and the third from 1886 to 1892 (about 50,000 miles). In 1893, with the job virtually finished, the United States had 176,500 miles of first track. As has been said, this was the result of competitive building, with all the wastes it entailed: mismanagement and the fraudulent practices of the earlier railroad promoters, frequent bankruptcies during recession years, and the high prices that had to be paid for capital. The last is the reason for overcapitalization, and not manipulative "stock-watering," as too commonly assumed. Economies of scale had to take place and technological innovations introduced by the railroads that sought to survive in the bitter, dog-eat-dog contest. The upshot was that despite the few great railroad fortunes that were made (and most came from successful management and not speculation) the social economies, which benefitted the whole country, were immence. The greatest of these was in the steady reduction of railroad rates. It should be said at this point that the railroads serving a region tried to mitigate the effects of their competition by the creation of pools, but these were short-lived and invariably failed.

The case of western products moving eastward from Chicago to New York was one in point. During 1866–1897 the price for the carriage of wheat fell from 65 cents per 100 pounds to 20 cents, or 70 per cent. (In the same period wholesale prices dropped 60 per cent.) During 1870–1899 the price for the carriage of dressed beef fell from 90 to 40 cents, or 55 per cent. (In the same period wholesale prices dropped 43 per cent.)

New construction, notably in the West, in large part due to the intention of the trunk systems, which took form to compete with one another, was accompanied by sharp rate reductions. Grodinsky makes the point clearly.* Thus from 1879 to 1889, when the new building was enormous, the Atchison, Topeka and Santa Fe reduced rates (per ton mile) 42.1 per cent; the Chicago, Burlington and Quincy, 49.2 per cent; the Chicago, Milwaukee and St. Paul, 42.5 per cent; the Denver and Rio Grande, 42 per cent; the Northern Pacific, 46 per cent; the Great Northern, 55.9 per cent; the Southern Pacific, 35.6 per cent. The Union Pacific's rates dropped 31.2 per cent and those of the Missouri Pacific, only 5.1

* Julius Grodinsky, *Transcontinental Railway Strategy, 1869–1893: A Study of Businessmen*, 1962.

per cent, but both were Jay Gould railroads and he—setting the pace in rate cutting and breaking up pools—started from much lower bases.* These declines were *greater* than those of agricultural prices, for the prices farmers received for wheat fell 37 per cent and for corn, 25 per cent.

The railroad capital came from three sources: European investors, American banks, and stock-market speculation by the railroad promoters themselves, who were in and out of the market in their own securities. Railroad capital consisted almost entirely of bonds; that is to say, loans against which railroad properties, equipment, land grants, and income were pledged. Efforts were made to sell stock, but usually it went gratis to promoters (and politicians), building contractors and suppliers, and purchasers of junior bonds. The bonds that were not sold abroad and the common stock—whether held by promoters, operators, contractors, or the public at large—were used as collateral for bank loans. In this fashion American banking played a significant role in the creation of railway capital.

European merchant-bankers (English largely, but also German, Dutch, and Swiss) bought railroad bonds from American merchant-bankers but also from individuals (Andrew Carnegie and Henry Villard were examples). There was a ready European money-market for American railroad bonds for a variety of reasons: confidence in the faith and credit and therefore the stability of the American government and the American economy, a favorable balance of payments, and—most important of all—the high rates of return. Thus Cairncross† points out that during the decade of the 1870s British investors were getting an annual yield on their American rails of 5.7 per cent and a capital appreciation (because bonds had been acquired at heavy discounts) of 3.6 per cent. At the same time British Consols (the public debt) were returning 3.26 per cent and a capital appreciation of 0.58 per cent.

Foreign ownership of American railway securities grew in consequence. In 1853 perhaps one-tenth of the value of American rails was held abroad; by 1870 this amount had increased to about one-fifth, in 1890, to about one-third, and in 1899 it stood at between one-fourth and one-third. It was estimated that in 1899 something like $3 billion in American securities was owned abroad, by far the greater part being those of American rails. The British held $2.5 billion of this amount, the Dutch, $240 million, the Germans, $200 million, the Swiss, $75 million, and the French, $50 million. Many American railroads might almost be considered to have been foreign controlled as a result of the concentration of ownership in important lines, a state of affairs that continued until the outbreak of World War I.

* Julius Grodinsky, *Jay Gould. His Business Career, 1865–1892*, 1957.

† A. K. Cairncross, *Home and Foreign Investments, 1870–1913*, 1953.

The western railroads—starting as they did in wholly undeveloped or sparsely settled country—encountered the greatest difficulties in the raising of capital. The railroad innovators perforce had to be promoters, political jobbers—and speculators. They were in and out of the market in their own securities; they sold short the independent lines they were interested in acquiring and then bought them up for a song. In times of recession they bought the securities of their own companies; in upturns of the business cycle they sold. They made great fortunes and sometimes lost them, but those who persevered as railroad builders ended by plowing back profits into their own railroads. In this wise part of the capital formation of the railroads occurred.

These same men were at the banks constantly, paying high rates of interest. They did not always triumph, for their course was studded with failure. Thomas A. Scott of the Pennsylvania, who tried to move into the Southwest, was unable to do so; the same was true of the Philadelphia banker Jay Cooke in the Northwest; Henry Villard, German representative of his native country's bankers in the Far Northwest, was no more successful.

A further word about the fortunes made: they really came from capital gains and not from manipulation. For men like Jay Gould, James J. Hill, and E. H. Harriman (like Andrew Carnegie in steel) had a passionate conviction, an *idée fixe,* that the western country they were building up would grow and thrive—and pay them back handsomely.

I have said heavy prices were paid for the needed capital; this is reflected clearly in the discounts at which the railroad bonds were sold. Grodinsky gives us some examples of the financing of a group of securities during 1869–1873, the first period of great western construction. An Atchison 7 per cent gold second-mortgage bond sold at 50 and the same railroad's 7 per cent currency land-grant bond sold at 73. A Northern Pacific 7.3 per cent gold first-mortgage bond sold at 83, and a St. Paul and Pacific (later Great Northern) 7 per cent gold first-mortgage bond sold at 65.

Grodinsky makes another point very clearly, and it is best to quote him. He is talking of the twistings and turnings of the railroad promoters.

> All this was accomplished by sharp and almost continuous reduction in selling prices [rates]. Some investors secured reasonable returns—others lost. Some speculators received substantial, even exorbitant profits—and many, particularly the very early pioneers, lost much more. Whoever gained, and whoever lost, the public was the gainer. Some of the roads were efficiently operated and gave good service; others gave poor service. This outcome was the essence of competition. Competition served the public well.

How much overcapitalizaton was there before the depression and bankruptcies of 1893–1896, as a consequence of which a good deal of the water was squeezed out? In 1892 a British investment adviser, S. F. Van Oss, put the real worth of the 171,000 miles of road in 1892 at $6.8 billion (on the basis of a knowledgeable estimate of cost of construction plus improvements); this was against a claimed value of $10.1 billion. H. V. Poor, the outstanding American railroad authority of the day, put the overcapitalization somewhat higher at $4.6 billion. The reorganizations that followed after 1897 made American rails the soundest investments in the United States, for their securities frequently sold at premiums. Institutional savers, particularly the country's insurance companies, had a large part of their portfolios in rail bonds. The gamble of the pioneer railroad promoters and financiers paid off before too long, and the country's gains were achieved in an even briefer period.

The strength of the railroad structure was due to the quick adoption of all the forward steps railroad technology was making; it was no wonder that Van Oss called American railroading the most advanced in the world. The substitution of Bessemer steel for iron rails was a key factor, for thanks to the same competition among steel companies that ruled in railroading—with Andrew Carnegie showing the way—the price of steel kept on falling, thus encouraging its further use. Steel rails could carry faster and more powerful locomotives and the stronger and larger cars, that were built and put into use. The appearance of block signaling (1864), air brakes (1869), and automatic couplers (1873) resulted in greater safety, speed, and more efficient use of yards and track facilities. Work was pushed ahead to make the standard gauge universal, and this was achieved in 1886. Railroad operations were synchronized all over the country as a result of the adoption in 1883—by the railroads themselves—of four standard time zones. Railroad associations set up three uniform freight classifications, one for the Northeast, one for the South, and one for the West. A through bill of lading was devised and put into general use. Fast freight lines—to assemble shipments for common destinations and route them over the country's vast and complex network—crisscrossed the United States and, because they were competitive, offered the benefit of low rates to small shippers. Bridges across the great rivers were built by independent companies, chartered by Congress because they were interstate authorities. The Ohio was bridged at Cincinnati in 1867 and again at Parkersburgh in 1871, the Mississippi at St. Louis in 1874. (Carnegie sold the bonds for the last in England.)

During 1876–1880 the production of steel rails was already exceeding that of iron rails; most were being made in the United States, which proved that the tariff could work. The replacement of iron track and the laying of new steel track followed, so that by 1890 80 per cent of the country's track was steel. Replacement created the opportunity to improve roadbeds—maximum gradients were cut from 1 to 0.5 per cent, and the introduction of "lap-sidings," instead of double-tracking throughout, made possible the splitting of single tracks so that two trains could pass without stopping. Track tanks were installed to allow locomotives to take on water without slackening speed.

The use of steel revolutionized the size and character of the locomotive and the freight car. Better track and locomotives thus increased the carrying capacity of trains (from 200 tons in 1865 to 2500 tons in 1900) and their speed (from 25 miles an hour in the earlier years to 65 in the later.) Nothing attested more to the achievements of American technology than the new freight cars. In 1865 the weight of a car was 60 per cent of its total laden weight; by 1900 the ratio had dropped to 26 per cent. In 1865 a freight car's capacity was 10,000 pounds; in 1900, 110,000 pounds. Van Oss was never more enthusiastic than when he was comparing America's railroading efficiency with England's, to the detriment of the latter. He pointed out that the average English freight car carried 8 tons and weighed 5 tons, or a ratio of 1.6 to 1, whereas the American carried 30 tons and weighed 12 tons, or a ratio of 2.5 to 1. As rates fell drastically, the costs of transportation had to be cut. According to Van Oss, on the Pennsylvania, for example, during 1870–1889 the cost of moving a ton-mile of freight was reduced from 1 cent to two-fifths of a cent. Because of the new technology and the economies in management and operation, American transportation charges were 50 per cent lower than in England, all this without benefit of regulation (the Interstate Commerce Commission had been established in 1887 but its hands were not untied until at least a decade later). To repeat the observation of Grodinsky: "This outcome was the essence of competition. Competition served the public well."

URBANIZATION

Whenever men have ceased wandering—as hunters, pastoralists, and warriors, and have sought some sort of orderly life—cities have appeared, usually as the seats of administrative authority, whether political, military, or religious. Until the appearance of the Industrial Revolution, cities were atypical, for they lay in the midst or on the edge of agricultural communities. In the Middle Ages in the West, and right up to the third quarter of the eighteenth century in England and the middle of the nineteenth century elsewhere, cities were commercial centers. Access to transportation was the key factor in their origin and growth.

That does not mean that during the centuries when merchant capitalism was dominant—from the thirteenth into the eighteenth—there was no industry; but, except for "bespoke" trades, industry was to be found in the country, where propinquity to raw materials or waterpower was the important locational factor. The merchant-manufacturers—an expressive title—found it expedient to move to cities in which the service industries they required—moneychangers and bankers, law courts and lawyers, and shipping and warehousing facilities—were to be found.

These were the prevailing characteristics of American cities, even the "large" ones (100,000 population or more), right up to the 1850s. They were commercial rather than industrial, and as has been said, their businessmen were called "merchants." This was true of New York, Boston, Baltimore, Charleston, New Orleans (which were seaports), Cincinnati, St. Louis, Pittsburgh, Louisville (which were river towns), and Chicago and Buffalo (situated on the Great Lakes). The absence of manufactures in most of them in 1860 has already been commented on above. (See Table 14, page 103.)

The industrial city is something else again. It was a particular attribute of this period of the dominance of industrial capital and it played an important part in contributing to the efficiency of the American economy. The industrial city may be distinguished from the commercial city because it was the result of and contributed to the following qualitative and quantitative changes in urban living and working.

The first was specializatioin of function. The merchant-capitalist was an undifferentiated merchant. The industrial-capitalist (and the skills serving him—bankers, lawyers, engineers, and marketing men) was a specialist. Industrial production was fragmented: the iron and steel industry became diversified, the textile manufacturer worked with cotton or wool, and the machine manufacturer made machine tools, agricultural implements, or locomotives. Light industry, in which particular aptitudes were required, was attracted to or developed in industrial cities. It may be said that the larger a city grew, the greater the tendency to shift from heavy to light industry and then to the services, or "tertiary" production.

The second was what the great English economist Alfred Marshall called the development of "external economies." These were the favorable effects—the lowering of input costs for other firms—that flowed out of the actions of other persons or firms. The economies resulting had factor indivisibility: it was impossible to differentiate their origin, whether from capital, labor, or natural resources. Cities, themselves, in the public activities they assumed, added to "external economies." They did so by the creation of "public goods" or what is called "social overhead capital." They improved transportation by paving and lighting streets, building bridges, and making possible rapid transit by introducing electrified trolley cars. They erected hospitals, provided public health and sanitation services, and expanded education (better high schools and municipal colleges). These additions to "social overhead capital" created general benefits for the city's population and workers and its firms and industries. As a rule they were furnished free of charge or at a nominal user cost, and the "external economies" that flowed from them also were indivisible.

The third was the expansion of the market. The improvement in agricultural production, which led to great surpluses in the staples, provided the cities with another role: the financing, warehousing, grading, processing, and marketing of the crops. Produce exchanges were an important concomitant of the last. The widening of the railroad net and the technological advances in rail transport—the development of the refrigerator car is another of these advances—facilitated the movement of dressed beef, fresh vegetables, and fruits to primary and secondary markets. The emergence of a national capital market—already discussed— lowered the costs of obtaining credit and also made for specialization in investment houses; these too were located in cities. An interesting form of such diversity was the emergence of houses that knew how to underwrite municipal bonds and place them among institutional savers, all of which was part of the growth of "social overhead" capital. The net municipal debt of the country increased from $200 million in 1860 to $725 million in 1880 and $1.4 billion in 1902. The interest rate municipalities paid on their bonds dropped from around 5.2 per cent in 1857 to 3.2 per cent in 1900.

The fourth was the growing labor force, which made possible the burgeoning of the industrial cities. This growth developed from two sources: the internal migration of young workers from the country to the cities and the natural gravitation of the "New Immigrants" to the larger urban communities. Among the former we are to note the beginning of the movement of Negroes in the South from country to city: to Birmingham, Atlanta, and Memphis, where they were employed in heavy industry not yet needing specialized training.

The urban growth of the United States was enormous. In 1850 there were 236 incorporated places of 2500 population or more in which 15.3 per cent of the country's inhabitants were located; in 1900 there were 1737 such communities with 39.7 per cent of the country's population. In "large" cities (100,000 and more), in 1850 there were six of them, in which 5.0 per cent of the population resided; in 1900 there were 38, with 18.8 per cent of the country's total inhabitants. By 1890 the number of gainfully employed workers 10 years and over in nonfarm pursuits already exceeded those in farming. In 1860 total farm workers came to 6.2 million and nonfarm workers, to 4.3 million; in 1890 the figures were 9.9 million and 13.4 million, respectively; in 1900, 10.9 million and 18.2 million, respectively.

As has been said, the "New Immigrants" tended to locate in cities, notably "large" cities. In 1900 63.1 per cent of the country's *rural* population but only 40 per cent of the *urban* population were of native-white stock. The following were the proportions of native-white stock in 1900 in the populations of some of the leading "large" cities of the country: New York, 21.5 per cent; Chicago, 20.9 per cent; Detroit, 21.5 per cent; Cleveland, 23.0 per cent; St. Louis, 32.9 per cent; Boston, 26.1 per cent.

THE BALANCE OF PAYMENTS

The balance of international payments in the 40 years after 1860 showed marked changes from American experience in the ante-bellum period, among which, in particular, the following may be noted: from 1874 on there was a sizable export surplus, in which the role of foodstuffs, both crude and manufactured, has already been noted; previously "invisible items"—shipping, insurance, tourist expenditures, and immigrant remittances—had been in balance; now they constituted large deficits. The same was true of interest payments to foreign investors. The consequence was an increasing inflow of foreign capital, which, with the export surpluses, matched the debits in the invisible services and the interest payments.

The summary figures for 1874–1895 show up these tendencies.* On the credit side: the excess of exports of merchandize and silver came to $2.5 billion; the excess of exports of gold, $112 million; new capital borrowings (net), $1 billion; and immigrant capital brought in, $180 million. On the debit side: freights (net), $560 million; tourist expenditures, $770 million; immigrant remittances and miscellaneous, $440 million; interest payments (net), $1.9 billion. The total exports for the

* Based on the estimates of Charles L. Bullock, John H. Williams, and Rufus S. Tucker, "The Balance of Trade of the United States," *Review of Economic Statistics*, Vol. I, 1919. Corrections, based on mathematical calculations, have been made by Matthew Simon (but they are relatively minor) in "The United States Balance of Payments, 1861–1900," *Trends in the American Economy in the Nineteenth Century*, National Bureau of Economic Research, 1960. The Nathaniel Bacon article was "American International Indebtedness," *Yale Review*, Vol. IX, 1900. Cleona Lewis's calculations are in her *America's Stake in International Investments*, 1938.

period came to $17.2 billion and the imports, to $14.7 billion; this was a very large foreign trade, but it should be noted that it constituted less than 10 per cent of the foreign trade of the world. Unlike Great Britain, the United States—thanks to its great national market—did not have to depend on its foreign commerce for the stability and growth of its economy.

Some further comments on a number of these items might be made. David A. Wells, in 1869 (with corrections by Bullock) estimated that foreign investments in the United States came to $1.5 billion, of which $1.4 billion were portfolio and direct (and most of it was in U. S. bonds) and $150 million were commercial credits. On the other side of the ledger—American investments abroad (almost entirely direct)—was a total of only $75 million. By 1899, when another estimate was made by Nathaniel Bacon (with corrections by Cleona Lewis), foreign holdings were put at $3.4 billion, of which the portfolio and direct investments were $3.1 billion (now largely in railroad securities) and short-term credits at $250 million. American investments abroad had increased to $685 million, all but $50 million of which were direct.

Matthew Simon thinks the Wells (plus Bullock) figure for 1869 much too high; that $1.2 billion was nearer the mark. He also had the same reservation about the Bacon (plus Lewis) estimate for 1897; Simon favors $2.7 billion. He also has doubts about the Bullock treatment of tourist expenditures and immigrant remittances. The effect of his corrections, says he, "is to increase the size of the deficit . . . on current account and therefore to raise the values for the accumulating balance of payments." Therefore fresh capital inflow was greater (by an extra $500 million) and interest payments were larger (by $350 million). As has been said, however, these are matters of detail and do not affect significantly the general situation. The United States was not a great trading nation, but the stepping up of its exports of foodstuffs played a crucial role in making possible large foreign investments in the United States (notably in the expansion and improvement of the American railroads).

XII

CHALLENGES TO A MARKET ECONOMY

CONSOLIDATIONS AND CONCENTRATION

Until 1896, atomistic business units (except for the railroad industry) generally prevailed in the United States. Some concentration in manufacturing, but nowhere else, had first begun to appear in the 1870s—in iron and steel, oil refining, agricultural implements, meat packing, and sugar refining, but it was gradual and not particularly significant. In those industries in which technology had become important and in which economies of scale were possible through vertical or horizontal integration and the more effective development of by-products, consolidations could take place. They did so without the use of a national credit market: entrepreneurial profits—as a result of successful innovation and powerful, imaginative owner-managerial direction—were the chief source of new acquisitions; local commercial banks, usually the rising state institutions, also helped to furnish funds through accommodation loans. The corporate form of organization, with its ability to obtain equity capital and debt financing through a money market, except for the railroads and a few mining companies, was virtually nonexistent in manufacturing or for that matter anywhere else.

The low measure of concentration is understandable. Agriculture continued to be the most important single economic activity and the units of production were obviously atomistic—in 1870 it accounted for 25 per cent of the national income. Manufactures, growing steadily, nevertheless were responsible for only 16 per cent of the national income. Public utilities were still insignificant, and the distributive trades, all in small units, were owned and managed by families or partnerships. Financial institutions were small and numerous; the national banks, despite their relatively large minimum capitalizations, were circumscribed in growth by their inability to establish extra-local branches and the creation of savings departments; the state banks, because they were permitted to start from such low bases of capitalization, were in similar circumstance.

Despite the hue and cry that began in the 1880s about pools and trusts and led to the Interstate Commerce Act of 1887 and the Sherman Antitrust Act of 1890, America's first pieces of regulatory legislation affecting business conduct, these efforts at concentration and therefore control of prices and entry were not the rule and their effects on competition were small. Pools, formal associations for the proration of business and the maintenance of prices, were common in railroading and appeared from time to time in iron and steel. Attempts at the formation of cartels—pools that also distributed profits on a proration basis—were created in a few industries, usually regionally located: in salt mining, whiskey distilling, and cord manufacturing. Pools were short-lived because they were illegal under the common law and such collusive arrangements could not be enforced in the courts; more important, they were broken no sooner than arrived at by innovator-entrepreneurs—like Gould in Southwest railroading and Carnegie in iron and steel—who felt that profits and larger market shares could better be achieved by aggressive competitive tactics than by "cooperation" with rivals.

The trust, an American device, reached into a number of American manufacturing industries and obtained its notoriety from its invention and wide use by Standard Oil. The Standard Oil Trust was set up in 1789 and was still in operation in 1882. Its example was followed only in a handful of industries—in the manufacture of cottonseed oil in 1884, linseed oil in 1885, and in 1887 in lead mining and refining, whiskey distilling, cord manufacturing, and sugar refining. The trust went beyond the cartel, for it showed many of the characteristics of the holding-company type of merger.

A trust was an open, and presumably legal, association of producers in a single field who maintained their individual charters, company organizations, and management but who, with the consent of stockholders, set up a board of trustees to run the businesses of the participating members as a single entity. Ownership was recognized on the basis of trust certificates and profits were shared prorata on the values the certificates represented. Thus the Standard Oil Trust was able to combine 90 per cent of the oil-refining and oil transportation (largely pipe lines) of the country. The total number of oil certificates was 972,500, each worth $100. The trust in this case—and in that of sugar-refining—could work because of domination by a single large producer: John D. Rockefeller and his partners, who owned the Standard Oil Company of Ohio, and Henry O. Havemeyer, who owned the American Sugar Refining Co. In the Standard Oil Trust both the crude oil prices of the many independent producers and the prices of the finished products were controlled. This trust was a monopoly, but it should be observed in passing that it achieved many economies of scale by the creation of an elaborate and comprehensive marketing organization, investment in research, and the development of by-products. Thus all of its owners were able to realize sizable capital gains.

The Standard Oil Trust was short-lived; it was vulnerable because state legislatures and law-enforcement agencies were able to invoke the common law against monopoly and therefore threatened to rescind the charters of member-companies on the grounds of participation in agreements to restrain trade. Such a proceeding was begun against the Standard Oil of Ohio in 1890 and upheld by the state's highest courts two years later. Louisiana moved against the Cottonseed Trust even earlier, in 1887, and New York against the Sugar Trust in 1889. In every case the action was taken against a company under the jurisdiction of the state in which the suits were begun; companies, once the court had approved, were ordered to withdraw from a trust under penalty of forfeiture of charter for noncompliance. All companies brought to book in this fashion yielded quickly, and thus by 1892 the death-knell of the trust movement was sounded, without benefit of the Sherman Antitrust Law, it will be noted.

The state of New Jersey made consolidation possible by legalizing the holding company—the commonest form of merger in the first great movement toward concentration, which set in in 1896 and lasted until 1905. In 1889 the New Jersey legislature permitted the creation of holding companies which could acquire the securities of other companies by an exchange of stock (as a rule in horizontal integration, but sometimes vertical as well) without acquiring the consent of their stockholders. In 1896 the New Jersey law was made broadly operative, for an amendment to its corporation code permitted holding-company acquisitions of subsidiaries, whether they were holders of New Jersey charters or not. New Jersey's lead was followed almost at once by other states—New York, Delaware, Pennsylvania, West Virginia, Maine, and Nevada, but it was in New Jersey that the big combinations were incorporated. (Possibly because it was on the scene first; more important, in all likelihood, because New Jersey offered lower corporation taxes, placed no limits on capitalization, and demanded less stockholder and director liability.)

More compelling reasons for this initial merger movement may be cited. With the end of the long depression of 1893–1896, the business cycle turned upward and continued into 1904; there was a renewal of business confidence and an interest in launching new ventures. It should be noted that all this activity—new ventures and mergers—took place largely in the manufacturing sector. Second, the capital market had now become a national one and funds were widely available for the financing of the holding companies' stock and debt securities. Stock exchanges, too, expanded their listings, thus providing markets for securities and giving the general public access to the new issues. Here insiders could unload (as H. C. Frick did with his large holdings of U.S. Steel before the market peaked out in 1904). As late as 1894 the stocks of only 16 mining and manufacturing companies were listed on the New York Stock Exchange, but at the beginning of 1910 more than 100 active mining and manufacturing stocks were being traded. Third, the successes of investment bankers in the reorganization of the railroads bred confidence in their promotional activities—for it was the merchant-bankers who put together the consolidated companies and sold and made markets for the new security issues. They, in turn, were motivated by a desire to make profits from underwriting, which they succeeded in doing handsomely, and from capital gains. Indeed, it may be assumed that all the insiders looked to this source as the basis of their profits. Finally, holding companies would put an end to cutthroat competition on the one hand and excess capacity on the other; both were the rule in too many manufacturing industries. The achievement of market power therefore must stand high as a motive that prompted promoters to push consolidations.

What of the assumed theoretical reasons about which economists like to speculate? That consolidations, leading to large firms, would make possible improved efficiency by research and development? That economies of scale would result? Both points are moot (more of them later). Here it is enough to say that government agencies, probing deeply during the years 1900–1920, were dubious about both. Henry Simons, in 1948, summarized their findings in this fashion *:

> Few of our gigantic corporations can be defended on the ground that
> their present size is necessary to reasonably full exploitation of production

* Cited by Donald Dewey, *Monopoly in Economics and Law*, 1959.

economies; their existence is to be explained in terms of opportunities for promoters profits, personal ambitions of industrial and financial "Napoleons," and the advantages of monopoly power.

In 1904 John Moody, in his *Truth about the Trusts*, presented an authoritative analysis (corrections since have been only in detail) which indicated that, from the 1880s to 1904, 318 major consolidations had taken place affecting about four-fifths of all the country's existing manufacturing industries. These had absorbed 5200 separate industrial plants and the merger capitalization had amounted to $7 billion. These mergers accounted for about 40 per cent of the manufacturing capital of the country. The greater part of this activity took place during the years 1895–1904, when, according to Ralph L. Nelson,* 3012 firms were absorbed and the merger capitalization came to almost $6 billion.

To what extent did the giant consolidations among them achieve market control? Nelson's calculations are of interest. Table 32 is derived from his book (page 102).

TABLE 32

GIANT CONSOLIDATIONS AND MARKET CONTROL, 1894–1904

Percentage of Industry Controlled	Consolidations and Parent Companies		Firm Disappearances		Capitalization (Millions of Dollars)	
	Number	Percent of Total	Number	Percent of Total	Value	Percent of Total
42.5–62.5	21	6.7	291	9.7	613.5	10.3
62.5–82.5	24	7.7	529	17.6	2,130.6	35.7
82.5–over	16	5.1	343	11.4	998.0	16.7
"Large"	25	8.0	302	10.0	455.5	7.6
Total	86	27.5	1,465	48.6	4,197.6	70.4

The greatest of all was, of course, the United States Steel Corporation, which was launched by the House of Morgan in April 1901 with a capitalization of $1.4 billion, of which $510 million represented common stock, $508 million, preferred, and $303 million first-mortgage bonds. The consolidation was made possible when Andrew Carnegie agreed to sell out his vast holdings, and the Carnegie Company (in the exchanges

* *Merger Movements in American Industry, 1895–1956,* 1959.

of securities that took place) received $492 million for its properties. Carnegie's personal share—all in the first-mortgage bonds—was in excess of $200 million, the promotional profits, which went largely to J. P. Morgan & Co., came to $62.5 million.

This consolidation—for a short time—truly dominated the market. It possessed vast reserves of iron ore, coal, and limestone; it owned almost one-half of the coke ovens of the country and produced more than one-half of its coke; it possessed 112 steamships and 1000 miles of railroad. It produced one-half of the country's pig iron, 68 per cent of its steel rails, 60 per cent of its structural steel, as much if not more of its steel plates, sheets, bars, wire and wire rods, hoops, and cotton ties, and nearly all of its tin plates, tubes, wire nails, barbed wire, and woven-wire fence. It also built 85 to 90 per cent of the country's bridges.

What was U.S. Steel worth? Moody, in 1904, put the figure at $760 million. In 1911 the Bureau of Corporations, representing the historical costs of the tangible properties, put it at $676 million. The market price of the securities of all the companies involved before the merger was $793 million. U.S. Steel in 1902 estimated the value of its tangible assets at $1.4 billion, but this was made up, by almost two-thirds, of the worth it put on its mineral reserves—$700 million in ore properties, $100 million in coal and coke fields, $20 million in natural-gas fields, and $4 million in limestone deposits. U.S. Steel, in short, was capitalizing its market power far into the future. I have talked of capital gains in connection with such promotions, but those of U.S. Steel were not impressive until World War I broke out. Its common stock was issued at $50 on April 1, 1901; on December 1 its market price was $43.50; in 1910 it was only $72.63. During these nine years the dividends paid out totaled $21.75. The average annual rate of return was therefore only 9 per cent; on the other hand—despite the fact that its ratios of the country's production of heavy and finished steel kept on falling, for U.S. Steel could not bar the entry of new and more progressive firms—it was king pin in steel and its price leader. Power was market power, but it was also psychic power: U.S. Steel spoke for American capitalism, and when it refused to deal with trade unions and kept a 60-hour work week it set the tone for all the heavy industries of the country until the 1930s.

This first concentration movement, largely in manufacturing, reached a plateau in 1905, a pattern that did not change much until perhaps the second half of the 1960s. It is true there was a dramatic increase in mergers in the 1920s, and here the concentration was almost entirely in public utilities. There was also a third wave of mergers in the 1950s. Nevertheless, all informed commentators agree, there was no evidence to indicate a persistent and inevitable tendency toward ever-increasing con-

centration and therefore a decline of competition in the United States.*
By 1960 there was no further increase in the ratios in manufacturing
than had been noted in 1905; in public utilities the movement slackened
off, if anything, and there was no significant upward trend in the distributive trades. The small-business sector, on the other hand, kept on
expanding after World War II, and it was among small firms (some of
which, when successful, grew very large) that a good deal of the innovation of the 1950s and 1960s occurred.

Thus Stigler, in 1949 † said:

> It is my present judgment that competition declined moderately from
> the Civil War to the end of the nineteenth century, and thereafter increased
> moderately. . . . There is no obvious evidence for the more popular thesis
> that competition has been declining steadily . . . for a half-century or more.

Bain in 1959 ‡ stated:

> [The] desire to combine and concentrate to restrict competition is, to
> be sure, always operative. . . . But there are powerful opposing or counter-
> vailing considerations—law, market growth, protection of enterprise sov-
> ereignty—and it is quite possible that these will over time tend to balance
> (or even overbalance) the drives toward increasing concentration so that in
> the net increasing concentration will not increase (or may even decline)
> over time. The experiences of the last twenty years is consistent with pre-
> dictions to this effect.

Caves, writing in 1967, confirms this.§

> Just as these rankings of industries according to their concentration
> have stayed rather stable for long periods of time, so has the average level
> of concentration in manufacturing industries remained largely unchanged.
> During the twentieth century there have been short periods when the trend
> of concentration was clearly up or clearly down, but these swings seem
> largely to offset one another. There has been no significant change in the
> years since World War II, a period in which improved data let the econo-
> mist draw such a conclusion with some confidence.

---

* As argued by A. A. Berle and G. C. Means, *The Modern Corporation and Private
Property*, 1932. The various contentions of Berle and Means about the changed nature
of the corporation because of concentration are put to a systematic examination—and
rejected—by E. S. Mason and his collaborators in E. S. Mason, Ed., *The Corporation
in Modern Society*, 1959. These writers also rejected the notion, first put forward by
J. A. Schumpeter (in his *Capitalism, Socialism and Democracy*, 1942) and reasserted by
J. K. Galbraith (in his *American Capitalism*, 1952) that monopoly (i.e., concentration)
was inevitable and had to grow because it was more efficient than a market economy.

† George Stigler, *Five Lectures on Economic Problems*, 1949.

‡ Joe S. Bain, *Industrial Organization*, 1959.

§ Richard Caves, *American Industry: Structure, Conduct, Performance*, 2nd ed,
1967.

The same stability holds for the other major elements of market structure. The level of product differentiation seems to change slowly in most industries. . . . We lack any direct data on changes in barriers to entry over time, but they give the same general impression of stability. Entry restrictions rest largely on product differentiation, scale economies, and other such elements which in turn seem to change quite slowly.

A fourth wave of consolidations made its appearance, unlike all the others, in the second half of the 1960s, and this was the so-called conglomerate, a merger of unrelated companies. A characteristic example, and one of the largest, was the International Telephone and Telegraph Corp. which combined communications services and appliance manufacturing at home and abroad (it was the second largest holder of the shares of the Communications Satellite Corp.) with electronics manufacturing, auto leasing, finance, home building, hotels, chemicals and wood-pulp manufacture, a supplier of silica for glass, and a large baking concern, among others. In 1967 combined assets were more than $3 billion and sales and revenues almost as much.

In the two years 1966 and 1967 the Federal Trade Commission, which was becoming more and more interested and concerned (as was the Department of Justice) counted 207 such conglomerate mergers which involved assets of $12.1 billions. In 1968 the Federal Trade Commission estimated that such mergers would represent assets between $11 and $12 billion.

Were the conglomerates—in addition to having other kinds of power—a serious threat to competition, as the mergers of 1895–1904 had been? Neil Chamberlain, quoted in the *Wall Street Journal* of August 12, 1968, did not think so. Said he:

> By and large, there has been general agreement that a conglomerate merger would not be likely to have a market effect on competition. The fairly prevalent view was that if a subsidiary had a relatively limited share of the market, putting it together with a bundle of other such subsidiaries wouldn't increase its impact. Now, however, some economists are coming to feel that sheer economic power can transcend the market. Power goes with the large firm.

The Department of Justice was on the alert, and in a statement issued in 1968 it indicated that it would enter the lists against conglomerates which threatened the market under these situations:

1. When the merger created the danger of "reciprocal trading" (i.e., pressure on suppliers to buy from subsidiaries which have goods and services to sell).

2. When the acquiring company's promotional resources were so great that they enhanced a subsidiary's dominance in *its* field.

3. When a large company—a "potential competitor"—that might have entered a new business by internal expansion does so in effect by acquiring a subsidiary already in that business.

MARKET RESTRAINTS AND OLIGOPOLY

All this does not mean that when firms were large and few in a particular sector or industry, market restraints did not occur; they did so through oligopolistic competition. Oligopoly, which is the control of the market by a small number of giant corporations, ensures profitability by the maintenance of steady prices even if less-than-capacity production exists. Business decisions were governed not by the reactions of buyers but by the reactions of these companies to one another directly and personally (as opposed to reactions to impersonal market forces of pure competition). Price wars could be forestalled by collusive agreements or by a tacit sharing of the market, but most often by the acceptance of price leadership by the largest, oldest, or most prestigious of the firms in a particular industry. Oligopoly was as effective as monopoly; it restricted competition severely by a number of devices.

Oligopoly had become the pattern of much of American business enterprise because, with bigness, restraints on free market decisions were possible. Oligopoly reigned when barriers to entry by new firms were effective. Such barriers worked when product differentiation (and here advertising played an important role), patents, control over scarce materials, scale economies, and "absolute cost" elements raised the costs of new firms so high that they could not afford to try breaking into the magic circle of the few. The case of automobiles is one in point. Up to 1920 entry had been easy; 126 firms had appeared since 1906, but with a high mortality among them. In 1920 there were still 84 firms in the industry and in 1926, 44. This was the decade of product differentiation (annual models in a large variety of cars) first started by a revived General Motors and reluctantly, but of necessity, followed by Ford. In consequence there was no permanently successful entry after the appearance of the Chrysler Corporation in the early 1920s. Drop-outs continued, and in the 1960s there were only three domestic mass producers which accounted for 90 per cent of the industry's production.

The nature of bigness can be measured by two characteristics: size and proportion of corporate assets held by a few giant corporations and percentage of total shipments (or sales receipts) enjoyed by them. In regard to the first, Joe S. Bain in the book referred to made a breakdown of the assets of giant corporations in 1952. Among 448,949 nonfinancial firms whose total assets were $347 billion he found 436 corporations each with assets in excess of $100 million. These giants made up 0.1 per cent of all the nonfinancial corporations but controlled 48.2 per cent of total assets. (This was a decline from 1933 when 375 giants—each with more than $50 million assets—controlled 56.2 per cent of all nonfinancial corporate assets.) For 1952 a sectoral breakdown showed the following proportions in total corporate assets held by the 436 giants. (Table 33.)

TABLE 33

TOTAL CORPORATE ASSETS HELD BY GIANT
CONSOLIDATIONS (PERCENT)

Public utilities (162 companies)	77.5
Manufacturing (215 companies)	49.4
Mining and quarrying	33.5
Agriculture, forestry, and fisheries	16.0
Wholesale and retail trade	15.5
Service trades	11.4
Construction *	4.0

* Included are corporations with assets between $50 million and $100 million apiece.

In regard to the second, a federal study "Concentration Ratios in Manufacturing Industry," published in 1958, showed the percentage of total shipments (sales receipts) achieved by the four largest firms in each industry. (Table 34A.)

TABLE 34A

PROPORTION OF SALES RECEIPTS WHERE OLIGOPOLY
EXISTED (PERCENT)

Tobacco and tobacco products	73.9
Transportation equipment	58.1
Motor vehicles	68.3
Other transportation	51.3
Rubber and rubber products	52.2
Instruments	47.8
Electrical machinery	47.8
Chemical and related products	45.7
Primary metals	44.7
Iron and steel	42.8
Nonferrous metal	49.2

In these industries oligopolistic competition was the rule. Indeed, it was Caves's * opinion that oligopolies in national markets created almost half the value of the shipments of all manufacturing industries. It was not so at the bottom of the scale, where the largest four companies controlled the following percentages of total shipments (Table 34B.)

TABLE 34B

PROPORTION OF SALES RECEIPTS WHERE OLIGOPOLY
DID NOT EXIST (PERCENT)

Paper, pulp, and products	25.7
Leather and leather products	24.3
Furniture and fixtures	18.8
Printing and publishing	17.7
Apparel	13.7
Lumber and wood products	11.4

On the other hand, the following important sectors of the American economy showed a reverse of concentration and therefore the absence of or the potentialities for oligopoly: agriculture, forest products, bituminous coal, crude-oil extraction (because of the existence of large underground pools which could be tapped by small as well as large companies), retail stores, and most service industries.

The outstanding consequences of oligopoly—of great concentration and real barriers to entry—have been high profit ratios and price rigidity. Prices are maintained or raised as a ratio of costs, even with less than utilization of full capacity and underemployment (both had been characteristics of the early 1960s). The defense for concentration has been the achievement of greater efficiencies effected by outlays on research and development. The quality of existing products is constantly improving; new ones are being developed, and as mass-production is introduced larger markets are opened up and *their* prices fall. The critics of high concentration are not impressed. The three economists already cited, Stigler, Bain, and Caves, agree that oligopoly does not necessarily advance technological efficiency; too often it is the reverse.

Stigler is for the dissolution of giant companies, since "an industry which does not have a competitive structure will not have a competitive behavior." He has this to say about built-in efficiency and progressiveness:

. . . on all these matters it has to be confessed that the relevant facts are scrappy and otherwise unsatisfactory. But they are sufficient to indicate the

* Richard Caves, *American Industry: Structure, Conduct, Performance* 2nd ed., 1967.

contrary nature of the evidence and to throw doubts upon the existence of a general rule. There are certain industries with a high, although indeed not the highest degree of concentration which devote large reserves to research and enjoy rapid technical advance. . . . There are, however, instances of the opposite trend.

And thus Bain:

It is not true that existing degrees of business concentration are adequately explained simply as the result of adjustments to attain maximum efficiency in production and distribution. More broadly, they are in part the result of adjustments to attain maximum profits . . . ; and in part the result of . . . financial considerations, and legal and sovereignty restraining factors. . . . Concentration will frequently tend to be higher than the minimum required for efficiency. Industries probably tend to be more concentrated than necessary for efficiency—and the larger firms bigger than necessary—because of the operation of monopolization, sales promotion, and financial motives, and because of specific entry barriers favoring a few firms in certain industries.

And thus Caves:

Progressiveness demands oligopoly, but of a competitive character, and it is frequently associated with structures in which price competition has been replaced by product competition. This last factor is especially important because American research and development establishments are directed primarily toward new and improved products rather than new techniques for producing old products [and in this way reducing costs]; and research facilities thereby become a crucial factor in product rivalry.

Big firms are more likely than small ones to carry on research; on the other hand, small firms that do research spend proportionately as much as big firms and frequently more. This was demonstrated again and again in the 1950s, when small firms—in electronics, copying machines, pharmaceuticals, and the development of rare alloys—found secure places for themselves in markets because of their dynamic and imaginative leadership. All big companies do not necessarily engage in enough research. The case of steel is illuminating. In 1964, steel, an oligopolistic industry, in the United States spent only 60 cents of every $100 of sales on research and development, compared with the $1.90 average for all manufacturing. In the 1950s, instead of pushing into new frontiers —the development of the basic oxygen furnaces and continuous casting —American steel overinvested in costly open-hearth furnaces. Profitability remained high at about 13.2 per cent of net worth. There were three consequences:

1. Heightened competition from other materials—aluminum, plastics, and concrete.

2. A sharp stepping up of imports because costs were lower when the basic oxygen method and continuous casting were used.

3. A fall in steel's profitability—in 1962 down to 7.4 per cent of net worth.

Oligopoly, in short, can run into trouble, and this confirms the remarks of Jacob Schmookler, one of the contributors to the Mason volume:

> As in an earlier day, so today the vitality of America's technology arises largely from the urge of its people for material progress and their consequent eagerness to buy better goods or to pay less for the same goods. The economy's dynamism arises likewise from the pressure of competition generated by a high degree of equality of opportunity.

ANTITRUST LEGISLATION AND THE COURTS

To cope with the complex problems created by high concentration the United States has an instrument in a body of law and judicial opinion that has been shaped over the last 70 years, starting with the passage of the Sherman Antitrust Act in 1890. Granted the accomplishment has not been too great, but the weapon is there and larger effectiveness is possible if the Justice Department had more funds, if the President's office refrained from curbing the ardor of the antitrust division, if the federal courts always responded intelligently and swiftly to the leads the antitrust division was trying to develop. Dewey * sees a number of positive gains. Two important accomplishments in the control of cartels have been achieved. First, "the threat of prosecution has succeeded in discouraging—and sometimes eliminating—overt collusion." He makes an interesting observation:

> Strictly speaking, the whole theory of oligopoly, or tacit collusion as manifested in price leadership, market sharing, delivered prices . . . is a tribute to the occasional effectiveness of antitrust policy, for these roundabout and inefficient ways of restraining competition are unknown within legal frameworks that permit overt collusion. . . .

Second, this doctrine that collusion to restrain competition is illegal per se has not only made the restriction agreement unenforceable but it has also eliminated any device that would make income pooling possible. Therefore says Dewey:

* Donald Dewey, *Monopoly in Economics and Law,* 1959.

> When the balance is struck . . . the rule that the courts unless directed otherwise by legislation, will not enforce a private agreement that restricts competition is the supreme achievement of antitrust policy in the United States.

The corpus of the antitrust law is not very great; within it, however, there has been room for the federal courts to operate, and certain specific guidelines—not many, it is true—have emerged. The antitrust laws have declared the following practices illegal:

1. To enter into a contract, combination, or conspiracy in restraint of trade. (Section 1 of the Sherman Antitrust Act of 1890.)

2. To monopolize, attempt to monopolize, or combine or conspire to monopolize trade. (Section 2 of the Sherman Antitrust Act.)

3. Business practices of individual firms (conspiracies or agreements do not have to be proved) that would substantially lessen competition or tend to create a monopoly and, specifically, price discrimination among purchasers. (Section 2 of the Clayton Act of 1914 as amended by the Robinson-Patman Act of 1936, which specifies particular kinds of price discrimination.)

4. Directed against individual firms, the making of exclusive and tying agreements with purchasers. (Section 3 of the Clayton Act.)

5. Also directed against individual firms, the acquisition of, in whole or in part the stock or the assets of a competing corporation. (Section 7 of the Clayton Act as amended by the Celler-Kefauver Act of 1950.)

6. To use unfair methods of competition. (Section 5 of the Federal Trade Commission Act of 1914.)

7. To employ unfair or deceptive acts or practices. (Section 5 of the Federal Trade Commission Act, as amended by the Wheeler-Lee Act of 1937. The latter was designed to safeguard the consumer against deceptive practices and to strengthen the protection of competitors even when there was no danger of monopoly.)

The first landmark decisions of the Supreme Court came in 1911 in the Standard Oil of New Jersey and American Tobacco cases. Both firms had come close to establishing monopolies—the first controlled about 90 per cent of the country's oil refining, the second, between 75 and 90 per cent of every tobacco product except the manufacture of cigars. Both companies were found guilty under Sections 1 and 2 of the Sherman Act and were ordered broken up into several competing firms. The Supreme Court, in its decision, emphasized Section 1 (combinations in restraint of trade were illegal) and laid down the so-called rule of reason; that is, only unreasonable restraints were under the ban. As Caves points out, conduct in the market and not structure (monopoly per se) was the guideline the Court meant to follow.

In a number of cases involving Eastman Kodak, United Shoe Machinery, and International Harvester the Department of Justice tried to make its case on Section 2 (to monopolize or attempt to monopolize), but the Court stuck to Section 1 and, finding no coercion, ruled for the defendants. It did similarly in the case of United States Steel in 1920. U.S. Steel's share of the market had declined steadily since 1901; it was not seeking to intimidate competitors or customers. In short, it was not actively engaging in a monopoly, and the Court found against the government, declaring "the law does not make mere size an offense or the existence of unexerted power an offense."

In 1945 a real step forward was taken; the Court shifted from market conduct to market structure as the test for determining whether monopoly or the process of monopolizing actually existed, all without necessarily violating Section 1. Having and maintaining sheer power alone (whether financial, managerial, or the possession of patents) was to be the guideline. It did so in the case of the Aluminum Company of America and found against it. Commenting on the concentration it found, the Court said that 90 per cent of the American virgin aluminum production that the company controlled "is enough to constitute a monopoly; it is doubtful whether 60 or 64 per cent would be enough; and certainly 33 per cent is not." The next year the three largest cigarette manufacturers (an oligopoly, for they dominated five-sixths of the market) were found in violation of the Sherman Act. They were acting oligopolistically; there was, in effect, tacit collusion because the practices of the three were much the same; yet the Court hesitated to follow through—to order the dissolution of the three companies into smaller units.

Section 7 of the Clayton Act, as amended in 1950 (forbidding mergers that tend to create monopoly) also has teeth in it, and the Department of Justice, followed by the Supreme Court in the 1960s, was alert to its possibilities. Vertical mergers were moved against, and, as already pointed out, the conglomerates were coming under close scrutiny in 1969. Caves declares hopefully:

> Section 7 of the Clayton Act may be taking on the same complexion as Section 2, concerned with both protecting competition and with protecting small businesses (under the Robinson-Patman Act of 1936) from competition.

Most economists would not be satisfied unless oligopolies and mergers were broken up on the ground that claimed efficiencies or progressiveness simply cannot be proved and that enough evidence exists to believe that the contrary is the case.

THE PROGRESSIVE MOVEMENT

Progressivism—that intellectual and social phenomenon of the brief period 1900–1915—was not a "movement" in the sense one commonly associates with that term. It had no cohesive body of doctrine or theoretical criticism of society and no clearly defined program of action for amelioration either immediately or in the future. In short, it had no ideology, no prophets and no epigoni involving the faithful in analysis, refinement, and disputation about the meaning of the true word. It was middle-class reform, and Progressives were reformers who, for different reasons and frequently with contradictory objectives found themselves uncomfortable in the American world that had emerged as a result of the successful American industrial revolution of 1865–1900. The best Hofstadter,* one of the historians of the movement, can do in gathering under a common banner all the disparate elements that made it up is to call it "a major episode in the history of the American conscience."

Hofstadter starts his analysis in this fashion:

> The Progressive movement, then, may be looked upon as an attempt to develop the moral will, the intellectual insight, and the political and administrative agencies to remedy the accumulated evils and negligences of a period of industrial growth. Since the Progressives were not revolutionists, it was also an attempt to work out a strategy for orderly social change.

He ends by calling the Progressives the "pioneers of the welfare state," for they were determined to remedy the most pressing and dangerous social ills of industrial society":

> . . . they asserted—and they were the first in our history to do so with real practical success—the idea that government cannot be viewed merely as a cold and negative policing agency, but that it has a wide and pervasive responsibility for the welfare of its citizens, and for the poor and powerless among them.

There were, then, all sorts of Progressives in one sense that at one time or another they accepted a common rubric; and in another, because they were middle class and the products and beneficiaries of what was already the beginnings of an affluent society, they possessed a sense of unease (shall we say, guilt?) because the existence of economic inequalities, social inequities, and the lack of a democratically directed and honestly administered political purpose. Finally, there was a Progressive movement because these men and women were articulate and because

* Richard Hofstadter, Ed. Introduction, *The Progressive Movement, 1900–1915*, 1963.

there sprang into existence a periodical press and publishing houses that gave them the opportunity to be heard.

Therefore, it may be said, the muckrakers—the writers of articles of exposure in popular journals with large circulations—started the movement off. There was an enormous outpouring of such pieces and the books that came from them—by Ida Tarbell, Lincoln Steffens, Ray Standard Baker, Charles Edward Russell, Samuel Hopkins Adams, all journalists without special training in the fields they explored but with a zest for and a skill in revealing horrors that cried out for remedy. These were the first wave, the shock troops of reform. The intellectuals followed in the second wave. They were interesting and in their day influential; like the muckrakers their preoccupation was with pathology—society was sick, a rededicated America was necessary. To do what? To create a new Nationalism said Herbert Croly. To give the American people a Square Deal, said Theodore Roosevelt. To embark us on a New Freedom, said Woodrow Wilson.

The best Herbert Croly could come up with (in *The Promise of American Life,* 1909) was a revival of what he was pleased to call a Hamiltonian state with a program of comprehensive governmental intervention in all economic matters. What America needed were careful planning and legislation in the national interest. There was Walter Weyl's *New Democracy,* 1912. Self-interest was the basis of his program of social and industrial democracy; the people were to be protected by government as they pursued these nebulous aims. And there was Walter Lippman's *Preface to Politics,* 1913. What the country needed was objective, scientific legislation. All this was pretty thin gruel: it can be seen why the organized workers—presumably the beneficiaries of such concern—were turning to the radicalism of socialism and anarchosyndicalism.

Roughly, the interests and activities of the Progressives may be divided into these categories. Some sought social justice and therefore a more active involvement on the part of the state in protecting women and children in industry, providing for the aged and indigent, giving assistance to mothers with dependent children, and passing workmen's compensation and safety legislation. One group worked alone for women's suffrage. Others saw all the solutions in the restoration of government to the people. "Bossism," notably in the cities, was corrupt not only because of the personal pilfering in which the "machine" politicians engaged but because of their unholy alliance with the contract and franchise seekers—those who built and operated the street railways and the light and power companies. Direct government therefore was the sovereign remedy: small councils representing the whole city instead of large municipal assemblies chosen on a ward basis; the initiative, referendum and recall; "scientific government," which meant the use of experts to draw up and administer legislation.

There were those who concentrated their attention on the inequities that had sprung up in the business world: business was too big; the "trusts" dominated it, and they in turn were the agents and the pawns of "high finance." Break up the great concentrations and restore the vitality of the atomistic small businessman, said William Jennings Bryan, Louis D. Brandeis, and Woodrow Wilson. Recognize that "bigness" was a characteristic of the economy but bring industry under the control and even the direction of the federal government, said Theodore Roosevelt (in good part following Herbert Croly).

While all these solemn asseverations were taking place, there were some who were not overly impressed. Thus Peter Finley Dunn's "Mr. Dooley":

> Th' noise ye hear is not th' first gun in a rivolution. It's on'y th' people in the United States batin' a carpet. What were those shots? That's th' housekeeper killin' a couple of cockroaches with a Hotchkiss gun. What is that yellin'? That's our ol' friend High Finance bein' compelled to take his annual bath.

The Protestant clergy, from acquiescence and approval of the processes of the market place and the successful entrepreneur who, by his victories, proved he was a man of God, swung to the opposite pole. Indifference to Christianity, the violence of industrial warfare, the wide disparities in wealth and income, proved that the churches, if they were to reach the consciences of men, had a positive mission: this was the preaching of the "Social Gospel" (a phrase coined in the 1890s). Walter Rauschenbush, a New York Baptist minister and professor at the Rochester Theological Seminary, led the clergy who sought to give the unrest among the intellectuals a moral direction. His books—the first one, *Christianity and the Social Crisis,* 1907, was widely read—sounded the call for a new evangelism which was heard in many pulpits.

What Rauschenbush was preaching was what he called Christian Socialism—the rejection of the prevailing political, social, and economic values and institutions without, however, an acceptance of Marxian socialism itself. It was Christianity which was to lead in the regeneration of men and society: an evangelical Christianity, founded on the universal acceptance of the Kingdom of God, which was to build a Christian social order, based on social justice and economic democracy. Rauschenbush, and many like him, proposed a mixed bag of reform: the public ownership of land and utilities, worker participation in management, and cooperation. The inspiration and leadership were to come from Christian Socialism, which he defined as follows:

> The Christian sense of the sanctity of life and personality and of the essential quality of men reinforces the socialist condemnation of the present social order. The religious belief in the Fatherhood of God, in the fraternal solidity of men, and in the ultimate social redemption of the races through Christ lends a religious quality to the Socialist ideals.

This preaching of a crusade carrying religious banners had a pervasive influence. Even Theodore Roosevelt, never before a religious man, listened, for when he arose in convention to accept the Progressive party's nomination for the Presidency in 1912 he ended a rousing address with the words: "We stand at Armageddon and we battle for the Lord."

Hofstadter admits that the first Roosevelt was both "a moderate conservative and moderate Progressive." Roosevelt was not certain that "trust busting" was an answer to concentration, and it was he who gave consent to U.S. Steel's absorption of the Tennessee Coal and Iron Company. During his Presidency the Republicans refused to engage in tariff reform; they avoided an overhauling of the country's banking laws; not a single piece of social legislation emerged out of his administrations. He spoke often to the Congress, the press, in public addresses, and with increasing flamboyance: it is on the basis of what he said (rather than what he did) that perhaps Hofstadter is prompted to say of him:

> . . . he was opposed to plutocratic arrogance, corruption, civic indifference, and materialism, and he understood the need of right-thinking Americans to be reassured about the ability of their government to cope with bosses, bankers, and trusts.

Kolko,* in a curious book, is of the exactly opposite opinion. Roosevelt was contemptuous of reformers: indeed, it was he who fastened the name "muckrakers" on them and sought to dissociate himself from them publicly and privately. They raked "the filth of the floor"; they were the friends of "disorder." Of Upton Sinclair, the author of the justly celebrated novel, *The Jungle,* whose descriptions of the Chicago stockyards were responsible for the passage of the Pure Food and Drug Act, he wrote to a friend: "I have an utter contempt for him. He is hysterical, unbalanced, and untruthful. Three-fourths of the things he said were absolutely falsehoods. For some of the remainder there was only a basis of truth." And thus Kolko on Roosevelt:

* Gabriel Kolko, *The Triumph of Conservatism: A Reinterpretation of American History, 1900–1916,* 1963.

Roosevelt preferred to solve problems by ignoring them, and rarely took leadership during the earliest stages of discussion of industrial or political problems if it was led by those not in his class. Circumstances often forced him to intrude into affairs after intervention could no longer be avoided—he was, after all, conscious of votes and public pressures. But he never questioned the ultimate good intentions and social value of the vast majority of businessmen, nor did he ever attack an obvious abuse in business or take a stand on regulation without discreetly couching his terms with luxurious praise for the basic economic status quo and the integrity of businessmen.

There were two things Roosevelt was keenly aware of and both were serious challenges to that nebulous New Nationalism of which he took to talking more and more—with the seat of power and the source of inspiration and leadership in Washington and more particularly in the Presidency. First, the increasing role the states were playing in radically changing their fiscal policies and launching programs of social legislation. Second, the threat of stability—to the middle-class peace Mark Hanna, industrialist, and Samuel Gompers, trade-union leader, had worked out in the National Civic Federation—emanating from the growing and increasingly more powerful Socialist party and the Industrial Workers of the World. Radicalism—based on a class analysis of society which sought to end the capitalist system—was really penetrating into the United States, and the American workers through their unions, were giving their loyalty more and more to socialism or anarchosyndicalism.

With the turn of the century a new group of governors had appeared in the states, and it was they who, by shaking off the domination of the older party leaderships, led their legislatures in the enactment of widespread programs of change. In the passage of social legislation: workmen's compensation laws and factory-inspection acts; the abolition of child labor; the raising of school-attendance ages and wider financial support for education; mothers' assistance laws; old age pensions; and the protection of women in industry by the establishment of maximum hours of work and minimum wages. In the widening of the tax base: by calling on the railroads, the lumber companies, and the public utilities to bear a larger share of the fiscal requirements of an expanding public authority. By passing regulatory legislation over corporations: state banks were to be more closely supervised; public utilities—to regulate their services and fix their rates—were to be put under the control of state public service commissions; insurance companies were to be as carefully scrutinized in their practices as the banks; the life insurance companies were to be mutualized; and business corporations charters were to be examined more closely. A long list of political reforms were designed "to give the gov-

ernment back to the people": the expansion of the civil service, the freeing of the judiciary from party control; home-rule for cities; the short
ballot, initiative, referendum and recall, direct primaries, and corrupt-
practices legislation. It was from the states and the resolutions of state
legislatures that the unending pressures for the passage of federal constitutional amendments emanated—for the direct election of United
States senators, income-tax legislation, women's suffrage, and the abolition
of child labor.

The role of these new governors was an impressive one with a widen-
ing influence, for many moved from their state capitals into the larger
national life. The first and the greatest was Robert M. La Follette of
Wisconsin, elected in 1900; he was joined by Albert B. Cummins in
Iowa, Hiram Johnson in California (the three became United States
Senators), by Charles E. Hughes in New York, Woodrow Wilson in New
Jersey, James M. Cox in Ohio, Joseph Folk in Missouri, and William S.
O'Ren in Oregon.

La Follette, in 1913, looking back on his fruitful years in Wisconsin,
wrote in his *Autobiography*:

> It has been a fight supremely worth making, and I want it to be judged,
> as it will be ultimately, by results actually attained. If it can be shown that
> Wisconsin is a happier and better state to live in, that its institutions are
> more democratic, that the opportunities of its people are more equal, that
> social justice more nearly prevails, that human life is safer and sweeter—
> than I shall rest content in the feeling that the Progressive movement has
> been successful.

THE CHALLENGE OF RADICAL LABOR

The earlier efforts at the creation of the radical movements of socialism
and anarchism in the United States, as we have seen, were abortive. The
most important reason for failure was the absence of a mass base; that is,
the inability to penetrate the workers' trade unions. When radicalism
raised its head again in the first decade of the twentieth century, its successes grew spectacularly because organization was superior and because
the workers themselves became the backbone of the Socialist party and
the Industrial Workers of the World.

The Socialist party of America formally appeared in 1901 and from
the start laid down a tactic that could not alienate the AFL, yet made
its unions its chief recruiting ground. "Trade unions," it declared "are
by historical necessity organized on neutral grounds as far as political
affiliation is concerned," and thus avoided the mistakes of European so-

cialism which organized competing unions. Instead, by "boring from within," it meant to convert the AFL unions to the adoption of a socialist ideology. At the same time, by organizing as a political party in the true American manner from the grassroots up, the Socialist party carried on ceaseless agitation to spread the idea that socialism could be achieved peaceably and at the polling places. It held out the ideal of the attainment of a "cooperative commonwealth" to supersede capitalism and the wage system. It offered a program of immediate demands—social insurance, minimum wage legislation, and government ownership—to mitigate the rigors and insecurities of a market economy. It joined hands with European socialism by becoming a member of the Second International, whose most important argument was that an international workingmen's association was a powerful force for the maintenance of world peace.

The socialists' propaganda was carried on in a variety of ways: by the creation of a large socialist press with daily and weekly newspapers (in both English and foreign languages): by the organization of socialist clubs with dues-paying members (there were 113,000 in 1912); by the creation of a youth organization, the Young People's Socialist League, and another, the League for Industrial Democracy, to reach the intellectuals; and by entering almost every political contest, from as lowly as municipal elections to the regular nomination of candidates for the United States Senate and the Presidency of the United States. For the last Eugene V. Debs was the standard-bearer, who raised his vote from 96,931 in 1900 to 901,062 in 1912. By the time of the outbreak of World War I the successes of the party were impressive: it had elected two congressmen, 22 mayors, 28 assemblymen in 13 states and five senators in four states, as well as innumerable aldermen at the municipal level.

The inroads into the traditional unions were even more impressive. By the outbreak of World War I the socialists had penetrated into some of the largest AFL unions, had rewritten their constitutions with a socialist preamble and recast them, seeking to widen their scope by admitting the unskilled, introducing workers' education classes, and embarking on research programs. At the same time they were also playing a greater role in the annual AFL conventions. The socialists controlled most of the unions in the needle trades as well as those of the brewery and bakery workers. They were important forces in the councils of the machinists, coal miners, metal miners, cigar makers, and printers unions. In fact, at the AFL 1912 convention a printer, Max Hayes, received 5000 votes for the presidency against Gomper's 12,000.

Anarchosyndicalism, supported by the Industrial Workers of the World, formed in 1905, was also on the march. The IWW (its members came to be called Wobblies) had started out under the influence of the socialists and even talked of uniting for political action, but its industrial policy—the organization of all the workers, unskilled as well as skilled, in industrial unions and for revolutionary purposes—ran counter to Socialist party principles. Friction broke out at once, particularly when Daniel De Leon, that perverse and stormy petrel of American radicalism, insisted on bringing his Socialist Labor party into the organization. De Leon was expelled in 1908, and from then on the IWW pursued strictly syndicalist lines, eschewing political action. In true anarchist style war was declared on the state and its whole apparatus as well as on the American Federation of Labor. It proclaimed as its goal a workers' commonwealth controlled entirely by the industrial unions, banded together in "One Big Industrial Union."

Thus said the Preamble to the 1908 Constitution:

> The working class and the employing class have nothing in common. There can be no peace so long as hunger and want are found among millions of working people and the few, who make up the employing class, have all the good things of life. . . .
>
> These conditions can be changed and the interest of the working class upheld only by an organization formed in such a way that all its members in any one industry, or in all industries if necessary, cease work whenever a strike or lockout is on in any department thereof, thus making an injury to one an injury to all.
>
> Instead of the conservative motto, "A fair day's wage for a fair day's work," we must inscribe on our banner the revolutionary watchword, "Abolition of the wage system." It is the historic mission of the working class to do away with capitalism. The army of production must be organized not only for the every-day struggle with the capitalists, but to carry on production when capitalism shall have been overthrown. By organizing industrially we are forming the structure of the new society within the shell of the old.

The enemies were the entire political institutionalism, the capitalist system, and the "pure and simple" trade unions. The IWW's chief weapon was the use of "direct action"—turmoil, disorder, organized and unorganized strikes, mass demonstrations, and "free speech fights" in which large numbers of Wobblies flooded small communities and openly invited being jailed to the disorganization of local law enforcement machinery. On the job IWW members used sabotage by slowdowns and the destruction of machinery at the same time that the general strike was proclaimed as the ultimate tactic to compel the breakdown of the industrial processes.

By dual unionism it challenged every aspect of the methods of the AFL craft unions it rejected. The IWW industrial unions were opposed to trade agreements and contracts, paid union officials, high dues, and benefit programs. The revolutionary spirit of the workers could be maintained only in a state of constant warfare.

With these methods and this ideology, the IWW moved into three areas and three kinds of workers, largely unskilled, casual, and unorganized. The first were the migratory laborers of the Far West, of the harvest fields and lumber and railroad construction camps. In the picturesque vocabulary of the IWW, these were the "bindle stiffs" who carried all their possessions in a bedding roll and lived in "jungles" on the edges of towns; the "straw cats" or the harvest hands; the "muckers" or the metal miners; and the "gandy dancers" or section hands who built and repaired the rails.

The second were the unorganized workers of the South—in textiles, lumbering, and turpentine camps; leading them in huge strikes and demonstrations, the IWW kept small towns in a constant state of turmoil. The third were the immigrant workers from southern and eastern Europe—who were employed in the textile mills of Lawrence, Paterson, and Fall River, in the iron mines of the Mesabi Range, and in the steel-car plants of McKees Rocks, Pa.—these were organized, maintained in long strikes, and taught the tactics of guerrila war. The police and the local courts replied in kind. IWW organizers were roughed up, denied due process by law authorities, run out of towns by vigilante groups. Some were executed by firing squads or lynched. Perhaps as many as 150 strikes, always accompanied by violence, were the work of the IWW, largely during 1908–1916. This organization claimed that it had issued one million cards during its lifetime, but at its peak, around 1916, its membership was possibly 60,000. Had America not entered World War I in 1917 (the Wobblies were opposed to the war and as a consequence were harshly treated by the federal government and the states under newly enacted criminal syndicalist laws), the IWW, with its engaging slogan of "one Big Industrial Union," its no-compromise attitude toward industry and the state, its propaganda program and "free speech fights," and its willingness to carry on constant industrial conflict, might well have broken the power of the AFL and brought class war to America.

During the decade 1907–1917 there were not a few Americans who sensed some of this: that radicalism in the United States had become a real threat to stability. Thus wrote Brooks * in 1913:

* John Graham Brooks, *American Syndicalism. The I.W.W.*, 1913.

The I.W.W. taps labor strata not only lower than those of the trade union, but still lower than those from which socialism generally gets recruits. It appeals to youth, to the most detached and irresponsible, to those free to follow a life of adventure. It appeals to those who rebel at the discipline of the trade union. It easily becomes a brother to the tramp and the outcast. Nor is there one of these traits that is not a source of temporary strength from its own point of view—that of rousing and educating discontent, of hectoring and obstructing the solidities of capitalism. . . . The I.W.W. movement is strictly a revolutionary uprising against that part of the present order which is known as capitalism.

Theodore Roosevelt was not unaware of all this. His correspondence with his friends refers again and again to his concern about the growth of radicalism and the necessity for blunting and dissipating its spreading influence. Gabriel Kolko properly calls attention to this (as Hofstadter and other historians of the Progressive movement do not); and for this reason he attributes to national Progressivism (and particularly to Theodore Roosevelt) a conscious effort to use a powerful federal authority to stave off the radical threat—by welfare legislation—at the same time that by government regulation it was building securely the defenses of big business. (The first notion is sound; the second fanciful.)

WOODROW WILSON'S ACHIEVEMENT

Theodore Roosevelt's effort to lead the Progressive host to victory in the 1912 election was doomed to failure: he simply ended by splitting the Republican vote, and the miscellany of reformers he gathered under his large umbrella carried no conviction. More and more workers, rather than follow the AFL leadership or the Progressive flag of many colors, voted Socialist. Woodrow Wilson, the Democratic choice after a bitter convention contest in which he accepted with reluctance the party leadership of William Jennings Bryan and his version of old-fashioned agrarian populism, was destined to win.

Wilson was no Bryanite; indeed he was a liberal of nineteenth-century English persuasion who was more comfortable following the earlier John Stuart Mill than those who saw the need for a larger participation by government, particularly the federal government, in the affairs of men, the economic processes, and society in general. His New Freedom was not a counterpose to the New Nationalism or to socialism but a nostalgic return to an atomistic world in which bigness—whether in the state, business, or labor—was suspect. Regulation, yes, to break up agglomerations that threatened the viability of personal choices; but not a positive government or a positive law that assumed responsibilities for decision making in economic and social arrangements and ended with an elaborate public institutionalism and bureaucracy. Here he was much under the influence of Louis D. Brandeis, who was prolabor but against the closed shop; for welfare legislation for women and children but not for a program of state social insurance; for business but not in alliance with or under the domination of the bankers; and for a romantic kind of cooperative commonwealth as long as it was not socialist.

Because the New Freedom was so vague (and Wilson's biographer Arthur S. Link adds the other adjectives "idealistic and meaningless"), it could move into some areas and completely avoid others. It was committed to tariff reform and a tariff act, with *ad valorem* schedules averaging about 27 per cent (as compared with the 37 per cent of the Republican 1909 act), a large free list, and a very modest graduated income tax (the Sixteenth Amendment had been ratified), was quickly passed. The Congress, under Wilson's direction, turned to two other matters, antitrust legislation and banking reform, and that was the lot. By November 1914, with the Federal Trade Commission Act, the Clayton Antitrust Act, and the Federal Reserve Act on the statute books, Wilson, in a public letter to his son-in-law, William McAdoo, the Secretary of the Treasury, announced the completion of his New Freedom program and hailed his accomplishment in these words: "The nightmare of the past is over, the future will be a time of cooperation, of new understanding, a time of healing because a time of just dealing."

This left Herbert Croly, writing in the *New Republic* which he had just founded, aghast. "Wilson," said Croly, "had no grasp of modern social and industrial life . . . he is a dangerous and unsound thinker upon contemporary political and social problems." Professor Link agreed. Said he:

> Croly's analysis of the superficial character of Wilson's progressivism was essentially correct. There is little evidence that Wilson had any deep comprehension of the far-reaching social and economic tensions of the time.

The Democratic Congress was precipitated into action on antitrust legislation, as a result of the sensational hearings, conducted by a skillful and unfriendly lawyer, and the report of the Pujo Committee (a subcommittee of the House Committee on Banking and Currency); and on banking reform because of the demands of the banking community rather than Democratic zeal. Congressional committees worked on these matters simultaneously; a banking bill was completed first and enacted into law in December 1913. The Federal Trade Commission Act was signed in September 1914 and the Clayton Antitrust Act, in October of the same year; these are discussed out of order because of the relevance of the Pujo report to both antitrust and banking legislation.

The Pujo Committee began its hearings in the summer of 1912 and issued its four volumes of testimony and a report a year later. Its findings were a seven-days' wonder (if its statistics were not so conclusive as the subcommittee thought) and at once a clamor rose for immediate action. (Brandeis wrote a book called *Other People's Money* based entirely on the Pujo revelations.) The subcommittee pointed out that four New York banking firms, the House of Morgan towering over all the others, controlled 341 directorships in 112 corporations which had an aggregate capitalization of more than $22 billion. These banks (they constituted what Brandeis called "Our Financial Oligarchy") were said not only to be guiding the destinies of some of the country's greatest industrial and transportation corporations but were also closely linked with other financial institutions—national and state banks, trust companies, and life insurance companies. Therefore the Pujo report was entitled "Concentration of Control of Money and Credit."

According to the report, the testimony the subcommittee obtained proved that an identity and community of interest existed among a few leaders of finance, particularly those who were in the investment-banking business. This control was exercised by voting trusts and interlocking directorates. The report called for the abolition of these two forms of control; it advocated granting the Comptroller of the Currency the power to veto the mergers of financial institutions, and outlawing security affiliates of national banks, banning financial transactions between banks and their directors, and the protection of the interests of the scattered (but uninfluential) stockholders. This cut a wide swath. How many changes in or whether the termination of such practices—if any—should go into antitrust legislation and banking legislation? At the same time, other "Populist" Democrats were pressing for the regulation of stock exchanges, limitations on holding companies or mergers to one-third of the total product of an industry, and the abolition of the Supreme Court's "Rule of Reason." To the relief of American bankers in general it was decided that none of these matters would go into a bank bill. An antitrust act, supplemented by another to create a Federal Trade Commission (Brandeis sold Wilson on this), would take care of undesirable practices in both the financial and industrial worlds.

So it turned out, as we have seen. The Federal Trade Commission Act created a commission of five to rule on "unfair methods of competition," declare them unlawful, and issue "cease and desist orders" that could be enforced by the federal courts The Clayton Antitrust Act, in addition to forbidding price discrimination and tying contracts, touched on—but only lightly—the points with which the Pujo Report had concerned itself. Corporations were forbidden to acquire stock in other corporations in which the effect would be "substantially" to lessen competition; interlocking directorates were banned in concerns in interstate commerce if such companies were competitors; directors of banks with resources of more than $5 million could not sit on the boards of railroads, construction and maintenance companies with which they did business, or competing companies. As concessions to the trade unions the antitrust laws were not to apply to them (Section 6); and the use of the federal injunction in labor disputes seemingly was limited (Section 20). As far as business was concerned, no bones were broken; and as for Gompers, his rejoicings about labor's "Charter of Liberties" were premature, for the federal courts continued to curb trade-union practices severely when it came to strikes and boycotts.

The Federal Reserve Act of 1913, in consequence, ended up a straight money and banking bill. It should be said that those who wrote and guided the destinies of the measure through both houses of Congress were not currency tinkerers but men who worked closely with and were constantly made aware of the needs of the country's national bankers.

As early as 1897 representatives from a large group of business organizations throughout the country met under the rubric of the Indianapolis Monetary Convention to discuss the inadequacies of the banking system and propose a program of thoroughgoing changes. The expert it hired to gather the necessary facts and submit a plan for reform was Professor J. Laurence Laughlin of the University of Chicago, and he (and one of his pupils, H. Parker Willis) was in and out of all the discussions in and proposals emanating from the banking world. A number of things troubled bankers and businessmen: the currency supply was inelastic (because it was not tied in closely enough to commercial assets); banking was too fragmentized and too diffuse (there were too many small banks; and national banks could create neither branches nor lend more than one-tenth of their capital to a single borrower). A larger role for a centralized authority was necessary to permit banking to respond to the needs of business operating in a national market.

Presidents McKinley and Roosevelt and their Republican Congresses responded sluggishly to such asseverations. Even the panic of 1907 and the heavy toll it took in bank failures led to no leadership from Washington. Minor temporary palliatives were enacted, but one significant forward step did emerge, which took President Roosevelt off the hook. This was the creation in 1908 of a joint Congressional National Monetary Commission. It was given a widesweeping mandate and the commission took its work seriously (this was notably so of its chairman, Senator Nelson A. Aldrich) by studying central banking abroad and scrutinizing in detail the operations and inadequacies of money and credit in the United States. The testimony and report of the commission were published in 1910, and out of them grew the Aldrich Plan, which proposed a private central bank, in the form of a National Reserve Association that would work through 15 reserve districts. This organization was to have no formal public representation other than the Secretaries of Agriculture, Commerce, Labor, and the Treasury, all serving ex officio. In addition to issuing bank notes against a reserve of gold and lawful money of 50 per cent, this central bank, through its reserve districts, was to rediscount commercial paper (thus providing a more elastic currency) and have the right to engage in open-market operations. Bankers (particularly big-city bankers), heretofore divided about remedies (but not causes) lined up behind the principles incorporated in the Aldrich Plan, but the chances for its enactment as a bill went aglimmering with the Democratic capture of the lower house of Congress in the 1910 election and the great cracks that emerged in the Republican party. The year 1912 was to be a Democratic year (as it turned out) and banking destinies were to be in the hands of Congressman Carter Glass, slated to be chairman of the House Committee on Banking and Currency, for President-elect Woodrow Wilson had no more ideas about (or, in fact, interest in) banking reform that had his predecessors Roosevelt and Taft.

This was fortunate, for Glass hired H. Parker Willis to become his committee's expert, and Willis got in touch with his one-time mentor Professor Laughlin. It was the Glass bill, based largely on the suggestions of Willis and Laughlin, that became the basis—with modifications—of the Federal Reserve Act. Behind it swung the support of the important banking groups of the country, for the differences between it and the Aldrich Plan were not particularly marked.

A good deal of jockeying went on behind the scenes even before the Congress was organized by the Democrats. Glass, working with Willis and Laughlin, drew up a number of drafts of a bill, and in December 1912 a broad plan emerged which Glass discussed with the President-elect. This (the quoted matter is from Glass's own recollections) called for the creation of a number of regional reserve banks "with a view to decentralizing credits" (these were to be controlled by the banks themselves); reserve balances were to be kept in these regional reserve banks; national banks had to be members; and state banks were to be invited to join. Also included were the following: "the rediscounting processes common to such plans"; the issuance by the regional banks of federal reserve notes, based on a gold and a liquid paper cover; the gradual retirement of national bond-secured notes; and the joint liability of all the regional banks. Wilson made an important contribution: there should be a central board, a Federal Reserve Board, as a capstone to the whole structure and its members were to be named by the government.

On this basis the Glass committee held public hearings and a bill was drawn up for submission to the House. Bankers generally were favorably disposed, but other quarters, particularly the political, were to be heard from and conciliation was necessary before full congressional support could be mobilized. Secretary of the Treasury McAdoo wanted a more powerful "National Reserve Bank." Senator Robert L. Owen, chairman of the Senate Finance Committee (backed by Bryan), wanted the notes issued by the Reserve Board to be obligations of the United States government, and that the government control its deposits and have full freedom in its fiscal operations. The "Pujoists" (headed by the committee's counsel, Samuel Untermeyer) insisted that the bill outlaw interlocking directorates among bankers. The Owen-Bryan demands were yielded to, and the "Pujoists" were bought off with the promise that antitrust legislation would take care of their proposal. Some grumblings among bankers were allayed by inclusion of a provision that discount rates would be set by the district banks, with the Board having the power only to veto changes in existing rates. As a final concession to westerners in the Senate the gold reserve behind the federal reserve notes was raised from 33⅓ per cent to 40 per cent. On this basis both Houses passed substantially the same bills and the Federal Reserve Act became law on December 23, 1913.

Gabriel Kolko, who has submitted the origin, inception, and final form of the act to the closest scrutiny, is certainly right in saying that the bankers, and the large bankers at that, got what they wanted. True, the Federal Reserve Board's five members were to be appointed by the President and the Secretary of the Treasury and the Comptroller of the Currency were to sit ex officio; but, says Kolko, "the Federal Reserve Act made it possible for the bankers to take over each reserve district [of which 12 were finally set up], put nothing in the way of this happening, and gave them the means of controlling two-thirds of the directors." This was the course of events in which the New York Reserve Bank— under the leadership of its governor Benjamin Strong—became the most powerful element in the Federal Reserve System. As we shall see, it was Strong who really was responsible for monetary policy in the 1920s and not the Federal Reserve Board.

XIII

THE PROGRESS OF THE
ECONOMY AND ITS INSTABILITIES

MEASURES OF GROWTH, PRODUCTIVITY, AND ECONOMIC PROGRESS

Despite all the viewers with alarm and the clamor for reform—loud and earnest declarations that concentration in business, in money and credit, and in wealth and income were creating barriers to entry for new enterprise and innovation, slowing down increases in real income, and dampening the consumption of goods and services—the American economy in the first 30 years of the twentieth century continued to move ahead almost as rapidly as it had in the 30 years earlier.

There were statistical measures (viewed retrospectively) that permit us to say these things. The country's rate of growth showed no signs of slackening seriously. Thanks to the infusion of large amounts of capital (as a result of private savings and investment) and advances in productivity, economic progress, as indicated by "a margin over maintenance" (consisting of support of national security and population increases but also of increases in consumption and in investment per capita), was being made. The United States had not yet become "mature"; it did not require massive intervention on the part of government—by regulating, spending, redistributing income, and expanding public employment—to ensure "effective demand," stimulate investment, maintain employment, and

TABLE 35

GROWTH IN REAL GNP AND PRODUCTIVITY 1889–1929[a]

	Real Net National Product	Total Factor Input	Total Factor Productivity
1889–1899	4.5	2.9	1.5
1899–1909	4.3	3.1	1.1
1909–1919	3.8	2.3	1.5
1919–1929	3.1	1.6	1.4

Source. Kendrick, op. cit., p. 99.

[a] Average annual percentage rates of change.

raise standards of living. At one point the economy failed, and this was due to a lack of economic knowledge but also of a want of public policy. Instabilities, leading to sharp changes in the business cycle, resulted in rises and falls in employment and investment followed by recessions and finally the Great Depression of 1930–1939.

Kendrick and Mills (following the pioneering work of Kuznets) have furnished us with statistics that give us rather clear notions of what did take place during 1899–1929.* Kendrick has provided convenient summaries and therefore we follow his analysis.

The figures in Table 35 present the roughest measures of economic growth through the average annual percentages of change for the real net national product, the total factor inputs of capital and labor, and the total factor productivity for capital and labor combined.

The figures in Table 36 are more refined in terms of real NNP per capita, real consumer outlays per capita, and capital and labor inputs per capita and again in terms of average annual percentage rates of change.

Kendrick, by adapting Mills's analysis, seeks to break down the "margins over the maintenance of the product" by separating the portions required for national security and population growth and finally—what Mills called the "margin for economic progress"—the portions for consumption and capital investment. The figures in Table 37 are for the various margins in percentages of the real Gross National Product.

* John W. Kendrick, *Productivity Trends in the United States,* 1961; Frederick C. Mills, "Productivity and Economic Progress," Occasional Paper 38 of the National Bureau of Economic Research, 1952; Simon Kuznets, *National Income and Capital Formation,* 1938, and *National Income,* 1941.

TABLE 36

GROWTH IN REAL NNP AND LABOR AND CAPITAL INPUTS, 1889–1929[a]

	Real NNP per Capita	Real Consumer Outlays per Capita	Labor Input per Capita	Capital Input per Capita
1889–1899	2.6	2.2	0.6	2.4
1899–1909	2.3	2.4	0.9	1.7
1909–1919	2.3	1.3	0.4	1.7
1919–1929	1.6	2.9	−0.3	1.2

Source. Kendrick, op. cit., pp. 84, 85.

[a] Average annual percentage rates of change.

It is interesting to go back to Mills, with his preoccupation with "economic expansion and economic progress." To him the chief lifting force in regard to expansion was steadily growing man-hour productivity—marked in the first decade of the century, 1901–1910, when the Progressive movement (claiming the opposite) was riding high; and decidedly so during the decade 1921–1930 (the period of "false prosperity," when, presumably, the causes for the Great Depression were building up).

We quote Mills at length:

> I have said that the relative gains in productivity were greatest in the twenties. . . . Special interest attaches to the period of six or eight years following the end of the first World War. In these years of acceleration in

TABLE 37

MARGIN OVER MAINTENANCE AS PROPORTIONS OF GNP, 1889–1928

			Margins over Maintenance			
		Maintenance of Population (Consumer and Capital Goods)			For Economic Progress	
	Real GNP		For National Security	For Growth of Population	Con- sumption	Capital Invest- ment
1889–1898	100.0	83.1	0.5	6.7	1.2	8.5
1899–1908	100.0	83.5	0.8	6.9	1.6	7.2
1909–1918	100.0	85.1	3.3	6.0	1.3	4.3
1919–1928	100.0	85.4	1.7	5.2	2.0	5.7

Source. Kendrick, op. cit., p. 100.

manhour productivity in the economy at large and in the important manufacturing sector reached their maxima [during the 50 years 1901–1950]. . . .

Back of these advances lay a highly favorable conjuncture of circumstances. The movement toward scientific management came to first fruition
in the industrial expansion of the early twenties. The movable assembly
line, dramatized by Ford a few years earlier, became a standard feature of
mass production. The power available to industrial workers was greatly
increased in amount and in flexibility of application. Working hours declined from 53 a week in 1914 and 1917 to an average of 47 in 1922. Occupational shifts contributed to the gain in manhour output in the general
economy. . . . The stock of real capital per worker, in the form of producers'
durable equipment and industrial and commercial structures, stood at a
relatively high level in the early twenties, having increased by some 40 per
cent in two decades. . . . Perhaps of greater importance than the increase
in the stock of capital goods was the advance in the *quality* of capital instruments. Technological improvements as well as the innovations of scientific
management were widely adopted in the early twenties; such improvements
were chiefly manifest in the tools of production.

Mills's analysis of the "margin above maintenance" is somewhat
different than Kendrick (he finds expenditures for war and defense
greater and does not allow for the growth of population). Following him,
and taking the whole span of 50 years (1901–1950) that he was examining,
Mills concluded:

> For the five decades as a whole approximately 51 per cent of our output
> margin was used to raise consumption levels, 23 per cent was used to create
> net additions to our capital plant, and 26 per cent was used for defense.
> About three-quarters of the margin was devoted to progress, one quarter to
> national defense.

Mills's figures are given in Table 38 in billions of 1929 dollars.

TABLE 38

MARGIN ABOVE MAINTENANCE IN REAL DOLLARS, 1901–1950

Decade	Margin Above Maintenance	War and Defense	Uses of Margin Above Maintenance Progress		
			Consumption Increase	Net Capital Increase	Total for Progress
1901–1910	$144	$ 4	$ 85	$55	$140
1911–1920	118	28	37	53	90
1921–1930	223	8	140	75	215
1931–1940	14	11	−9	12	3
1941–1950	558	228	285	45	330

Progress in Mills's terms, it will be noted, was especially rapid in the first and third (and fifth) decades when the gains in consumption were also the sharpest. In the twenties, to quote Mills, "consumption levels were sharply advanced in a productivity spurt of exceptional intensity." Put in per capita consumer expenditures (as measured by 1929 dollars), Mills went on to indicate that the gain during 1901–1910 over the preceding decade was 32 per cent and that during 1921–1930 over the decade before was 27 per cent. He concluded: "The thesis that industrial development is necessarily marked by increasing misery would be hard to defend in the light of this record." Finally Mills at the end of his essay said:

> Thanks to modern technology we have had to employ only a relatively small part of our resources to maintain and enlarge our productive plant. We have used most of our vast new powers to ease the lot of citizens at large through gains in leisure, and to improve it through diversified consumption patterns. . . . The record leaves no doubt that much of our new productive power has gone, over this half century, to advance human welfare. In major degree, the benefits of industrial progress in the United States in this half century have served to lighten toil for producers and elevate living standards for consumers.

A few further comments about some of the matters discussed. The "economic progress" Mills talked of was stimulated in considerable measure by increases in productivity represented by both capital and labor inputs. During 1920–1929 the gross capital formation (in 1929 dollars) was $179 billion and the net capital formation (deduction for depreciation of plant and tools), $79.6 billion. This represented $18 billion and $8 billion, respectively, as annual averages. (Contrast with the depression decade 1930–1939 is marked. The gross capital formation was $117.9 billion—or $11.8 billion annual average—and the net capital formation was $10.3 billion—or $1 billion annual average.) For the years 1922–1929 the productivity increase in labor inputs came to about 2 per cent annually, and the increase in wages of workers in manufacturing (measured by average hourly compensation) came to about the same. This represented a real wage increase, for consumer prices remained virtually unchanged during the years referred to. Thus the long-term experiences of worker compensation in the United States—that increases in productivity have been matched by rises in real wages—were also typical of the 1920s. Economic progress was not at the expense of the workers; indeed they shared in it and their heavy outlays for durable consumer goods was an important factor in keeping the economic engine going.

THE BOOM OF THE 1920S

In connection with the "economic progress" in the 1920s, of which Mills wrote, the great increase in the use of electric power and the appearance of a group of new and, technologically speaking, modernized industries which furnished fresh opportunities for employment and investment, played leading roles. We shall look at a few of these industries briefly.

The electric light and power industry (as measured by the horsepower of electric central stations) grew from 6,228,000 in 1910 to 17,050,000 in 1920 and to 43,427,000 in 1930. The value in plant and equipment of the industry in the same years was $964 million in 1910, $3.2 billion in 1920, and $7 billion in 1930. Consolidations and refinancing in the 1920s made possible the building of great central stations and the extension of transmission lines and electrical services into suburban and rural areas. The utility holding company was a product of the 1920s; the greatest group clustered about the activities of Samuel Insull, based in Chicago and operating largely in the Middle West. Insull obtained his financing from Chicago rather than Wall Street and his companies were widely owned; they had 600,000 stockholders and 500,000 bondholders. By the end of the 1920s the Insull companies were worth $3 billion, served more than four million customers in 5000 communities in 32 states, and produced one-eighth of the gas and electricity consumed in the country.

This sort of imaginative expansion—accompanied by economies of scale due to innovations in technology, management, and financing—led to sharp reductions in prices and expanding consumer demand for power and concomitant growth in the production and sale of durable goods dependent on the use of electricity. Thus the value of electric appliances and supplies (refrigerators, washing machines, and stoves) grew from $63.2 million in 1921 to $176.7 million in 1929 and of radios, from $12.2 million to $36.6 million in the same years.

Taking the whole range of the value of output of durable consumers goods, we find that in the 1920s (comparing 1921 with 1929) the increase was from almost $3 billion to $5.6 billion. A breakdown of the more important ones (in addition to the two already cited) runs as follows. The figures are for the value of output of finished commodities at current producer prices in millions of dollars:

Passenger vehicles, motor
    1921—$1,115.5
    1929— 2,567.0

Motor vehicle accessories
    1921—$169.5
    1929— 407.6
Household furniture
    1921—$466.6
    1929— 600.4
Heating and cooking apparatus
    1921—$186.5
    1929— 347.3
House furnishings
    1921—$374.6
    1929— 643.3
China and household utensils
    1921—$166.8
    1929— 274.0

The most spectacular growth industry in the 1920s was of course the passenger automobile, and its early history was associated with the accomplishments of Henry Ford, who introduced his light, sturdy, and inexpensive Model T in 1908. Built on the basis of interchangeable parts, it was simple in design and easy to operate, maintain, and repair. In 1913, when Ford was able to standardize production and step up productivity by the installation of his moving assembly line, output took a sharp jump as costs and prices were cut sharply. In 1908 the whole industry had turned out 65,000 passenger automobiles. By 1915 it was manufacturing 1 million annually, of which Ford's share was almost 40 per cent. What the assembly-line technique did for productivity is evidenced by these figures. By the end of 1913 the average labor time employed to put together a Model T chassis had fallen from 12 hours and 28 minutes to 2 hours and 38 minutes; by the spring of 1914 it was 1 hour and 33 minutes. At the chief Ford plant at Highland Park, Michigan, 1000 vehicles were assembled each day, and the price of the Model T runabout dropped from $500 on August 1, 1913, to $260 on December 2, 1924.

The magic of the Model T was not only that it was a utility car, cheap to operate, and a great value for the money, but it was within the means of large numbers of people in both city and country. By the mid-1920s the Ford reached its zenith—and declined as rapidly. This decline was due to the appearance of a rejuvenated General Motors, which had been put together in 1908 by W. C. Durant. Durant was as remarkable in his way as Ford: he, too, gambled everything on the automobile, saw its great future, but saw it in a variety of forms rather than in one utility model. Durant's organization included the Buick, Olds (later the Oldsmobile), Oakland (later the Pontiac), and Cadillac, and electric-lamp and auto parts and accessory companies. He had no large financing and his integration was based on exchanges of stock. When he was caught short—and unable to pay his suppliers and workers—he sought outside help and got it from Pierre S. du Pont. Incapable of weathering the recession of 1920–1921, Durant was compelled to step out and du Pont moved in as president (by this time the du Ponts owned 30 per cent of the General Motors stock). Thus funds raised by the du Ponts and Morgan permitted General Motors to weather the storm of 1921–1922. Du Pont was succeeded by Alfred M. Sloan, Jr., and from then on the history of the automobile was that of General Motors and not Ford.

The success of General Motors was based on a number of things: a decentralized administration (in regard to production, sales, purchasing, research, and dealer organization), tight budgetary and costs controls from the top, diversification of model making and a highly competitive adaptation to a market in which a car was to be made available "for every purse and purpose," and concentration on the low-priced Chevrolet to compete with the Ford. The key to the success of General Motors, of course, was growth, but even more than that it was marketing competition. To ensure growth General Motors developed the trade-in and installment financing; its competitive leadership was based on the manufacture of new cars for comfort, power, and style and not for basic transportation alone. By 1927 the Chevrolet was closing in on the Ford (compelling Henry Ford to retool completely to follow the General Motors broad scheme of diversification). Before the end of the decade, General Motors had pulled into the lead, never again to be headed off. In 1928 the Ford Motor Company showed a loss of $70 million, and General Motors a profit of $296 million.

The forward linkages of the automobile industry must not be lost sight of. The first and the greatest was road construction. In 1916, after many decades of debate in Congress, the federal government took the plunge: an act authorizing federal aid to the states for building modern highways was passed. The government's contribution was modest—in the 1920s it came to an average of $75 million annually—but the law also forced the states to create highway departments with proper supervision and financial control. From 1916 on a large industry—the builders of roads and their suppliers—took shape. In 1915 all 48 states combined had spent only $75 million for highways; 15 years later the amount had climbed to $1 billion. Next in importance were the lifts given the petroleum (gasoline for cars, trucks, and farm tractors) and rubber (automobile tires) industries.

In the 1920s, with their new cars, more comfortable and more powerful, Americans took to the road for pleasure, and the new trucks and motor buses (with interstate highway systems available) hauled goods and passengers over greater and greater distances. Service industries developed to meet the requirements of auto, truck, and bus drivers and their passengers: gas and repair stations (where parts and tires could be obtained), quick lunch counters (the roadside "diner" became an American institution), and tourist cabins for overnight stays (which blossomed out later into the highly successful motel industry—a unique American contribution to travel).

World War I gave a great boost to two American industries—chemicals and aluminum—and the growth then initiated continued at an accelerated pace into the 1920s. The chemical industry's development had been retarded by a number of factors: its failure to see the real links it had with American industrial production at large, its acceptance of its dependence on foreign sources for many of its raw materials, and the tight grip German basic patents had on products, those derived from coal tars in particular. The military contracts, the profits derived from them, the sequestration of some 4500 German patents by the Alien Property Custodian (and their general use for the whole American industry under the nonprofit Chemical Foundation created after the war) gave chemical companies extra room in which to maneuver. In this they were assisted by the high protective duties for chemicals written into the Tariff Act of 1922.

On the other hand, here was an industry that began to spend sizable sums on the expansion of the domestic production of nitrates and potash, thus regularizing supply and lowering costs, and on research and development. Many basic chemical inventions were European in origin, but an impressive number came out of the laboratories of American companies. It was the long years and patient labor (and money) spent on their development that made them available. Innovation is as much technology as it is invention, and it was in that sector in particular that American enterprise shone.

The 1920s marked the commercial beginnings of synthetics and plastics in chemistry. Work with synthetic fibers (wood pulp and cotton linters were reduced to cellulose) led to the development of rayon, which was in general use in the 1920s. Fundamental nylon research (in the du Pont laboratories it cost them, all told, some $30 million) was well under way in the 1920s and filaments for commercial use (the manufacture of stockings) appeared in the 1930s. Similarly, research (also at the du Ponts) was begun on neoprene in 1925; the result was a truly synthetic rubber. Development and commercial feasibility also occurred in plastics, cellophane, synthetic leather, lacquers, fertilizers, and a large range of substitutes for coal-tar products, all made synthetically. The consequence was that in the 1920s the chemical industry's product value was as great as that of iron and steel.

The aluminum industry had had humble beginnings, starting with the Pittsburgh Reduction Company in 1888 which had a capitalization of $20,000. It converted the bauxite ores (great deposits of which were to be found in the United States) into "primary" aluminum, largely in sheets. The company grew by the acquisition of bauxite mines in the United States, Canada, and elsewhere and was able to function as a manufacturer because it was the beneficiary of high protective tariffs. In 1907 it emerged as the Aluminum Company of America and its grip on the market was strengthened by its merger in 1925 with the Canadian Manufacturing and Development Company. It was then discovered that the United States was confronted with a monopoly in the classical sense.

Alcoa's opportunity came with the new automobile, the aeronautical industry, and the widening hunt for substitutes for steel, iron, and copper. It was particularly alert to the possibility of the use of cable, to replace copper, for electrical transmission. In addition to its deposits all over the world, Alcoa therefore established or acquired large numbers of producers of aluminum and aluminum-alloy manufactures—sheets, rods, wire and cable, foil, tubes, cooking utensils, castings, and paint. Their impact on industrial technology and the development of new consumer goods must be apparent.

This recital, albeit sketchy, is not complete without reference to the contributions made by the construction industry in stimulating the economy in the 1920s. The fact is an enormous construction boom took place in the decade that changed the face of American cities. Taken in the large, construction (dwelling units, commercial and industrial buildings, public works, and public utilities) made up a large part of the national income—greater than that of any single group of manufacturing industries with the exception of metals; it furnished employment to almost 6 per cent of the country's total civilian labor force; and had important backward linkages. To this extent its own cycle had significant effects on the upward-moving business cycle of 1921–1929. The estimated value of construction (at current prices) rose from $12.2 billion in 1919 to $17.4 billion in 1928, dropping off slightly to $16.2 billion in 1929. Although the creation of new housing reached a peak in 1926 and began slowing down, the general momentum in construction was sustained because of the continued erection of commercial and industrial buildings, public works (highways playing a large part), and public-utility installations.

The part of the national income arising directly from construction went up to $4.2 billion in 1926 and declined slowly to $4.0 billion in 1928. As for its backward linkages, construction furnished a large part of the market for steel, electrical equipment, glass, and almost the whole market for cement, stone, brick, lumber, earth-moving machinery, plumbing supplies, and hardware. Shipment of building materials made up one-sixth of all the railroad ton-miles.

The house-building boom, which started at the end of the recession of 1920–1921, reached its high point in 1926. New housing was possible because of the backlog of demand (and the existence of savings from high wages and full-employment during the war years), plentiful and easy credit in the form of mortgage money for builders of urban multiple dwellings and suburban developments, and the large-scale movement into suburbia of the middle-class, made possible by the automobile. In the last connection, despite the fact that houses were still being built by handicraftsmen, economies of scale were possible; individual houses in a "development" did not deviate markedly from a common pattern, streets and public utilities were laid out with an economy of means, there was mass purchasing of supplies, and contractors worked on a time schedule and percentage basis.

As for rebuilding the urban slums, it is to be reported, alas, that neither imagination on the part of public authority nor of private builders and the purveyors of credit rose to the occasion. Escape from the slums was possible—thanks to rapid transit for many white urban workers, but Negroes, coming north (as we shall see), began to move into the slum buildings. In the 1920s the dry rot of the inner core of cities began to set in—for few to have the wisdom to see and for even fewer to comment on.

In connection with commercial and industrial building, in particular, the influences of technological and management advances were marked. Materials were improved and standardized, concrete began to be used more and more, and lifting and portable machinery were perfected. The many new skyscrapers of the large cities—following the precepts of the great architect Louis Sullivan—had a simplicity of design and a maximum of functional space; they were easy to manage and operate and comfortable to work in. Because of the ease and cheapness of mortgage credit, the erection of urban commercial buildings reached overcapacity toward the end of the decade. Builders frequently met total costs of construction through large first mortgages. The banks furnishing the funds were able to protect their stakes by floating real-estate mortgage bonds, which were sold—passing on the risk—to the public. This was one kind of financial practice that contributed to the general orgy of speculation that set in in 1928 and grew in 1929.

PRICES, THE CIVILIAN LABOR FORCE, AND EMPLOYMENT

One of the broad consequences of the changes recorded here (in improved technology, heightened productivity, and interindustry competition, e.g., aluminum competing with steel, synthetic products with natural products) was the effect on prices. Wholesale prices, as the impact of World War I on the American economy began to be felt, started to move up sharply in 1916 and continued their rise until 1920. From 1915 to 1920 the increase was 122 per cent (as great as during the Civil War). Prices fell suddenly during the postwar recession of 1920–1921 (by almost 37 per cent), and from then on during the 1920s remained stable. Thus, with 1926 as 100, wholesale prices were 97.6 in 1921 and 95.3 in 1929. Consumer goods prices normally mount even when wholesale prices remain steady (because of greater marketing costs), but they did not do so during the 1920s; in fact, they even dropped a bit. With 1947–1949 as 100, consumer prices were 76.4 in 1921 and 73.3 in 1929. Reference has already been made to the rise in real wages in this connection.

Was the stability of prices due to lack of "effective demand," or was it due to improved productivity in the mass-production industries and to the appearance of new areas of competition for the consumer dollar (automobiles, radios, electrical appliances)? As a result of the malaise in agriculture (as we shall see), undoubtedly weakness in "effective demand" played a part, but the agricultural population had become a relatively minor one in the American labor force. What of employment? Except for the recession of 1920–1921 and a brief one in 1924 employment remained high. Immigration was cut sharply by the quota acts of 1921 and 1924; but the industrial labor force—industry was deprived of this source of supply—was augmented by internal migration—movement from the South to the North (largely by both blacks and whites from rural areas) and also laterally from the country to the cities in all sections of the nation.

During the years 1905–1914 more than one million immigrants as annual average had entered the United States. There was a fall-off during the war, of course; in 1921 800,000 had come (but emigrant departures were about 250,000), and then (except for 1924) a real drop—294,000 in 1925, 304,000 in 1926, 335,000 in 1927, 307,000 in 1928, and 279,000 in 1929. In 1920 54.2 million of the country's population was urban, as against 51.6 million rural (of which 20.2 million were rural nonfarm and 31.4 million rural farm). By 1930 the proportions had changed markedly: 69 million were urban and 53.8 million rural (with 23.7 million rural nonfarm and 30.2 million rural farm). Internal migrations, as measured by changes of residence into noncontiguous states, showed these proportions: in 1920 for the whole population 11.5 per cent, for whites 11.7 per cent, and for nonwhites 9.5 per cent; in 1930 for the whole population 12.1 per cent, for whites 12 per cent, and for nonwhites 13.3 per cent. The movement of southern rural Negroes into the North, usually to become urban workers, begun in 1910, was accelerated between 1916–1919 (as laborers in war industries) and took on even greater proportions during 1921–1924. Between 1910 and 1920 the net increase of southern-born Negroes in the North was 322,000 (five times the average for 1901–1910); between 1921 and 1924 the net increase was probably as high as 600,000.

TABLE 39

DISTRIBUTION OF GAINFULLY EMPLOYED BY OCCUPATIONAL GROUPS,
1919 AND 1929

Occuptional Group	1919 (%)	1929 (%)
Agriculture	21.3	18.3
Mining	2.8	2.3
Manufacturing	25.4	22.3
Construction	2.8	4.4
Transportation and public utilities	8.2	7.3
Trade	12.6	14.8
Finance	2.4	3.3
Service	12.2	15.6
Government	8.8	7.0
Miscellaneous	3.5	4.6
Total number (millions)	39.8	44.9

Source. Simon Kuznets, National Income and its Composition, 1919–1938, 1941.

There were 42.4 million gainfully employed workers in 1920 in the United States, of whom 31 million were nonfarm and 11.4 million farm. In 1930 the number of gainfully employed was 48.8 million, of whom 38.3 million were nonfarm and 10.5 million farm; that is to say, over the course of the decade the number of gainfully employed increased 15 per cent, but nonfarm workers showed an increase of 24 per cent.

Thanks to the work of Stanley Lebergott (under the auspices of the

National Bureau of Economic Research), we have good estimates of the civilian labor force and the unemployed for the 1920 and 1930 decades. After the recession of 1920–1921 had spent itself unemployment fell sharply to 3.2 per cent of the civilian labor force in 1923, 4.0 per cent, in 1925, 1.9 per cent, in 1926, 4.1 per cent, in 1927, 4.4 per cent, in 1928, and 3.2 per cent, in 1929. That is, for four of the seven years 1923–1929 there was high employment (virtually full, allowing for changing of jobs) in the United States. The contrast with the Great Depression years is a melancholy one. The following were the percentages of unemployed in the total civilian labor force: 1931, 15.9 per cent, 1932, 23.6 per cent, 1933, 24.9 per cent (high point), 1937, 14.3 per cent (low point), 1938, 19.0 per cent, and 1939, 17.2 per cent.

The fall in unemployment was due to shifts in occupation from agriculture and manufacturing to construction, trade, and the service industries—all evidence of an advancing, upward-moving economy. (The changeover from primary and secondary production to tertiary production is a characteristic of such progress.) Table 39 shows the distribution of the gainfully employed by occupations for 1919 and 1929. The low proportion in government will be noted.

WHAT CAUSED THE ONSET OF THE
GREAT DEPRESSION?

This is an easier question to ask than answer. Were there fundamental structural weaknesses in the American economy (really inadequacy of "effective demand" and the drying up of investment opportunities)? Had the American economy become "mature" so that secular stagnation was inevitable without a large push from public investment to create employment opportunities? Did the trouble lie in the failure of economic wisdom on the part of the purveyors of credit and in the areas of fiscal and monetary policy by its managers? Did the recession, starting in 1929, build up to the Great Depression (lasting in the United States right up to 1939) in part because of exogenous factors and in part because of the adoption of wrong policies by the New Deal?

Undoubtedly there were weaknesses or soft spots in the American economy. Agriculture—the growers of staples—was in a bad way. So was the textile industry. So were elements in the labor force. The return of high protectionism in the Emergency Tariff Act of 1921 and the Tariff Act of 1922 curbed imports and, as exports continued to increase, forced Americans to expand capital movements abroad (in effect to subsidize exports). Many of the portfolio loans turned out to be bad investments.

American agriculture had enjoyed boom times from 1897 through the end of World War I, and then distress hit segments of the agricultural population. To meet wartime needs American farmers had expanded acreage and brought large additions of arable land under the plow; new land and new machinery had been bought at inflated wartime prices and taxes on agricultural property had also mounted. A good part of the increase in agricultural products had gone abroad. With the war ended, these outlets had sharply contracted, for other countries had also increased acreage and their products in the world market competed with the American, thus forcing prices down. In addition, European countries, confronted by war debts and unfavorable balances of payments, cut imports, placed duties on American farm imports, and subsidized their own farmers. These figures show that the movement of the farm surplus overseas was part of the problem. In 1919–1920 the value of American agricultural exports was as high as $3.8 billion. Then it declined to $1.9 billion in 1921–1922 and went even lower in the subsequent years (except 1924–1925). Not only value but quantity of exports fell. Taking 1909–1913 as the base and including 44 principal farm commodities, the index number for exports had been 134 in 1919–1920 and then dropped to 117 for 1928–1929.

Another factor was the inelasticity of demand for farm products at home: the slowing down of immigration reduced a population whose food consumption had been high, and prohibition (adopted in 1920) cut the use of grains for fermented and distilled beverages. The average caloric intake of Americans decreased, due to dieting among women, less physical labor on the part of American workers (with the shifting from primary and secondary production to tertiary), and the heating of homes, offices, and automobiles (so that not so much food was required for bodily warmth and comfort). The spreading of the use of synthetic fibers reduced the consumption of cotton. A National Bureau of Economic Research study * came up with these figures. In the years 1910–1914 the daily per capita food consumption was 5.18 pounds in good years and 5.04 pounds in bad. This amount fell to 4.87 pounds in 1919 and in 1920, did not rise again to 5 pounds until 1926, and never went beyond for the rest of the decade.

Some key index figures will point up farmer inequalities. In an effort to measure agricultural well-being, or purchasing power, a ratio

* Harold Barger and H. H. Landsberg, *American Agriculture, 1899–1939*, 1942.

was set up of prices paid by farmers to prices received. It had been assumed that during 1910–1914 this ratio stood at 100. The farmer was then at an equal level with the nonagricultural community, but in 1921 the ratio fell to 75, and although it climbed up slowly during the 1920s (to 81 in 1922, to 88 in 1923, and finally to 93 in June 1928) it never reached prewar parity. At the same time mortgage debt payments and taxes were taking a larger share of the farmer dollar: in 1910 these payments had made up 6 per cent of the farmer's fixed charges, but increased to 12 per cent by 1930. The farmer had expanded his holdings during the war years, and he had bought at peak prices (or had seen his values go up as a result of the improvements he had put into his property). Thus, with 1912–1914 as 100, the index for the value of agricultural lands had risen to 170 in 1920 and then dropped to 122 in 1925 and 116 in 1929.

The Bureau of Economic Research * demonstrated a decline in the capital value of farm property by taking another measure—that of net savings by farm operators. Such savings had stood at $2.3 billion in 1919, but then there had been dissavings (or capital losses) for every year in the 1920s except 1925 and 1929 (e.g., dissavings had been as high as $1.4 billion in 1921 and even in 1926 stood at $115 million). Also, the share of agriculture in the national income had declined from 16 per cent in 1919 to 8.8 per cent in 1929.

It is true that in the 1920s increases in yields per acre had occurred and productivity per farm worker had jumped. This was a second period of agricultural advances, which resulted from further mechanization (the introduction of the all-purpose tractor and the small combine harvester), the growing use of fertilizers and of hybrid seed for corn and wheat, and improved feeding of dairy stock and hogs. Measured in terms of the output per farm worker (with 1924–1929 as 100), the index rose from 84 for 1917–1921 to 105 for 1927–1931. Larger farmers, therefore, were able to manage, despite declining prices, because of greater production per acre or unit of livestock; but there were too many marginal farmers on lands of low yield and too many tenants who could not afford the outlays (fertilizer, hybrid seed, and mechanical devises) for stepping up productivity. Tenancy increased from 38.1 per cent of farm operators in 1920 to 42.4 per cent in 1930. In the entire South the ratio in the latter year was in excess of 50 per cent. Low man on the totem pole was the cropper in the cotton South; in 1930 there were as many as 725,000, of whom one-half were black. These were the submarginal farmers for whom even bare subsistence was difficult to achieve.

* Simon Kuznets, *National Income and Its Composition, 1919–1938*, 1941.

A word about labor. The 1920s saw no advances either in organizing workers under independent unions or in the changeover from craft to industrial unionism. The first was due to a variety of factors, the second to the refusal or inability of the AFL craft unions to organize the mass production industries on industrial lines. As to the first, there were not many more than four million workers in independent unions by the end of the 1920s, and, during the same decade, company unions grew—encouraged by management, having no connection with the whole body of organized labor—until their membership totaled in the neighborhood of 1.5 million. Vigorous open-shop drives also were launched and were successful, along with which went the adoption by large companies of welfare schemes of one kind or another to wean workers away from trade unionism—stock purchase programs, company health and recreational devices, and some profit sharing. Finally, we are to note the conservative line pursued by the federal courts in narrowing the rights to organize and to carry on strike activities. Thus yellow-dog contracts were declared legal; secondary boycotts were outlawed; unions could be sued under the antitrust laws; injunctions were handed down forbidding practices by strikers, such as paying strike benefits, engaging in sympathetic strikes, and mass picketing, which had been accepted before. Thus the presumed promise of a charter of liberties for labor, written into Section 20 of the Clayton Act, was broken.

The point is this. It was observed earlier that industrial unionism, in which whole industries are organized and engage in collective bargaining—as is the case today—leads to a narrowing of the wage differentials between skilled and unskilled workers. Wage contracts provide for across-the-board wage increases; the result is that proportionately unskilled wages go up higher than the wages for the skilled. There was little industrial unionism in the 1920s and next to no industry-wide agreements, so that, although wages did rise with productivity gains, they did not do so (we may presume, for this had been the experience of 1896–1914) comparably for unskilled workers. In short, there was a large segment of workers whose "effective demand" for the new consumer durables and services was undoubtedly inadequate. Here was an element of civilian labor, as in agriculture, that could respond only sluggishly, if at all, to the forces making for "economic progress" and to strengthen them.

Tariff tinkering upward and its undesirable effects on the balance of payments created another soft area in the economics of the 1920s. In part as a result of the pressure of agricultural interests but as much due to that of the new industries—chemicals, aluminum—the Republicans wrote two tariff laws in the 1920s. The Emergency Tariff Act of 1921, reinforced by the Tariff Act of 1922, did a number of things: it imposed high duties on wheat, corn, meat, wool, and sugar (which led to retaliatory duties on American farm exports by European countries, as we have seen); it put agricultural implements and fertilizers on the free list; and it pushed up the rates on the imports of many manufactured goods, so that the high levels of the 1909 tariff were restored. The results were an increase in exports and a falling off of imports as the export gap widened.

The United States had become a creditor nation during World War I. We had lent heavily to the Allied and Associate Powers, but we had also made private loans. On private account alone foreigners began to owe us interest. Curbing imports therefore was the wrong policy to pursue. In consequence American investments abroad (portfolio loans as well as direct investments) really played the dual role of subsidizing our exports and maintaining in power foreign governments (particularly in Latin America) whose ability to achieve stability in their own countries and to attract the loyalty of their own people was highly dubious.

A glance at the balance of payments will provide confirmation. For the years 1921–1929, inclusive, the total American export gap was $7.7 billion. The foreign net offset of invisible items (freights, insurance, tourist expenditures, immigrant remittances, interest) was slight (only $115 million) because net interest paid to the United States was almost $5 billion.

The consequences were two: American net long-term capital movements for 1921–1929 totaled $5.6 billion, and foreign countries were compelled to send gold—which they could ill afford—notably in 1925, 1927, and 1928. During the whole decade the United States financed gold exports, particularly to European countries (Germany and Great Britain) by government loans and private short-term credits, these to build up the gold reserves of central banks and to make possible the adoption of the gold standard or the gold-exchange standard. When the flow was reversed after the middle of 1928, it meant what the whole world was beginning to sense: that the economic well-being of the West hung on American decisions and that these threatened to contract seriously and perilously the world supply of American dollars. These decisions were to continue the limitations on foreign imports and (starting with 1928) to decrease American long-term capital movements (not so much direct investments as portfolio loans). Two reasons were given for the latter: disenchantment with foreign dollar loans and the greater returns, presumably, that could be obtained on funds put out at home. Again, starting with 1928, a good part of such funds began to finance the stock market in the form of brokers' loans.

During the 1920s almost every country in the western world came to New York to seek financial aid—a few for the proper purposes of expanding industrial programs, most to embark governments, nations, states, and municipalities, on public enterprises of one kind or another, many of little validity. Between 1925 and 1929 about $5 billion in foreign loans were raised in the United States for Great Britain, France, Switzerland, the Netherlands, and Canada, which were sound; and for Germany, Italy, Poland, Japan, and many Latin American countries, which were not (for there was no conceivable way by which repayments could be made other than in imports). The fault in underwriting such highly risky ventures lay in the American investment houses, in their inexperience and their cupidity, for they were more interested in promoters' profits (and therefore sometimes pressed loans on foreign countries) than in protecting the American purchasers of these dollars bonds.

The changeover from a debtor to a creditor nation in the period 1914–1929 is shown in a breakdown of private investments by foreigners in the United States and by Americans abroad (see Table 40). The importance of portfolio investments at this time will be noted.

TABLE 40

PRIVATE BALANCE SHEET, FOREIGN INVESTMENTS,
(MILLIONS OF DOLLARS) 1914 AND 1929

	1914 July 1	1929 July 1
Foreign investments in the United States		
Portfolio	$5,440	$ 4,304
Direct	1,310	1,400
Sequestered properties	—	150
Short-term	450	3,077
Total	$7,200	$ 8,931
American investments abroad		
Portfolio	862	7,839
Direct	2,652	7,553
Short-term	—	1,617
Total	$3,514	$17,009
Net	−$3,686	+$ 8,078

Source. Cleona Lewis, *America's Stake in International Investment,* 1938.

Thus the stock market boom, which began in 1928. (It need not have occurred, had there been sounder monetary and fiscal policies at work, but then perhaps greater economic intelligence was required than Americans had at that time. Of this more below.)

One simple measure indicates that brokers' loans were feeding the speculative boom (made to security houses to cover the purchase of stock on margin and therefore sometimes referred to as call loans). These loans rose from $1 billion in the early 1920s to $3.5 billion at the end of 1927 and reached $8 billion at the end of 1929. They were made because funds were available from companies with cash assets which were no longer expanding their own capital investments, from commercial banks which were not expanding their business loans, from the surplus incomes of the well-to-do, and from foreign short-term money which was pouring into the United States—and because the interest rates were high. Interest paid on loans to brokers rose from 5 per cent at the beginning to 12 per cent at the end of 1928 and reached 20 per cent in May 1929.

Another factor that attracted idle money but also the unwary and the avaricious was the flotation of new securities by investment bankers and the security affiliates of great commercial banks, all presumably with impeccable reputations. The wave of mergers that took place in the 1920s already has been commented on: these created new securities. Another source was the appearance of the investment trust in large numbers, beginning with 1928 and accelerating in 1929. Investment trusts were started by investment banking houses and commercial banks—which seemed sound enough—but also by brokerage houses, security dealers, and other investment trusts. Investors bought the securities of the trusts. With this capital, their managers acquired the securities of existing companies, and thus investors thought they were diversifying their risks. All was based on confidence, but the managers betrayed it by making unwarranted claims and sometimes not using all of the funds put in their charge for stock and debenture purchases. They also entered the call market. At the beginning of 1927 there were about 160 such investment trusts in existence; by the end of that year, 300. Another 186 were organized in 1928 and 265 more in 1929. In 1929 alone these investment trusts sold $3 billion of their securities. It was estimated, before the crash, that they held assets in the securities of other companies worth $8 billion.

The consequence was an enormous expansion in the stock market business with a kiting of values—as a result of the speculative fever—that had no relation to the real worth of the assets of companies or their profitability. The market value of all shares listed on the New York Stock Exchange alone rose from $27 billion in 1925 to $67 billion in

January 1929 and to $87 billion in October. (By March 1933 it had fallen to $19 billion.)

MONETARY AND FISCAL POLICIES

It was in the 1920s that the Federal Reserve System really felt free to exercise control over monetary policy. The outcome, presumably, was monetary ease (and stable prices), and, perhaps of greater importance, economic stability. The boom—growth, increases in real income and production and high employment—taking on full proportions in 1923, was to be guided or watched over benevolently by the Federal Reserve. One measure of this control (achieved by changes in the discount rate and purchases and sales of government securities in the open market) was the orderly rise in the money stock. From July 1921 (a cyclical trough) to August 1929 (a cyclical peak) the money stock increased 45 per cent, or at a rate of 4.6 per cent annually.*

This comment on the role of the Federal Reserve System during the 1920s is that of Friedman and Schwartz †:

> It had to face explicitly the need to develop criteria and standards of monetary policy to replace the automatic operation of the gold standard. One result was a conscious attempt, for perhaps the first time in monetary history, to use central-bank powers to promote internal economic stability as well as to preserve balance in international payments and to prevent and moderate strictly financial crises. . . . As the decade wore on the System took—and perhaps even more was given—credit for the generally stable conditions that prevailed, and high hopes were placed in the potency of monetary policy as then administered.

How well did the System succeed? There was steady growth in the economy during 1923 to 1928, interrupted by two mild recessions, from

---

* The supply of money was controlled by two devices, the discount rate and open-market operations. The discount rate was set by the Reserve Banks, and when they lowered the rate, bank loans of commercial banks could be expanded. Open-market operations were run by a committee of the Federal Reserve Board in fact (with really Benjamin Strong Governor of the New York Bank dominating the committee and its activities during 1922–28). When the committee bought government securities (largely, but also bankers' acceptances and bills of exchange), this increased both the deposits and the reserves of commercial banks, thus also making possible the augmentation of the money supply. The reverse—raising the discount rate, sale of government securities—had the opposite effect.

† Milton Friedman and Anna Jacobson Schwartz, *A Monetary History of the United States, 1867–1960*, 1963.

May 1923 to July 1924 and from October 1926 to November 1927, and in both instances the System took action to create monetary ease, lowering the discount rate and buying government securities. Probably, because action was late, little effect was had on the recessions, which were very slight anyway. The influence on Europe and particularly on Great Britain was something else again. Here, all commentators are agreed, it was Strong who was the *deus ex machina*. He was committed to the re-establishment of a worldwide gold standard, and with the Federal Reserve System's approval he played the leading role in its relations with other countries. Thus American credits had been extended to Poland, Czechoslovakia, Belgium, Italy, Rumania, and later Germany to speed economic revival but also to help these nations get back to the gold standard. It was Strong who pressed in 1924 for an easy money policy: in this case to assist Great Britain on its way to a return to gold; for, with easy money and low interest rates, gold would leave the United States, go to Britain, and make possible the building up of its gold reserves. So it turned out and Great Britain was once more on the gold standard in 1925, with unhappy results. British prices rose, because of the overvaluation of the pound, exports fell but imports increased. There was a series of exchange crises, accompanied by disaffection on the part of workers, industrial turmoil, and the General Strike of 1926.

Meanwhile, in the spring of 1927 industrial production was slackening in the United States and another mild recession had set in. In May 1927 and continuing into the second half of the year—once again too late and unnecessary, for the business cycle was turning up—the authorities of the Federal Reserve System moved to ease prices, lowering the discount rate from 4 per cent to 3.5 per cent, with Reserve Banks also buying government securities totaling $435 million. The New York Bank, guided by Strong, took the lead a second time, and now the pressure from Europe—to help bail out Great Britain—was overt, for Strong was visited by the governors of the central banks of Great Britain, Germany, and France and was urged to do so.

Monetary ease in the United States had untoward consequences. The expansion of the money supply did not go into commercial loans but was used by banks to purchase securities and finance the stock market. Here were the beginnings of the runaway stock market boom which, in another year, was beyond control. Retrospectively, two reputable economists put their finger on the System's open-market operations of 1927 as an important cause of America's—and the world's—troubles.

Said A. C. Miller, in 1927 a member of the Federal Reserve Board and the only economist on it, in testifying before a Senate committee in the early 1930s:

It [the open-market operations] was the greatest and boldest operation ever undertaken by the Federal Reserve System, and, in my judgment, resulted in one of the most costly errors committed by it or any other system in the last 75 years!

Robbins,* the distinguished English economist, quoted Miller and then added the following:

> The reflation succeeded. . . . By 1928 the authorities were thoroughly frightened. But now the forces they had released were too strong for them. . . . Thus, in the last analysis, it was deliberate cooperation between Central Bankers, deliberate "reflation" on the part of the Federal Reserve authorities, which produced the worst phase of this stupendous fluctuation [in the stock market]. . . . It was not old-fashioned practice but new-fashioned theory which was responsible for the excesses of the American disaster.

The Federal Reserve authorities, in 1928 and 1929, from then on were unhappily steering between Scylla and Charybdis: easier money policy would only feed further the speculative boom; a tighter one— and business was beginning to slow down in midsummer 1929—would make a recession more severe. What they did is summed up in this fashion by Friedman and Schwartz (undoubtedly ironically):

> The conflict was resolved in 1928 and 1929 by adoption of a monetary policy, not restrictive enough to halt the bull market yet too restrictive to foster vigorous business expansion. . . . A stalemate persisted throughout most of the crucial year 1929, which . . . prevented decisive action one way or another in that year.

In the late summer the System raised discount rates to high levels; it couldn't stop the stock market, but, as far as business was concerned, says one commentator, its action came "probably at just the right time to do maximum damage." For the curve of industrial production started to decline in July 1929 and inventories began to mount. What may have been "the familiar inventory recession" (in Galbraith's words) really was the start of the Great Depression.

Federal fiscal policy served as no regulator of money and credit; the Treasury did not use its powers to tax and spend either to slow down the economy (and to put a damper on stock speculation) or, in reverse, to stimulate production and employment when the economy required assistance. Under Secretary of the Treasury Andrew W. Mellon (who served in the three administrations of Presidents Harding, Coolidge, and Hoover) the Treasury was committed to a single course: to ease money by not only balancing the budget but also by reducing taxes and there-

---

* Lionel Robbins, *The Great Depression*, 1934.

fore the commitments of the government. Thus it lowered income taxes and death duties, refunded the wartime short-term indebtednesses (thus cutting interest payments), reduced the national debt—and ended with surpluses in the Treasury almost every year. It rejected the notion that the government had a responsibility, for example, to come to the aid of the farmers and help them, by subsidy, to carry their agricultural surpluses. The complacency of the Treasury, its occasional mollifying remarks about the stock market, and its failure to participate in the work of the Federal Reserve Board (the Secretary was a member *ex officio*) deprived the economy of a tool that might have been used to check the excesses of the bull market and to provide a truly stabilizing influence.

Congress, following the recommendation of the Treasury, in a special session called for that purpose in April 1921 started out by repealing the wartime excess profits tax and reducing the graduated surtax on personal incomes. The Revenue Acts of 1924, 1926, and 1928 swept away the war excises and cut sharply the rates of the personal income tax, the corporation tax, and estate duties. The 1924 and 1926 laws lowered the normal tax on personal incomes and reduced the surtax (on high incomes) from a maximum rate of 65 per cent (in 1921) to 20 per cent. Exemptions for lower income payers were also raised. The 1926 law wiped out a gift tax, lowered the estate duty, and allowed a rebate of 80 per cent (to cover state death tax payments); thus, as far as the federal government was concerned, the whole area of death duties was turned over to the states. Finally in 1928 (in face of the growing use of company profits in the stock market) the corporation income rate was reduced to 12 per cent.

Despite all this surpluses continued in the Treasury; this was due to reductions in military expenditures and interest payments. Even when surpluses were used to reduce the national debt, the Treasury ended with a favorable balance of receipts over expenditures. One of its first tasks was the refunding—at lower interest rates—of the wartime Victory notes and certificates; the next was to retire in part and refund in part the wartime Liberty Loans with high coupons. At a large saving of interest the Treasury converted a good part of its long-term debt into intermediate and short-term issues. These were the results. From June 1920 to June 1929 the national debt was cut from $24.1 billion to $16.7 billion. Although interest payments had been $997 million in fiscal 1921, they were $680 million in fiscal 1929, and for the same nine years the expenditures for the Army and the Navy went down from $1.2 billion to $771 million. (Veterans were not forgotten—payments to them rose from $516 million to $743 million in the same interval.) Here were the surpluses in a number of selected fiscal years, in millions:

	Expenditures	Receipts
1921	$4,467	$5,625
1923	3,245	4,007
1925	2,464	3,780
1927	2,974	4,129
1929	3,302	4,033

Other governments however—states, counties, and municipalities—were expanding expenditures, notably their capital outlays, and here was an important reason for the great role of the construction industry in the 1920s. They built roads and more roads, but also schools and other public buildings, raised the funds by bond issues, and developed new sources of taxation—the motor vehicle registration fee and the gasoline tax—to carry this indebtedness. The upshot was that in 1922 capital and current expenditures for the states, counties, and municipalities came to $5.5 billion in 1922 and $8.9 billion in 1929. This expanding area of public outlays mitigated somewhat the parsimony of the federal government; alas, during the depression sharp reductions here took place—in fact, many municipalities had to be rescued from bankruptcy.

WHY THE DEPRESSION?

Galbraith * disclaims any intention to offer explanations for the persistence of the Great Depression which, in the United States, lasted into 1939. He is ready to admit that the economy of the United States was not "subject to such physical pressure or strain as a result of its past level of performance that a depression was bound to occur." He then goes on to say:

> The high production of the twenties did not, as some have suggested, outrun the wants of the people. During these years people were indeed being supplied with an increasing volume of goods. But there is no evidence that their desire for automobiles, clothing, travel, recreation, or even food was sated.

The fatal weakness was "ineffective demand" (although he does not use the phrase "saturation of investment opportunity" of the oversimplified American version of the Keynesian analysis). There was "a capacity for a large further increase in consumption" and he offers some

* John Kenneth Galbraith, *The Great Crash, 1929*, 1955.

conjectures why this was so: wages were not keeping up with productivity; the profits and income of the well-to-do were excessive; nevertheless, beginning with the summer of 1929, investment was insufficient. (From this last he retreats: "there is no final proof on this point, for unfortunately we do not know how rapidly investment had to grow to keep abreast of the current increase in profits.")

Then, despite all his reservations, Galbraith takes the plunge. Says he: "There seems little question that in 1929 . . . the economy was *fundamentally* unsound." [Italics added.] He singles out these five weaknesses which "seem to have had an especially intimate bearing on the ensuing disaster [i.e., the Great Depression]."

1. Unequal income distribution.
2. The bad corporate structure.
3. The bad banking structure.
4. The dubious state of the foreign balance.
5. The poor state of economic intelligence.

In varying degree the first four have persisted—through the great recovery of the forties, the prosperity (with mild recessions) of the fifties, and into the long period of boom times starting in 1961 and continuing (without recession) through 1969. It will be necessary to seek elsewhere to learn why the Great Depression cut so deeply and lasted so long in the United States.

XIV

THE GREAT DEPRESSION

On October 24, 1929, on "Black Thursday," the New York Stock Market went into a rout. From then on security values plummeted; business confidence—so important a factor in keeping the economic engine going even in time of adversity—was badly shaken and then entirely disappeared. National income, physical production, investment, worst of all, employment dropped sharply, and banks shut down; there was wholesale bankruptcy of companies, homeowners, farmers, and municipalities. A slight recovery seemed to appear in midsummer 1930—probably in response to the measures taken by President Hoover—but from the second half of 1930 into 1932 (in part occasioned by the Tariff Act of 1930, in part by the collapse of the international monetary mechanism in 1931), the depression worsened. The hardest hit country was the United States, and because the American economy sank so low the climb back was longest. It was not until 1940 (World War II had broken out) that the indicators of recovery—production, investment, employment—showed that the Great Depression was over.

In the three years 1930–1932 in the United States there were some 85,000 business failures and more than 5000 banks suspended; the market values of stocks on the New York Exchange fell from $87 billion (October 1929) to $19 billion (March 1933). Unemployment rose to perhaps as high as 12 million persons by 1932 (25 per cent of the civilian labor force). The national income fell from $87.8 billion to $75.7 billion between 1929 and 1930 and then to $42.5 billion in 1932. The decline in agricultural income was at least 50 per cent. The GNP (in 1929 dollars) dropped from $104.4 billion in 1929 to $76.4 billion in 1932, and per capita GNP declined from $857 to $611. The index of physical output in manufacturing, which had stood at 58 in 1929 (1947–1949 = 100) was down to 30 in 1932.

In the face of all this, the money stock of the country fell by more than one-third from cyclical peak in August 1929 to cyclical trough in March 1933. The Federal Reserve System, which had pursued an active role in the 1920s, in the early 1930s withdrew from monetary management: it became "passive, defensive, hesitant" (in the words of Friedman and Schwartz). Whatever the reasons—lack of strong leadership, inadequate economic intelligence, the pulling and hauling of regional forces —the System failed to loosen the credit strings, and the sharp descent toward collapse continued.

President Hoover during his administration launched three programs, the first to help agriculture, the second to restimulate investment (and therefore start production and employment going) and provide relief to the hard hit, and the third to erect safeguards for the domestic market against foreign competition. The first two were well-intentioned but the funds made available were hopelessly inadequate; the third was misguided and ended by making matters worse. An Agricultural Marketing Act, passed in 1929, authorized the establishment of a Farm Board which, with a revolving fund of $500 million, could make loans to farm cooperative associations. By this authority, a Grain Stabilization Corporation was set up which sought to protect wheat growers by making advances to them up to 90 per cent of the going sale price. This proved a failure because the Board could not absorb the whole surplus. A similar scheme to support cotton ended in the same frustration. At the end of a year the Board confessed its defeat; the real problem was, it said, "Adjustments of production to market requirements are indispensable, in agriculture as in industry, to the solution of surplus problems." Canute-fashion, Hoover was seeking to sweep back the onrushing tide with a broom.

Hoover's acceptance of high protectionism in an effort to adjust the American market to all other kinds of goods by sharply cutting back imports ended even in a worse disaster. The stimulus to revision of the tariff started in 1928 and came largely from agriculture: the hope was for succor by this device from the burden (and falling prices) of the farm surpluses. The House was in possession of the Hawley bill in May 1929, which contained higher duties on farm products and other raw materials but no subsidy to farmers to carry their surpluses. The latter was supplied by the Senate Smoot bill, which included the "export debenture" plan (the purchase of surplus staples by the government at domestic prices and their sale abroad at world prices); but President Hoover's objection defeated the proposal in the conference committee. It was the Hawley bill—with rates as high as those prevailing in the 1890s; the general average of *ad valorem* duties was 40.08 per cent, compared with the average of 33.22 in the 1922 Act—that Congress made law in the Hawley-Smoot Act in June 1930. The depression was biting deeper and deeper into both the domestic and world economy. Aroused American economists, one thousand strong, pleaded with President Hoover not to sign: protectionism was precisely the wrong medicine—it would constrict and not expand world trade, having unfortunate effects on the producers of primary products the world over and thus limit purchasing power to buy American exports. Besides, in retaliation, self-defense, or anger, other countries would push their duties up. President Hoover signed. The economists were right on all counts: economic nationalism—instead of attempts to shore up world commerce—followed, and before 1931 was over, some 25 countries had made extensive tariff revisions upward or were planning to do so, citing the action of the United States as justification. Here was an example of man-made policy, instead of "inexorable forces," compounding the confusion.

Now convinced that more heroic measures were necessary—not only for the rescue of banks, railroads, owners of homes and farm properties in distress but also to provide relief for the unemployed—Hoover got Congress to create the Reconstruction Finance Corporation in January 1932. Its original capital, wholly government subscribed, was $500 million with the right to borrow an additional $1.5 billion. It was to operate on the basis of loans. From this fund $125 million was to go to home loan banks and another $125 million to set up a farm loan system. An additional $2.1 billion was appropriated by Congress for relief and public works, $1.8 billion of which was to be used to augment the capital of the RFC. In the year in which the RFC functioned under Hoover it authorized $1.9 billion to be lent out, of which actual disbursements were $1.5 billion. Help was doled out in the following order: banks and trust companies (by far the largest beneficiaries), railroads, building and loan associations, mortgage loan-companies, relief and work relief (by loans to states and local governments for self-liquidating projects), insurance companies, and agricultural credit agencies. The area to cover was wide; the funds available could not be stretched to have any significant effect anywhere; the Hoover administration ended in frustration with thickening clouds across the whole sky. But it showed the way to the incoming

President in at least three particulars: that handling the agricultural problems required more than palliatives—crop control was necessary; that loans for business and property owners might help—assuming enormous funds were made available; and that programs of direct financial aid and work-relief for the unemployed were part and parcel of any devices to speedy recovery.

THE NEW DEAL'S EFFORTS AT RECOVERY AND RELIEF

The economy was in danger of coming to a grinding halt when President Franklin D. Roosevelt assumed office on March 4, 1932. Starting in February and continuing up to March 3, some 19 state governors had ordered banks closed and 11 others restricted withdrawal of funds. Stock and commodity exchanges too had shut down. Prices were continuing to fall, unemployment was increasing, and the well springs of credit appeared to have dried up. There was a crisis of confidence and it was to restore America's faith in itself that Roosevelt moved swiftly. Congress was summoned in special session on March 9 and it sat until June 16; in these "One Hundred Days" a veritable stream of messages to Congress, followed at once by legislation, indicated that if there was no general, over-all plan to guide the President and his "Brain Trust" (and there never was; many of the ideas coming from the White House were sheer improvisations), certainly there was action on almost every front of the economic scene. Relief and, hopefully, recovery were the watchwords for what Roosevelt had proclaimed was a New Deal for the American people, and programs forthwith were devised to cope with the problems of banking, agriculture, industry, labor, and unemployment.

An Emergency Banking Relief Act (March 9) permitted banks in the Federal Reserve System to reopen under licenses from the Treasury Department which also was to call in all the gold and gold certificates in the country; it enlarged the open-market operations of the Federal Reserve Banks and gave the RFC authority to subscribe to the preferred stock of national banks and trust companies. The RFC acted swiftly and sound banks were reopened; confidence in the country's banking was restored—one of the first great triumphs of the new administration. These ideas, and others, were further fleshed out in the Glass-Steagall Banking Act of June 16, 1933. It formalized the activities of the Federal Open Market Committee (now under the Board's control); guaranteed individual deposits up to $5000 by creating the Federal

Deposit Insurance Corporation (FDIC); permitted branch banking within a state; extended membership in the System to include savings and industrial banks; and forced commercial banks to divorce themselves from their investment affiliates. Under his emergency powers the President had taken the United States off the gold standard. Congress on June 5 gave its formal approval by passage of the Gold Repeal Joint Resolution. This canceled the gold clause in all federal and private obligations; contracts and debts thenceforth could be paid in legal tender.

The first Agricultural Adjustment Act was passed by Congress May 12 (and declared unconstitutional by the Supreme Court in 1936). Its purpose was to restore the farmer's purchasing power and the notion of "parity prices" was devised; that is, through government benefit payments and loans farm prices were to be pushed up until they approximated those existing during 1909–1914 when the prices received by farmers equaled those paid out. Thus, if farmers reduced acreage, accepting quotas, they were to be subsidized through these benefit payments; the funds for the subsidies were to be obtained from taxes imposed on the first processors of agricultural goods. Further, to check farm bankruptcies and mortgage foreclosures Federal Land Banks were authorized to refinance the standing indebtednesses of farmers. On June 16 a Federal Farm Credit Administration was established to handle not only mortgage refinancing but also short-term and medium-term loans to cooperatives and production credit corporations and associations to facilitate the marketing of agricultural commodities.

Subsequent AAAs (those of 1936 and 1938), under the notion that taking land out of cultivation and planting it in leguminous crops or letting it lie fallow was really "soil conservation," continued to subsidize farmers; and they did fairly well. The parity-price index began to rise a little and the income of farmers went up as agricultural prices rose higher than industrial prices. The general consequences were the following: "soil conservation" increased productivity, so that although acreage (in wheat, corn, cotton, and tobacco) fell by one-fifth during 1932–1939 there was an increase of some 10 per cent in agricultural output. The government therefore was compelled to lend against surpluses up to 75 per cent of parity prices. This pushed American prices above world prices, with no measurable increase in exports.

The National Recovery Industrial Act (NIRA) of June 16 was one of the most fanciful (and least successful) of the Washington brain children. The assumptions on which it was based were that industrial production was chaotic and prices were too low. To restore to normal this leading sector of the economy representatives of each industry were authorized to draw up codes of "fair competition" which, in effect, meant self-regulation (and in those in which oligopoly ruled, cartelization) and therefore the suspension of the antitrust laws. An agency was created (NRA) to which such codes were to be submitted and which, also, was to prepare a general code to cover other industries not in a position to devise their own. Under such a dispensation many codes fixed minimum prices and incorporated other pricing devices; not a few barred entry of new firms and erected barriers to existing company expansion by putting limits on fresh investment in plant and machinery; also, many provided for limitations on production and the fixing of maximum hours for the operation of machinery. All this was an invitation to monopolistic practices.

The NIRA had another intention—to raise wages and thus increase consumer purchasing power. The law had two sections that were relevant to this purpose: Section 7(a) which assured workers they had the right to form trade unions, name representatives of their own choosing, and engage in collective bargaining; and Section 7(b) which authorized the codes to fix minimum wages and maximum hours (and therefore over-time pay) and to abolish child labor.

These two broad purposes—the raising of prices and the raising of wages—were obviously at variance with each other. There was a basic confusion in the tactics (or theory) of the New Deal. Raising prices was a commendable notion; raising costs (by encouraging labor to organize for higher wage demands and by fixing minimum wages and maximum hours) threatened profitability. The heart of the recovery problem was really stimulation to investment; and without profitability no new ventures or risk taking seemed likely. And so it turned out. The slight spurt to business because of the codes was at a dead halt by the fall of 1933 and the boomlet was over. (In May 1935 the Supreme Court declared the NIRA unconstitutional.) From being prepared to waive the antitrust laws, the Roosevelt administration then turned to pursuing the opposite tack. Rigorous enforcement became the order of the day; the Justice Department's antitrust division was reinforced and suits were initiated against many large companies alleging violation of the Sherman Act and/or the Clayton Act. This attitude and the Administration's wage and fiscal policies (as we shall see) undoubtedly helped contribute to the slowness of recovery; for many businessmen became convinced that Roosevelt and his advisers and aids were changing the climate of opinion and making more difficult the functioning of capitalist enterprise, innovation, and risk taking (and therefore investment).

Provisions for the relief of the unemployed were many and varied. The first was the creation of the Civilian Conservation Corps (March 31) under which make-work programs (reforestation, road construction, and flood control) were to provide for some 250,000 jobless male youths who were to live in work camps. An act of May 12 created the Federal Emergency Relief Administration with a fund of $500 million for outright grants (not loans) to states and cities for distribution. Work-relief projects, again by state and local authorities, could be set up and financing authorized by the RFC. Title II of the NIRA established a Public Works Administration and voted a fund of $3.3 billion to be administered by the Secretary of the Interior. By "public works" was meant roads, bridges, and public buildings: thus not only employment would be furnished but also the construction industry and its suppliers would be stimulated. (This came to be known as "pump-priming," anticipating J. M. Keynes' "multiplier effect.") The difficulties were two: the Secretary of the Interior, Harold L. Ickes, insisted that such proposals for public works be self-liquidating and also that contracts and supervision be carefully processed to check fraud and collusion as much as possible. Authorizations proceeded slowly, in consequence.

In addition, in 1934 came the Works Progress Administration (WPA) which frankly was based on the make-work principle. The unemployed, young people, and creative artists were found some sort of work—laying pavements and digging ditches for water mains, cleaning empty lots and setting up playgrounds; establishing theaters for out-of-work actors and playwrights without producers; letting artists paint, writers write, scholars research, and students remain in school. Up to 1943 some 8.5 million people were found some sort of busy work, for which, as a rule, they received about $22.50 a week and which permitted them to maintain a modicum of self-respect. The influence on recovery—although something like $13.5 billion was spent by the WPA—was little if anything.

The establishment of the Tennessee Valley Authority (May 18), on the other hand, was an imaginative and fruitful idea. The installations (dams and nitrate plants) erected at Muscle Shoals in the Tennessee River in Alabama during World War I were its basis. Attempts had been made to have the power plant run by the government, only to have such bills vetoed by Presidents Coolidge and Hoover. President Roosevelt (perhaps inspired by Senator George W. Norris, who had vainly pushed government operation) saw the opportunity to rehabilitate the population and economic life of a whole region which had long been depressed because of soil erosion, heavy floods, the decline of the coal industry, and the movement of cotton growing (with its effects on the share croppers and marginal farmers) out of the Southeast. The power development of the Tennessee Valley (covering in whole or in part the states of Tennessee, North Carolina, Kentucky, Virginia, Mississippi, Georgia and Alabama)—and the control and utilization of its water resources (by the

building of dams, hydroelectric works, and nitrogen fertilizer factories
and by the distribution of cheap power to municipalities and farmer
cooperatives)—meant new industries, home electrification, improved
farmland, flood control, and public parks and recreational facilities. It
was a magnificent conception and it was fully carried out over the years
1933–1944 (one of the by-products was the erection of the country's first
atomic energy plant at Oak Ridge, Tennessee). Also among the relief
measures were the Home Owners Refinancing Act (June 13) and the
Farm Credit Act (June 16).

THE REFORMS OF THE NEW DEAL

Recovery faltered despite all these measures of the "One Hundred Days"
and others that were added in subsequent years. One of the interesting
oddities of New Deal thinking and behavior was the preoccupation with
money. More money in itself would ease prices (and, hopefully, make
credit more plentiful); cheaper money would help the farmers, for—
so it was believed—lowering the gold content of the dollar would automatically cause the rise of commodity prices and thus relax the pressure
on agriculture. The first Agricultural Adjustment Act proposed many
things about money. The President was authorized (but not ordered):

1. To require Federal Reserve Banks to buy on the open market
U.S. governments up to the value of $3 billion.
2. To issue an additional $3 billion in U.S. notes as legal tenders.
3. To reduce the gold content of the dollar by as much as 50 per
cent, set up a bimetallic system, and make possible the unlimited coinage
of gold and silver at ratios fixed by him.
4. To accept silver from foreign governments in payment of inter-
governmental (wartime) loans.

The adventure in gold throws further light on the thinking of President Roosevelt. In April 1933 the United States officially abandoned the
gold standard (as had a number of European countries, Britain among
them, as early as 1931). The whole international economic fabric was
weakening, and to prevent further deterioration a World Economic
Conference had been organized—to meet in London in June 1933—to
which President Hoover had accepted an invitation for the United
States. The hope was, with the concurrence of the United States—it was
to lead the way in stabilizing the dollar instead of permitting it to fluctuate erratically—that there would be "the eventual restoration of a

revised international standard." Secretary of State Hull left for London as head of the American delegation and assumed that an agenda had been prepared in which the President had concurred; the target was the restoration of an international economic community—based on the orderly movement of goods and capital and linked with stabilized currencies. Somewhere along the way, however, the President had changed his mind.

Roosevelt sent Assistant Secretary of State Raymond Moley to London with new instructions: the American representatives were by no means to accept stabilization of the dollar or the renewal of gold shipments. The United States would not even join in a declaration that it favored a return to the gold standard some time in the future. Said the President, justifying the path he had decided on—a nationalist policy of go-it-alone instead of world agreement: [The United States] was seeking "the kind of a dollar which, a generation hence, will have the same purchasing and debt-paying power as the dollar value we hope to attain in the near future." This broke up the Conference and it adjourned *sine die*.

The consequences were portentous. To quote Lewis * the best and most understanding discussion of the Great Depression we have the following:

> The failure of the World Economic Conference marks, in a minor sense, the end of an era. It was the last economic conference before the war; the last major effort to cope with economic problems internationally. From 1933, countries abandon hopes of international revival and concentrate on stimulating domestic demand, if necessary at the expense of still greater restrictions on international trade. From 1933 the divergent domestic policies of the nations become more important than the international economy, to the extent even that the world market disintegrates into many different markets with different price levels and restricted interchange. . . . Neither is the change confined to economic affairs. By 1933 the political situation had already begun to deteriorate. In 1931 Japan invaded Manchuria; in 1933 Hitler came to power; in 1935 Italy attacked Abyssinia. Already in 1933 the world was clearly moving towards war, and discussion of economic cooperation gave way to increased political tension.

American prices were not responding; in fact, in July 1933 farm prices declined precipitately. In October, under the broad powers given him in the AAA, the President authorized the RFC to buy and sell gold

---

* W. Arthur Lewis, *Economic Survey, 1919–1939*, 1949. I have had the benefit of Professor Lewis's insights and have used many of them here, as I also have used those of J. A. Schumpeter's *Business Cycles*, 2 vols., 1939. Lewis acknowledges his debt to Schumpeter, too, although at one point he disagrees, but I do not. More of this later.

on the world market so that the United States could take "in its own hands the control of the gold value of her own dollar." Devaluation was finally announced: the price of gold was set at $31.36 an ounce, and later changed to $34.06 an ounce. This meant a gold dollar of 66 cents. By proclamation on January 31, 1934—having received further authority in the Gold Reserve Act—Roosevelt fixed the value of the dollar at 59.06 cents (to make the price of gold $35 an ounce) and set up an Exchange Stabilization Fund of $2 billion with which to prevent the dollar's fluctuation.

The President's assumption—and so the advisers to whom he listened told him—that devaluation would raise prices automatically was an illusory one. One of the most respected economists of the time (but not a New Dealer) Professor O.M.W. Sprague, pointed out the following— and he was a prophet without honor in his country:

> Mere depreciation of the currency in relation to the currencies of other countries will not bring about a general rise in prices . . . at a time when there is large excess plant capacity and millions of unemployed wage earners. An advance in prices that has any promise of being maintained requires the development of conditions that will permit a sustained demand for more labor and more materials, with resultant increase in the production of goods and services and a higher standard of living.

Along with this went the purchase of silver at home and abroad. The Treasury fixed a price of $1.29 an ounce (the domestic market price was 50 cents) and before long acquired 62 million ounces of silver against which it issued $80 million of legal-tender certificates. More were emitted later, the only consequences being a subsidy to the silver producers of the United States and great harm to the countries on a full silver standard (which they were compelled to abandon). The effect on prices was nil; indeed the target the administration had set itself—a price level comparable to that of 1926—was not reached until 1943, when the United States was at war.

Secretary of State Hull, although he found much of the economic nationalism of the President and his advisers distasteful, continued in the administration in the hope that he could do something to repair the harm that had come from the collapse of the World Economic Conference. He urged and saw the creation of a useful institution, the Export-Import Bank (February 1934) which was empowered to finance foreign trade. He achieved a signal triumph, and a radical change in American policy, with the passage of the Trade Agreements Act of June 1934. Tariff making was put in the hands of the President; he was authorized, through the State Department, to enter into reciprocal trade agreements with foreign nations; he could reduce specific duties by as much as 50 per cent in such bargaining—as long as the most favored nation principle was observed, all without the need for seeking congressional approval. The thought was that as more nations drew up such understandings with the United States the reductions in tariff rates would extend out in widening circles. All together, 26 such reciprocal treaties were signed before the United States entered the war. The effect on foreign trade? The total exports of American merchandize and general imports was $9.5 billion in 1929; these had dropped to $2.9 billion in 1932, recovered to $6.3 billion in 1937, and fallen back to $5.0 billion in 1938. It was not until 1942, with the United States fully involved in war, that the total trade reached $10.7 billion.

Reform programs followed thick and fast during 1934 and 1935, and with the end of the latter year the New Deal's efforts were largely finished. Most of these measures remain on our statute books and have been woven deeply, for better rather than for worse, into the fabric of the American economic life. They did something else: habituating Americans to large-scale public intervention and taking them on the road to what has come to be known as the "welfare state." A few of the outstanding reforms are mentioned (for they are all familiar today) and the more important ones are discussed briefly. This time chronological order is dispensed with.

The Banking Act of 1935 was a thoroughgoing revision of the Federal Reserve System, which improved and strengthened it in many ways. The central authority (now to be known as the Board of Governors) was given clearly defined powers over open-market operations, rediscount rates, and reserve requirements, in this way downgrading the roles of the Reserve Banks. The Board itself could order as much as a doubling of reserves; it received majority control over the Open Market System, and the Reserve Banks were required to buy or sell securities when the Open Market Committee embarked on such operations. To strengthen further the independence of the Board the Secretary of the Treasury and the Comptroller of the Currency were dropped as *ex officio* members and terms of members were lengthened to fourteen years. Also, in 1935 national bank notes were discontinued and thenceforth banks no longer had the power to issue private currency. Further, Reserve Banks, as lenders of last resort for the banking system, were given greater leeway in advancing funds to individual members when hard pressed. A uniform currency and a more flexible one were important results of this overhauling of the Federal Reserve System.

The Federal Securities Act (May 1933), which required that companies issuing new securities furnish full information, was given real teeth with the creation of the Securities and Exchange Commission (June

1934). The new commission, in addition to regulating stock exchanges, had the power to scrutinize the organization, financial structure, and character of business of public companies. This law gave another important function to the Board of Governors of the Federal Reserve System—it could fix the margin requirements for trading in securities.

When the Public Utility Holding Company Act of 1935 was written—in effect, imposing a death sentence on them—it was the SEC that was told to simplify holding-company structures and compel them to reduce their operations to single systems economically and geographically integrated. It should be noted that this hostility to mergers on the part of the administration was another reason for the mounting suspicion and hostility on the part of business. The electric-power industry fought back—taking every measure of the SEC into the courts, and it was not until 1946 that the Supreme Court validated the death sentence clause. By that time more amicable arrangements gave the electric-power companies wider scope for expansion and investment than the New Dealers had contemplated.

If the immediate economic effects of support for trade-union organization and other devices to help labor (to push up wages and improve the purchasing power of workers) backfired, the social consequences were immense. There is no doubt that clearing the air—as far as the rights to carry on labor disputes peaceably, to organize in unions of their own choosing and the beginnings of a social security program—gave the workers of America a sense of personal dignity and pride in their own associations. There was too a feeling that now, for the first time, workers were being protected against the hazards of unemployment, industrial accident, old age, and care for their survivors in the event of untimely death before retirement. Put together, the Norris-LaGuardia Act of 1932 (enacted during the Hoover administration), the National Labor Relations Act of 1935, the Social Security Act of 1935, and the Fair Labor Standards Act of 1938 constituted a code that made up perhaps—at least as far as human relations were concerned—the most important achievement coming out of the New Deal's many strivings.

The Norris-LaGuardia Act widened the allowable area of industrial conflict which had been shrunk by the Supreme Court in the 1920s in the face of the assumed promise of a "Charter of Liberties" written into the Clayton Act of 1914. The Norris-LaGuardia Act limited the power of federal courts to issue injunctions in labor disputes to areas only in which it could be proved that the complainant, the employer, was likely to be more injured than the union.

The National Labor Relations Act of 1935 wrote into law what Section 7(a) of the NIRA sketchily had tried to achieve—that workers could "organize and bargain collectively through representatives of their own choosing" without coercion by employers or their agents and that they were to be protected from employer "unfair labor practices." (Later it was found that there were also trade union "unfair labor" practices and these were spelled out in the Taft-Hartley Act of 1947.) To ensure both of these intentions the Wagner Act established the National Labor Relations Board. This was to investigate employee complaints of "unfair practices" (including discrimination for trade-union activity), hold hearings, conduct collective-bargaining elections, determine the appropriate bargaining units (craft, single plant, industry-wide), and certify the organization chosen as representative. As a result, free unions increased their membership from four million in 1929 to 11 million in 1939 and— thanks also to the imaginative organizational activity of the Committee for Industrial Organization of the AFL—were able to break the barriers that had prevented them from getting a foothold in the great mass-production industries of steel, automobiles, rubber, chemicals, and electrical equipment.

The Fair Labor Standards Act of 1938—well-intentioned but of dubious merit (dubious because minimum wages narrow opportunities for work of the young and the unskilled)—also sought to carry out one of the intentions of the outlawed NIRA. It set a minimum wage of 25 cents an hour and fixed 40 hours as the length of the working week (with overtime pay for hours worked in excess). Also, the Department of Labor was given the authority to designate industries in which the labor of children was likely to be hazardous or injurious to their health—thus, in effect, forbidding the work of children under 16 years of age.

The Social Security Act aimed at many things. First, it set up a program of unemployment insurance maintained entirely by a tax on employer payrolls, which was to be administered by the states but supervised by the federal government. Second, it provided the establishment of old-age annuities to workers reaching 65 years and for benefit payments to their survivors either in the event of early death or the survival of a spouse. Such payments were to be paid from funds accumulated as a result of an annual tax equally divided between employed and employer. Third, federal grants-in-aid for welfare programs were made to the states to assist them in the care of the needy aged, blind persons, and neglected, dependent, or crippled children.

Along with such assistance was a series of laws having to do with housing: not only the rescue of homeowners from mortgage debt by re-financing mortgages at lower rates of interest and longer amortization periods but also efforts to stimulate new residential construction. The National Housing Act of 1934 created the Federal Housing Administration; this, in turn, had the right to guarantee FHA first-mortgages by, in effect, insuring them. Such mortgages had a long amortization period (25 years) and carried low interest rates (5 per cent). By 1949 the FHA had insured $11.5 billion in mortgages. Going even further were the efforts to encourage the construction of new multiple-dwelling houses in urban or suburban communities and to provide such individual family units at low rentals. These were the intentions of the National Housing Act of 1937 through the U.S. Housing Authority it set up. Loans and grants were to be made to local communities which would build and maintain dwellings for low-income people (demolishing or repairing one substandard building for each new one erected with USHA aid). Federal loans to cover 90 per cent of the cost of public-housing projects—the remainder furnished by local governments—were to run for 60 years at 3 per cent interest.

WHY THE GREAT DEPRESSION LASTED SO LONG

The Great Depression of the 1930s was like a huge tidal wave that swept over much of the free world. It is idle, and too simple, to say that had it not been for the instabilities existing in the American economy the countries of Europe and Japan, as well as those having a colonial or semi-colonial relationship to the West, would have escaped its rigors. We must not forget that Europe in much of the 1920s was still struggling with the problems of adjusting to peace after the long and debilitating 1914–1918 war. It was not only Germany that was paying a heavy price; the same was equally true of Britain, France, Japan, and those lands producing primary products—copper, tin, rubber, copra—whose economies were closely tied in with the markets and the capital centers of the West.

World War I had had wide-sweeping effects: its destruction of wealth and, perhaps even more important, the young manpower of nations, had been enormous. The international currency system—which heretofore had made possible the virtually automatic flow of goods and capital at staple prices—had been rudely shaken; efforts to recreate it in the 1920s seemed beyond the capacities, physically and mentally, of those peoples and nations that had been responsible for its devising. Distortions, as a result of wartime needs, had appeared in domestic economies, notably in the overexpansion of agricultural lands, and the same had happened in regard to the producers of other primary products in South America, Southeast Asia, Oceania, and Africa. Before the war the capital markets of London, Paris, Berlin, Vienna, and Amsterdam had been able to supply the credit needs of their own economies but of many others as well with which they had had long-established connections. Engineers, technicians, and company managers had gone out with the capital and skills to explore new natural resources, erect factories, and supervise methods of production and marketing. A whole generation of young men capable of doing these things and doing them more efficiently had been destroyed. Suddenly, the maintenance of this intricate web of relations and responsibilities had shifted to the United States, a country itself freshly emerged from a debtor status and with a managerial class (banking, industrial, and commercial) yet untrained to assume such interests and obligations.

Besides, up to the 1920s America had given virtually all its energies to the completion of its own industrial revolution, started as recently as 1865; it still looked inward rather than outward. Indeed, its few efforts at colonialism or imperialism—in the Caribbean and the Philippines (in fact, it can be argued plausibly that overseas ventures and adventures had been motivated by military rather than economic considerations)—had not given Americans a taste for such enterprises and further confirmed the feeling that American growth and development were linked with their concerns at home and their own enormous domestic market. Suddenly the United States was catapulted into a world role; its trade and capital movements were expanded—to serve its own needs, of course, but also to patch up, or rather cover over, the deep maladjustments that continued to exist in the lands of the free world.

The Great Depression took place and continued therefore for three reasons. First, these weaknesses everywhere now emerged and took over. Second, from 1929 to 1932 America itself fell into a very deep pit (its GNP dropped almost 40 per cent, net investment in capital goods became negative, and unemployment exceeded 12 million). Third, the policies of the New Deal, rather than speeding recovery, had the reverse effect of retarding it. Ironically, the rest of the industrial world of the West (except for Germany) began to climb up out of depression from 1932 on; in the United States it was not until 1940 that a return to normality began to show itself.

The analysis that follows—as I have said before—follows the speculations of J. A. Schumpeter and W. Arthur Lewis; what they have written seems to make real sense and I acknowledge my thanks to them.

Why was the downturn from the high prosperity of the 1920s in the United States so severe? For by 1932, when bottom was reached, a decline in investment—a continuing characteristic of the Great Depression in the United States—had become truly portentous. Net investment had turned negative in 1931, fell to minus $5.8 billion in 1932 (in 1929 prices), and did not become positive until 1936. Nothing showed this more clearly than the contrast in production between consumer and capital goods. Here are the index figures with 1929 = 100.

	1929	1930	1931	1932	1933	1934
Consumer goods	100	90	85	75	85	87
Capital goods	100	74	51	31	41	50

Along with this were the mounting bank suspensions—5096 in the three years 1930–1932—and the high level of indebtedness (among farmers, industrial companies, and consumers) whose burden was hard to carry as a result of the sharp fall in prices. There was nothing fundamentally wrong in the American economy to have caused such a disaster.

Business cycles in a free-market economy will turn down as investment opportunities temporarily spend themselves, as business confidence wanes and risk taking becomes more cautious, and as soft spots appear—in the United States in agriculture, coal, and textiles. With less investment employment opportunities shrink and production of consumer goods declines. When the banking system, at such a pass, does not take positive action—when it does not expand the money supply and thus make it easier and cheaper for investment capital to be created—the cyclical instability will continue until it exhausts itself in company bankruptcies, unemployment, reductions in wages, and the like. Granted that this particular downturn received an impetus—after the economy had become sluggish by midyear 1929—from the runaway stock-market boom. Granted also the failure to act positively on the part of the Federal Reserve System and its member banks during 1929–1932. But this did not mean—and Schumpeter denies this heatedly—that a saturation in investment opportunities had permanently set in. So had argued the American Keynesians and notably their leader, Alvin Hansen.

W. Arthur Lewis, looking at the 1920s and grappling with the depth and length of the Great Depression in the 1930s, makes these observations:

> The credit inflation of the 1920s was no greater than previous credit inflations, which had not had this severe result. The underconsumption was no greater, as far as we know, than it had been before; there is no evidence that the distribution of income in the United States had become more uneven over the course of the previous sixty years; the evidence on the contrary suggests less inequality, and suggests also that the proportion of the national income being devoted to consumption was about the same in the

1920s as it had been before the war. Neither was the rate of growth of production greater in the twenties than it had been before; on the contrary, prewar rates of growth had often been higher. Comparing the origins of the 1929 slump with the origins of earlier slumps, none of the factors so far mentioned, and not even the coincidence of all these factors, can tell us why the slump was so severe.

What had occurred to involve the United States had been the steep, worldwide fall in prices of primary products—of wheat and cotton (American commodities) and wool, silk, rubber, sugar, copper, and tin—beginning with midyear 1930 and continuing into 1932. In 1931, starting off with the failures of great banks in Austria and Germany and leading to suspension of gold payments, was the collapse of the international monetary system and, of course, the hoarding of hard currency and discouragement of further investments. Lewis gives these figures to make the point.

The index of prices of commodities entering world trade dropped from 1929 to 1932 by 56 per cent for raw materials, by 48 per cent for foodstuffs, and by 37 per cent for manufactured goods. The impact on the United States and its multiple effect on the rest of the world was even greater. In 1929 American imports and American overseas loans had been $7.4 billion; in 1932 (in 1929 dollars) they had dropped to $2.4 billion—a fall of 68 per cent. Similarly, the United States export surplus had narrowed from $842 million in 1929 to $333 million in 1931. The contraction in world trade and world production was accompanied by and further sharpened by high tariffs, quotas, and exchange controls—triggered by the American Hawley-Smoot Tariff, as we have seen.

The international monetary crisis, which had started off in 1931 in Austria and Germany and had led to widespread bank failures, forced Britain in that year to go off gold and devalue the pound. Canada, India, Ireland, Denmark, Egypt, Norway and Sweden had quickly followed. By the end of 1932 more than 30 countries had depreciated their currencies. The only important countries still on gold were the United States, Germany, France, Belgium, Holland, Italy, and Poland. In April 1933 the United States abandoned the gold standard, as we have seen, in the futile and misguided belief that by so doing American prices would rise. With trade limited by tariffs, quotas, and exchange controls and an international monetary mechanism gone, economic nationalism had replaced a freely operating world market for goods and credit.

Many foreign countries began to revive toward the end of 1932 (Japan's recovery was quick through the use of inflationary measures—unhappily, a large part for military outlays) and most of them were well on the way to recovery in the second half of the 1930s; that is, except the United States.

The United States lagged behind the rest of the world, and again, the key reason has been cited here: the sluggish flow of investment capital to stimulate the production of capital goods. These index figures of industrial production once more show capital goods lagging behind consumption goods. The year 1929 = 100.

	1929	1932	1935	1936	1937
Consumption goods	100	75	97	108	114
Capital goods	100	31	63	81	92

Lewis and Schumpeter agree on these reasons for the tardiness of the American recovery; Schumpeter, as we shall see, and I follow him, gives particular weight to the last.

1. The American depression had sunk the American economy very deep; the climb back therefore took longer.

2. American deficit spending, or pump priming, did not go far enough. It is true federal deficits were quite large, but we must not forget that American public outlays also include the expenditures of states and municipalities, which contributed little toward "income increasing expenditures" during the depression years.

3. New Deal wage policies were an important factor in affecting profitability, and with low profitability the revival of private investment was almost impossible.

4. The New Deal attacks on American capitalism—the revival of large-scale antitrust suits and the obtaining of consent decrees; fiscal measures that were punitive, directed as they were against larger personal incomes and undistributed company profits; the general climate of hostility created by government economists and other functionaries, and by the utterances of President Roosevelt himself—played an important part in keeping investment at low levels.

Added to all this—after a revival had occurred in 1936 and 1937—was the sudden decision to stop deficit financing and balance the budget. The result was another Descent into Avernus. Between 1937 and 1938 the index of production of capital goods fell from 92 to 59 and unemployment rose from 5 to 7.5 million.

Returning now to the question of wages and profitability, Lewis says flatly: "Without a doubt industrialists invested so little because profits were so low." He cites the case of the manufacturing industries, in which hourly wages in 1937 were 10 per cent higher than in 1929, whereas the prices of finished goods were 8 per cent lower. The consequence was that profits had been $7.6 billion in 1929, had become negative, or –$2 billion, in 1932, had remained negative for three years, and then risen to only $4.2 billion in 1937 (all in 1929 prices). Lewis then went on:

> Recovery was not possible until investment was restored, and investment would not be restored while profits were so low. Investment had to be restored, because it was impracticable in the U.S.A. for government spending fully and permanently to take place. . . . The idle stock [of capital overhanging the market] could not be reduced without an increase in employment, which, in turn depended on a revival of investment. Here was a vicious circle.

The reason was that average capital formation annually over 1925–1928 had been $18 billion and in 1932, $4 billion (1929 prices); the gap of $14 billion was too great for public expenditures alone.

The first year of a federal deficit was 1931, when it was $462 million, and the gross debt stood at $16.8 billion. By 1936 the deficit was $4.4 billion and the gross debt, $33.8 billion. The government relaxed its spending in 1937, and the deficit was $2.8 billion; but as a result of the recession of that year spending was resumed, and in 1939 the deficit was $3.9 billion and the gross debt, $40.4 billion.

This seemed like a good deal of spending; but we must not forget that as the federal government increased its expenditures those of the states and municipalities were contracting. If we take the "net income increasing" expenditures, those of the federal government stood at $249 million in 1930 and $3.4 billion in 1936, but the state and municipal "net income-increasing" expenditures dropped from $845 million to $116 million in the same period. Lewis points out:

> However, taking all governments together diminishes the significance of the increase in federal expenditure only from $3.1 billion to $2.4 billion, or by 23 per cent, and is not as important a point as is sometimes suggested.

The federal government sought to balance its budget in 1936; in any event, it cut back expenditures and deficit spending sharply. A recession set in in the late summer of 1937 and continued to late spring 1938. Its causes were the following:

1. The tapering-off of federal spending.
2. The decision by the Board of Governors of the Federal Reserve System, in August 1936 to double the reserve requirement of banks, thus contracting the money supply.
3. Inventories had been accumulating and purchases therefore had contracted.
4. Foreign trade had not increased so that declines in agricultural output failed to drain accumulated surpluses.

5. Price levels in basic commodities like steel, cement, and building materials had continued unresponsive to changes in demand. The government was compelled to resume spending.

Only the resumption of spending made possible the revival of the summer of 1938. It was the defense expenditures that began to appear in 1940—after war had broken out in Europe—that began to account for the end of the Great Depression in impressive increases in industrial production, employment, and the national income.

We come now to the anticapitalist attitude of the Roosevelt administrations. Roosevelt had indicated the line he planned to follow as early as September 23, 1932, when in a campaign address he said:

> Our task now is not discovery or exploitation of natural resources, or necessarily producing more goods. It is the soberer, less dramatic business of administering resources and plants already in hand, of seeking to reestablish foreign markets for our surplus production, of meeting the problem of underconsumption, of adjusting production to consumption, of distributing wealth and products more equitably, of adapting existing economic organizations to the service of the people. The day of enlightened administration has come.

Roosevelt started on this line—"of distributing wealth and products more equitably"—as early as the Revenue Act of 1934 and continued through the Revenue Act of 1936. The Revenue Act of 1935, which clearly revealed his purpose, was called "The Wealth Tax Act" and, justifying it, Roosevelt said:

> Our revenue laws have operated in many ways to the unfair advantage of the few, and they have done little to prevent an unjust concentration of wealth and economic power.

As Schumpeter says properly, the purpose was "a transfer or redistribution of wealth which in the highest brackets amounted to the socialization of the bulk of private income, and in some cases taxation for taxation's sake and regardless of insignificance of results for the Treasury." The Act of 1935 included the following: increases in individual surtaxes going up to 73 per cent of incomes over one million, taxes on the net income of corporations on a graduated scale pushed up to 15 per cent, increases in excess profits taxes, a capital stock tax on corporations, taxes on the undistributed corporate profits, and higher inheritance and gift taxes.

The Revenue Act of 1936 shoved these rates higher: the maximum rate of personal income tax was pushed up to 79 per cent, the corporation tax was put at a flat 15 per cent, the tax on capital gains was raised, and

additions were made to the corporate undistributed profits tax, the rates
running from 7 to 27 per cent. A corporation that paid no dividends was
to be subject to the maximum undivided profits tax, plus the normal
corporate income tax. No provision was made for carrying forward of
business losses.

Schumpeter was particularly severe about the undistributed profits
tax. Of it he said:

> The antisaving theories and the *ressentiments* of the day found a very
> characteristic expression in the special surtax on undistributed corporate
> income. . . . The measure may well have had a paralyzing influence on
> enterprise and investment in general. The actual presence of accumulated
> "reserves," and the possibility of accumulating them quickly, strengthens
> the position of a concern with respect to the risks and chances of innovation
> and expansion which it confronts. . . . Adequate book reserves are as neces-
> sary a requisite as adequate stocks of raw material, and in their absence, or
> with reduced facilities of acquiring or replenishing them, an entirely different
> and much more cautious business policy would impose itself.

Schumpeter ended up by having this to say about what he called
the "Social Atmosphere" the New Deal was creating:

> We know that behind these measures, administrative acts, and anticipa-
> tions there is something much more fundamental, viz., an attitude hostile to
> the industrial bourgeoisie which is no ephemeral composite of individual
> circumstances and political exegencies of the day but the product of the
> same social process that created that bourgeoisie. Businessmen . . . need
> not hold any [theory] in order to realize that they are on trial before judges
> who have the verdict in their pocket beforehand, that an increasing part of
> public opinion is impervious to their view, and that any particular indict-
> ment will, if successfully met, at once be replaced by another.

THE ACCOMPLISHMENTS OF THE NEW DEAL

There was no doubt that the New Deal had come to grips with a series
of important and pressing problems. From the social point of view its
accomplishment had been significant: it had sought to end insecurity and
it had helped the American labor movement mature. From the economic
point of view its assumption that there already existed saturation of
investment opportunity, that there were no new horizons for enterprise
and innovation to explore, led to a stifling of risk taking and the continuance of depression in the United States long after it had spent itself
elsewhere. The 1950s and 1960s were to demonstrate amply how badly

mistaken the New Dealers were: that American technology and management, with their inventiveness and boldness, were not only to conquer new worlds but to gain the admiration and, more important, emulation of European businessmen. The knowledge and skills of American enterprise were leading to further advances in growth and development at home and, when their examples and leadership were followed, everywhere in Europe and Asia.

It was in the political realm that the greatest impact of the New Deal revolution was to be felt, for the state of the nineteenth century, the laissez-faire or passive state, was relegated to the lumber room of history. The state was to assume positive functions: to act as umpire in labor relations and those between companies and their equity holders. It was to take on social service functions regarding the unemployed and the dependent. Nor was this all. Under the New Deal the state initiated projects and undertakings of a distinctly economic character. The national state, in short, was beginning to take on, in many domains, the essential color of private enterprise. It borrowed money not only for the traditional civil and military establishments of government but also for the buying and selling of commodities, processing goods, creating electric power and light, dealing in real estate, and engaging in warehousing, banking, shipping, and railroads. It set up corporations and corporate agencies (at least 50 under the New Deal), which possessed charters, directors, assets, thousands of employees, and industrial and mercantile policies. As in big business, there were interlocking directorates and the shifting of funds.

Much of this was cut back in the years of a revitalized economy following the end of World War II. Nevertheless, one of the heritages of the New Deal was the Big State—with its swarm of faceless, anonymous functionaries whose authority continued to expand as refinements on old duties occurred or new ones were taken on. The Big State came to be called the "Welfare State" in the 1960s, as it moved into the areas of education, urban rehabilitation, and problems of poverty—furnishing funds and at the same time concentrating power in the federal offices and agencies. Whatever its motives, the Big State, to those who prized liberty, privacy, enterprise, risk taking (what the sixteenth and seventeenth centuries called "adventurers," when they looked at the new businessmen in their midst) was suspect and something to guard against.

XV

THE PROBLEMS OF AN AFFLUENT
ECONOMY

WORLD WAR II AND ITS CONSEQUENCES

The war did many things. It not only pulled the United States out of the long depression but it gave the American economy a fresh elan; there were new energies and men—in industry and management—who possessed the kind of boldness and imagination that had taken America so far in the tumultuous years of its industrial revolution. The forebodings of the soothsayers—that saturation of investment opportunity had been reached; that America would have to settle for stability (without growth) at less than full employment; that the enterprise of individuals and companies was finished, and that the Big State meant *dirigisme* everywhere—vanished into thin air. A modernized plant, new opportunities as a result of research and development, constantly advancing productivity, and rises in real wages (and therefore consumer power) sent up all the key indicators—real GNP, industrial production, capital investment, individual savings, and consumer expenditures.

The war gave America fresh responsibilities. Not only was the United States an integral part of the whole world once more—after almost one hundred years of isolating itself—but perforce it had become the leader of the free nations. The high hopes (or ill-founded beliefs) of Franklin D. Roosevelt that we could live in amity with communism and

322

the Soviet Union—so many concessions had been made at Yalta in February 1945 to appease Stalin and to get out of him the promise of a declaration of war against Japan—were quickly dashed; the Iron Curtain came clanging down before a full year of peace had run its course. Bretton Woods (July 1944) saw the creation of two important pieces of international machinery—to restore once more a world community of trade and capital movements based on the convertibility of currencies—the World Bank and the International Monetary Fund. Dumberton Oaks (August-September 1944) sketched out plans for a United Nations. At San Francisco (April-June 1945) its charter was drawn up and within a month the American Senate ratified it to make the United States a charter member with a permanent seat on its Security Council.

But the Cold War was on. The Soviet threat to Greece and Turkey led to the promulgation of the Truman Doctrine (March 1947)—the United States would resist aggression anywhere in Europe—and at once military and economic aid was sent to southeastern Europe. This was followed by the Marshall Plan (June 1947)—a towering conception whose political purpose was the containment of communism by massive financial assistance (economic, largely, but military, too) for all nations who sought it. Said Secretary of State George C. Marshall, when he proposed it, American policy was to be directed against "hunger, poverty, desperation, and chaos. Its purpose should be the revival of a working economy in the world . . . ." The Soviet Union had representatives at a Marshall Plan Conference—and then walked out, leaving 16 nations to set up the important (and still functioning) Committee for European Economic Cooperation and to draw up a proposal for Europe's needs for dollar aid. For the years 1948–1952 this was to be between $16.4 and $22.4 billion. How quickly Congress responded may be noted from the fact that its appropriations for foreign help for the five years 1948–1952, inclusive, came to almost $30 billion. By the end of 1952 the requirements of Europe had been met; thenceforth aid—grants, loans, food—went everywhere and by the end of 1968 the total was in excess of $100 billion. The North Atlantic Treaty (April 1949) led to NATO, whose purpose was to integrate the defenses and mutual assistance of the Atlantic nations. To make the problems of a divided world more complex—for counterposed to NATO was the Warsaw Pact (May 1955), which binds together all the European communist countries (except Yugoslavia)—was the atomic bomb.

Even before Pearl Harbor the United States had begun to arm and to give help to the countries fighting Germany. Lend-lease (March 1941) made it possible to render assistance—with war materiél, ships, and scarce raw materials—first to the British Commonwealth countries, then also to the Soviet Union. Before Lend-Lease was finished more than $50 billion in goods had gone overseas (with only $9 billion coming back in reverse Lend-Lease). Once in the war, total mobilization of manpower and economic production took place; yet the civilian population at home never really felt the pinch. This was due to the great skills in organization but as well to a willingness—never before encountered in all-out war—to permit science and technology free rein. New weapons, new synthetics, the atomic bomb, heightened productivity (in agriculture and industrial production) came out of the war. The last is interesting. The United States still had eight million unemployed in 1939 (17 per cent of the labor force); in 1942 submarginal workers had to be enlisted in the war effort at home. Yet the new technology—which took the form of new plants and tools—was able to overcome their lack of skills and training.

The War Production Board (later Office of War Mobilization) had full authority over production and procurement; its principal instrument of control was in the establishment of priorities (to expand steel capacity and get more aviation gas, rubber, copper, and magnesium). One of its important creations was the Defense Plant Corporation, which financed and built new factories and contracted for their operation by private firms. Something like $30.7 billion in industrial installations added to American productive capacity, two-thirds of which was provided by government. The War Manpower Commission had authority over the distribution and use of the civilian labor force. A Selective Service Act had been passed in 1940; in 1942 all males 18–38 became subject to the draft for military duty. (Labor was not conscripted; the President had asked for this power in 1944 and Congress had refused.) The Department of Agriculture saw to the mobilization of agricultural production, of foodstuffs, of course, but particularly of vegetable oils and livestock. The War Food Administration allocated foods to claimant groups at home, in the field, among the Allies. (The result was immense. With only 10 million farm workers—as against 11.5 million during 1935–1939—American farms doubled their output, as productivity per farm worker increased 90 per cent over the experiences of 1910–1914.)

The mobilization of foreign trade under the Board of Economic Warfare—to stockpile scarce raw materials and to engage in preclusive buying (so that, e.g., mercury, chromium, wolfram, ball bearings could be kept out of German hands)—was highly imaginative and successful. Axis assets were searched out in neutral countries; the Germans were frozen out of Latin America—all Brazilian and Bolivian rubber was bought up. German aviation companies were forced to retire from Peru, Ecuador, Bolivia, and Brazil, and neutrals yielded to all sorts of pressures and diverted scarce materials to the United States.

The result of all this was that the American war output reached staggering proportions. The armed forces mobilized 14 million men and women (12 million were male draftees) who were fed, housed, clothed, and armed. Between 1939 and 1944 manufacturing, mining, and construction more than doubled their output. (It had been only 7 per cent during World War I.) The production of durable manufactured goods increased 260 per cent. Productive capacity increased 50 per cent. Overall productivity grew by 25 per cent. And the real wages of workers (unlike the Civil War, unlike World War I) also rose, for weekly earnings between 1938–1945 increased by 50 per cent, while the rise in the general price level was 30 per cent. A few figures will show what was done: 296,000 planes, 5400 cargo ships, 6500 naval vessels, 64,500 landing craft, 86,000 tanks, and 2.5 million trucks were built.

The financial cost? Congress appropriated $347 billion for war expenditures (1941–1945). The public debt increased from $50 billion to $260 billion. Taxes were responsible for 44 per cent of the federal income during the war years and were pushed up to achieve these purposes: to produce as much as possible by this device to lessen inflationary pressures and to check war profits. Eight war loans (1941–1946) brought in $157 billion, two-fifths of which came from banks. (To prevent this vast accumulation in banks from adding to inflation the Federal Reserve Board raised reserve requirements to the limits set by law and also put checks on installment selling.) The upshot was that federal taxes absorbed 25 per cent of the national income, federal expenditures, 50 per cent, during 1943 and 1944.

Further, to curb inflation the Office of Price Administration (OPA) was set up in 1941. In 1942 it received the power to control prices and rents and ration scarce goods (gasoline, sugar, and meatstuffs) among consumers. From 1939 to 1945 the wholesale prices of all commodities increased 37.2 per cent; but those of consumer goods, 28.4 per cent. This was a great triumph and showed how far and deep acceptance of the war spread among the American people, for any sort of restriction or control is based on compliance.

RECONVERSION AND SOME RESULTS

The inflation of the 1940s was a postwar phenomenon which confounded all those who had seen through a glass darkly and were prepared to assume that peace and reconversion would once again bring depression. It was commonly stated by New Deal economists that there would be eight million unemployed six months after Japan's defeat and that the economy could be sustained only by government planning linked with massive public outlays.

They were wrong for the following reasons.

1. The backed-up demand for consumer goods as a result of the austerities of the war period.

2. The existence of purchasing power because of individual savings built up during the war.

3. The expanded plant and machine tools, created by the war, which made possible the satisfaction of consumer demand.

4. The existence of a labor force, which had acquired new skills in the war and to which was added the returned soldiers who received the benefit of training as a result of the G.I. Bill of Rights.

5: The population explosion which took place during the 10 years following the end of war and created great demands for new houses and cars.

6. The appearance of new or modernized industries and processes— natural gas and transmission, plastics, aeronautics, electronics, data processing, aluminum, and notably new construction on a vast scale, which further fed capital outlays and investment.

7. The adoption of the Marshall Plan (to help Europe get back on its feet) and the broad commitment to foreign aid; this meant an expansion of exports along with the movement of foreign credits.

The technological advances of American industry after World War II were particularly impressive, and this showed up in the increase in productivity, or output per man-hour. During the quarter-century before the outbreak of World War I the increases in output per man-hour had been about 22 per cent per decade; after World War II they ran to 35–40 per cent per decade. Automation, based on the feedback principle in the production processes, made possible the self-regulation of machines operating at greater speeds and more precision in many industries. A further advance was in the utilization of continuous-flow methods of production. The large sums spent on research and development constituted a key factor here. By 1960 these sums had reached $12 billion, an increase from $3.4 billion in 1950; one-half came from the federal government.

Here are some figures to point up these observations. GNP (1957 prices) was $340.1 billion in 1945, $301.1 billion in 1946, and $340 billion in 1950. Personal consumption expenditures (1957 prices) were $179.5 billion in 1945 ($1357 per capita), $200.3 billion in 1946 ($1492 per capita), and $225.6 billion in 1950 ($1492 per capita). Personal savings were $27.8

billion in 1942, $33 billion in 1943, $36.9 billion in 1944, $28.7 billion in 1945, but $13.5 in 1946 and $12.6 billion in 1950. Gross private domestic investment was $3.8 billion in 1945, $11 billion in 1946, and $24.2 billion in 1950 (of which $14.1 billion was for new residential construction). The index of industrial production (1947–1949 = 100) was 110 in 1945, 90 in 1946, and 113 in 1950. The civilian labor force was 52.8 million in 1945 (with 1 million, or 2 per cent, unemployed), 55.3 million in 1946 (with 2.3 million, or 4.1 per cent, unemployed), and 60 million in 1950 (with 3.1 million, or 5 per cent, unemployed). Productivity per man-hour (1929 = 100) was 159 in 1945, 150.9 in 1946, and 175.4 in 1950. The annual average of live births had been 2.4 million during 1931–1940 and 3.8 million during 1946–1955. The birthrate (per 1000 female population 15–44 years) was 84.6 in 1931 and 118 in 1955; at the same time the deathrate dropped from 11.1 per 1000 population in 1931 to 9.3 per 1000 population in 1955. During the six years 1945–1950 the wholesale prices of all commodities rose 52.6 per cent, an average of 8.8 per cent annually; those of consumer prices rose 33.7 per cent, an average of 5.6 per cent annually. Homes with electrical refrigeration increased from 40 per cent in 1939 to 75 per cent in 1951. Of the total number of farms 25 per cent were equipped for electricity in 1939 and 80 per cent in 1951.

Reconversion came swiftly. By V-J Day (August 15) 2.7 million veterans were demobilized; in 1946 11 million more joined civilian life. Partial price controls were ended between June and July 1946 and in total (except for rent, sugar, and rice) in November 1946. One of the most significant pieces of legislation of this 79th Congress was the passage of the Employment Act of 1946. Still concerned with the fear of depression, the Congress in 1945 began to debate the Murray bill, introduced in the Senate, whose purpose was to ensure "full employment" by setting up a $40 billion "annual investment fund" to be managed by the Secretary of Commerce. In short, it was based on the (American) Keynesian assumption that only great government outlays would keep the economic wheels going.

The Employment Act of 1946, as it finally emerged, was less than that; there was no commitment to the maintenance of "full employment" and no "investment fund"; yet it created machinery for keeping the President, the Congress, and the American people on the alert to threats to stability and means of achieving growth. The Act declared the following:

> It is the continuing policy and responsibility of the federal government to use all practicable means . . . for the purpose of creating and maintaining . . . conditions under which there will be afforded useful employment

opportunities, including self-employment, for those able, willing, and seeking to work, and to promote maximum employment, production, and purchasing power.

Toward this end two agencies were established. The first, a Council of Economic Advisers, in the President's Office, was to "assist and advise" the President in the preparation of an annual "economic report" on the state of the nation. This was to be submitted to the Congress with recommendations for legislation. The second was a standing Joint Economic Committee (to be chosen from both Houses of the Congress and from both parties) which was to make a continuing study of matters relating to the economic report, with power to assemble its own technical staff, hold hearings, report to Congress, and make such recommendations on the economic affairs of the country as it chose. It turned out to be a highly skilled body and demonstrated one of the great strengths of the American constitutional separation of powers, for its ideas not infrequently were at variance with those of the Council of Economic Advisers and a corrective to the Executive will. In any event, both agencies were constantly alert to the changes in and the needs of the health of the economy so that a constant flow of information and expert opinion was available as guides to discussion and public decision making.

THE ECONOMY IN THE 1950S AND 1960S*

The economy went on expanding—with short-term cyclical swings—following the end of the war and through the 1950s and 1960s. There were four recessions but they were brief and mild. No large-scale breakdown threatened, for the economic life of the nation continued to be sustained by all the healthy and powerful forces to which reference has been made. Nevertheless, problems emerged and much debate concerning them took place, for the choices to guide decision making frequently were mutually contradictory.

They were these. First, the growth in real GNP had ups and downs; during the second half of the 1950s the rate of growth dropped sharply. Query: Was it desirable not only for economic but for psychological reasons that high sustained growth be maintained? Second, the unemployment rate, too, had its wide swings. In the second half of the 1950s, even during cyclical recovery after recession America was confronted by

* For a detailed analysis of the 1950s see Harold G. Vatter, *The U.S. Economy in the 1950s*, 1963, from which a good deal of the statistical information here has been drawn and for which the writer acknowledges his debt.

rates going up to 7 per cent. Query: Should every device, particularly stepped up public spending, be used to maintain high employment? Third, one of the prices of achieving this aim was inflation. Inflation began to appear mildly in the second half of the 1950s (when it was kept at a low level by public policy) and then accelerated in the 1960s. Inflation seriously affected the distribution of income and the American balance of payments. Query: Was it of prime importance to curb inflation even if high employment was temporarily abandoned? If high employment was the prime desideratum, was the only solution to inflation public control of prices and wages? Fourth, during the 1950s and 1960s there was a chronic deficit in the balance of payments and a gold drain. Query: Was unilateral action desirable or possible or were the arrangements made at Bretton Woods (of maintaining fixed exchange rates) obsolete and new international agreements necessary? Fifth, despite prosperity and high employment (in many years of the 1960s), depressed areas continued to exist, urban blight had become common, and the unemployment rate of nonwhites was notably high. (All this spelled "poverty," a term not heard in the 1950s and early 1960s but apparently on all tongues in the late 1960s) Query: Should a good part of investment—public and private—be diverted to overcome the first two, even if sustained growth might be affected? Was a solution for the problem of "poverty" generally a guaranteed annual income, the negative income tax, or family allowances—any of which, of course, requiring large public spending as they had to, would also add to the inflationary fires? Finally, despite the vitality of private enterprise—so thoroughly demonstrated by the prolonged and upward-moving recovery following World War II—how much public direction and control, *dirigisme* in short, had to be accepted to sustain the delicate balances and eliminate the inequities all the above questions raised? Some attention is given to these concerns below.

The four recessions to which reference has been made were those of 1948–1949 (11 months), 1953–1954 (13 months), 1957–1958 (9 months), and 1960–1961 (9 months). The upward turn following the third was not complete, for private investment lagged and the unemployment rate remained high. Following the fourth, and beginning with February 1961, recovery was sustained right into 1969—with high employment and high growth rates during the greater part of the period, but also with accelerating inflation, starting in 1965. It was the longest period of unbroken prosperity in American economic development.

The recessions, as has been said, were brief and mild. In each there were slight falls in industrial production and the GNP and short-term rises in unemployment. In the first, 1948–1949, the GNP dropped by 4 per cent and unemployment rose to about 7 per cent. In the second, 1953–1954, the fall in the GNP was 1.8 per cent and unemployment went up to about 6 per cent. In the third, 1957–1958, the GNP decline was 3.7 per cent and unemployment was about 7 per cent. In the fourth, 1960–1961, the GNP drop was 2 per cent and the unemployment rate was again about 7 per cent. Taking the decade of the 1950s as a whole, the average annual unemployment rate was 4.6 per cent of the American labor force. Gross private investment was $54.1 billion in 1950, $67.4 billion in 1955, and $74.8 billion in 1960.

The fact is, in all likelihood, these recessions had little impact on the lives of most Americans. The figures in Table 41—comparing personal income in billions of dollars from onset to termination—show why the postwar recessions were less severe than those of the 1920s and 1930s.

TABLE 41

CHANGES IN PERSONAL INCOME DURING RECESSIONS,
1920–1961

| Year | Personal Income | | Change in P.I. (per cent) |
	From	To	
1920–1921	$ 73.4	$ 62.1	−15
1929–1933	85.9	47.0	−45
1937–1938	74.1	68.3	− 8
1948–1949	210.2	207.2	− 1.4
1953–1954	288.2	290.1	+ 0.6
1957–1958	351.1	361.2	+ 2.8
1960–1961	401.0	416.8	+ 3.9

Source. Wall Street Journal, November 25, 1968, p. 1.

The rise, instead of fall, in personal income in three of the postwar recessions will be noted. The reasons, among others, were these: the continued growth of defense (and war) and aerospace expenditures, the increase in white-collar workers with their fixed salaries, and the great influence of all transfer payments (the transfer of income to people who do not work for it); this includes payments from private pension and welfare funds as well as federal transfer payments. The rise of this item as a part of personal income can be realized from the figures given in Table 42.

The $60.2 billion in transfer payments may be compared with the $22 billion in dividends paid out by all corporations in the United States

TABLE 42

TRANSFER PAYMENTS AS PERCENTAGES OF PERSONAL INCOME,
1929–1968

Year	All Personal Income (billions)	All Transfer Payments	T.P. As percent of P.I.
1929	$ 85.9	$ 1.5	1.7
1939	72.8	3.0	4.1
1950	227.6	15.1	6.6
1960	401.0	28.5	7.1
1968	702.2	60.2	8.5

Source. Op. cit.

in 1967 and the $14 billion in the country's total farm income. This factor thus was a powerful force in sustaining consumer purchasing power.

These other influences also were at work to prevent the recessions from plunging too deeply and continuing for too long a time. The Federal Reserve Board, in every case, acted at once to ease credit by increasing the money supply. The only resort to fiscal policy was by the establishment of an accelerated depreciation rate in the Revenue Act of 1954. Consumption continued at a high level because personal income remained steady and personal savings were substantial. There now existed built-in stabilizers to check precipitous down turns: reductions in tax bills with the decline of personal and corporate earnings, supports for agricultural prices, the public transfer payments to persons in the form of unemployment and old-age and survivor benefits, and benefit-payments to veterans. Further, we are to note continued federal, state, and local spending. Federal military expenditures, in addition to production for defense and war, also included atomic research and outlays, stock piling, and foreign assistance (with the lift this gave to exports). State and local spending were for public-works construction, education and health, and welfare relief.

The role of public spending (federal plus state and local) for expansion and to overcome contraction may be ascertained from these figures. All government purchases made up 15 per cent, in real dollars, of the Gross Private Product in 1950 (compared with 11 per cent in 1929) and 20 per cent, annual average, during 1953–1960. State and local expenditures totaled $47.3 billion in 1960, compared with the $30.2 billion, which represented federal transfer payments and federal civilian expenditures. Taken together we have some notion of how far along the road to the welfare state the United States was traveling; it will be seen it was not very much. In 1960 state and local expenditures made up 9.4 per cent of the GNP, federal transfer payments 4.4 per cent, and federal civilian expenditure 1.6 per cent, a combined total of 15.4 per cent.

This was the postwar's price history. From 1945 through 1968 wholesale prices rose 87.7 per cent for an annual average of 3.8 per cent. The greater part of this rise had taken place during 1945–1949, for during the 1950s the annual average increase had been only 1.6 per cent and during the eight years 1961–1968 a bit more than 1 per cent. The record of consumer prices was similar until the mid-1960s and then the inflationary pressures began to be felt. From 1945 through 1968 consumer prices went up 93.3 per cent, for an annual average of 4.0 per cent. During 1945–1949 the annual average rise was 6.5 per cent; during 1950–1954 it was almost 2 per cent; during 1955–1959 it was 1.6 per cent; during 1960–1964 it was 1.6 per cent. Then from 1964 to 1965 consumer prices rose 1.8 per cent; from 1965 to 1966, 3.2 per cent; from 1966 to 1967, 3.2 per cent; from (December) 1967 to (December) 1968, 4.7 per cent; and from (March) 1968 to (March) 1969, 5.1 per cent.

How growth in the GNP and employment and prices are related may now be seen from the following. The real GNP rate of growth for 1950–1959, annual average, was 2.9 per cent, compared with 4.7 per cent for 1920–1929 and 3.7 per cent for 1879–1919. For the first half of the decade of the 1950s it was 4.7 per cent, annual average, but for the second half it was 2.25 per cent. In the 1960s the annual average rate of growth was as follows: for 1961–1968, 5.3 per cent, but for 1968 the rate fell from 6.4 per cent in the first quarter to 3.8 per cent in the fourth.

A word about monetary policy. Broadly speaking, it was the intention of the Federal Reserve Board to maintain monetary ease during the greater part of the 1950s, and its quick action played an important part in shortening the length and softening the impact of the recessions. It used all the devices of credit control in its possession—open-market operations, the discount rate, and changes in reserve ratios. After the end of the Korean War, and with recovery once more on its way, it reversed course and its growing concern over inflation (and here it say eye to eye with the Adminstration) prompted it to adopt a mildly restrictive monetary policy, using as its chief weapon the discount rate and going from 1.5 per cent to 3 per cent by six rises during April-November 1955. It resumed this course after the 1957–1958 recession (its chief concern, again, being the maintenance of stable prices) and raised the discount rate to a peak of 4 per cent in September 1959. It should be observed, at this point, that monetary policy did not restrain the rise in prices, while an only imperfect recovery during 1958–1960 drifted into the fourth recession of 1960–1961. The Administration, in its turn, used budgetary control exclusively to maintain price stability. Efforts were made to reduce the size of the budget, keep it in balance (or run a surplus to retire debt), and lengthen the maturity of the greater part of the publicly held debt. In the case of budget and debt management the Administration did well. True, there was a deficit of $13.1 billion in fiscal 1959, but this was due to the smaller receipts because of the recession and to previously planned expenditures (defense, agricultural payments, an additional subscription to the International Monetary Fund, and salary increases for federal civilian employees and the military).

A continuing matter for concern of the 1950s (and, in fact, of the 1960s as well) was the chronic deficit in the balance of payments, the annual averages being as follows: 1951–1960, $−1.8 billion, 1951–1957, $−957 million, 1958–1960, $−3.7 billion. The reasons were many, and plausible enough, but the consequence was an increase in dollar holdings abroad and therefore an outflow of gold. These were the contributing factors: military expenditures; grants and loans to foreign countries, including the government underwriting of American farm surpluses under Public Law 480 (passed in 1954); the private long-term capital outflow largely into Europe (but of course this was offset almost entirely by earnings on services and investments); the movement of private short-term capital abroad (because interest rates were higher); and the narrowing of the export gap (it was only $3.2 billion, annual average 1951–1960, which may be compared with a trade surplus of $5.2 billion in 1949). The last was undoubtedly affected by the rise in American prices. The American share in the world export of manufactures—despite a superior technology—did not improve significantly over 1928. In that year the proportion was 16.6 per cent, in 1957 it was 17.3 per cent, and in 1960, 17.1 per cent. More revealing was the fall in exports as a proportion of the GNP. In 1928 this had been 5.2 per cent, but in 1957, 4.4 per cent, and in 1960, 3.9 per cent. The upshot at the end of the 1950s was that the American holdings of gold were down to $18.6 billion (compared with $24.4 billion in 1949); against these reserves dollar claims against the United States totaled $16.8 billion.

The summary figures of American foreign assistance programs during 1946–1960 are truly impressive. The over-all total was in the neighborhood of $80 billion, broken down as follows: investment in four international financial institutions, $4.9 billion, and assistance to foreign countries $75.1 billion (of which the net grants of military supplies and services came to $26.5 billion and all other nonmilitary aids to $48.6 billion).

American private investments overseas also kept pace with public expenditures. In 1946 they had stood at $14.2 billion (of which $8.8 billion were direct investments); by 1949 they were $17.7 billion (of which $12.5 billion was direct), and in 1957, $37.7 billion ($25.3 billion direct).

Direct investments at the end of the 1950s—American-owned companies, financed by American capital or capital raised abroad—were distributed by industries as follows: petroleum, 36 per cent, manufacturing, 31 per cent, mining, 11 per cent, public utilities, 7 per cent, distribution, 6 per cent, and others, 9 per cent. These were the areas in which direct investments were to be found: Latin America, 35 per cent, Canada, 33 per cent, Western Europe, 16 per cent, Western Europe dependencies, 3.5 per cent, and Middle East and Africa, 9 per cent.

THE HIGH PROSPERITY OF THE 1960S

Except for faltering once or twice (without recessions occurring, however) the American economy kept on expanding from February 1961 to the end of 1968 and into mid-1969. From the first quarter of 1961 through 1968 the real GNP showed an average annual rise of 5.3 per cent. Real disposable personal income per capita went up 3.7 per cent. Industrial production grew by 6.3 per cent annual average. Federal expenditures increased by 5.4 per cent annual average and state and local expenditures were even higher—5.7 per cent, annual average. Civilian employment grew by 10.2 million in the eight years, yet the unemployment rate from 1966 on showed full employment existing, that is, 4 per cent or less of the civilian labor force. (So much for all the fears about the effects of automation—voiced so frequently in many quarters in the second half of the 1960s. Improved technological processes created more job opportunities, for displaced workers could be absorbed in other industries and services.) The following shows the great advances that were effected, comparing the first quarter of 1961 with the last quarter of 1967 and with 1968.

Indeed, in January and February 1969 the economy's performance was even better than that. Thus the unemployment rate for adult men

Unemployment Rates	1961–I	1967–IV	1968
Total	6.8%	4.0%	3.6%
Total males			
20 years and over	5.9	2.4	2.2
Teenagers	17.2	14.0	12.7
Nonwhites	12.4	7.6	6.7

dropped to 2.0 per cent and then to 1.9 per cent, that for teenagers fell to 11.7 per cent for both months, whereas the jobless rate for all white workers was 3 per cent and 2.4 per cent and for nonwhite workers, 6 per cent and 5.7 per cent. Even in July 1969, the jobless rate was 3.6 per cent, with the civilian labor force continuing to grow to 79.6 million. Viewed selectively, the unemployment problem really boiled down to these two groups: the out-of-work teenagers—really short-term—and the hard-core untrained adult males, most of them blacks. To this state of affairs one question was raised, notably by Arthur F. Burns: Did we really know the extent of unemployment until we had accurate figures on what job vacancies actually existed? Then—and these methods were being pursued with increasing vigor and some successes in the 1960s— as a result of the training of the unskilled and the retraining of the displaced (through the Manpower Development and Training Act of 1962), concentration on the distressed areas like Appalachia with the movement of new industries (plus training) into such regions, making possible greater mobility of workers, provision of summer work for teenagers, and efforts to get drop-outs back into school with greater expenditures on education, there was every realistic hope that high unemployment and persistent hard-core unemployment could be licked. All this assuming continued stability in the economy with steady advancement in investment and production and therefore effective demand.

The following comparison shows the changed nature of the labor force and one of the elements of stability. It gives the distribution of jobs by industries and services for 1957 and 1967. The rise in government and services and the fall in manufacturing and agriculture and mining will be noted.

Jobs in	1957	1967
Manufacturing	28.6%	26.4%
Trade	18.1	18.6
Government	17.8	21.0
Services	14.6	16.8
Agriculture and mining	4.5	2.7
All other	16.4	14.5

INFLATION

One of the prices of closing the gap between actual and potential GNP —and the President's Council of Economic Advisers was arguing that this was being achieved with unemployment at 4 per cent or lower and industrial utilization of plant at 85 per cent of capacity or higher—was mounting inflation; that is, the rise in consumer prices. The sharp increase from 1965 through 1968 has already been commented on. These were the reasons most commonly being adduced:

Heavy public expenditures with huge deficits in the budget (in part because of the Vietnam war but also because of the outlays to hasten on the "Great Society"); the cost-push of wages, which were far ahead of productivity, and the rise in prices to meet the wage demands because fully utilized plants and a scarcity of skilled workers shoved up costs; but also demand-pull because of full employment and the increasing dearth of skilled workers. The Administration had announced in 1962 the guidelines for labor and industry it was setting out—that wage increases should be held to 3.2 per cent a year, about equal to productivity growth; and that prices should offset each other, that is, reductions in industries with superior production to balance off increases in those that lagged behind. Compulsion, of course, could not be used; "education"—publicity and pressure on large industrial companies—was to be the device for obtaining compliance. All this worked fairly well during 1961–1965, in which percentage changes per year in the private nonfarm sector were as follows: for average hourly compensation, 4 per cent, for output per man-hour, 3.5 per cent, for increase in unit labor cost, 0.5 per cent, and implicit GNP price deflator, 1.2 per cent. Then everything went awry in 1965, 1966, 1967, and 1968; the guidelines were not working and the Administration stopped talking of them in 1968. In that year wage increases (including benefits) covered by bargaining settlements rose by 7.5 per cent. The figures in Table 43 are for the private nonfarm economy.

Inflation was a cause for serious concern. It produced an unfair change in the distribution of income: the retired, the elderly, the disabled, the poor (because increasing regressive taxes took larger bites out of their shrinking real incomes) were being hurt. The balance of payments was further affected because mounting costs led to decreases in the dollar value of exports and increases in imports, which caused a widening in the transfer gap. The result was increased dollar claims abroad and jeopardy to the price of gold, its maintenance at $35 an ounce being a pledge every Administration had committed itself to defend.

Despite the cumulative balance of payment deficits (totaling more than $17 billion since 1959) and the fact that some $30 billion in dollar claims (Eurodollars) * were owned abroad, gold transfers were held down

---

* "Eurodollars" were all dollars deposited with banks located outside the United States, whether they were banks of a foreign country or the branches of American banks. Most "Eurodollars" were American-owned; but Europeans, Canadians, Japanese (and Russians!) also owned "Eurodollars."

TABLE 43

WAGE INCREASES AND OUTPUT PER MAN-HOUR, 1965–1968

	Percentage Changes per Year		
	1965 to 1966	1966 to 1967	1967 to 1968
Average hourly compensation	6.0	6.0	7.2
Output per man-hour	2.6	1.1	3.4
Increase in unit labor cost	3.4	4.8	3.7
Implicit GNP price deflator	2.2	3.5	3.6

to $5 billion. The Kennedy and Johnson Administrations were able to do so by these devices: they urged foreign monetary authorities not to convert Eurodollars into gold; they arranged for official borrowings of one kind or another with foreign central banks and governments; they pushed the creation of a new international facility in the form of "Special Drawing Rights" on the International Monetary Fund; and they sought to tie foreign aid to imports of American merchandize and technical assistance.

How strong then was the American dollar? In one sense only as strong as the American economy itself—and therefore in danger when winds blew cold. In another sense the bulwarks against sudden threats to the dollar from foreign claims were more powerful than appeared on the surface. Of the $30 billion in claims, one-half was being held by foreign central banks—and they were as much interested in the stability of the dollar as the United States; of the other half, possibly two-thirds was controlled by American-owned corporations abroad or by United States banks. Besides, the United States gold reserve (as a protection against foreign claims) had been increased by $10 billion when Congress in 1968 abolished the 25 per cent gold cover for American currency in circulation. Nevertheless, concern continued because of the steep fall in the net merchandise account and the continued liquidity deficit in the balance of payments.

The payment deficit had lasted continuously since 1950 (except for 1957) over the 18 years 1950–1967, averaging annually $2.1 billion and getting as high as $3.6 billion in 1967. This was because the great financial transfers of the United States (military expenditures, government grants and loans net, and the movement of private American capital abroad net) were not being matched by the country's export surpluses. In 1964 the gross merchandize trade surplus was $7 billion, but in 1965 it was $5.3 billion, in 1967, $4.2 billion, and in 1968, only $100 million. (It should be had in mind, however, that a good part of the import increases came from American-owned factories abroad. Thus the income on United States foreign investments was $6.2 billion in 1966, close to $7 billion in 1967, and more than $8 billion in 1968.)

The net financial transfers, the net "real transfers" (goods and services, excluding earnings from capital), and the liquidity deficits are shown for typical years in Table 44, compared with the GNP in current billions of dollars.

It will be observed that the low in the Transfer Gap came in 1957 (the year following the Suez crisis) and the high in 1967 (the year of monetary overexpansion in part because of the escalation of the Vietnam war).* Professor Machlup points out that despite the increases in the GNP and the trade volume (exports plus imports) there was no tendency for the Transfer Gap to narrow; in fact in 1967 it was wider than ever and he remarks:

> One cannot help being impressed by the stubbornness and apparent intractability of the relatively small shortfall of the export surplus. With the huge increases in GNP and in the volume of foreign trade, why should it have been impossible to squeeze or switch another two or three billion dollars of goods and services out of domestic and into foreign use?

He offers this explanation (or his hypothesis):

> In the absence of sufficient expansion of demand, incomes, and prices in other countries, only painful doses of deflation in the United States or an unwanted reduction in the exchange rate of the dollar could secure the reductions in relative incomes and prices that would be needed to raise the export surplus to the required size.

At this point it may be observed that the American share of exports of manufactured goods of the leading industrial nations has been falling— down to 20.8 per cent in 1968, compared with 28.1 per cent in 1951.

* In 1968, for the first time in more than 10 years, the deficit disappeared and there was a surplus of something like $200 million. This undoubtedly was transitory and due to these two special considerations: the mandatory limitation on direct foreign investments of United States companies and the voluntary restrictions on United States bank loans abroad (both started January 1968); and the unusually large flow of foreign private capital for investment in the United States, due to high interest rates and the profits of American corporations. Foreigners bought $1.9 billion (net) in stocks in the United States in 1968; this was twice as much as such purchases in 1967 and four times as much in 1967 over 1966.

TABLE 44
TRANSFER PAYMENTS AND TRANSFER LIQUIDITY DEFICITS, 1950–1967

Years	GNP 1	Net Real Transfers 2	Net Financial Transfers 3	Transfer Gap (3–2)	Liquidity Deficit
1950	$248.8	$1.1	$4.7	$3.6	$3.5
1957	441.1	6.8	7.5	0.7	0.6
1958	447.3	3.4	7.3	3.9	3.4
1960	503.7	4.7	7.8	3.1	3.9
1965	683.9	5.7	7.2	1.5	1.3
1966	743.3	4.6	6.0	2.4	1.4
1967	785.0	4.5	9.3	4.8	3.6

Source. Fritz Machlup, *Banca Nazionale del Lavaro Quarterly Review,* September 1968. I have followed Professor Machlup largely in this discussion.

Machlup does not deny the impacts of "unduly lax fiscal policy," the "demand-pull," the wage-price or "cost-push" inflationary spirals, and the "easy-money policy" of the Federal Reserve Board. He calls attention to the important part performed by the Financial Transfers (for they do play a role in financing exports). Even if military expenditures were reduced at the end of the Vietnam war (but not likely, as a result of the need for strengthening NATO—brought on by the Czechoslovakia crisis in 1968 and the presence of an increasing Russian fleet in the Mediterranean), there still remains the moral and political obligation to aid the developing countries.

The target set has been widely accepted—most recently reaffirmed by the United Nations Conference on Trade and Development—that rich nations should give as aid 1 per cent of their national income for the economic development of poor nations. In this connection American performance had been poor; indeed it was averaging not much more than one-half the target. If and when the United States pushes up its aid appropriations—as it should—approximating the points France and the Netherlands have already reached, then normal capital exports to both developed and developing countries would exceed 1.5 per cent of GNP.

How raise the level of Net Real Transfers to improve the export surplus of the United States and make bearable the necessary and desirable Financial Transfers? A reduction in the external value of the dollar (Machlup says by 4 per cent) would do it. Machlup does not look with favor on deflation; he sees it accompanied by "almost unbearable suffering. A deflation that could push extra quantities of American goods into export markets and empty American pockets sufficiently to reduce the demand for imports, together enough to close the Transfer Gap, would be intolerable." Machlup opts for—as do many other academic economists—revision in the arrangements available to the International Monetary Fund as they were laid down at Bretton Woods in 1944. Then convertibility of currencies through fixed exchange rates was provided for, with deviations in the rates being permitted to fluctuate only by 1 per cent of parity in either direction.*

Interestingly, the American proposal for the creation of the "Special Drawing Rights" ("paper gold") began to loom large in 1969 as one of the ways out of the balance of payment dilemma. The plan, which members of the International Monetary Fund agreed on in 1967, received immediate attention from the 111 countries belonging to it. At the end of July 1969, this was crowned with success and the International Monetary Fund was able to announce that agreement among the required number of member governments had been filed. The steering committee of the fund then indicated that the amount of resources to be available for the financing of expanding world trade and the settling up of balance of payment deficits would almost be doubled by 1972. In this wise: $3.5 billion of the "Special Drawing Rights" would be issued in 1970; $3 billion more in each of the next two years; and the quotas for the IMF members would be increased from $4 billion to $8 billion. In mid-1969, the assets of the IMF came to about $21 billion; in 1972, they would be nearly $40 billion.

This certainly was one way of adding flexibility to the monetary system of the free world. Academic economists had supported the creation of the SDR proposal; to it, however, they wanted to add further changes in the Bretton Woods agreements—the currency rates to fluctuate in a "wider band" than the 1 per cent permitted. About the latter many American bankers began to have their doubts in 1969; they argued that exchange-rate flexibility created too many uncertainties for businessmen and thus would impede international trade.

Fritz Machlup was a characteristic example of the academic economist; he favored (in the article already cited) the widening of the

* The agreements at Bretton Woods were based on these two assumptions: that the principal nations would regulate their economies to preserve the external values of their currencies in proper alignment with each other; and, if "fundamental disequilibriums" occurred and could not be corrected by changes in domestic policies, then currencies would be revalued—up or down. Subsequent experiences indicated that these were counsels of perfection because, apropos the first hope, treasuries and central banks gave first priorities to the maintenance of economic growth and high employment rather than to monetary stability; and apropos the second the acceptance of devaluation was too bitter a pill for national pride to swallow.

"band" of permissible deviation to as much as 5 per cent of par, up or down. He said:

> Variations of exchange rates of this order of magnitude would allow the adjustment mechanism to operate on the international flows of goods and services. No government would have to take unpopular action; supply and demand would be allowed to determine exchange rates within the fixed limits; and any variations within these limits would reverse themselves when conditions change.

The pure monetary theorists, like Milton Friedman, went considerably farther, brushing aside the cautions and hesitancies of both camps: they favored allowing exchange rates to float freely. The world market would make its own adjustments. Here the discussions stood, with every prospect that the SDR program would be established in 1970; the creation of a "wider band" was less certain of immediate adoption.

XVI

CONTINUED SUSTAINED GROWTH: ITS CHALLENGES AND PERILS

THE IMMEDIATE CHOICE BEFORE US: A GROWTH ORIENTED OR A CYCLE-ORIENTED ECONOMY?*

Up to 1967 the economists who favored and worked toward achieving the "Great Society" of Presidents Kennedy and Johnson had every reason to congratulate themselves. They were closing the gap between the actual and potential capacities of American output by using largely fiscal policy —they were certain they had the methods to "fine-tune" the economy— to keep on advancing the real growth of the country's GNP. Growth through the manipulation of taxes (up or down) and the expansion or contraction of the federal expenditures—Walter W. Heller (along with

* For the debate and some of the background discussions about the "Modern Economy Policy" of the United States, as it developed in the 1960s, the reader is referred to the following: *Economic Report of the President Transmitted to the Congress, February 1968* and the 1969 *Report*, January 1969; *Report of the Joint Economic Committee 1967*, March 1967 and the 1968 *Report*, March 1968; W. Arthur Lewis, *The Theory of Economic Growth*, 1955; Edward F. Denison, *The Sources of Economic Growth in the United States and the Alternatives Before Us*, Committee for Economic Development, 1962; Walter W. Heller, *New Dimensions of Political Economy*, 1967; Arthur F. Burns and Paul A. Samuelson, *Full Employment, Guideposts and Economic Stability*, American Enterprise Institute, 1967.

342

Paul A. Samuelson, one of the chief architects of the "New Economics") called the program "Keynes cum growth"—was to be the key to continued economic stability, progress, and steady prices rather than the smoothing out of the business cycle. The business cycle, in effect, would take care of itself largely through the built-in stabilizers and monetary action; it no longer threatened large-scale depression to shake business confidence and the morale of the American people; the four mild recessions of the postwar proved the point. Continued, indeed faster, growth would make possible overcoming the inequities of the past and achieve a more satisfactory life for all in the future. Of course it would be the federal government largely that would lay out the plans for this "Great Society" and realize them by public expenditures. The role of private entrepreneurship—which, as we have seen, has had so much to do in the past in speeding innovation, greater productivity, and constantly increasing real GNP per capita—was a clouded one, perhaps secondary and minor.

Thus Heller, one-time chairman of the Council of Economic Advisers under Presidents Kennedy and Johnson, wrote in 1966:

> The search for faster growth of our productivity capacity [rising productivity will be the key] will lead us ever more directly to wellsprings that only government can provide through its investment in education, research, and physical resources. When we add to this the federal government's responsibility for overcoming some of the *ravages* of economic growth, and its commitment to those *uses* of growth that will raise the quality of life, federal expenditures become a top claimant on the fiscal dividends in our future. (Italics original.)

As government investments in "research" and "physical resources" Heller cited atomic energy for peaceful uses, communication satellites, urban redevelopment, better use of water resources, pollution control, and weather modification. By overcoming the "ravages" of the earlier growth process he meant the pollution of air and water, "ugliness and social disorder," displaced workers and their skills, and urban blight.

The achievements of what came to be called the "New Economics" —Keynes cum growth, the "fine-tuning" of the economy by fiscal methods —as it moved swiftly and unerringly, now to stimulate now to check the economy, were writ large in the events of 1961–1965. Said Heller: "We have, more effectively than ever before, harnessed the existing economics . . . to the purposes of prosperity, stability, and growth."

Heller was only repeating what the President's Council of Economic Advisers had proclaimed: " a new era for economic policy is at hand" and "fiscal policy stands ready to meet any changing needs and unanticipated developments."

Heller and his successors in the Council could point out how this in fact had been done. In 1964 and 1965—to speed up growth—Congress had granted tax reductions in personal and income taxes and excise taxes; and along with them had authorized increased federal expenditures for defense and space outlays, personal transfer payments, grants-in-aid, and domestic nondefense purchases. During 1961–1965, Heller indicated, the federal government had been responsible for $48 billion of "fiscal dividends" to expand the economy—$16 billion consisting of tax reductions and $32 billion of increases in expenditures. True, this was accompanied by budget deficits: $3.4 billion in fiscal 1961, $7.2 billion in 1962, $4.7 billion in 1963, $5.9 billion in 1964, $1.6 billion in 1965, $3.8 billion in 1966, $8.8 billion in 1967, and $25.2 billion in 1968. Budget deficits did not alarm Heller; said he, "the fear that [they] necessarily spell inflation, insolvency, and irresponsibility has been refuted by the facts."

Heller was saying this in 1966; but inflation was already raising its head, as we have seen. Now, in line with the whole conception of "fine-tuning," a reverse course was necessary; tax increases and budgetary reductions were in order—these hopefully would stop inflation before too long. Congress was asked to assist in 1966 by imposing a surcharge of 6 per cent, then 10 per cent, on income taxes; it finally agreed in 1968 to the latter after the Administration had promised to squeeze $6 billion out of its budget.* In 1966 the Administration had not applied fiscal restraint (it could not, politically, because of its promises to move on the "Great Society"); and in 1968—in the face of the 10 per cent surcharge and budgetary reductions—fiscal policy simply could not halt the unexpected and alarming rise in consumer prices. Nor were the price-and-wage guideposts working.

Arthur F. Burns, one-time chairman of the Council of Economic Advisers in the Eisenhower Administrations, was saying in 1967 what he had begun to say as early as 1961. He was a fair but discerning critic of the "New Economics." He hailed the accomplishments since 1960. Said he, in 1967:

> Since 1960 we surely have made progress in moving toward our national objections [as set forth in the Employment Act of 1946]. Production and employment rose substantially, the advance of prosperity became widely

* In fiscal matters, the Executive proposed but it was Congress that disposed. It took the Congress almost two years to come around to voting the surtax—by then it was too late for the brakes on inflation to take hold. The same attitude on the part of Congress (the Senate largely), in its refusal to grant at once President Nixon's request in early 1969 for the immediate renewal of the surtax, did not help in the checking of the inflation that continued to mount. This was the Achilles heel of the whole theory of fiscal policy as a weapon of control. "Fine-tuning" had turned out to be a blunt and unwieldy instrument indeed.

diffused, full-employment was reestablished, and new doors of economic opportunity were opened up to underprivileged citizens. The government played a vital part in bringing about these gains by its imaginative, and yet pragmatic, approach to the nation's problems.

But the "New Economics" troubled him, exactly because of its high confidence in "fine-tuning"—that short-run variations of macroeconomic policy (instead of long-term structural reforms) were adequate to keep all of the economy's forces in balance. He was critical of the "New Economics" because he questioned its central doctrines that "the stage of the business cycle has little relevance to sound economic policy, that policy should be growth-oriented instead of cycle-oriented," and that fiscal deficits and monetary tools were enough to close the gap between actual and potential output. The trouble was that while all this was taking place its assumption that inflationary pressures could not occur was not borne out by the facts. Inflation had heavy prices to pay both at home and abroad. "We need," he said, "to learn to act, at a time when the economy is threatened by inflation, with something of the sense of urgency that we have so well developed in dealing with the threat of recession."

Burns also called for "long-run" structural changes which would, of themselves, tend to favor high employment and reasonable price stability. These among others: the dismantling of the impediments to competition—high tariffs, import quotas, farm supports, restrictive work practices, the minimum wage; stricter enforcement of the antitrust laws; a stronger and more modern unemployment insurance system; new automatic stabilizers; a systematic policy of tax reduction; and the collection of data on job vacancies and short-run projections of the federal budget. Finally: "free markets are our nation's most valuable economic asset and we should therefore be wary of governmental edicts, perhaps all the more so when they come in the coquettishly modern dress of voluntary guidelines."

Burns had been notably critical of the abrupt shifts in monetary and fiscal policy; he was particularly concerned by the mechanism the Administration sought, as Heller put it, to use: "push-button tax increases or decreases activated by the President and subject to congressional veto." This would make business decisions about investments and prices wholly subordinate to an Executive will or whim. Another group of observers had also become disenchanted with the mix of fiscal and monetary devices being employed. This was the highly influential Joint Economic Committee in its comments on the 1967 Economic Report of the President (repeated in its observations on the 1968 Economic Report) which the whole Committee, majority and minority members, signed.

On the following all the members agreed. The money supply was to be increased at a more stable rate. The Bureau of the Budget should file with the Congress quarterly budget reports indicating major changes on earlier projections. To achieve an efficient allocation of resources, "there should be a greater assertion of priorities in terms of economic growth and national interest." Federal expenditures had to be reduced. Domestic cost and price stability were clearly linked with America's international position and agreement "on international monetary reform is a matter of increasing urgency." Investment in manpower training and other human resource programs was highly desirable.

About the money supply the Committee in 1967 had this to say:

> The Committee urges that the monetary authorities adopt the policy of moderate and relatively steady increases in the money supply, avoiding the disruptive effects of wide swings in the rate of increase or decrease. The Committee is impressed with the increasing weight that many economists give to the importance of a steady rise in the money supply. Such rate of increase should be more or less consistent with the projected rate of growth— generally within a range of 3–5 per cent per year. Sudden changes in the money supply give rise to instabilities in the economy. We are convinced that restoration of economic growth and avoidance of a recession demand such increases in the money supply. . . .

And this on prices and growth:

> Achievement of full employment potential depends heavily on our ability to resolve the problem of maintaining price stability; otherwise price and wage inflation will frustrate our efforts to achieve the most effective use of our economic resources. . . . Our price data [which need improvement] must guide monetary, fiscal, and employment policies; and they must measure the standard of living of the American people.
>
> Policies which attempt to bring the economy to full employment do run the risk of price increases if we approach full employment too rapidly. . . . The perpetual search for short-run benefits results in persistent long-run disadvantages for all. The resulting price increases spread and tend to be built into the structure of the economy. . . .

The Joint Economic Committee was not the only one to comment sharply on the monetary decisions of the Federal Reserve Board. It was being pointed out that the Board shifted too rapidly from a tight-money policy to an easy one and back again. It let the money supply shoot up too fast late in 1965 (to help finance the mounting budgetary deficit); contracted it too sharply in mid-1966 when a serious credit crunch (much like that of 1969) followed; and then moved to the excessive expansion of credit in early 1967, which it continued into 1968. In 1967 the money supply increased at an annual rate of 6.4 per cent, as compared with the annual rate of 2.6 per cent from 1960 through 1964.*

Thus fundamental differences between two kinds of policy were shaping up. How get inflation down? The government could do it by slowing up demand sufficiently through curbs on its expenditures. The price would be a temporarily higher unemployment rate and a lower growth rate. At the same time, if improvements in structural unemployment were steadily pushed—through manpower training, provisions for temporary jobs for teenagers, regional policies to cope with distress areas, a concerted effort on the parts of private companies and private investment to provide training and jobs for the hard-core unemployed—there was no reason, it was felt, why the unemployment rate had to go up markedly, even if demand were dampened temporarily. As has been pointed out here, previous recessions—mild, lightly if at all felt by most Americans—had put a stop to inflationary tendencies. This was true of the recessions of 1953–1954 and 1957–1958. The result after the latter had been a long period of price stability. Then the economy had been put in serious jeopardy by pushing growth too energetically. As for monetary and fiscal policies—having always in mind possible inflationary consequences and business uncertainty—they could be managed better and be made more predictable than they had been. Annual income tax adjustments (made by the President and debated by the Congress) might be one way of handling fiscal management on a routine basis; a steadier rise in the nation's money supply—with swings up and down in the interest rates charged by banks and thrift institutions—would be sounder monetary policy than that previously pursued.

Ideas along these lines were the basis of a report by Herbert Stein written for the Brookings Institution late in 1968. Mr. Stein (as was Arthur F. Burns) was an adviser to President-elect Nixon. Certainly these

* In late 1968, the Board began to retreat and the money supply was held steady by sharp increases in the discount rate, supplemented in April 1969, by rises in bank reserve rates. The great changes that took place—accompanied by another credit crunch—can be seen from these figures. Whereas the money supply had increased, at an annual rate of 6.5 per cent in 1968, it dropped to 2.8 per cent during the first half of 1969. In consequence, interest rates soared—in June 1969, up to 8½ per cent for prime borrowers. It became apparent that it was easier to stimulate than to damp down the economy (thus lessons were being learned the hard way). Inflation was not being slowed as late as the summer of 1969; but an indication that restraints were beginning to work (cuts in federal expenditures; checks on the money supply; a budget surplus of $3 billion for fiscal 1969) is evidenced from the decline in the real GNP. The annual rate of real growth dropped in the first two quarters of 1969 to 2.5 per cent as compared with the 6 per cent of a year earlier. But inflation was a stubborn growth; it was difficult to stunt it; for consumer prices speeded up by nearly 5 per cent in the first half of 1969.

notions were going to be given consideration as the continued search for greater stability with growth took place.*

WAS THERE A ''TRADE-OFF'' BETWEEN UNEMPLOYMENT AND INFLATION?

In the discussions taking place in 1967, 1968, and 1969, there was one question raising its head again and again: Was there an inevitable "trade-off" between unemployment and inflation? That is, to ensure an annual unemployment rate of 4 per cent or less was it necessary to accept an annual inflation rate of 2 or 3 (or even 4) per cent? In short, inflation meant more jobs and price stability fewer ones. Those who felt that way —the defenders of the "New Economics" were among them—cited the findings of the so-called "Phillips Curve" (named after an English economist) which purported to prove that there was an immutable relationship between wages (and wages were a price) and employment. Thus, as evidence, it was pointed out that in the early 1960s, prices rose only 1 per cent annually when the jobless rate was 5 per cent or more.

The position was being disputed, however. The "Phillips Curve" was too simplistic, it described a short-run state of affairs, it did not take into account other variables besides only wages and employment. Also, there was no proof that there was a stable long-run relationship between varying rates of anticipated price changes and the level of unemployment. Roger W. Spencer, writing in the *Bulletin* of the St. Louis Federal Reserve Bank (March 1969) submitted the "trade-off" to a rigorous examination, and came out unconvinced. He cited the findings of a number of research workers seeking to apply the "Phillips Curve":

> Our final caution is that we have been astounded by how many very different Phillips Curves can be constructed on reasonable assumptions from the same body of data. The nature of the relationship between wage changes and unemployment is highly sensitive to the exact choice of the other variables . . . and to the forms of all the variables. For this reason, the authors of Phillips Curves would do well to label them conspicuously *"Unstable. Apply with extreme care."* (Italics original.)

The proponents of the "long-run Equilebrium View," to quote Mr. Spencer, consider

* Both Mr. Stein and Mr. Burns entered the Nixon Administration in 1969: Mr. Stein as a member of the Council of Economic Advisers and Mr. Burns in the especially created post of Counselor to the President with a seat in the Cabinet.

. . . the trade-offs between wages or prices and unemployment as transitory phenomena, and that no such trade-off exists after factors have completely adjusted to the trend of spending growth. In the short-run there can be a discrepancy between expectations and actual price of wage changes, but not in the long run. After the discrepancies have worked themselves out, the only relevant ones are "real" or price-deflated ones.

It was in line with this thinking that Paul W. McCracken, chairman of the new Council of Economic Advisers, announced that the Nixon Administration would pursue a "gradualist" approach toward the rate of inflation. It was recognized that the adoption of structural measures to complement monetary and fiscal action would serve to lower the optimal level of unemployment. These, for example: the use of a shorter work week rather than the laying off of experienced workers; the spread of pension plans to make lay-offs too expensive; job-training programs to prevent the disemployment of the unskilled; wider and sustained information concerning job-opportunities. Further, it was being pointed out that brakes applied to a high economic growth rate would not necessarily involve a sharp jump in unemployment because of the changed character of the civilian labor force. The greater part of it was now in white-collar jobs where lay-offs did not take place as quickly as in the case of blue-collar workers; and skilled workers in the service industries were definitely in short supply. Easing the labor shortage (the reduction of military forces not only in Vietnam but elsewhere too was one way) was bound to bring pay increases into line with the growth of productivity and help in the slowing down of the final demand for goods.

THE POOR

Applying the brakes—without serious damage to the economy—seemed feasible; granted that political pressures did not swerve the policy-makers from their course. The one that was becoming increasingly insistent was the demand that the plight of the poor have the nation's first concern.

A memorandum released by the Subcommittee on Employment, Manpower and Poverty of the Senate Committee on Labor and Public Welfare (October 1968) declared that there were 29.7 million poor persons in the United States in 1966, if the measure was available minimum income. On this basis, the poverty line was fixed by the Social Security Administration for a nonfarm family of four as $3335, for a four-person farm family as $2345, and of course lesser amounts for smaller households and the elderly and larger amounts for greater households. The 29.7

million were made up of the following: 5.4 million were elderly over 65, 2.1 million lived alone, 4.6 million were heads of families, 5.1 million were other family members, and 12.5 million were children. Thus two-thirds of the poor were at the beginning (14–24) or at the end (55–64) of the normal working ages.

It should be noted that in less than 10 years the percentage of the nation's households living below the poverty level had fallen sharply: from 22 per cent in 1959 to 15 per cent in 1966 and 13.3 per cent in 1967. That is to say, better education, more job training, job placement, and therefore increased employment were cutting into the numbers and pro-portions of those who were rated as poor. Although most of the poor were white, the incidence of poverty was far higher among nonwhites: about one household in three as compared with one in seven. But declines were taking place comparably in both groups: between 1962 and 1967, white poverty was reduced about 28 per cent, but the same fall took place among nonwhites. In short, substantial gains were being achieved.

This notwithstanding, crash programs were being called for to guar-antee rapid progress: supplementary income support of one kind or another along with employment and education. Said the memorandum above referred to:

> Underlying these three main thrusts is need to improve the capability of local communities to reach and serve the poor and to carry out effective programs which deal with byproducts of poverty, such as ill health, sub-standard housing, legal injustice, and the other social ills which afflict the poor.

To close the job gap, the memorandum recommended—as does everybody else—more education, more imaginative job placement efforts, day-care provision for the children of female heads of families willing and able to work, special incentives to private employers to encourage them to recruit, hire and train the unemployed poor. The memorandum went farther, however; all this was not enough. A "massive public service employment program" was necessary: to create 300,000 jobs at once (at a minimum wage reaching up to $2 an hour) with 1,200,000 jobs as the goal in the third and fourth years. The memorandum set out some finan-cial estimates of costs for the training of large numbers of unemployed persons for existing jobs. It put the average cost of training and placing per person at $3500; to train and place 1.2 million would come to $4.2 billion. Adding retraining and the operations of the U.S. Employment Service, the total would be $5.5 billion.

Thus, an over-all umbrella was still necessary: this was supplemen-tary income support for the elderly and for families. True, there were programs of one kind or another already in existence, the largest being public assistance to families with dependent children; but these were "vastly inadequate." Hence, for the elderly (living alone or in couples), it was recommended that either straight grants on a national standard basis be adopted to close the poverty gap 100 per cent, or the negative income tax be installed. The cost of either one would come to $3 to $4 billion annually.

Supplementary income support for families (because the "amounts paid to families [now on welfare relief] keep them in poverty") might be handled in one of three ways: by a straight-out guaranteed annual income, in every case breaching the poverty line; by the use of the negative income tax; or by the employment of a children-allowance benefit system. The cost of the first would be $8 billion the first year, although the memorandum admits it might come to twice that because poor families would quit working, being guaranteed a minimum income in any event. The memorandum did not venture to estimate the costs of the second or third plan, although it admitted they would be high. As regards the negative income tax, there was, it was true, the question of incentives to work; and, in the case of the family allowance, while "it eliminates the means test and other procedural indignities of the present welfare system," it did also include the nonpoor.

It is curious to observe, in this often emotional debate about poverty, how little was being said about the welfare system as a device for institutionalizing poverty. The New York *Times* (April 4, 1969) suddenly took alarm as it contemplated the continuous rise in welfare payments on the one hand and the jump in fatherless families on the other. Fatherless Negro families in central city areas went up from 23 per cent in 1960 to 30 per cent in 1968; among whites, the increase was from 10 to 12 per cent. Said the *Times*: "Social disorder is rampant in New York City, where more than 150,000 families headed by females are on relief rolls. These families have about 500,000 children. . . . The appalling rise in fatherless families across the nation offers further proof that the welfare system needs fundamental reform . . ." The *Times* offered these as examples of "fundamental reform": more child day-care centers and family planning programs.

Here was the heart of the difficulty: it was the welfare system: it was a motley cloak put together willy-nilly over some 35 years, and it had turned out to be a thing of "rags and patches." There were more than 10 million Americans receiving some form of welfare aid in 1968 at a cost of nearly $10 billion ($2 billion more than in the previous year). Some of this came from the states and cities, some from the federal government, with a confusion of agencies daily becoming more complex. If welfare was to be narrowed down to the care of the wholly dependent—but also if the problem of the poor was to be approached in terms of equity, social justice, the creation of income minimums to begin to approximate the requirements of health, decency, human dignity for all Americans—then a thoroughgoing re-examination of the public commitment was called for.

This President Nixon did in a general statement he made to the nation August 8, 1969 and in a series of messages to Congress immediately thereafter. What he said and what he proposed be done were widely hailed. His recommendations—because they were novel and bold, because they would (in the beginning) increase the numbers on public assistance possibly double them, because they would (again in the short-run) cost large sums and probably more than the $4 billion annually he anticipated—were bound to be argued over and closely debated in Congress. Even those who were always hostile to everything that came out of the Executive Offices were quick to admit that the President's analysis and program were all-encompassing, imaginative and courageous. Here, at last, was a master plan: its basic essentials were bound to be enacted in one form or another by Congress and with the approval of the states and even the large industrial cities.

In his address Nixon made two broad observations out of which flowed the reforms he was calling for: that the "present welfare system had to be judged a colossal failure"; and that it had led to a "third of a century of centralizing power and responsibility in Washington [which had] produced a bureaucratic monstrosity—cumbersome, unresponsive and ineffective." He wanted therefore to cut down to proper size the first and get rid of the second, propounding two general principles for guidance: the creation of national standards (with federal financial help) for the support of the poor; and the "federalization" (among the states and cities) of responsibility for and management of the specific tasks that had to be done. This to convert the underemployed and the unemployed (taking them off welfare) into useful members of the civilian labor force. With all this went a "sweetener." *

Put briefly, there were three specific suggestions that were put before

* The existing system of so-called Aid to Families with Dependent Children had these outstanding faults built in: it excluded from welfare aid families containing a father capable of working (thus encouraging his flight and the breakup of families); it penalized work by deducting any earnings of any member of a family from welfare payments; and it inevitably led to migration from the rural South (where payments were low) to urban centers particularly in the North (where payments were much higher), thus producing the urban crisis. The President proposed flatly the abolition of AFDC. The thrust of his new "family assistance" program was to be on three levels: "equality of treatment, a work requirement, and a work incentive."

Congress. The first was in effect the creation of a nationwide minimum income floor for all families with children, whether the head of the family (including the father) was working or not. Such families were to receive welfare benefits; those with low-paying jobs were to get supplements until their incomes rose at least to the minimums set for the various family sizes. The federal Social Security Administration would be charged with the duty of creating a centralized system of local registrations and monthly welfare payments; in this way would be reduced inequities among the states and localities and among welfare recipients. The "welfare mother" (particularly among the Negroes) would end.*

The second called for the requirement that most welfare recipients (mothers included) accept job training or "suitable" jobs when available, with payments continuing for those underemployed or inadequately paid and with subsidies while in training for new or better jobs. These manpower training programs were to be managed by the states and localities. To help mothers become available for training—and therefore to free them once and for all from the humiliations of the welfare system—a major expansion of child day-care centers was to be established.

The third reform (the "sweetener") proposed that a share, to mount by regular steps, of the federal income tax receipts be turned back to the states and cities. In the first year this "free cash" was to be only $1 billion; but it was to rise annually in absolute amounts and as a proportion of the federal revenue until it got to $5 billion in 1976. Thereafter the annual increase was to be $500 million.

CONTINUED GROWTH

Continued growth, even accelerated growth, undoubtedly has its charms. W. Arthur Lewis has ticked off many of the reasons why growth (at any rate, in a free and not directed society) is desirable, and some of them may be recorded here. Growth increases the range of human choices. It gives men greater control over their environment and thereby increases their freedom to pick or to reject. They may, for example, opt for greater leisure or the cultivation of the things of the spirit. It permits men to

* The national minimum for a family of four was to be $1600. A working mother or father could keep up to $60 monthly of earnings without loss of welfare benefits. A subsidy of $30 a month would be paid to a family member on job training. Thus a family of five in which the father earned $2000 yearly would get family assistance payments of $1260 for a total income of $3260. This might encourage the shiftless or those with low-keyed expectations to stay on welfare; but certainly not those fully at work and making $4500–$5000 annually to transfer over to the public rolls.

have at their disposal more services as well as more goods. It improves the status of women and gives them release from the drudgery of hard work. It allows mankind to indulge in the luxury of greater humanitarianism. If struggle for mere survival (and the chicanery, fraud, and brutishness with which this is involved) is lessened, hopefully growth helps in the elimination of social tensions and strife.

To these may be added the following. A society that is growing (again, assuming it is free) has a greater elan, a higher spirit, a sparkle and a derring-do about it. Creativity is encouraged and supported. For the venturesome, doors to opportunity are opened, there exists a vertical social mobility, there is room at the top. Innovators, risk-takers, adventurers emerge, are welcomed rather than rebuffed and are given the recognition (possibly fortunes, too) that is their due.

Yet, continued growth and particularly accelerated growth are not easy to maintain. Too many of its demands, discipline, sacrifices, most people find distasteful. Growth requires what Lewis calls acceptance of "the economizing spirit"—the pursuit of economic gain with the immediate deprivations for many this entails. For the few it may mean wealth —or idleness. Growth requires the acceptance of individualism, rationality, discipline; and all these are suspect. The cultivation of science and the pursuit of technology demand education and re-education; only the committed, those with a "calling," those prepared to school themselves rigorously, are willing to pursue such a hard course. Growth requires economies of scale and these are linked with a division of labor, specialization (again, more education), automation, large-scale organization. Says Lewis on this last: "Large-scale organization brings with it also peculiar social tensions; such organizations have to be run on hierarchical lines, which means that a few command while the majority obey." Growth, finally, is dependent upon and leads to inequality of income.

The desire for security as against uncertainty, the human propensity for inaction and indolence, the suspicion of unusual men and intellectualism—in short, the equating of democracy or a free society with egalitarianism—all these make it hard to sustain growth. Says Lewis: "We [most men] demand the abolition of poverty, illiteracy, and disease, but we cling desperately to the beliefs, habits, and social arrangements which we like, even where these are the very cause of the poverty which we deplore."

Yet, adding and subtracting, we must come to the conclusion that grow we must; for unless there is growth there is sooner or later stagnation. It is not only that material wealth declines but there is a fall in the spirit and a disappearance of creativity. But to grow how fast? And here we come to all the questions already raised in this chapter. Shall we pursue accelerated growth relentlessly—note the swift pace set by the "New Economics" of the 1960s—with more and more government *dirigisme,* the Big State, devising the tools of policy and making the decisions?

Edward F. Denison, writing at the beginning of the 1960s, pointed out that in the last 75 years or the last 50 years of America's economic development the annual rate of growth—the real output of goods and services making up the country's GNP—was 2.9 per cent. Taking shorter periods, the rate was markedly greater or markedly less. It was 4.5 per cent as the annual average for 1922–1929; 1.6 per cent annual average for 1930–1939; 3.8 per cent annual average for 1948–1957; 5 per cent annual average for 1947 to early 1953; but 1 per cent annual average from mid-1953 to the first quarter of 1958. And 5.5 per cent annual average for 1961–1966; but 2.5 per cent in 1967 and 5.0 per cent in 1968.

Looking at 1929–1957, Dennison gave these weights to the factors of growth that were producing an annual average rate of 2.9 per cent: increased employment, 34 per cent; more educated workers, that is, improved quality of the labor force, 23 per cent; increases in capital outputs, 15 per cent; improvements in all kinds of knowledge about production, 20 per cent; economies of scale associated with the expansion of the national market, 9 per cent. There was a positive association between high employment (and the quality of the work force) and the rapid growth of productive potentialities.

In a sense anticipating the "New Economics," Dennison pointed out that the federal government had available three tools to bring the actual rate of production closer to the potential; that is, to accelerate the growth rate. These were: an increase in the money supply to ease credit and thus encourage private capital investment and those of the state and local governments; the reduction of federal taxes and/or the increase in federal transfer payments to augment private disposable income; and the expansion of federal purchases or expenditures to add directly to aggregate demand and indirectly to the stimulation of private purchases.

Pursuing such a course—Dennison was neutral; he was prepared as an economist and statistician, "if growth is an independent objective," to indicate what could be done by government to stimulate it—Americans had to be put on notice that there were involved "costs of one type or another and/or risks of interfering with other objectives." Curiously, the first risk of maintaining fuller utilization of resources Dennison recorded was inflation. The other costs or risks were largely similar to those Lewis had mentioned. Of the institutional obstacles that needed eliminating to accelerate the growth rate, Dennison said: "But in every case their ex-

istence is in the real or supposed interest, and reflects deeply felt attitudes, of some group in the population whose views would have to be
overridden to remove them."

Yet Dennison could not forego offering his own opinion—nor is he
to be faulted for stepping outside the limitations he had imposed upon
his inquiry. In the final chapter, which he calls "High Employment and
Growth," Dennison says:

> Doubtless we could all agree that we would like unemployment held
> always to the minimum consistent with efficient production and, simultane-
> ously, stability in the average level of prices. Stated so inflexibly, this is not
> a feasible objective. The maximum objective we can hope to attain is to
> hold cyclical fluctuations in employment and prices to small proportions,
> while avoiding any extended period of excessive unemployment and any
> cumulative rise in average prices.

This is where America stood as the new Nixon Administration took
over in 1969. In addition to the very real problem of high employment
and stability of prices, it also had to face up to poverty, urban redevelopment, and further education. Whether it would choose real scope for
individual and private choices—which had been the prevailing mores in
the long history of American economic development presented here—or
accept the *dirigisme* implicit in the "New Economics" remained to be
seen. In any event, a new chapter was about to open in the tale of America's progress toward a more affluent and, hopefully, a more stable society.

As the Nixon Administration's first year drew to a close, it nevertheless was apparent that a sharp change in course was not easy. Washington
was burdened with these legacies from the booming, overconfident
1965–1968 years: an erratic monetary policy and great federal budgetary
deficits (both the results of easy money and lavish public spending); over-
blown wage increases in the face of falls in productivity; and a steadily
mounting (and a generally complacent acceptance of) inflation. To check
the inflationary processes the economy had to be cooled off with two
inevitable consequences. The first was a drop in the real GNP from an
annual average increase rate of 5–6 to around 2 percent. This meant a
slowing down of business and a decline in company profits. The second
was a rise in the unemployment rate from 3.3 to 4 percent or even more.
This meant that the unskilled, the hard-core unemployed, the black
workers, would be hit hardest.

During 1969, Administration and the Federal Reserve Board worked
together.* Monetary restraint kept the money supply below a 3 to 5

* There was assurance that this would continue with the President's announcement
that his Counselor, Arthur F. Burns, was to succeed William McChesney Martin, Jr. as

percent growth rate, as its cost remained high. There were severe reductions in federal spending—by more than $7 billion annually—accompanied by curtailed government construction commitments and the shutting down of unneeded military installations at home and abroad. Every effort was being made to persuade Congress to extend the surtax into 1970 and, in overhauling the tax structure in the interests of greater equity, not at the same time to decrease federal income and jeopardize the creation of budgetary surpluses.

Restraints seemed to be working, albeit haltingly and erratically. There took place a downturn in industrial production and an increase in inventories. There occurred a fail in retail sales, a slowing down in housing starts, and less anticipated business capital outlays and capital-goods purchases for 1970. But, through the third quarter of 1969, consumer prices continued rising to an annual rate of 6 percent; as did new wage contracts, which carried increases as high as 8 percent; as did unemployment—up from 3.3 percent of the civilian labor force in the first quarter of the year to 3.7 percent in the third and to 3.9 percent in October. Given the steady pressures of monetary and fiscal programs and business slowdown, the first two, hopefully, would respond and, in time, would drop.

The price to be paid—the rise in unemployment—was the sticky point. How much criticism and for how long could the Administration and the Federal Reserve Board take, when public and congressional impatience and protest began to mount? The Administration was pressing two plans to prevent the unskilled (black workers largely) from bearing the brunt of the battle. First, by decree of the Labor Department (and not waiting for congressional action), the job-training program was being modernized, vastly broadened, and being put under the control of state employment services. (More than $2 billion was being earmarked for this.) Second, the Labor Department was starting to expand the establishment of the so-called "computer job banks"; by the end of 1970 these would be working in some 55 cities. The thought was to try intensively and steadily, through daily computer controls, to match workers seeking jobs with job vacancies. Experiments previously carried on in Baltimore, and in five other pilot cities, had demonstrated that the number of hard-core unemployed placed in jobs could be as much as doubled by such devices.

If politics was suspended for a time, if job-seekers were quickly

---

chairman of the Federal Reserve Board in February, 1970. Burns had worked closely with the President on his economic program; he was also clearly committed to orderly increases in the money supply rather than to the previous jerky stop-go tactics; and at the same time he was alert to the dangers that recession might bring.

trained and retrained and jobs for them were found, if wage settlements and other prices turned realistic and were fixed by market responses, if the capital outlays of companies were held in tight check—all large ifs— the fight against inflation, without prolonged recession, had a good chance of succeeding. At this fateful position, in time and space, the American economy was situated as the year 1969 was ending.

BIBLIOGRAPHICAL SUGGESTIONS

The many books, monographs, and articles in learned journals cited in the text are not repeated here; students and instructors will have noted them. In addition, two general works having to do with growth and development are to be mentioned: Benjamin Higgins, *Economic Development: Problems, Principles, and Policies,* 1959 and as were Bernard Okun and R. W. Richardson, *Studies in Economic Development,* 1961. Indispensable are U.S. Bureau of the Census, *Historical Statistics of the United States, Colonial Times to 1957,* 1960 and the annual volumes of *Statistical Abstract of the United States.*

This book will be read by students who intend to concentrate in history or economics. In view of the fact that I am utilizing the methodology of both disciplines, students may want to cross the lines from their own major interests. I therefore suggest these general texts in *economics* for students in *history*:

Bach, G. L., *Economics: An Introduction to Analysis and Policy,* 5th ed., 1966.

Harriss, C. L., *The American Economy,* 5th ed., 1966.

Lipsey, R. G., and P. O. Steiner, *Economics,* 2nd ed., 1969.

McConnell, C. R., *Economics: Principles, Problems and Policies,* 3d ed., 1966.

Reynolds, L. G., *Economics: A General Introduction,* 3d ed., 1969.

Samuelson, P. A., *Economics: An Introduction to Analysis,* 7th ed., 1969.

These general texts in *American History* are recommended for students in *economics*:

Blum, John, et al., *The National Experience,* 1st ed., 1963.

Caughey, John, and Ernest May, *A History of the United States,* 1st ed., 1964.

Garraty, John, *The American Nation,* 1st ed., 1966.

Hicks, John, George Mowry, and Robert Burke, *A History of American Democracy,* 3d ed., 1966.

Hofstadter, Richard, William Miller, and Daniel Aaron, *The American Republic,* 1st ed., 1959.

Williams, T. H., Richard Current, and Frank Freidel, *A History of the United States,* 2 vols., 2nd ed., 1965.

Morison, S. E., H. S. Commager, and W. E. Leuchtenburg, *The Growth of the American Republic,* 2 vols., 6th ed., 1969.

There are many textbooks in American economic history, and to avoid selectivity and partiality I shall name none of them. Instead, I offer two lists: the separate volumes of "The Economic History of the United States" Series and one made up of books of readings and essays, in which the editor is named in each case.

"The Economic History of the United States"

The Colonial Period to 1775 (in preparation).

Nettels, C. P., *The Emergence of a National Economy, 1775–1815,* 1962.

Gates, P. W., *The Farmer's Age: Agriculture, 1815–1860,* 1960.

Taylor, G. R., *The Transportation Revolution, 1815–1860,* 1951.

Shannon, F. A., *The Farmer's Last Frontier: Agriculture, 1860–1897,* 1945.

Kirkland, E. C., *Industry Comes of Age, 1860–1897,* 1961.

Faulkner, H. U., *The Decline of Laissez Faire, 1897–1917,* 1951.

Soule, George, *Prosperity Decade, 1917–1929,* 1947.

Mitchell, Broadus, *Depression Decade, 1929–1941,* 1947.

World War II and the Post War, 1941–1961, (in preparation).

Books of Readings and Essays

Andreano, Ralph, Ed., *New Views on American Economic Development,* 1965.

Callender, G. S., Ed., *Economic History of the United States, 1765–1860,* 1909.

Chandler, A. D., Jr., Stuart Bruchey, and Louis Galambos, Eds., *The Changing Economic Order,* 1969.

Cobin, Stanley, and F. G. Hill, Eds., *American Economic History,* 1960.

Cochran, T. C., and T. B. Brewer, Eds., *Views of American Economic Growth,* 2 vols., 1966.

Hacker, L. M., Ed., *The Shaping of the American Tradition,* 1947.

Hacker, L. M., Ed., *Major Documents in American Economic History*, 2 vols., 1961.

Harris, S. E., Ed., *American Economic History*, 1961.

Lambie, J. T., and R. V. Clemence, Eds., *Economic Change in America*, 1954.

Nash, G. D., Ed., *Issues in American Economic History*, 1964.

Robertson, R. M., and J. L. Pate, Eds., *Readings in U.S. Economic and Business History*, 1966.

Scheiber, H. M., Ed., *United States Economic History*, 1964.

Williamson, H. F., Ed., *The Growth of the American Economy*, 2nd ed., 1951.

Readings in American growth and development will also be found in the following three books, designed for students in elementary economics: C. L. Harriss, Ed., *Selected Readings in Economics*, 3d ed., 1967; P. A. Samuelson et al., Eds., *Readings in Economics*, 4th ed., 1964; and R. E. Slesinger, Mark Perlman, and Asher Isaacs, Eds., *Contemporary Economics, Selected Readings*, 2d ed., 1967.

Pioneering essays in American economic history are to be found in the National Bureau of Economic Research's "Studies in Income and Wealth." The first cited is Vol. 24 of the series and the second, Vol. 30.

Trends in the American Economy in the Nineteenth Century, 1960.

Output, Employment, and Productivity in the United States After 1800, 1966.

INDEX

Wages, real: (Cont'd),
and unskilled workers, 192; drop during
the Civil War, 220; increase in 1920s, 278;
in the 1920s and wage differentials, 290;
question of adequacy, 298–299; efforts
to raise under the New Deal, 305, 311;
unfortunate effects of wage policy for
recovery, 317–318; rise in, during World
War II, 325; rise in 1960s, 336, 356, 357
Walker, Amasa, 194
Wall Street Journal, 251
Ware, Caroline, 148
Warren, Earl, 204
Washington, George, 28, 50, 55, 64, 66
Wayland, Francis, 194
Welfare legislation: limitations on, as expounded by state courts, 200; Supreme
Court and, 203; about-face of Court
after 1837, 204; and under the Warren
Court, 204; in the states, 260, 263–264;
criticism of and Nixon program for re-
form, 352–353
Welfare state: pioneered by Progressives,
259; created under New Deal and its
accomplishments, 310, 320–321; not
much advanced in 1950s, 332; effort
to extend under the "Great Society,"
342–346 *passim*
Welfare system, *see* Poor
Wells, D. A., 197, 243
West Coast Hotel Co. v. Parrish, 204
West Point Military Academy, and engineering education, 155
Weyl, Walter, 260
What Social Classes Owe to Each Other
(Sumner), 198
Wheat: colonial production, 22; exports
in 1860s, 105; the growing states, 1839–
1859, 106; during the Civil War, 229; in
the Great Plains, 227–228; revolution in
productivity, 230; fall in price after 1887,
232
Wheeler-Lee Act, 256

Whiskey Rebellion of 1794, 63
Whitney, Eli, 149
Wildcat banks, 120, 131–132
Willburn, J. A., 127–130 *passim*
Williams, J. H., 132, 242
Willis, H. P., 271, 272
Wilson, Woodrow, 260, 261, 264, 268–273
passim
Woodman, H. D., 163, 164
Wool manufactures, and cottage production,
141
Woolen Act of 1699, 28
Work, American attitude toward, and con-
trasted with European, 13–14
Workers: attitude toward money, 121; bet-
ter educated in ante-bellum period?, argued
and disputed, 150–154; attitude toward
European radicalism, 208; attitude toward
money, in post-Civil War period, 219–222;
turn to radicalism, 1900–1917, 260, 264–
268; right to organize and bargain collectively, under NIRA, 304–305; advances
in, and New Deal social legislation, 311–
312; not conscripted during World War II,
328
Works Progress Administration (WPA), 306
World of Andrew Carnegie, 1865–1901
(Hacker), 9, 172, 199
World Economic Conference of 1933, 307–
308
World War I: effects continuing into 1930s,
313–314
World War II: ending of the Great Depression with its outbreak, 319; organization
for and political and economic consequences,
322–325; conversion to peace, 325–328
Wright, Frances, 88

Yeoman farmers, of the South: 168, 169–
170; well-off (Owsley) and disputed
(Linden), 169–170; Radical Republicans
and, 186
Young, Arthur, 14